Judicial Practice, Customary International Criminal
Law and *Nullum Crimen Sine Lege*

Thomas Rauter

Judicial Practice, Customary International Criminal Law and *Nullum Crimen Sine Lege*

 Springer

Thomas Rauter
Bezirkshauptmannschaft Salzburg-Umgebung
Land Salzburg
Salzburg, Austria

ISBN 978-3-319-64476-9   ISBN 978-3-319-64477-6   (eBook)
DOI 10.1007/978-3-319-64477-6

Library of Congress Control Number: 2017948010

Printed on acid-free paper

This Springer imprint is published by Springer Nature
The registered company is Springer International Publishing AG
The registered company address is: Gewerbestrasse 11, 6330 Cham, Switzerland

Preface

> We must never forget that the record on which we judge these defendants today is the record on which history will judge us tomorrow. To pass these defendants a poisoned chalice is to put it to our own lips as well. We must summon such detachment and intellectual integrity to our task that this Trial will commend itself to posterity as fulfilling humanity's aspirations to do justice.[1]

These were the words addressed by the chief US prosecutor Robert H. Jackson to the International Military Tribunal at the opening of the trial of the major war criminals on 21 November 1945 in Nuremberg. Those words remind us that it is the task of every international criminal tribunal to uphold fundamental principles of criminal justice in order to preserve the integrity of the system of international criminal justice and not to sacrifice these principles to obey a "cry for vengeance which arises from the anguish of war".[2]

When the International Criminal Tribunal for the Former Yugoslavia (ICTY) took up its work in the 1990s, it was faced with the problem that the development of international criminal law had virtually stood still since the post-World War II criminal convictions. Indeed, by setting up the ICTY, the UN Security Council (SC) ended a 60-year period of drought in which no international tribunal existed that could enforce international criminal law. Only occasionally were domestic cases held that reminded us that international criminal law even existed.[3] Apart from the rare judicial enforcement, conventional developments in this field of law were also scarce. To date we do not have an international convention on crimes against humanity. It is only reasonable, therefore, that the ICTY and the

---

[1] IMT Nuremberg, 2 Trial of the Major War Criminals Before the International Military Tribunal (1947) ("Blue Series"), 101 (Justice Robert H. Jackson, Prosecutor's Address of Nov. 21, 1945 to the International Military Tribunal.)

[2] Ibid.

[3] See, for example, Supreme Court of Israel, *Attorney General of Israel v. Eichmann*, 36 International Law Reports (1968), 277; French Court de Cassation, *Barbie Case*, 78 International Law Reports (1988), 125.

international criminal tribunals that followed, such as the International Criminal Tribunal for Rwanda (ICTR), the Extraordinary Chambers in the Courts of Cambodia (ECCC) and the Special Court for Sierra Leone (SCSL), had to rely on customary international law as their main source of international criminal convictions.

However, taking recourse to an unwritten source of law such as customary international law is problematic from a human rights perspective. One of the fundamental principles of criminal law, the *nullum crimen sine lege* principle, has been aptly described by *von Liszt* as "the citizen's bulwark against the State's omnipotence", protecting the individual against arbitrary charges.[4] The principle of *nullum crimen sine lege* inter alia requires that the law is accessible and criminal prosecution is foreseeable for the individual.[5] However, customary international law as the underlying legal basis for individual criminal responsibility in international criminal proceedings is problematic. It has been stated that this particular source of law is "situated in a theoretical minefield".[6] *Simma* and *Alston* have remarked that customary international law suffers from an "identity crisis".[7] There is no coherent theory on customary international law, but varying doctrinal and methodological approaches exist that compete to establish and determine customary international law "properly".[8] For this reason, the Secretary General of the United Nations made it clear that, in order to comply with the *nullum crimen sine lege* principle, the ICTY shall only apply norms that are "beyond any doubt part of customary law".[9]

Nevertheless, international criminal law, being at the interception of human rights, humanitarian law and criminal law, appears to be torn by moral aspirations that determine the way the law needs to be interpreted and applied. The human factor in yielding to the moral pull is quite understandable. Critics such as *Robinson* consider that international criminal tribunals apply a "victim-focused teleological reasoning aggravated by utopian aspirations".[10] However, the source of authority for judges of international criminal tribunals rests upon the application of existing customary international criminal law. Thus the UN Secretary General's demand that international criminal tribunals apply norms, "which are beyond any doubt part

---

[4]*F. von Liszt*, The Rationale for the Nullum Crimen Principle, 5 Journal of International Criminal Justice (2007), 1009–1010, reproducing from his essay Die deterministischen Gegner der Zweckstrafe, 13 Zeitschrift für die gesamte Strafrechtswissenschaft (1983), 325ff.

[5]See further Chap. 3, *Nullum Crimen Sine Lege*.

[6]*M. Koskenniemi*, The Pull of the Mainstream, 88 Michigan Law Review (1990), 1947.

[7]*B. Simma* and *P. Alston*, The Sources of Human Rights Law: Custom, Jus Cogens, and General Principles, 12 Australian Yearbook of International Law (1988–1989), 88.

[8]See further Chap. 4, The Formation of Customary International Law and Its Methodological Challenges.

[9]Report of the Secretary-General Pursuant to Paragraph 2 of Security Council Resolution 808 (1993), 3 May 1993, UN Doc S/25704), para 34 (SG Report on ICTY).

[10]C.f. *D. Robinson*, The Identity Crisis of International Criminal Law, 21 Leiden Journal of International Law (2008), 944f.

of customary international law", is its legitimizing source of authority. Consequently, judges adjudicating on the strength of law must keep a clear distinction between *de lege lata* and *de lege ferenda*. Humanitarian and moral considerations can only be taken into account by judges when they have found adequate expression in legal form.

The aim of this book is to analyse the methodology used by international criminal tribunals when determining customary international criminal law and to consider the compatibility of these methodological approaches with the *nullum crimen sine lege* principle.

Salzburg, Austria   Thomas Rauter

Acknowledgements

This book is the revised version of the PhD thesis that has been submitted to obtain the degree of doctor iuris at the Paris Lodron University of Salzburg. I am much obliged to all those who encouraged and helped me in working on this book. Chief among those are my two PhD supervisors, Prof. Kirsten Schmalenbach and Prof. Otto Triffterer. By her dedication to legal research, Prof. Kirsten Schmalenbach has been a role model to me throughout the years. Without her, I would not be the lawyer I am today, and I can hardly put my gratitude into words. Prof. Otto Triffterer has been an inspiration to so many international criminal law students, including myself. It was an honour to receive his critical and useful feedback in particular at the early stage of writing this thesis.

I am also grateful to Prof. William Schabas for accepting to be the second examiner to the PhD thesis. The first paragraph of his report reads as follows: "Bismarck famously said that if one loves laws and one loves sausages, it is better not to see how they are made. After reading this thesis, we might add 'including customary law'". This quote offers proof that being one of the leading authorities in international criminal law does not necessarily deprive you from a great sense of humour.

I am particularly indebted to my fellow colleagues at the Paris Lodron University of Salzburg, Dr. Lando Kirchmair, Mag. Robert Kogler, Mag[a]. Sandra Hummelbrunner and Dr. Lucia Schulten, not only for their insightful comments on many of the chapters but most importantly for their great company and friendship.

I also want to thank Dr. Ian Macgregor Morris for proofreading and correcting my adventurous grammatical creations.

Needless to say, while all of these people mentioned above have substantially contributed to this book, the responsibility for any remaining errors rests with me.

Last but not least, I gratefully acknowledge the financial support received from the Anniversary Fund of the Oesterreichische Nationalbank (OeNB).

Contents

List of Abbreviations

AC	Appeals Chamber
AP	Additional Protocol
Art.	Article
c.f.	Confer (compare further)
CRC	Convention on the Rights of the Child
Doc.	Document
ECCC	Extraordinary Chambers in the Courts of Cambodia
ECHR	European Convention on Human Rights
ECtHR	European Court of Human Rights
ed. (eds.)	Editor (editors)
e.g.	Exempli gratia (for instance)
et al.	Et alii (and others)
f. (ff.)	Folio (foliis) (and the following)
FN	Footnote
FS	Festschrift
GAOR	General Assembly Official Records
GC	Geneva Convention
i.a.	Inter alia (among other things)
IAC	International armed conflict
ibid.	Ibidem (in the same place)
ICC	International Criminal Court
ICCPR	International Covenant on Civil and Political Rights
ICJ	International Court of Justice
ICRC	International Committee of the Red Cross
ICTR	International Criminal Tribunal for Rwanda
ICTY	International Criminal Tribunal for the Former Yugoslavia
id.	Idem (the same)
i.e.	Id est (in other words)
IHL	International humanitarian law
ILA	International Law Association
ILC	International Law Commission

ILO	International Labour Organization
ILR	International Law Reports
IMT	International Military Tribunal (Nuremberg)
IMTFE	International Military Tribunal for the Far East (Tokyo)
JCE	Joint criminal enterprise
LNTS	League of Nations Treaty Series
NCSI	*Nullum crimen sine iure*
NCSL	*Nullum crimen sine lege*
NIAC	Non-international armed conflict
para	Paragraph
PCIJ	Permanent Court of International Justice
pp.	Per procurationem (the following pages)
PTC	Pre-Trial Chamber
SC	Security Council
SCSL	Special Court for Sierra Leone
SG	Secretary General
TC	Trial Chamber
UDHR	Universal Declaration of Human Rights
UN	United Nations
UNTAET	United Nations Transitional Administration in East Timor
UNTS	United Nations Treaty Series
v.	Versus (against)
Vol.	Volume

Chapter 1
Introduction

1.1 Research Questions

The aim of this study is to analyze the methodology used by international criminal tribunals when determining customary international criminal law and to consider the compatibility of these methodological approaches with the *nullum crimen sine lege* principle. In that regard the following research questions are of particular importance: Is there one approach common to international criminal tribunals or are different approaches detectable in their jurisprudence when determining customary international law? Do international criminal tribunals regard both traditional elements of customary international law, State practice and *opinio iuris*, as necessary elements for the establishment of customary international law? Do international criminal tribunals argue along the lines of the International Court of Justice (ICJ) requiring a high frequency and consistency of State practice, that is both "extensive and virtually uniform"?[1] In addition, the evidence used by international criminal tribunals in order to establish the constituent elements of customary international law will be analyzed. Finally, do international criminal tribunals distinguish, according to *Schwarzenberger*, between the "law-creating processes" of public international law on the one hand, and the "law-determining agencies" as subsidiary means for the determination of a rule of law on the other?[2]

Assuming that they exist, how can different methodological approaches to determine customary international law be assessed in light of the *nullum crimen sine lege* principle? Does the principle require judges to apply the traditional method to establish customary international law as being based on extensive,

---

[1]See ICJ, North Sea Continental Shelf Cases (Federal Republic of Germany v. Denmark, Federal Republic of Germany v. the Netherlands), ICJ Reports (1969) 3, para 74.

[2]*G. Schwarzenberger*, The Inductive Approach to International Law (1965), 5, 19ff.

© Springer International Publishing AG 2017
T. Rauter, *Judicial Practice, Customary International Criminal Law and* Nullum Crimen Sine Lege, DOI 10.1007/978-3-319-64477-6_1

uniform and enduring state practice accompanied by *opinio iuris*?[3] Can the principle balance the urge for justice and the specificities of law creation of the international legal order with fairness for the accused?[4] How can the law be accessible and criminal punishment foreseeable, when the underlying legal basis for criminal convictions, customary international criminal law, is unwritten in nature?

These are the questions that shall be addressed in this thesis.

1.2 Structure of the Thesis

The study begins by considering how public international law, a legal order that traditionally was focused on inter-State relations, began to be directly applicable to individuals by the establishing of international crimes (Chap. 2). Since the comprehension of the *nullum crimen sine lege* principle is central for this thesis, Chap. 3 deals with this fundamental principle of criminal law. Its domestic origin, theoretical foundations and application in the Nuremberg era will be assessed and it is asked whether its firm inclusion in international (human rights and humanitarian law) conventions changed the perception of this principle by international criminal tribunals, evincing a shift from "substantive justice" to "strict legality".[5] In terms of the sources of international law, which comprise conventional and unwritten norms, the principle in international criminal law is best considered as *nullum crimen sine iure*. Its *praevia* requirement prohibits *ex post facto* law creation and thus this chapter also considers which sources of public international law are adequate sources of international criminal law. International criminal tribunals have generally made criminal convictions dependent on the existence of customary international criminal norms. Chapter 4 discusses the formation of customary international law and its methodological challenges, describing traditional and modern approaches. Chapter 5 analyzes the role judges play in that regard, and whether they should merely determine or develop or even create customary international law. Chapter 6 elaborates on the methodological approaches to customary international law detectable in the jurisprudence of international criminal tribunals. Chapter 7 considers the evidence used by the chambers to verify the existence of customary international criminal law and tries to allocate these instances to the

---

[3]See also *T. Hoffmann*, The Gentle Civilizer of Humanitarian Law, in Stahn/van den Herik (eds.), Future Perspectives on International Criminal Justice (2010), 67, who determines that the SG Report on the ICTY demanding the ICTY to apply norms that are "beyond any doubt part of customary law", results in the "inescapable conclusion" that the ICTY "was obliged to use only the most conservative positivist methodology in finding the applicable law".

[4]These different requirements have been addressed by *M.C. Bassiouni* and *P. Manikas*, The Law of the International Criminal Tribunal for the Former Yugoslavia (1996), 265; see also ICTY, *Prosecutor v. Vasiljević*, Case No. IT-98-32-T, Judgment, Trial Chamber, 29 November 2002, para 193.

[5]*A. Cassese* International Criminal Law (2008), 36ff.

elements of State practice or *opinio iuris*, and whether they could be used as subsidiary means for the determination of customary international law. The conclusions are drawn in Chap. 8.

1.3 Terminology

The term international criminal law carries various meanings.[6] From a domestic point of view it may describe the boundaries for the application of domestic criminal norms when the crime has international points of contact, establishing a link to a concrete domestic criminal law system on basis of site of the crime, nationality of the victim or nationality of the perpetrator.[7] Furthermore, States might choose to foster their cooperation in criminal matters, especially were crimes have transborder effects.[8] It could also be understood from a comparative law point of view as a criminal law common to civilized nations that might influence the international legal sphere as general principles of law recognized by civilized nations according to Art. 38 lit. c ICJ Statute. Last but not least, international criminal law may also describe substantive international criminal law that imposes criminal responsibility directly on individuals for violations of international law without the need of an intermediate step *via* the domestic legal forum.[9] Due to these different conceptions of international criminal law, the diversity of labels are also reflected in the legal literature, using terms such as crimes under international law, international crimes, international crimes *largo sensu*, international crimes *strictu*

---

[6]*Schwarzenberger* identified six meanings of ICL: in the meaning of the territorial scope of municipal criminal law, of internationally prescribed municipal criminal law, of internationally authorized municipal criminal law, of municipal criminal law common to civilized nations, of international co-operation in the administration of municipal criminal justice, and in the material sense of the word; G. *Schwarzenberger*, The Problem of an International Criminal Law, in: G.O.W. Mueller and E. M. Wise (eds.), International Criminal Law (1965), 3ff; when looking at the terms used in other languages it is evident that some of them give a clearer picture of distinction between international criminal law and transnational criminal law. German legal language differentiates between "Völkerstrafrecht" and "Internationales Strafrecht", French legal language between "droit international penal" and "droit penal international", and Spanish legal language between "derecho internacional penal" and "derecho penal internacional".

[7]Compare for instance: PCIJ, S.S. Lotus (France v. Turkey), 1927 PCIJ (ser. A) No. 10 (Sept. 7), Judgment.

[8]For example: European Convention on Mutual Assistance in Criminal Matters, ETS 30; 41 ECA 283; 72 UNTS 185.

[9]*Schwarzenberger's* definition of ICL in the material sense of the word (supra note 6), 13ff; cf. *S. R. Ratner, J. S. Abrams, J. L. Bischoff*, Accountability for Human Rights Atrocities in International Law: Beyond the Nuremberg Legacy (2009), 10; *Luban* describes these offences as "pure international crimes" both in relation to the origin of the prohibitions as well as the enforcement mechanisms, namely international criminal tribunals; see *D. Luban*, Fairness to Rightness: Jurisdiction, Legality and the Legitimacy of International Criminal Law, Georgetown Law Faculty Working Papers (July 2008), 5.

sensu, transnational crimes, international delicts, *jus cogens* crimes and *jus cogens* international crimes.[10] For the purpose of this study the term international criminal law is used in relation to the "core crimes" under international law: genocide, crimes against humanity and war crimes. Those crimes are established by international law itself,[11] meaning that international law directly establishes the criminality without the necessity of an interim step through the domestic legal order. Furthermore, this study will deal exclusively with substantive international criminal law and not with its procedural aspects. Thus, the focus is placed on the prohibited acts under international law for which the individual can be held criminal accountable directly under international law, the modes of liability, and international criminal law defenses.

---

[10]*M. C. Bassiouni*, Introduction to International Criminal Law (2003), 114.

[11]See also Sect. 3.10.5, The *praevia* Requirement and the Sources of International Law.

Chapter 2
State Responsibility and the Criminal Liability of the Individual

2.1 Nuremberg: Setting the Stage

It was only with the establishment of the International Military Tribunal at Nuremberg (IMT), that the international community became capable of coping with the question of individual criminal responsibility after the committing of atrocities on the international plane. Efforts were made to establish individual criminal responsibility during the inter-war period through the Versailles Treaty of 28 June 1919 by holding German Emperor Wilhelm II of Hohenzollern responsible for the "supreme offence against international morality and the sanctity of treaties" and other "persons accused of having committed acts in violation of the laws and customs of war".[1] These efforts, however, did not fall on fertile soil. The major powers focused on ensuring the future peace of Europe and therefore neglected holding individuals criminally responsible.[2] The Netherlands did not surrender the Kaiser for trial and the Leipzig trials conducted under German law proved ineffective.[3] According to *Triffterer*, the sovereignty of the national States were not shaken to their very foundations by World War I, thus maintaining the *status quo* and the assumption that states and not individuals were to be held internationally accountable.[4] Efforts to establish an International Court of Criminal Justice were thwarted when in 1920 a Committee of the Assembly of the League of Nations considered the idea to be

---

[1]Treaty of Peace with Germany (Treaty of Versailles), 28 June 1919, 11 Martens Nouveau Recueil (3d), Arts. 227 and 228.

[2]*M. C. Bassiouni*, Introduction to International Criminal Law (2003), 403.

[3]The 1919 Commission on the Responsibilities of the Authors of War and on the Enforcement of Penalties has established a list of 895 alleged war criminals; only 12 were tried with 6 being convicted to serve sentences ranging between 6 months to 4 years. Cf *Bassiouni* (supra note 2), 402; *A. Cassese* International Criminal Law (2008), 317.

[4]*O. Triffterer*, Dogmatische Untersuchungen zur Entwicklung des materiellen Völkerstrafrechts seit Nürnberg (1966), 10.

© Springer International Publishing AG 2017
T. Rauter, *Judicial Practice, Customary International Criminal Law and* Nullum
Crimen Sine Lege, DOI 10.1007/978-3-319-64477-6_2

"premature".[5] The sanctions available to the international legal order at that time were still restricted to collective sanctions, while penal sanctions were generally not considered: international treaties addressed states, not individuals.[6] Thus, within public international law, conceived historically as a horizontal legal order regulating inter-State relations, the individual would not come within its legal sphere. Generally, when organs of a State committed a violation of international law, international law only permitted sanctions addressed to the state itself, as the sanctions available only concerned collective responsibility.[7] The individual was not within the focus of public international law, although two exceptions should be mentioned: piracy and slavery. A pirate, due the threat he poses to the safety of the high seas, has been considered an outlaw for centuries, a *hostis humani generis*. Consequently, each state, whether affected by the acts of the pirates or not, had the right to bring them to justice.[8] The interest to prevent piracy was economically driven as the major trading powers needed to secure trade on the high seas. In contrast, the prohibition of the slave trade was a humanitarian endeavour and early attempts of an international court to suppress slave trade provide an important precursor to later developments.[9]

There have been striking different views of the genesis of individual responsibility for war crimes. Some have suggested that individual criminal responsibility for war crimes can be dated to the middle ages, the natural law theories of *Grotius* and *Vattel*,[10] or the second half of the nineteenth century when the codification process of the laws and customs of warfare began.[11] Others insist that in the middle

---

[5]Cf. Lord *Phillimore*, An International Court and The Resolutions of the Committee of Jurists, 3 British Yearbook of International law (1922–23), 84.

[6]See Art. 3 of the 1907 Hague Convention (IV) respecting the Laws and Customs of War on Land, 36 Stat. 2277, 3 Martens Nouveau Recueil (ser. 3) 461: "A belligerent party which violates the provisions of the said Regulations shall, if the case demands, be liable to pay compensation. It shall be responsible for all acts committed by persons forming part of its armed forces." See, however, *Lauterpacht* who argues that "[t]here ought to be no doubt that these provisions refer to the responsibility of the State as a whole, and that they were not intended to exclude the responsibility of individuals or the customary right of States to punish enemy individuals for the violation of rules of war." *H. Lauterpacht*, The Law of Nations and the Punishment of War Crimes, 21 British Yearbook of International Law (1944), 65.

[7]*H. Kelsen*, Collective and Individual Responsibility in International Law with Particular Regard to the Punishment of War Criminals, 31 California Law Review (1943), 533–4.

[8]*Kelsen* (supra note 7), 534ff; *L. Oppenheim*, 1 International Law (1995), 609. Cf *A. de Gentili*, De Iure Belli (1612), Book I, Chapter XXV (Carnegie translation 1933), 124; The crime of piracy has also been criminalized in international treaties: The Nyon Arrangement, 14 September 1937, 181 L.N.T.S., 135; Agreement Supplementary to the Nyon Agreement, 17 September 1937, 181 L. N.T.S., 149; The Convention on the High Seas, 29 April 1958, 450 U.N.T.S. 82; Convention on the Law of the Sea, 10 December 1982, U.N. Doc. A/Conf. 62/122.

[9]Cf. *J.S. Martinez*, Antislavery Court and the Dawn of International Human Rights Law, 117 Yale Law Journal (2008), 550ff.

[10]*E. van Sliedregt*, Individual Criminal Responsibility in International Law (2012), 4 with further references.

[11]*Cassese* (supra note 3), 28–31 referring *inter alia* to the Lieber Code, the Hague Codifications of 1899 and 1907 and further to national prosecutions.

of the twentieth century international law still exclusively addressed States and not individuals. *Kelsen* argued that only individuals that do not belong to the enemy state's regular armed forces and have taken up arms against the occupant state may be punished,[12] but that war crimes committed by the regular armed forces of a state had to be "imputed to the State and not to the individual who has performed it, the individual, according to general international law, cannot be made responsible for his act by another State without the consent of the State whose act is concerned".[13] The acts of regular armed troops were thus attributed to the state and not to the acting individuals, a view shared by *Verdross*.[14]

Whatever point of departure is taken it is clear that at least since the inter-war period there has been a growing acceptance that individual responsibility for the commission of war crimes was given under international law, stipulating an exception to the concept of "collective responsibility".[15] During World War II several declarations insisted that German crimes would not go unpunished. In fact the prosecution of the German war criminals was proclaimed to be a major war aim,[16] and individuals were held criminally liable for the violations of the laws and customs of warfare before domestic courts.[17] The United Nations War Crimes Commission, formed in order to state the development of the law of war crimes during 1939–1945, simply declared that the right to "punish as war criminals persons who violate the laws or customs of war is a *well-recognised principle* of international law".[18] However, it also stated that the right to try alleged war criminals depended on the existence of an armed conflict between two states, was possible when offenders were captured or when the enemy territory was occupied,

---

[12]*Kelsen* (supra note 7), 536.

[13]*H. Kelsen*, Peace through Law (1944), 81.

[14]*A. Verdross*, Völkerrecht (1937), 298: "Eine Bestrafung ist aber ausgeschlossen, wenn die Tat nicht aus eigenem Antrieb beganfgen wurde, sondern ausschließlich dem Heimatstaat zugerechnet werden kann." *Cassese* (supra note 3), 29 (footnote 36) however argues that both, *Kelsen* and *Verdross*, are simply wrong.

[15]Cf *Cassese* (supra note 3), 28; *R. K Woetzel*, The Nuremberg Trials in International Law with a Postlude on the Eichmann Case (1962), 36ff.

[16]Cf Inter-Allied Commission, Punishment for War Crimes, signed at St. James's Palace, London, 13th January, 1942, as printed in: History of the United Nations War Crimes Commission and the Development of the Laws of War (1948), 89ff; The Moscow Declaration of 1st November 1943, printed in: History of the United Nations War Crimes Commission and the Development of the Laws of War (1948), 107f.

[17]See US Supreme Court, *Ex parte Quirin et al.* (1942) 317 U.S. 1; at 27–28: "From the very beginning of its history this Court has applied the law of war as including that part of the law of nations which prescribes, for the conduct of war, the status, rights and duties of enemy nations as well as enemy individuals." See also *Fujii v. State of California*, 217 Pac. (2d) 481 and *Oyama v. State of California*, 332 US 633. War crimes trials were also held in the Soviet Union, c.f. *K.H. Lüders*, Strafgerichtsbarkeit über Angehörige des Feindstaates, Süddeutsche Juristenzeitung, 1946, 217–28 with further references.

[18]United Nations War Crimes Commission, History of the United Nations War Crimes Commission and the Development of the Laws of War (1948), 29 (emphasis added).

but ceased with the end of hostilities.[19] *Kelsen* argued that an individual serving in the regular armed forces could not, according to general international law, be held responsible for his act by another state without the consent of the state he served[20]; however, unconditional surrender could be deemed as such consent. When the Third Reich unconditionally surrendered to the Western Allies, the victorious powers assumed "supreme authority with respect to Germany, including all the powers possessed by the German Government, the high Command and any state, municipal, or local government or authority."[21] The Nuremberg Charter, annexed to the Agreement for the Prosecution and Punishment of the Major War Criminals of the European Axis,[22] can therefore be considered to be both an international agreement and the expression of the German legislative authority as exercised by the Occupying Allied Powers. With the IMT Nuremberg Charter, international criminal law, as we understand it today, was formed, establishing direct individual accountability for violations of international law. The charter did not restrict individual responsibility to the notion of war crimes, but also included individual liability for crimes against peace and crimes against humanity.[23] The Nuremberg Tribunal famously placed the shift from collective international responsibility to individual criminal responsibility in the following words:

> Crimes against international law are committed by men, not by abstract entities, and only by punishing individuals who commit such crimes can the provisions of international law be enforced.[24]

The Tribunal described the essence of international criminal law as "individuals [having] international duties which transcend the national obligations of obedience imposed by the individual state."[25] Although the Nuremberg Charter and the IMT had been established by the Allied Powers, the IMT Nuremberg sought to show that the Nuremberg Charter was "not an arbitrary exercise of power on the part of the

---

[19] *Ibid*; cf. US Supreme Court, *Ex parte Yamashita* (1946) 327 U.S. 1.

[20] *Kelsen* (supra note 13), 81.

[21] Defeat of Germany: Assumption of Supreme Authority by Allied Powers, Declaration signed at Berlin 5 June 1945, 60 Stat. 1649 as cited in *C. I. Bevans*, Treaties and Other International Agreements of the United States of America 1776–1949, Volume 3 Multilateral 1931–1945 (1969), 1140.

[22] Nuremberg Charter as annexed to the Agreement for the Prosecution and Punishment of the Major War Criminals of the European Axis (London Agreement), 39 American Journal of International Law Supplement (1945), 257ff between the United States of America, the French Republic, the United Kingdom of Great Britain and Northern Ireland and the Union of Soviet Socialist Republics, which consequently was ratified by 19 other States.

[23] Art. 6 Nuremberg Charter (supra note 22). Those three categories of crimes are also contained in the Tokyo Charter, Art. 5 as annexed to the Special Proclamation by the Supreme Commander for the Allied Powers, 19 January 1946, Treaties and Other International Agreements of the United States of America 1589.

[24] IMT Nuremberg, Trial of the Major War Criminals Before the International Military Tribunal, Vol. 1 (Nuremberg, 1947) ("Blue Series"), 223.

[25] *Ibid*.

victorious Nations, but [...] the expression of international law existing at the time of its creation".[26] Nevertheless, there has been persistent critique that the IMT Nuremberg applied *ex post facto* law, thereby violating the *nullum crimen sine lege* principle.[27] Aware of the need to legitimise the jurisprudence of the IMT and the Nuremberg Charter, the United Nations General Assembly decided to "affirm" unanimously the principles of international law recognized by the Charter of the Nuremberg Tribunal and the judgment of the Tribunal on 11 December 1946.[28] Furthermore, the General Assembly appointed the International Law Commission to the task of formulating these principles,[29] published in 1950.[30] Although these instruments were not binding by themselves, they nevertheless shaped the perception of international criminal law. Indeed, it is interesting to note that in 1946 the General Assembly used the term "affirmation", implying that the Nuremberg Charter stipulated, and that the tribunal applied, law that was already in existence. It thus gave the impression that the laws were not created retroactively.[31] While there are grounds to sustain the accusation of *ex post facto* law creation *via* the Charter and the IMT Nuremberg,[32] the affirmation of the Nuremberg principles by the General Assembly were formative for their evolution as customary law.[33] Indeed, actors on both, the international as well as the domestic level, have

---

[26]IMT Nuremberg Judgment, Vol. 1, 218.

[27]*C. Burchard*, The Nuremberg Trial and its Impact on Germany, 4 Journal of International Criminal Justice (2004), 800ff with further references. See also Sect. 3.5, *Nullum Crimen Sine Lege* and the IMT Nuremberg and the IMTFE Tokyo, p. 24.

[28]UN GA Res. 95 (I), A/RES/95 (I).

[29]UN GA Res. 177 (1947), A/RES/177 (II).

[30]International Law Commission, Principles of International law Recognized in the Charter of the Nürnberg Tribunal and in the Judgment of the Tribunal, Yearbook of the International Law Commission (1950), Vol. II, para 97, which were, however, not approved by a General Assembly resolution.

[31]*E. Greppi*, The Evolution of Individual Criminal Responsibility under International Law, International Review of the Red Cross, Volume 81, Issue 835 (1999), 531ff; *A. Cassese*, Affirmation of the Principles of International law Recognized by the Charter of the Nürnberg Tribunal (2009), 1ff available at: http://legal.un.org/avl/ha/ga_95-I/ga_95-I.html (last visited 16 June 2017).

[32]*Burchard* (supra note 27), 800ff.

[33]*M. P. Scharf*, Seizing the "Grotian Moment": Accelerated Formation of Customary International Law in Times of Fundamental Change, 43 Cornell International Law Journal (2012), 454–5, however he generally acknowledges problems determining customary international law *via* General Assembly resolutions (pp. 447–448). Nevertheless, the International Court of Justice also has recourse to General Assembly resolutions as evidence for customary international law: see *Scharf* in footnote 50 referring *inter alia* to Military and Paramilitary Activities in and against Nicaragua (Nicaragua v. US), ICJ Reports (1986), 14; Legality of the Threat or Use of Nuclear Weapons, Advisory Opinion, ICJ Reports (1996), 254–255; Legal Consequences of the Construction of a Wall in the Occupied Palestinian Territory, Advisory Opinion, ICJ Reports (2004), 171; Armed Activities on the Territory of the Congo (Democratic Republic of Congo v. Uganda), 45 ILM 271, 308–309. For the importance of General Assembly when determining customary international law, see Sect. 7.6, UN Resolutions.

regularly referred to this resolution as a declaration of customary international law.[34]

The IMT Nuremberg has rightly been celebrated as the obstetrician of international criminal law, with individual responsibility and punishment of international crimes as its "cornerstone" and the "enduring legacy of the Charter and the Judgment of the Nuremberg Tribunal".[35] International criminal tribunals today have provisions on "war crimes"[36] and "crimes against humanity" within their jurisdiction.[37] To date, only the Rome Statute of the International Criminal Court has included "crime against peace" as the "crime of aggression".[38] The ICC State parties have agreed on the definition of the crime of aggression and the conditions on exercising jurisdiction at the Review Conference in Kampala, Uganda.[39] In contrast to the IMT Nuremberg and the IMTFE Tokyo statutes, international criminal tribunals include a provision on genocide within their jurisdiction,[40] a term coined by *Lemkin* in 1944.[41] The concept originated from the notion of crimes against humanity, but found distinct recognition as an international crime in the

---

[34]See for example: Report of the Secretary-General Pursuant to Paragraph 2 of Security Council Resolution 808 (1993), 3 May 1993, UN Doc S/25704, para 35 (SG Report on ICTY); Reference to both, the GA Resolution 95 (I) and the Nuremberg principles as formulated by the ILC can be found in various instances of case law: *R. v. Finta*, Supreme Court of Canada (1994) 1 S.C.R. 701; Israeli Supreme Court, Eichmann Case; European Court of Human Rights, *Kolk and Kislyiy v. Estonia*, Application Nos. 23052/04 and 24018/04, Decision on Admissibility, 17 January 2006; ICTY, *Prosecutor v. Tadić*, IT-94-1-T, Trial Chamber, Opinion and Judgment, 7 May 1997, para 623. Cf. *Scharf* (supra note 33), 455.

[35]Cf. International Law Commission, Draft Code of Crimes against the Peace and Security of Mankind with commentaries, Yearbook of the International Law Commission (1996), Vol. II, Part 2, Art. 2 Individual Responsibility (1996 ILC Draft Code), 19.

[36]Statute of the International Criminal Tribunal for the former Yugoslavia UNSC Res 827 (1993) (25 May 1993), Arts. 2 and 3 (ICTY Statute); Statute of the International Tribunal for Rwanda UNSC Res 955 (1994) (8 November 1994), Art. 4 (ICTR Statute); Statue of the Special Court for Sierra Leone, 2178 UNTS 138, UN Doc. S/2002/246 (2002), Appendix II, Arts. 3 and 4 (SCSL Statute); Rome Statute of the International Criminal Court, 2187 UNTS 90 (1 July 2002), Art. 8 (ICC Statute).

[37]Art. 5 ICTY Statute, Art. 3 ICTR Statute, Art. 2 SCSL Statute, Art. 7 ICC Statute.

[38]Art. 5 ICC Statute.

[39]Cf. Resolution RC/Res.6, Depositary Notification C.N.651.2010 Treaties-8, ICC, Assembly of State Parties, 11 June 2010, Annex I. For an overview of the drafting process see *K. Schmalenbach*, The Crime of Aggression Before the International Criminal Court, in: *Liber Amicorum Rüdiger Wolfrum*, Coexistence, Cooperation and Solidarity Vol. II (2012), 1259ff; see also *S. Barriga, C. Kress* (eds.), The Travaux Préparatoires of the Crime of Aggression (2012).

[40]Art. 4 ICTY Statute, Art. 2 ICTR Statute, Art. 6 ICC Statute.

[41]*R. Lemkin*, Axis Rule in Occupied Europe: Laws of Occupation, Analysis of Government, Proposals for Redress (1944), 79, who assembled the Greek word *genos* (race, tribe) and the Latin word *cide* (killing).

1948 Genocide Convention.[42] War crimes, crimes against humanity and genocide have been labeled the "core crimes" of international law,[43] which will be the main focus of this thesis.

2.2 International Criminal Law: A Collision of Legal Systems

While the IMT Nuremberg set the stage for international criminal law it must be remembered that it is a rather young branch of international law,[44] still in its infancy and facing issues in relation to its doctrinal foundations.[45] At the outset, there is something to the critique that international criminal law is cursed by a "profound and innate schizophrenia".[46] Within the sphere of international criminal law different and seemingly contradictory legal regimes collide. On the one hand, we encounter the doctrine of public international law, which in its classical form is addressed at states, based on the consent between equal states and is thus characterized as a system of horizontal relations. The law creation process at the international level differs from the domestic due to the lack of any central legislator. On the other hand, criminal law developed in communities, which later consolidated as states. The individual is subordinated in a vertical relationship to a national legislator that coercively imposes duties upon him or her.[47] In democratic societies, the parliament as the representative body of the individuals enacts penal laws as an *ultima ratio* for the protection of the common good, in which the individual participates as a legal subject.[48] To enforce its penal laws the domestic legal order uses its

---

[42]Convention on the Prevention and Punishment of the Crime of Genocide, 9 December 1948, 78 UNTS 277 (entered into force 12 January 1951). According to *Simma* and *Paulus* the Genocide Convention takes a unique position among international treaties since Article VI establishes the "truly *international* legal character of the crime". B. *Simma* and A.L. *Paulus*, The Responsibility of Individuals for Human Rights Abuses in Internal Conflicts: A Positivist View, in 93 American Journal of International Law (1999), 308 (emphasis in original).

[43]See e.g. G. *Boas*, The Difficulty with Individual Criminal Responsibility in International Criminal Law, Stahn/van den Herik (eds.), Future Perspective on International Criminal Justice (2010), 502.

[44]*Cassese* (supra note 3), 4.

[45]*Bassiouni* (supra note 2), 685.

[46]S. R *Ratner*, The Schizophrenias of International Criminal Law, 33 Texas International Law Journal (1998), 251.

[47]M. *Boot*, Genocide, Crimes Against Humanity, War Crimes. Nullum Crimen Sine Lege and the Subject Matter Jurisdiction of the International Criminal Court (2002), 14; R. D. *Sloane*, The Expressive Capacity of International Punishment: The Limits of the National law Analogy and the Potential of International Criminal Law, in 43 Stanford Journal of International law (2007), 40.

[48]C. J. M. *Safferling*, The Justification of Punishment in International Criminal Law – Can National Theories of Justification be Applied to the International Level, 4 Austrian Review of International & European Law (2000), 153.

state apparatus, such as the police, the prosecution and criminal courts. This incongruity between public international law and national criminal law led *Schwarzenberger* to conclude that international criminal law is a "contradiction in terms".[49]

For centuries these two legal regimes did not collide. Predominantly, in relation to international law individuals were objects and not subjects of law.[50] The only way individuals could be affected by international law was if the international legal order gave the national state a right to protect the individual's interest, or it imposed on the national state a duty to regulate certain conduct within its own domestic legal system. Individuals could not be the immediate beneficiary of international law, as they could not bring forward claims against a state. Instead, the national state was required to mediate for the individual on the international plane *via* diplomatic protection. However, once the state exercises diplomatic protection it would not claim the violation of the rights of its citizens, but would assert its own rights.[51] Similarly, individuals could neither be the immediate addressees of international law, instead requiring the state to enact national laws to transform international obligations into the domestic sphere.[52] *Triepel* considered the idea of subordinating the state and the individual under a single legal regime to be an "impossible thought".[53] Such a doubt reflects the idea of dualism, the consideration of international law and national law as two distinct legal systems or "circles" that could not coalesce.[54] In this view state responsibility would only be possible as a form of

---

[49]*G. Schwarzenberger*, The Problem of an International Criminal Law, in: G.O.W. Mueller and E. M. Wise (eds.), International Criminal Law (1965), 35; see also *Cassese* (supra note 3), 7–9 referring to "conflicting philosophies" of international criminal law and public international law.

[50]*G. Manner*, The Object Theory of the Individual in International law, 46 American Journal of International Law (1952), 428ff; *R. Higgins*, Rethinking the Conceptual Thinking about the Individual in International Law, in 4 British Journal of International Studies (1978), 2ff.

[51]PCIJ, Mavrommatis Palestine Concessions Case (Greece v. United Kingdom), 1924 PCIJ (ser. A) No. 2 (30 August 1924), Judgment, 12: "a state is in reality asserting its own rights, its right to ensure, in the person of its subjects, respect for the rules of international law"; *S. Vattel*, The Law of Nations (1916), 136: "Whoever ill-treats a citizen indirectly injures the state, which must protect that citizen".

[52]Cf. Dissenting Opinion Nielsen, Mexico-United States General Claims Commission, International Fisheries Company (USA) v. Mexico, July 1931, 4 Reports of International Arbitral Awards, 728: "International law contains no penal provisions forbidding acts on the part of either individuals or corporations, and no rules of any kind imposing any obligations except obligations binding on states." The reliance on the domestic legal order in order to enforce international criminal law is referred to in the legal literature as the "indirect enforcement model". Cf. *Bassiouni* (supra note 2), 29f; *Safferling* (supra note 48), 143f.

[53]*H. Triepel*, Völkerrecht und Landesrecht (1899), 329: "[S]o ist es undenkbar, daß eine 'Norm' des Völkerrechts vom Einzelnen übertreten werde. Delikte des Individuums, 'Verbrechen gegen das Völkerrecht' giebt es nicht. Weder gegen 'allgemeines' Völkerrecht, noch gegen 'Staatsverträge' kann sich das Individuum verfehlen." And further at 333: "Denn was der Staat befiehlt, gilt es zu wissen. Gegen sein Gebot, nicht gegen das des Völkerrechts sündigt der Unterthan."

[54]*Triepel* (supra note 53), 111.

collective responsibility in response to breaches of international law. Individual criminal responsibility could only take place within the domestic legal sphere.

On the other hand *Kelsen*—although highlighting the fact that international law is generally directed at states and that a system of collective responsibility of states is in place—saw in the establishment of individual criminal responsibility an exception to the indirect relationship between individuals and international law. He contended that to some extent "international law penetrates areas that heretofore have been the exclusive domain of national legal orders, its tendency toward obligating or authorizing individuals directly increases."[55] At least since the establishment of the IMT Nuremberg, it has been widely accepted that international law imposes duties upon individuals who are directly accountable under international law.[56] At the time of the Nuremberg Trial such a finding was indeed groundbreaking.[57] International law penetrated the legal shield of sovereignty of the domestic legal order, directly accessing the individual, leading to their partial subjectivity under international law. As partial subjects individuals possess rights and duties under international law only if they are specifically assigned to them.[58] The result is a restricted legal personality of individuals in specific legal fields. International law addresses individuals only in exceptional circumstances. In relation to the application of international criminal law, this requires that individual responsibility can only be invoked if a prohibition under international law attributes individual criminal responsibility.[59] In order to respond to the breach of the legal obligations by the individual, the international legal order is thereby using the same sanctions that previously have been reserved for states, *i.e.* criminal sanctions.[60] Within domestic borders the state authority exercises the monopoly of the *ius puniendi* and has the power to create binding criminal norms for its citizens. Criminal law as

---

[55]*H. Kelsen*, Pure Theory of Law (1967 as translated by Knight), 324–328. He considers that the establishment of tribunals commences the centralization of international law.

[56]Trial of the major war criminals before the International Military Tribunal, Vol. 1 (Nuremberg, 1947), 223.

[57]Individual criminal responsibility does, however, not displace State responsibility, as a double attribution to individuals as well as States is possible. See for instance ICJ, Application of the Convention on the Prevention and Punishment of the Crime of Genocide (Bosnia and Herzegovina v. Serbia and Montenegro), Judgment, 26 February 2007, ICJ Reports 2007, 43. Compare also *van Sliedregt* (supra note 10), 5–7 with further references.

[58]*P.K. Menon*, Individuals as Subjects of International Law, Revue de Droit International 1992, 319. *K. Ipsen*, Völkerrecht (2004), 96. "Legal personality" or "subjectivity of law" is associated with the capacity of possessing rights and/or duties, cf. *I. Brownlie*, Principles of Public International Law (2008), 57; *M.N. Shaw*, International Law (2008), 195.

[59]See also advisory opinion of the Inter-American Court of Human Rights in the Re-Introduction of the Death Penalty in the Peruvian Constitution Case, 16 Human Rights Law Journal (1995), 14.

[60]*Kelsen* (supra note 55), 327.

a matter of public policy is closely connected to state sovereignty.[61] It presupposes a consolidated community in which it functions as the *ultima ratio* for the protection of legitimate values and interests ("Rechtsgüter") of the national society.[62] At the heart of domestic criminal law lies the principle of individual culpability, holding the individual accountable because of his conscious "deviance from societal expectations".[63] The question is how to fit international criminal law into this perceived picture of a criminal legal order.

In terms of protected values and interests ("Rechtsgüter") the entire concept of international criminal law presupposes the existence of an international community with common values.[64] It has been repeatedly stated that international crimes not only affect the interests of one state or the interests of the concerned individuals alone but also shock "the collective conscience of mankind".[65] The purpose of international criminal law is the protection of supra-national values of the international community binding all states and individuals.[66] There is thus an international

---

[61]*J. Crawford*, The ILC Adopts a Statute for an International Criminal Court, 89 American Journal of International Law (1995), 406. See on the question of the *ius puniendi* at the supranational level without a sovereign, *K. Ambos*, Punishment without a Sovereign? The Ius Puniendi Issue of International Criminal Law: A First Contribution towards a Consistent Theory of International Criminal Law, 33 Oxford Journal of Legal Studies (2013), 293ff.

[62]*N. Jareborg*, Criminalization as Last Resort (*Ultima Ratio*), 2 Ohio State Journal of Criminal Law (2004), 524–525, referring to *C. Roxin*, Strafrecht: Allgemeiner Teil I: Grundlagen. Der Aufbau der Verbrechenslehre (1997), 11–30. Those "Rechtsgüter" are *inter alia* human life and dignity, physical and sexual integrity, protection of property etc.

[63]*D. Robinson*, A Cosmopolitan Liberal Account of International Criminal Law, 26 Leiden Journal of International Law (2013), 134.

[64]*Bassiouni* (supra note 2), 31, who considers that ICL presupposes the existence of an implied social contract (at p. 690); for a rationale of ICL on basis of *Kant* see *K. Gierhake*, Begründung des Völkerstrafrechts auf der Grundlage der Kantischen Rechtslehre (2005).

[65]Compare for instance ICJ, Reservations to the Convention on the Prevention and Punishment of the Crime of Genocide, Advisory Opinion 28 May 1951, ICJ Reports (1951), 23; ICTR, *Prosecutor v. Ruggiu*, Case No. ICTR-97-32-T, Trial Chamber, Judgment and Sentence, 1 June 2000, para 48; *Prosecutor v. Nzabirinda*, Case No. ICTR 2001-77-T, Trial Chamber II, Sentencing Judgment, 23 February 2007, para 56; ICTY, *Prosecutor v. Tadić*, IT-94-1, Appeals Chamber, Decision on the Defence Motion for Interlocutory Appeal on Jurisdiction, 2 October 1995, para 57; *Prosecutor v. Erdemović*, IT-96-22-T, Trial Chamber, Sentencing Judgment, 29 November 1996, para 27.

[66]*P. Gaeta*, International Criminalization of Prohibited Conduct, in Cassese (ed), The Oxford Companion to International Criminal Justice (2009), 66. *Cassese* (supra note 3), 11, who also believes that a universal interest to punish these crimes is necessary for the notion of international crimes; *S. Glaser*, Droit international pénal conventionnel (1970), 16: "L'ensemble des règles juridiques, reconnues dans les relations internationales, qui ont pour but de protéger l'ordre juridique ou social international (la paix sociale internationale) par la répression des actes qui y portent atteinte; ou, en d'autres termes, l'ensemble des règles établies pour réprimer les violations des préceptes du droit international public." *Triffterer* (supra note 4), 178: "Im Gegensatz zu den Weltverbrechen ist nicht entscheidend, daß die Handlungen wegen der meistens über die Grenzen eines Staates hinausreichenden Begehungsweise nur durch die Zusammenarbeit aller Staaten wirksam bekämpft werden können. Vielmehr verletzen diese Verbrechen Rechtsgüter der Völkerrechtsordnung, denen wegen ihres besonderen Wertes für die Staatengemeinschaft der stärkste Schutz verliehen wird, den eine Gemeinschaft gewähren kann, der Schutz durch das Strafrecht."

community component attached to international criminal law and it is claimed that its higher objective is the maintenance of peace, security, and the well being of mankind.[67] The protection of these supra-national values is the primary concern of international criminal law, although evidentially subsidiary protection to the protected values and interests of the concerned individual is given simultaneously.[68]

Admittedly, international criminal law is reactionary in nature, responding to pressing needs of the international community in the aftermath of horrendous atrocities.[69] Due to its reactionary nature international criminal law has not had the time to develop its own doctrinal foundation gradually, but has applied existing doctrines of various components. International criminal law is not a cohesive system but is the international community's response to serious breaches of human rights and humanitarian law. Rather than establishing a unifying theory, *Bassiouni* claims that through its piecemeal nature, such as human rights law, humanitarian law, national and comparative criminal law, "the different components that make up international criminal law constitute a functional whole, even though they lack the doctrinal cohesiveness and methodological coherence found in other legal disciplines whose relative homogeneity gives them a more defined systemic nature."[70] However, it appears that the actual development of international criminal law is ahead of its doctrinal foundation.

It is questionable whether it is indeed possible to reconcile these various fields of law into one single framework of international criminal law, bearing in mind incompatibilities in terms of scope, actors, values, contents and methods. While criminal law principles (culpability, fair labeling, *nullum crimen sine lege* in its various forms, *in dubio pro reo*) might require a narrow application of international criminal norms, the object and purpose of human rights law and humanitarian law (*i.e.* victim protection, be it individuals and their human dignity[71] or protecting the

---

[67]Listed by the ICTY Trial Chamber as the tribunal's objectives in the *Erdemović* Sentencing Judgment, para 58. See also the various versions of the ILC Draft Codes on *Offences against the Peace and Security of Mankind*. The Rome Statute in its preamble declares that "such grave crimes threaten the peace, security and well-being of the world".

[68]K. *Ambos*, Möglichkeiten und Grenzen völkerstrafrechtlichen Rechtsgüterschutzes, in F. Neubacher and A. Klein (eds.), Vom Recht der Macht zur Macht des Rechts? (2006), 111; see also O. *Triffterer*, Bestandsaufnahme zum Völkerstrafrecht, in Hankel, Stuby (eds.), Strafgerichte gegen Menschheitsverbrechen (1995), 209: "Die dogmatischen Grundlagen des Völkerstrafrechts erlauben nur den Schutz eigenständiger Rechtsgüter der Völkergemeinschaft und ausnahmsweise einen subsidiären Schutz für *in erster Linie* den staatlichen Rechtsordnungen anvertraute Rechtsgüter, wenn deren Verletzung typischerweise unter Beteiligung des Staates geschieht und diese daher gerade gegen die Staatsmacht selbst geschützt werden müssen."

[69]M.A. *Drumbl*, A Hard Look at the Soft Theory of International Criminal Law, in: L.N. Sadat and M.P. Scharf (eds), The Theory and Practice of International Criminal Law: Essays in Honor of M. Cherif Bassiouni (2008), 2.

[70]*Bassiouni* (supra note 2), 1.

[71]See e.g. ICTY, *Prosecutor v. Furundžija*, IT-95-17/1-T, Trial Chamber, Judgment, 10 December 1998, para 183: "The general principle of respect for human dignity is the basic underpinning and indeed the very *raison d'être* of international humanitarian law and human rights law; indeed in

civilian population from the horrors of war), and the possible deterring effect on future violators, demand a wide applications seeking individual criminal convictions. International criminal law is exposed to this tension and its rapid development reveals an under-theorized shift from state responsibility to individual criminal responsibility.[72] Within this nexus one can detect different reactions to the development of international criminal law. According to *Robinson* the development of and the consequent reaction to modern international criminal law occurred in three stages.[73] Firstly, we encountered the expansion of humanitarian and human rights law as international criminal norms on basis of teleological aspirations. Criminal norms consequently were created on basis of "victim-focused teleological reasoning aggravated by utopian aspirations."[74] However, such a teleological expansion loses sight of the fact that although international criminal law is part of public international law, its double nature requires it to adhere to fundamental criminal principles. Consequently, in the second stage, the progressive development of international criminal law was criticized for its deviations from fundamental liberal criminal principles, such as individual culpability and the principle of legality that focus on the protection of the accused individual.[75]

In the third stage, however, other writers defended the departure from fundamental criminal principles in terms of international criminal law. They focused on the occurrence of these crimes as forms of macro criminality and the participation of individuals therein. These writers oppose the imposition of criminal principles derived from national legal systems that focus on the individual, and argue that mass atrocities as forms of macro-criminality require different concepts.[76] Indeed,

---

modern times it has become of such paramount importance as to permeate the whole body of international law."

[72]*G. Fletcher and J.D. Ohlin*, Reclaiming Fundamental Principles in the Darfur Case, 3 Journal of International Criminal Justice (2005), 541.

[73]See *Robinson* (supra note 63), 127ff.

[74]*D. Robinson*, The Identity Crisis of International Criminal Law, 21 Leiden Journal of International Law (2008), 944.

[75]*Robinson* (supra note 63), 128; *Fletcher and Ohlin* (supra note 72), 539ff; much of the criticism came as a reaction to the jurisprudence of international criminal tribunals in relation to the joint criminal enterprise doctrine or the application of command responsibility: *cf A. M. Danner and J. S. Martinez*, Guilty Associations: Joint Criminal Enterprise, Command Responsibility, and the Development of International Criminal Law, 93 California Law Review (2005), 75ff; *M. E. Badar*, "Just Convict Everyone!" – Joint Perpetration: From *Tadić* to *Stakić* and Back Again, 6 International Criminal Law Review (2006), 293ff; *K. Ambos*, Joint Criminal Enterprise and Command Responsibility, 5 Journal of International Criminal Justice (2007), 159ff.

[76]*Robinson* (supra note 63), 128–9 referring *inter alia* to *M.A. Drumbl*, Atrocity, Punishment and International Law (2007), 24–39; *M. Osiel*, The Banality of Good: Aligning Incentives against Mass Atrocity, 105 Columbia Law Review (2005), 1752–5. See, however, *H. Jäger*, Hört das Kriminalitätskonzept vor der Makrokriminalität auf?, in F. Neubacher and A. Klein (eds.), Vom Recht der Macht zur Macht des Rechts? (2006), 59ff, opposing the possibility that there should be two separated criminal concepts, one for macro-criminality and one for "normal" criminality, whereas the former would be a trimmed-back version.

the ICTY *Tadić* Appeals Chamber stated in its judgment that "[m]ost of the time these crimes do not result from the criminal propensity of single individuals but constitute manifestations of collective criminality: the crimes are often carried out by groups of individuals acting in pursuance of a common criminal design."[77] It is in these contexts, where the individuals that perpetrate horrendous acts do not in reality deviate from social norms but participate as a "matter of obeying official authority, not transgressing it".[78] The question is whether such a finding poses problems to the question of individual responsibility as the foundation for the application of criminal law, be it at the domestic or international level. Despite this active, albeit rather academic, debate concerning collective guilt *versus* individual guilt, it is clear that the international criminal law jurisprudence maintains the paradigm of individualized culpability. The ICTY *Tadić* Appeals Chamber held in its judgment that "the foundation of criminal responsibility is the principle of personal culpability: nobody may be held criminally responsible for acts or transactions in which he has not personally engaged or in some other way participated (*nulla poena sine culpa*)".[79] Consequently, although international crimes occur as "macro criminality", "systemized criminality" or "State criminality" that does not alter the underlying principle of criminal law: individual guilt. International criminal law is based on the "liberal idea that the only true units of action in the world are individuals, not groups."[80] Indeed, what is required by international criminal law is some form of "deontological, desert-based justification"[81] by the international community that focuses on prohibited conduct that is morally and more importantly also legally reproachable to the individual, thereby establishing culpability of individuals as the basis for criminal convictions. Consequently the famous words of the IMT Nuremberg still hold true: "crimes against international law are committed by men, not by abstract entities".[82] This focus on individual guilt is not to be conceived as a dismissal of the notion of collective guilt.[83] However, as matters stand today, this issue centres on the question of state responsibility under general international law. This was seen, for example, in the proceedings of Bosnia and Herzegovina *versus* Serbia and Montenegro before the International Court of

---

[77]ICTY, *Prosecutor v. Tadić*, IT-94-1-A, Appeals Chamber, Judgment, 15 July 1999, para 191.

[78]*Drumbl* (supra note 76), 24: "A paradigm of individualized culpability may well be suitable for deviant isolated crimes, although some criminologists challenge this premise. This same paradigm, however, is all the more ill fitting for crimes committed by collectivities, states, and organizations."

[79]ICTY, *Tadić* Appeals Chamber Judgment, para 186.

[80]See G. *Fletcher*, Collective Guilt and Collective Punishment, 5 Theoretical Inquiries in Law (2004), 163ff; cf. *Gierhake* (supra note 64), 175ff referring *inter alia* to *H. Jäger*, Makroverbrechen als Gegenstand des Völkerstrafrechts, Hankel/Stuby (eds.), Strafgerichte gegen Menschheitsverbrechen. Zum Völkerstrafrecht nach den Nürnberger Prozessen (1995), 325ff.

[81]*Robinson* (infra note 87), 116.

[82]IMT Nuremberg Judgment (supra note 24), 223.

[83]See *Drumbl* (supra note 76), 38.

Justice, concerning the application of the convention on the prevention and punishment of the crime of genocide that took place alongside the criminal trials against individuals before the ICTY.[84]

The predominant role of individual culpability within any criminal law system—be it on the national or international level—means that recourse to the justification theories of punishment, such as retribution, reconciliation and particularly deterrence (general and specific prevention), falls short as the underlying methodological basis for international criminal law.[85] These theories are consequence-orientated, protecting society by preventing future crimes but neglecting the individual's need of protection from society. While deterrence generally answers the question as to why we punish, it does not address the more fundamental issue of individual criminal accountability as such.[86] Individuals are to be treated not as means but as ends for a rationale of punishment, so a conclusive justification for international criminal law cannot be based on deterrence for the sake of society alone.[87]

In conclusion it can be said that the development of international criminal law was accompanied by various doctrinal challenges. The transition from state responsibility to individual criminal responsibility on the international plane occurred rather hastily. However, international criminal law as a system of criminal law necessarily rests upon fundamental liberal criminal principles that must be adhered to in order to establish individual guilt and individual responsibility. In that regard the *nullum crimen sine lege* principle is of the utmost importance and its validity and application in international criminal law will be assessed in the next chapter.

---

[84]See in this regard the references in supra note 57.

[85]By this analogy it is claimed that ICL receives its legitimacy; see for example ICTY, *Prosecutor v. Kupreškić*, IT-95-16, Trial Chamber, Judgment, 14 January 2000, paras 848f; *Erdemović* Sentencing Judgment, para 58; for the legal literature, both accepting and rejecting a domestic analogy, see *G. Werle*, Völkerstrafrecht (2007), 40 (footnote 182).

[86]This distinction is also made by *H.L.A. Hart*, Punishment and Responsibility (1968), 80–83.

[87]*D. Robinson*, The Two Liberalisms of International Criminal Law, Stahn/van den Herik (eds.), Future Perspective on International Criminal Justice (2010), 116 referring to *G. Fletcher*, Basic Concepts of Criminal Law (1998), 43: "We may use objects as means; but we must respect human beings as subjects, as ends in themselves" thereby articulating a "rejection of deterrence as a sufficient rationale for punishment". Originally that idea stems from *Kant* and his 'Formula of the End in Itself', see *I. Kant*, The Moral Law (1948) as translated by Paton, 96.

Chapter 3
Nullum Crimen Sine Lege

3.1 Preliminary Remarks

The most powerful objection to criminal prosecution available to the individual is the defense of *nullum crimen, nulla poena sine lege* (no crime, no punishment without law). Within the domain of public international law in particular, a legal system that at least historically appears to be at odds with pure criminal law as it was not concerned with penal norms, it seems as if this fundamental principle of criminal law is an insurmountable barrier to the existence of international criminal law. This study is concerned with the crime itself—the elements of the crime, modes of liability and possible defenses—and not with sentencing. Therefore this chapter will elaborate on the *nullum crimen sine lege* (NSCL) principle and not on *nulla poena sine lege*.[1]

3.2 *Nullum Crimen Sine Lege* and Domestic Law

The NCSL principle was a gradual historical development, drawing on the legal codes of the Greek city states and Roman law, through Enlightenment thought, eventually becoming one of the fundamental principles of modern criminal law.[2] *Paul Johann Anselm Ritter von Feuerbach* is generally given credit for the establishment of NCSL in modern criminal law:

---

[1] It appears that the *nulla poena sine lege* principle is under-theorized in international criminal law. Cf. *G. Endo*, Nullum crimen nulla poena sine lege Principle and the ICTY and ICTR, 15 Revue Québécoise de droit international (2002), 205ff; *S. Dana*, Beyond Retroactivity to Realizing Justice: A Theory on the Principle of Legality in International Criminal Law Sentencing, 99 The Journal of Criminal Law & Criminology (2009), 857ff.

[2] Cf. *J. Hall*, Nulla Poena Sine Lege, 47 Yale Law Journal (1937), 165ff; *A. Mokhter*, Nullum Crimen, Nulla Poena Sine Lege: Aspects and Prospects, 26 Statute Law Review (2005), 41ff.

© Springer International Publishing AG 2017
T. Rauter, *Judicial Practice, Customary International Criminal Law and* Nullum Crimen Sine Lege, DOI 10.1007/978-3-319-64477-6_3

Any infliction of punishment presupposes a penal law. For only a threat of evil by law constitutes the foundation of the notion, as well as the legal possibility, of punishment.[3]

A comparative analysis reveals that the NCSL principle enjoys universal recognition. Only two member States of the United Nations (Bhutan and Brunei) do not contain provisions on NCSL in their domestic legal orders.[4] From a norm hierarchy point of view this principle has the status of a constitutional norm in four fifths of the UN member States.[5] While it should be stated that there are certain differences in the scope of application of the different domestic NCSL principles, the underlying core of this principle is firmly anchored in the domestic legal orders.[6]

3.3 The Four Guarantees of *Nullum Crimen Sine Lege*

In its strictest form one can distinguish four guarantees of this principle, which have to be upheld in criminal proceedings in order to establish a fair trial[7]: As *nullum crimen sine lege praevia* it contains the prohibition of retroactivity, meaning that the criminalization of a certain conduct must have been already established when the crime was committed, forbidding *ex post facto* crime creation. *Nullum crimen sine lege stricta* entails a prohibition of constitutive or aggravating crime analogy, meaning that norms shall be narrowly construed, preventing the judges from filling a gap by expanding the scope of a norm. *Nullum crimen sine lege certa* requires the law to be precisely defined so that foreseeability of the punishment and accessibility of the concrete penal norms can be established for individuals. Finally, *nullum crimen sine lege scripta* requires that the applicable law is laid down in written form, thereby rendering inapplicable any unwritten law, such as customary law.[8]

---

[3]*P. J. A. Ritter von Feuerbach*, The Foundations of Criminal Law and the Nullum Crimen Principle, 5 Journal of International Criminal Justice (2007), 1008, reproducing from his book Lehrbuch des gemeinen in Deutschland gültigen peinlichen Rechts (1847), § 20.

[4]See *K. S. Gallant*, The Principle of Legality in International and Comparative Criminal Law (2009), 241ff.

[5]*Ibid.*

[6]*Ibid.* For a difference in the scope of application between the civil and common law system see *A. Schüller*, Das Rückwirkungsverbot im Völkerstrafrecht, in Kühner/Esser/Gerding (eds.), Völkerstrafrecht (2007), 200.

[7]*R. Heinsch*, Die Weiterentwicklung des humanitären Völkerrechts durch die Strafgerichtshöfe für das ehemalige Jugoslawien und Ruanda (2007), 313, *K. Ambos*, General Principles of Criminal Law in the Rome Statute, 10 Criminal Law Forum (1999), 4.

[8]*P. Hauck*, The Challenge of Customary International Crimes to the Principle of Nullum Crimen Sine Lege, 21 Humanitäres Völkerrecht – Informationsschriften (Journal of International Law of Peace and Armed Conflict) (2008), 58ff; *M. Swart*, Judicial Lawmaking in the Context of the International Criminal Tribunals for Yugoslavia and Rwanda (2006), 146–148; *Dana* (supra note 1), 864.

3.4   Theoretical and Philosophical Foundations

The NCSL principle is based on various theoretical and philosophical foundations. In the following the most important theories will be shortly elaborated:

Von Liszt understood criminal codes, paradoxical though it may appear, as the *magna charta* of the criminal. Criminal codes do not protect the society but the individual, as criminal law is "the legally limited punitive power of the state": limited insofar as in the interest of individual freedom the NCSL principle is "the citizen's bulwark against the State's omnipotence" protecting the individual from the arbitrary power of the State.[9] The protection of the individual was one of the central demands of the enlightenment.[10] Conceptualizing criminal law as the *ultima ratio* of the domestic society, with its far-reaching sanctioning mechanisms (including deprivation of liberty or even the death penalty), the need of such protection is evident. The foreseeability, accessibility and predictability of the law and its sanctions are requirements in a democratic State under the rule of law so that the individual can adapt his/her conduct to the requirements of the legal order. The NCSL principle understood as the limitation on the punitive power of the State protecting the individual against State arbitrariness can function as a theoretical basis for *nullum crimen sine lege praevia, certa and stricta*. The *lege scripta* requirement, the prohibition of unwritten, customary, norms as a legal basis cannot be established on this basis alone.[11]

For several authors the NCSL principle is founded upon the principle of individual guilt. Criminal law is based on the assumption that a conduct, be it intentional or careless commissions or omissions, leads to the responsibility of the individual. The criminal imputation of guilt is the result of a penal norm that exists at the moment of the commission of the crime and specifies the element of wrongdoing.[12] However, the principle that "ignorance of law is no excuse" suggests that subjective knowledge of law is not a prerequisite of the NCSL principle. Only

---

[9]*F. von Liszt*, The Rationale for the Nullum Crimen Principle, 5 Journal of International Criminal Justice (2007), 1009–1010, reproducing from his essay Die deterministischen Gegner der Zweckstrafe, 13 Zeitschrift für die gesamte Strafrechtswissenschaft (1983), 1009–1010.

[10]*Boot*, Genocide, Crimes Against Humanity, War Crimes. Nullum Crimen Sine Lege and the Subject Matter Jurisdiction of the International Criminal Court (2002), 83ff with further references.

[11]Compare *C. Kress*, Nulla poena nullum crimen sine lege, in R. Wolfrum (ed.), Max Planck Encyclopedia of Public International Law, online edition (2010) MN 3.

[12]*B. Krivec*, Von Versailles nach Rom – Der lange Weg von Nullum crimen, nulla poena sine lege. Bedeutung und Entwicklung des strafrechtlichen Gesetzesvorbehalts im völkerrechtlichen Strafrecht (2004), 9 with further reference to *W. Sax*, Grundsätze der Strafrechtspflege, in: Bettermann/Nipperdey/Scheuner, Die Grundrechte, Band III, Halbband 2 (1972), 998f: "der strafrechtliche Schuldvorwurf auf einer bewußten oder vorwerfbar unbewußten Fehlentscheidung zur Verwirklichung straftatstbestandsspezifischen Unrechts aufbaut, ist es die unausweichliche Konsequenz, dass zum Zeitpunkt der Tatentscheidung ihr Richtpunkt: das den Unrechtstatbestand spefifizierende Strafgesetz, bereits vorhanden gewesen sein muß".

an objective possibility to know is required.[13] Consequently, it is not necessary to establish the perpetrator's concrete awareness of the existence of the crime, but individual guilt can be established by objectified proof. As the case may be, accessibility to the law is given, even if the individual would be in need of legal counsel to comprehend the content of the criminal norm.[14] However, if one bases the NCSL principle upon the principle of individual guilt alone, it is evident that one might be tempted to connect the principle to the moral blameworthiness of a conduct, while the classification as a penal norm might not be required.[15] Such a wide understanding of guilt or blameworthiness would not adequately establish an explanation for the *nullum crimen sine lege* guarantees.

In connection with the social contract and the principle of the separation of powers, it is argued that only the legislative in possession of the democratic legitimacy is entitled to develop criminal norms binding on the individual.[16] In 1748 *Montesquieu* demanded that the judge should be nothing more than "the mouth that reproduces the meaning of the law."[17] The possibility of judicial law creation would thus not be provided for. The role of the judges is reduced to the application of norms previously created by the legitimized legislators. However, on basis of this theory alone a *nullum crimen sine lege praevia* cannot be established. If the national parliament decides to enact laws retroactively this fact alone would not be in contradiction to the principle of democratic legitimacy.[18]

The final theory takes recourse to the purpose of criminal law, namely the justification theories of punishment of the domestic legal order to develop NCSL. On basis of *Feuerbach's* "psychological compulsion" a general deterrence can be established as the committed crime is "followed by an evil that is greater than the displeasure consequent upon the non-satisfaction of the impulse to the deed."[19] The clearer the description of the crime the greater the deterring factor as the potential criminal is informed about the concrete legal frame of the crime to know the exact border between legality and criminality.[20] However, as elaborated above, the justification of punishment alone cannot form a complete legal basis for

---

[13]See *H. Kelsen*, The Rule Against Ex Post Facto Laws and the Prosecution of the Axis War Criminals, 2 Judge Advocate Journal (1945), 9.

[14]*Kress* (supra note 11), MN 29 referring to the jurisprudence of the European Court of Human Rights stipulating that the *nullum crimen sine lege certa* requirement is also fulfilled if "need be with the assistance of pre-existing judicial interpretations and/or the aid of legal counseling" (references omitted).

[15]*Krivec* (supra note 12), 9f.

[16]*Kress* (supra note 11), MN 5; *Boot* (supra note 10), 83.

[17]*C. de Secondat, Baron de Montesquieu*, De l'Esprit des lois. Livre XI, Chapitre 6 (1748), in the original language: "la bouche, qui prononce les paroles de la loi" (as translated by the author).

[18]*Kress* (supra note 11), MN 5.

[19]*Feuerbach* (supra note 3), §§ 10–13.

[20]Swart (supra note 8), 143.

criminalization as such.[21] Furthermore, based on this idea NCSL would not exclude customary norms, as reliance on unwritten norms does not exclude deterrence.[22]

While these theories form the philosophical and theoretical foundations of the four guarantees of the NCSL principle, it should be mentioned that none of them could explain all of the four guarantees established above. Consequently, the theories should not be viewed in clinical isolation but as complementary to one other.[23] Furthermore, these theories have been developed in the context of domestic criminal legal systems. It needs to be seen to what extent the principle of *nullum crimen sine lege* has found application when individuals have been held responsible for violations of international criminal law and how these theoretical foundations can be applied *mutatis mutandis* at the international level.

3.5   *Nullum Crimen Sine Lege* and the IMT Nuremberg and the IMTFE Tokyo

There has been a persistent critique that the IMT Nuremberg applied *ex post facto* law thereby violating the *nullum crimen sine lege* principle.[24] The issue of *nullum crimen sine lege* came up at the London Conference, the International Conference on Military Trials, which was held by the Four Powers (the United States, France, Great Britain and the Soviet Union) and which was tasked with establishing the statute of the IMT Nuremberg. It seems that the United States, Great Britain and the Soviet Union had no concerns with the issue of *ex post facto* law creation. The American delegation in particular, in its proposed agreement of 14 June 1945, went as far to propose that the tribunal "shall be bound by the declaration of the parties to this Agreement that the following acts are criminal,"[25] namely crimes against peace, war crimes and crimes against humanity. According to the US proposal the tribunal would have been bound by the substantive criminal law as laid down by the statute and could not have challenged the legality of its own subject matter jurisdiction. Only the French delegate, Professor *Gros*, expressed his concerns in relation to such an approach on basis of the NCSL principle.[26] He considered that aggression did not entail individual criminal responsibility in international law before World War II and thus constituted *ex post facto* law creation.[27] He

---

[21]See Sect. 2.2, International Criminal Law: A Collision of Legal Systems.

[22]See also *Kress* (supra note 11), MN 6.

[23]*Kress* (supra note 11), MN 2.

[24]See Sect. 2.1, Nuremberg: Setting the Stage.

[25]Cf. *R. H Jackson*, Report of Robert H. Jackson United States Representative to the International Conference on Military Trials (1945), 57f.

[26]See *Gallant* (supra note 4), 76ff.

[27]Comments of *Gros* in Report of Jackson (supra note 25), 295: "We do not consider as a criminal violation the launching of a war of aggression. If we declare war a criminal act of individuals, we are going farther than the actual law." Cf. *id.*, 328 and 335.

acknowledged that it would be morally and politically desirable to punish individuals who instigated war, but that this would not reflect the state of international
law.[28] Interestingly it was *Gros*, a representative of a civil law country, who did not
wish to restrict the judges and voted for an agreement containing a provision on
subject matter jurisdiction, rather than a concrete set of crime definitions.[29] *Gros*
determined that the London Conference was not tasked with creating a codification
of international criminal law and that the judges themselves should decide on the
applicable law.[30]

In the final wording of the IMT Charter, the American proposal that the tribunal
"shall be bound" was transformed into "[t]he following acts, or any of them, are
crimes coming within the jurisdiction of the Tribunal for which there shall be
individual responsibility".[31] *Gros* believed that this change of wording would
secure that although the IMT Charter defined which crimes came within the
jurisdiction of the court, the judges themselves would decide upon the law. Consequently, he considered that by such a formulation the judges would not be forced to
apply the IMT Charter as the substantive legal basis for criminal convictions.[32]

At the trial *nullum crimen sine lege* was raised by the defense. It filed a joint
pre-trial motion, claiming that the law contained in the IMT Charter had been
created *ex post facto*, as the crime against peace was new penal law.[33] The defense

---

[28]*Id*, 297.

[29]*Gallant* (supra note 4), 83ff.

[30]Comments of *Gros* in Report of Jackson (supra note 25), 378f: "We have just to say what crimes
will go before the court. This article says that and only that. The American draft would be a perfect
article if we were charged with the duty of making a codification of rules of international law for
the punishment of international war criminals, which we are not charged to do. [. . .] We must leave
the law to the judge to decide."

[31]Nuremberg Charter, Art 6.

[32]Comments of *Gros* in Report of Jackson (supra note 25), 378–379; *Gallant* (supra note 4), 88.

[33]Motion adopted by all Defense counsel, 19 November 1945, IMT Nuremberg, Trial of the Major
War Criminals Before the International Military Tribunal, Vol. 1 (Nuremberg, 1947) ("Blue
Series"), Vol. 1, 168–170. Interestingly the defense only claimed the violation of the principle
of legality in relation to the crime against peace and not in relation to crimes against humanity. The
reason for this restraint might be seen in the opinion that technically crimes against humanity were
subordinated to or were to be aligned with any other crime within the jurisdiction of the IMT
Nuremberg. The IMT Nuremberg stated in its Judgment that "[t]o constitute Crimes against
Humanity, the acts relied on before the outbreak of the war must have been in execution of, or
in connection with, any crime within the jurisdiction of the Tribunal. The Tribunal is of the opinion
that revolting and horrible as many of these crimes were, it has not been satisfactorily proved that
they were done in execution of, or in connection with, any such crime. The Tribunal therefore
cannot make a general declaration that the acts before 1939 were Crimes against Humanity within
the meaning of the Charter, but from the beginning of the war in 1939, War Crimes were
committed on a vast scale, which were also Crimes against Humanity; and insofar as the inhumane
acts charged in the Indictment, and committed after the beginning of the war, did not constitute
War Crimes, they were all committed in execution of, or in connection with, the aggressive war,
and therefore constituted Crimes against Humanity." See IMT Nuremberg Judgment, Vol.
1, 254–255.

brought forward the argument of *nullum crimen sine lege* on basis of general princi-ples of law,[34] on basis of customary law[35] and in relation to the question of personal guilt,[36] since the accused must be aware of the wrongfulness of his commissions and omissions as a substantive requirement for individual criminal responsibility.

The IMT Nuremberg swept away the *nullum crimen sine lege* objection based on three arguments: Firstly, it held that the court was bound by the statute; secondly, that the charter did not violate the principle of legality as it was a declaration of international law; and thirdly that the principle of legality was not binding upon the tribunal.

Concerning the first point the IMT Nuremberg followed the arguments of the US prosecutor *Jackson*[37] and USSR prosecutor *Rudenko*[38] that the IMT Charter was decisive and "binding upon the Tribunal as the law to be applied to the case".[39] Thereby, the tribunal was barred from evaluating its own legal basis as well as the legality of the law it had to apply.[40] As such the IMT Nuremberg considered it unnecessary to delve into the question as to whether the crimes listed in its statute were already crimes before the establishment of the IMT Charter.[41] The IMT Nuremberg destroyed the hopes of the French delegate, Professor *Gros*. It identified the IMT Charter as an "exercise of the sovereign legislative power by the countries to which Germany unconditionally surrendered", which was binding on the Tribunal.[42]

Nevertheless, the court also clarified that the charter is "not an arbitrary exercise of power on the part of the victorious Nations, but in the view of the Tribunal, [. . .] it is the expression of international law existing at the time of its creation."[43] However, even the US prosecutor *Jackson* apparently admitted that the rather

---

[34]*Pannenbecker*, Counsel for Defendant Frick, IMT Nuremberg Judgment, Vol. 18, 164: a "legal principle [which has] found general recognition in all civilized countries as a prerequisite and basic precept of justice." Furthermore *Freiherr von Lüdinghausen*, Counsel for Defendant Von Neurath, IMT Nuremberg Judgment, Vol. 19, 219, referring to the "principles of law of all democratic states".

[35]*Pannenbecker*, Counsel for Defendant Frick, IMT Nuremberg Judgment, Vol. 18, 165.

[36]*Jahrreiss*, Counsel for Defendant Jodl, IMT Nuremberg Judgment, Vol. 17, 460.

[37]Opening Statement of US Chief Prosecutor *Jackson*, IMT Nuremberg Judgment, Vol. 2, 147: "the Charter, whose declarations concededly binds us all."

[38]Opening Statement of USSR Chief Prosecutor *Rudenko*, IMT Nuremberg Judgment, Vol. 7, 148: arguing that the IMT Charter "is to be considered an unquestionable and sufficient legislative act" and that the "principle *nullum crimen sine lege,* or to the principle that 'a statute cannot have retroactive power,' are not applicable because of the following fundamental, decisive fact: The Charter of the Tribunal is in force and in operation and all its provisions possess absolute and binding force."

[39]IMT Nuremberg Judgment, Vol. 1, 174.

[40]*M C. Bassiouni*, Crimes Against Humanity in International Law (1999), 149.

[41]IMT Nuremberg Judgment, Vol. 1, 219.

[42]IMT Nuremberg Judgment, Vol. 1, 218.

[43]IMT Nuremberg Judgment, Vol. 1, 218.

recent establishment of individual responsibility was prone to being perceived as victor's legislation. This would explain his position strongly favoring that the IMT Charter was decisive and binding upon the IMT Nuremberg: "I am frank to say that international law is indefinite and weak in our support on that [*i.e.* individual criminal responsibility], as it has stood over the recent years. This definition seems to me to leave the Tribunal in the position where it could be argued, and the Tribunal might very reasonably say, that no personal responsibility resulted if we failed to say it when we are making an agreement between the four powers which fulfils in a sense the function of legislation."[44]

Nevertheless, in relation to the crime against peace, the tribunal took recourse to various treaties, the Pact of Paris (Briand-Kellogg Pact),[45] the Treaty of Versailles,[46] and the Protocol for the Pacific Settlement of International Disputes,[47] in order to determine that individual criminal responsibility existed for the crime against peace. Of these instruments only the Treaty of Versailles foresaw individual responsibility for breaches of international law. At the time *Kelsen* argued that there is an exception to the rule forbidding *ex post facto* law creation when the illegality of an act is given under public international law and it is "only" the criminality that is established retroactively.[48] However the Nuremberg Tribunal used a different argument: It claimed that it did not create the criminality retroactively and that it adhered to the NCSL principle.[49] It drew parallels between the crimes against peace and war crimes, and asserted that the NCSL principle finds no application to the present facts.[50] The international conventions of the latter also did not provide for individual responsibility; however, they have been treated as crimes in the practice

---

[44]Report of Jackson (supra note 25), 331.

[45]Pact of Paris, 27 August 1928, 94 L.N.T.S. 57; in the IMT Nuremberg Judgment, Vol. 1, 219–21.

[46]Treaty of Peace with Germany (Treaty of Versailles), 28 June 1919, 11 Martens Nouveau Recueil (3d), especially with reference to Article 227 (responsibility of the Kaiser "for a supreme offense against international morality and the sanctity of treaties"), in the IMT Nuremberg Judgment, Vol. 1, 222.

[47]Protocol for the Pacific Settlement of International Disputes, 2 October 1924, 1008 League of Nations O.J. 1521 (1925) (never entered into force), in the IMT Nuremberg Judgment, Vol. 1, 221.

[48]*H. Kelsen*, Will the Judgment in the Nuremberg Trial Constitute a Precedent in International Law?, 1 International Law Quarterly (1947), 165: "A retroactive law providing individual punishment for acts which were illegal though not criminal at the time they were committed, seems also to be an exception to the rule against ex post facto laws. The London Agreement is such a law."

[49]IMT Nuremberg Judgment, Vol. 1, 220: "In the opinion of the Tribunal, the solemn renunciation of war as an instrument of national policy necessarily involves the proposition that such a war is illegal in international law; and that those who plan and wage such a war, with its inevitable and terrible consequences, are committing a crime in so doing." See also *B. Van Schaack*, Crimen Sine Lege: Judicial Lawmaking at the Intersection of Law and Morals, 97 The Georgetown Law Journal (2008), 126ff.

[50]IMT Nuremberg Judgment, Vol. 1, 219.

of States.[51] Consequently, taking the development of war crimes as a blueprint, it seems that the IMT Nuremberg equated illegality under international law with criminality.[52]

Considering the third point, since the IMT Nuremberg declared itself to be bound by the statute, the tribunal elaborated on the application of NCSL solely in an *obiter dictum*,[53] "in view of the great importance of the questions involved".[54] Various legal scholars at that time have shared the position that the principle of legality was generally not applicable within international law at the time the Nuremberg Trial was conducted.[55] Indeed, the NCSL principle was not included in international conventions at that time. The tribunal observed that "the maxim *nullum crimen sine lege* is not a limitation of sovereignty, but is in general a principle of justice."[56] The French translation takes a step further, claiming that "*nullum crimen sine lege* ne limite pas la souveraineté des États; *elle ne formule qu'une règle généralement suivie.*"[57] Accordingly, the IMT Nuremberg acknowledged that the sovereign in Germany at that time, the Allied States, had the power to override this principle and to establish criminal law even if this would mean *ex post facto* law creation, and that it had the right to establish a tribunal that was obliged to adhere to the crimes in the statute as defined by the Allied Powers.[58]

Furthermore, the IMT Nuremberg apparently determined that the NCSL principle would only protect acts that are not morally reprehensible: in relation to the Nazi atrocities "the attacker must know that he is doing wrong, and so far from being unjust to punish him, it would be unjust if his wrong were allowed to go

---

[51]IMT Nuremberg Judgment, Vol. 1, 220–221: "Many of these prohibitions had been enforced long before the date of the Convention; but since 1907 they have certainly been crimes, punishable as offenses against the laws of war; yet the Hague Convention nowhere designates such practices as criminal, nor is any sentence prescribed, nor any mention made of a court to try and punish offenders. For many years past, however, military tribunals have tried and punished individuals guilty of violating the rules of land warfare laid down by this Convention. In the opinion of the Tribunal, those who wage aggressive war are doing that which is equally illegal, and of much greater moment than a breach of one of the rules of the Hague Convention."

[52]*van Schaack* (supra note 49), 127–8.

[53]*van Schaack* (supra note 49), 126.

[54]IMT Nuremberg Judgment, Vol. 1, 219.

[55]Cf. *Kelsen* (supra note 48), 164; *B. D Meltzer*, A Note on Some Aspects of the Nuremberg Debate, 14 The University of Chicago Law Review (1946–1947), 456ff; see also *S. Garibian*, Crimes against Humanity and International Legality in Legal Theory After Nuremberg, 9 Journal of Genocide Research (2007), 95 with further references.

[56]IMT Nuremberg Judgment, Vol. 1, 219.

[57]As quoted in *S. Lamb*, Nullum Crimen, Nulla Poena Sine Lege in International Criminal Law, in *Cassese* (ed.), The Rome Statute of the International Criminal Court: A Commentary (2002), 737 (emphasis added); *van Schaack* (supra note 49), 126.

[58]*Gallant* (supra note 4), 113; *van Schaack* (supra note 49), 126. See also *H. Kelsen* (supra note 13), 8, concerning the application of NCSL in the common law system: It "was never interpreted as a limitation of the sovereign legislative power of Parliament."

unpunished."[59] *Kelsen* elaborated further on this issue. He claimed that the basis of NCSL "is the moral idea that it is not just to make an individual responsible for an act if he, when performing the act, did not and could not know that his act constituted a wrong. If, however, the act was at the moment of its performance morally, although not legally wrong, a law attaching ex post facto a sanction to the act is retroactive only from a legal, not from a moral point of view."[60] *Kelsen* recognized that the Nuremberg jurisprudence was caught up in a conflict between two principles of justice: the rule against retroactive legislation and the principle widely acknowledged by the civilized world to punish individuals morally responsible for international crimes. He considered that the latter is a higher postulate of justice, which must prevail.[61] According to *Kelsen*, as the NCSL principle rests upon a moral foundation it could not be applied before Nuremberg. Since these crimes were manifestly immoral the principle to bring justice to those morally responsible for the commission of crimes was of higher importance.[62] One could view the NCSL principle as a mere procedural guarantee that had to yield in case substantive justice requires it.[63]

The IMTFE Tokyo was faced with similar objections in relation to the NCSL principle. However, the Tokyo Tribunal "took the easy way out" by simply referring to the Nuremberg judgment: "In view of the fact that in all material respects the Charters of this Tribunal and the Nuremberg Tribunal are identical, this Tribunal prefers to express its unqualified adherence to the relevant opinions of the Nuremberg Tribunal rather than by reasoning the matters anew in somewhat different language to open the door to controversy by way of conflicting interpretations of the two statements of opinions."[64]

---

[59]IMT Nuremberg Judgment, Vol. 1, 219.

[60]H. *Kelsen*, Collective and Individual Responsibility in International Law with Particular Regard to the Punishment of War Criminals, 31 California Law Review (1943), 544.

[61]*Kelsen* (supra note 48), 165: "In case two postulates of justice are in conflict with each other, the higher one prevails; and to punish those who were morally responsible for the international crime of the second World War may certainly be considered as more important than to comply with the rather relative rule against ex post facto laws".

[62]H. *Kelsen* (supra note 13), 11: "[I]n all cases where the rule against *ex post facto* laws comes into consideration in the prosecution of war criminals, we must bear in mind that this rule is to be respected as a principle of justice and that, as pointed out, this principle is frequently in competition with another principle of justice, so that the one must be restricted by the other. It stands to reason that the principle which is less important has to give way to the principle which is more important. There can be little doubt that, according to the public opinion of the civilized world, it is more important to bring the war criminals to justice than to respect, in their trial, the rule against *ex post facto law*, which is merely a relative value and consequently, was never unrestrictedly recognized." See also *Garibian* (supra note 55), 100. Generally it seems as if *Kelsen*'s law and norm conception would not exclude the possibility of retroactive law creation, see also *H. Kelsen*, Reine Rechtslehre (1960), 13.

[63]*Bassiouni* (supra note 40), 125. See also *R. K Woetzel*, The Nuremberg Trials in International Law with a Postlude on the Eichmann Case (1962), 112: "The principle of *Rechtssicherheit* must yield to *Gerechtigkeit*."

[64]International Military Tribunal for the Far East, Judgment of 12 November 1948, in Pritchard/Zaide (eds.), The Tokyo War Crimes Trial, Vol. 22, 48,439.

Nevertheless, the issue of *ex post facto* legislation has been debated in the separate and dissenting opinions of judges *Bernard, Röling* and *Pal.* Judge *Bernard* denied that the IMTFE Tokyo had violated the NCSL principle, as the crime of aggression can be based upon the "expressions of natural law".[65] Judge *Röling* declared that the NCSL principle is not even a principle of justice but a mere unbinding "rule of policy" only applicable to protect citizens from arbitrariness of legislators and judges.[66] In contrast Judge *Pal* considered that the NCSL principle has been violated since even assuming that the prohibition of aggression had been established under public international law in inter-State relations—which he doubted—that would not turn that violation into a crime entailing individual criminal responsibility.[67]

3.6 *Nullum Crimen Sine Lege* and Post World War II US Military Tribunals

While the Nuremberg Judgment concerned the trial of the major war criminals before the IMT Nuremberg, the application of the NCSL principle was also discussed before the US military courts in the occupied zones that operated under Control Council Law No. 10. Control Council Law No. 10, a legislative act jointly promulgated by the occupying powers,[68] was enacted in order to give effect to the IMT Charter in the zones, and to "establish a uniform legal basis in Germany for the prosecution of war criminals and other similar offenders, other than those dealt with by the International Military Tribunal".[69]

The US Military Tribunal in the Justice Case, very much in line with the argumentation of the IMT Nuremberg, determined that the Control Council Law No. 10 had been set forth as "an exercise of supreme legislative power in and for Germany" and denied to have the authority to review its legality.[70] It further

---

[65]Dissenting Opinion of Judge *Bernard*, 105 IMTFE Records, 10 as cited by *Gallant* (supra note 4), 148.

[66]Separate Opinion of Judge *Röling*, 109 IMTFE Records, 45 as cited by *Gallant* (supra note 4), 145.

[67]Judge *R. Pal*, Dissentient Judgement (1953), 83.

[68]See also *Bassiouni* (supra note 40), 33, who considers that Control Council Law No. 10 "was not intended to be an international instrument but national legislation" enacted by the Allies in their role as "the supreme legislative authority" over Germany.

[69]Control Council Law No. 10, Punishment of Persons Guilty of War Crimes, Crimes Against Peace and Against Humanity, 20 December 1945, 3 Official Gazette Control Council for Germany 50–55 (1946).

[70]US Military Tribunal, *Altstötter and Others Case* ("The Justice Case"), Trials of War Criminals Before the Nuernberg Military Tribunal under Control Council Law No.10 ("the Green Series"), Vol. III, 965: "It can scarcely be argued that a court which owes its existence and jurisdiction solely to the provisions of a given statute could assume to exercise that jurisdiction and then, in the exercise thereof, declare invalid the act to which it owed its existence."

determined that the legislation *via* Control Council Law No. 10 had not been a creation of law but a codification of existing norms.[71] In the Justice Case the US Military Tribunal opted for a differential treatment of the NCSL principle, contrasting the international legal plane and the domestic legal order concerned with "ordinary" domestic crimes, and stressing the difference of the two different legal systems:

> International law is not the product of statute for the simple reason that there is as yet no world authority empowered to enact statutes of universal application. International law is the product of multipartite treaties, conventions, judicial decisions and customs which have received international acceptance or acquiescence. It would be sheer absurdity to suggest that the ex post facto rule, as known to constitutional states, could be applied to a treaty, a custom, or a common law decision of an international tribunal, or to the international acquiescence which follows the event. To have attempted to apply the ex post facto principle to judicial decisions of common international law would have been to strangle that law at birth.[72]

Despite the use of these words, which would rather imply a non-application of the NCSL principle by the US Military Tribunal in the Justice Case, the military tribunal opted for a restricted application and viewed the NCSL principle as a "principle of justice and fair play". The US Military Tribunal departs from the IMT Nuremberg Judgment in two important aspects. Firstly, it specified that the NCSL principle does not require subjective knowledge of the crime but requires an objective possibility to know (the criminal "knew or *should have known* that he would be subject to punishment if caught"[73]). Secondly, it determines that foreseeability of punishment is fulfilled if the conduct for which the criminal was charged before a military tribunal "was also known to him to be a punishable crime under his own domestic law."[74]

The US Military Tribunal in the Hostage Case was more concrete on the relationship between customary international law as an underlying legal basis for criminal convictions and the NCSL principle:

> It is true, of course, that customary international law is not static. It must be elastic enough to meet the new conditions that natural progress brings to the world. It might be argued that this requires a certain amount of retroactive application of new rules and that by conceding the existence of a customary international law, one thereby concedes the legality of retroactive pronouncements. To a limited extent the argument is sound, but when it comes in conflict with a rule of fundamental right and justice, the latter must prevail. The rule that one may not be charged with crime for committing an act which was not a crime at the time of its commission is such a right.[75]

---

[71] US Military Tribunal, *Altstötter and Others Case*, 966ff.

[72] US Military Tribunal, *Altstötter and Others Case*, 974–5. See also Opening Statement of US Chief Prosecutor *Jackson*, IMT Nuremberg Judgment, Vol. II, 147: "International law is not capable of development by the normal processes of legislation, for there is no continuing international legislative authority."

[73] US Military Tribunal, *Altstötter and Others Case*, 977–8 (emphasis added). See also *K. J. Heller*, The Nuremberg Military Tribunals and the Origins of International Criminal Law (2011), 124ff.

[74] US Military Tribunal, *Altstötter and Others Case*, 977.

[75] US Military Tribunal, *List and Others Case* ("The Hostage Case"), in Trials of War Criminals Before the Nuernberg Military Tribunal under Control Council Law No.10 ("the Green Series"), Vol. XI, 1241.

While in other decisions the US Military Tribunals did not conduct lengthy debates on the NCSL principle, they did not view NCSL to be a mere non-binding principle of justice but determined that the Tribunal could not give *ex post facto* application to Control Council Law No.10 as "[n]o act is adjudged criminal by the Tribunal which was not criminal under international law as it existed when the act was committed."[76]

The application of the NCSL principle in the post World War II US military trials reveals a rather fragmented picture in relation to its application. This fragmentation left many questions unanswered, in relation to the normative value and the guarantees of the NCSL principle applicable in international criminal proceedings. It needs to be seen whether these open questions were answered by the firm inclusion of the NCSL principle in human rights and humanitarian law conventions.

3.7   Changing the Picture? *Nullum Crimen Sine Lege* and Its Inclusion in Human Rights Law and Humanitarian Law Conventions

Whatever position is taken on the debate of *ex post facto* law application of the post World War II tribunals, it is evident that "[t]ime and the unfulfilled quest for international criminal justice have put a favourable gloss on the infirmities and flaws of these proceedings."[77] The discrepancies within the application of *nullum crimen sine lege* before the post World War II tribunals paved the way for the development of the NCSL principle outside the context of international criminal justice: the evolution of international human rights and humanitarian law conventions. The inclusion of the principle of legality in various international and regional conventions[78] might have been driven by an awareness that Nuremberg and Tokyo

---

[76]US Military Tribunal, *Flick and Others Case*, in Trials of War Criminals Before the Nuernberg Military Tribunal under Control Council Law No.10 ("the Green Series"), Vol. VI, 1189; see also *Krupp and Others Case*, in Trials of War Criminal Before the Nuernberg Military Tribunal under Control Council Law No.10 ("the Green Series"), Vol. IX, 1331; *Krauch and Others Case* ("The Farben Case"), in Trials of War Criminal Before the Nuernberg Military Tribunal under Control Council Law No.10 ("the Green Series"), Vol. VIII, 1098.

[77]*M. C. Bassiouni*, Establishing an International Criminal Court: Historical Survey, 149 Military Law Review (1995), 56.

[78]The NCSL principle has been included *inter alia* in the following international and regional human rights instruments: Universal Declaration of Human Rights, General Assembly Resolution 217 A (III), 10 December 1948, UN GAOR, 3rd sess, Art. 11; International Covenant on Civil and Political Rights, 16 December 1966, 999 UNTS 171, Art. 15; Convention for the Protection of Human Rights and Fundamental Freedoms, 3 September 1952, 213 UNTS 222, Art. 7; as well as humanitarian law conventions: 1949 Geneva Convention Relative to the Treatment of Prisoners of War (GC III), 21 October 1950, 75 UNTS 135, Art. 99 (1); 1949 Geneva Convention Relative to the Protection of Civilian Persons in Time of War, 21 October 1950, 75 UNTS 287, Art. 67; Protocol Additional to the Geneva Conventions of 12 August 1949, and relating to the Protection of Victims of International Armed Conflicts (Additional Protocol I), 6 June 1977, 1125 UNTS 3 Art. 75 (4) (c).

constituted violations of the *ex post facto* rule.[79] *Cassese* argues that at first international criminal law followed the doctrine of substantive justice, punishing conduct that was regarded as harmful to the society even though that conduct was not clearly set out as a crime. Only recently has this approach been gradually replaced with the doctrine of strict legality, favoring the accused, meaning that a person may only be convicted for a crime if it was firmly established as a criminal offence at the time of its commission by the relevant legal order.[80] This change of attitude in relation to international criminal justice relates to the firm inclusion of the NCSL principle in human rights and humanitarian law conventions.

Rather than detailing every provision on NCSL contained in the various documents, Art. 15 of the International Covenant on Civil and Political Rights (ICCPR) can be used to illustrate the current status of the NCSL provision on the international plane. It reads as follows:

1. No one shall be held guilty of any criminal offence on account of any act or omission which did not constitute a criminal offence, under national or international law, at the time when it was committed. Nor shall a heavier penalty be imposed than the one that was applicable at the time when the criminal offence was committed. If, subsequent to the commission of the offence, provision is made by law for the imposition of a lighter penalty, the offender shall benefit thereby.
2. Nothing in this article shall prejudice the trial and punishment of any person for any act or omission which, at the time when it was committed, was criminal according to the general principles of law recognized by the community of nations.

Unlike its predecessor, the Universal Declaration of Human Rights (UDHR), the ICCPR is binding in form as an international convention that came into force on 23 March 1976. The *travaux préparatoires* of both, the UDHR and ICCPR, suggest that the term "penal" (UDHR) or "criminal" (ICCPR) offence under international law of paragraph 1 is to be understood widely and includes penal/criminal offences deriving from all sources of international law as enshrined in Art. 38 ICJ Statute, international conventions, customary law as well as general principles of law recognized by civilized nations.[81]

Within the UDHR there were already efforts to include the so called "Nuremberg provision" as contained in paragraph 2 of Art. 15 ICCPR. However, it was omitted from the final wording of the UDHR. Several delegates proposed not

---

[79]*Gallant* (supra note 4), 156.

[80]A. *Cassese* International Criminal Law (2008), 36ff.

[81]For the UDHR compare further *N. Robinson*, The Universal Declaration of Human Rights (1958), 116. For the ICCPR see *M.J. Bossuyt*, Guide to the "Travaux Préparatoires" of the International Covenant on Civil and Political Rights (1987), 325, referring to the statements of State representatives at the Third Committee, GAOR, 15th Session (1960) from Afghanistan (A/C.3/SR.1007, § 19), India (A/C.3/SR.1008, § 4), The Philippines (A/C.3/SR.1008, § 19) and Uruguay (A/C.3/SR.1012, § 6).

including a special provision on international crimes within the covenant at all, thinking it undesirable to refer to the special case of war criminals in a general convention on fundamental human rights.[82] The Nuremberg Clause remained disputed in the fifth session of the Commission on Human Rights in 1949,[83] as well as in the fifteenth session of the Third Committee in 1960.[84] Despite some wavering during the drafting of the covenant, the provision survived within paragraph 2 of Art. 15 ICCPR. In a vote to delete the provision in 1960, nineteen votes were for deletion, fifty-one were against and ten state representatives abstained.[85]

In terms of the *trauvaux préparatoires*, the inclusion of paragraph 2, the Nuremberg Clause, reveals a fragmented picture of what to understand by it: the discussions of that clause touch upon various issues, the applicable law, the retroactive justification of the Nuremberg jurisprudence, as well as the possible impact of the Nuremberg Clause on future atrocities.

One position taken by many representatives at various stages of the drafting history was that "criminal offence under international law" as contained in paragraph 1 shall be read in accordance with Article 38 of the Statute of the International Court of Justice. The legal basis for the establishment of a crime under international law would thereby include international conventions, customary law and general principles of law recognized by civilized nations. An understanding of paragraph 2, the Nuremberg clause, as an explicit reference to "general principles of law" as a source of applicable law would, however, make the entire paragraph superfluous, since all sources of Art. 38 ICJ Statute were already covered by the first paragraph.[86] The Secretary General in a memorandum of 1951 shared this

---

[82]Cf. the statements of State representatives from India (para 53) and China (para 51) at the Sixth Session of the Commission on Human Rights, E/CN.4/SR.159, 27 April 1950, Summary Record of the 159th meeting. Similarly the State representative from Spain argued that the ICCPR "was not designed to be relied upon at the great historical trials of the future; its purpose was to safeguard the dignity of man and to guarantee his everyday freedoms by enabling him to go before courts which interpreted a clearly defined law" and that trials like the ones in Nuremberg and Tokyo "were rare, and the courts set up on those occasions their own rules of law and their own body of practice in light of the prevailing circumstances." See A/C.3/SR.1011, para 26, Third Committee, 15th Session as quoted in *Gallant* (supra note 4), 200.

[83]Cf. the positions of State representatives from Egypt, India, Guatemala, Poland and Uruguay in U.N. Doc. E/CN.4/SR.112 (7 June 1949), Summary Record of the 112th meeting.

[84]See *Bossuyt* (supra note 81), 331 referring to the statements of State representatives at the Third Committee, GAOR, 15th Session (1960) from Argentina, Saudi Arabia, in U.N. Doc. A/C.3/SR.1007; Brazil and Paraguay in U.N. Doc. A/C.3/SR.1011; Peru and Haiti in U.N. Doc. A/C.3/SR.1011; and Italy in U.N. Doc. A/C.3/SR.1013.

[85]See *Bossuyt* (supra note 81), 331, referring to the Third Committee, GAOR, 15th Session (1960), A/C.3/SR.1013, para 47.

[86]Cf. the statements of State representatives at the Sixth Session of the Commission on Human Rights, E/CN.4/SR.159, 27 April 1950, Summary Record of the 159th meeting from USA (para 49), China (para 51), Denmark (para 68), Uruguay (para 76) and Australia (para 85).

position.[87] The United Kingdom, however, pushed for the explicit reference to "general principles of law" to be included. It seems that the United Kingdom feared that general principles were not adequately covered by the wording "criminal offence under international law" as stipulated in the first paragraph.[88] There are some grounds for the British concerns, since several State representatives in the drafting process objected to the use of general principles as a legal basis for individual criminal convictions, stating that no individual should be convicted on basis of vague, imprecise general principles.[89]

Furthermore, the Nuremberg Clause was construed by other delegates as a retroactive justification or remedy to any possible defects within the Nuremberg jurisprudence.[90] In contrast other State representatives explicitly feared that paragraph 2 could be construed in that way, arguing that the post World War II cases needed no special justification as they had been adjudicated on basis of international law existing at that time.[91]

The controversies over the meaning of the Nuremberg clause did not stop there. Other delegates wanted to secure a loose application of the Nuremberg Clause for future atrocities even if a strict positivistic understanding would not support the existence of a crime on the basis of the available sources of international law.[92] Paragraph 2 should not only remedy any defect in relation to the Nuremberg or Tokyo trials, but should also guarantee a re-application of the Nuremberg principles

---

[87]Draft International Covenant on Human Rights and Measures of Implementation, The General Adequacy of the First Eighteen Articles (Parts I and II), Memorandum by the Secretary-General, UN Doc. E/CN.4/528, 2 April 1951, 51–52, stating that "there seems to be no clear reason for regarding the provision made in paragraph 2 as being different in content from that made in the first sentence of paragraph 1 of the Articles, particularly in view of the reference made therein to 'international law'. It seems to be accepted that the generally recognized principles of law are a part, or are a source of, international law."

[88]*Gallant* (supra note 4), 196f, referring to the Statement of the UK representative in E/CN.4/SR.159, para 75.

[89]See *Bossuyt* (supra note 81), 331, referring to the statements of State representatives at the Third Committee, GAOR, 15th Session (1960): Spain (A/C.3/SR.1011, para 25), Italy (A/C.3/SR.1013, para 38), Japan (A/C.3/SR.1010, para 25), Pakistan (A/C.3/SR.1011, para 10), Peru (A/C.3/SR.1010, para 20), Argentina (A/C.3/SR.1007, para 9) and Haiti (A/C.3/SR.1011, para 3).

[90]See *Bossuyt* (supra note 81), 331, referring to the statements of State representatives at the Third Committee, GAOR, 15th Session (1960): USSR (A/C.3/SR.1008, para 24), Great Britain (A/C.3/SR.1009, para 13), Romania (A/C.3/SR.1010, paras 32–33), The Netherlands (A/C.3/SR.1011, para 31) and Israel (A/C.3/SR.1011, para 35).

[91]Sixth Session of the Commission on Human Rights, E/CN.4/SR.159, 27 April 1950, Summary Record of the 159th meeting, Statement of State representatives from Belgium (para 74): paragraph 2 "defeated its own purpose by implying that the defendants at Nurnberg and Tokyo had not been condemned under international law but in virtue of principles of less certain authority." See also the positions of the USA (para 60) and Denmark (para 68).

[92]While *Gallant* (supra note 4), 199, sees little support for either supporters or opponents in the record that the Nuremberg Clause was intended to be applied for future cases, other writers do not share this contention – see for instance *Boot* (supra note 10), 141.

for future trials.[93] The State representative of Yugoslavia argued that paragraph 2 "should form an integral part of an international instrument; that might perhaps prevent a repetition of past events and deprive war criminals of any opportunity of escaping justice on the ground that their offences were not provided for under the laws of their country or under international law."[94] Ghana considered paragraph 2 to be a "saving clause" that enables the State parties to convict individuals "despite" paragraph 1.[95]

Considering these varying positions, the *trauvaux préparatoires* do not provide a clear basis for interpreting the Nuremberg clause. There is one line of thought detectable in the drafting history that would thus opt for the interpretation of the Nuremberg clause as a "saving clause" for prosecution of international crimes, even if these offences were not clearly established as crimes under international law. Such an understanding would favour the non-application of the guarantees of the NCSL principle when horrendous international "crimes" have occurred. However, the subsequent practice of international as well as national courts demonstrates that the NCSL principle also applies when international core crimes are at stake.[96] Whereas some decisions would apply the domestic *nullum crimen sine lege* standard for "ordinary" domestic crimes and international core crimes alike,[97] other courts differentiated between two distinctive versions of *nullum crimen sine lege*: one domestic version applicable to "ordinary" domestic crimes and one version applicable when international core crimes were committed.[98] This differential application has been justified on basis of the Nuremberg Clause, as contained in the second paragraph of human rights instruments.[99]

---

[93]See *Bossuyt* (supra note 81), 331: "if in the future crimes should be perpetrated similar to those punished at Nürnberg, they would be punished in accordance with the same principles", referring to the statements of State representatives at the Third Committee, GAOR, 15th Session (1960): Poland (A/C.3/SR.1008, para 2), Yugoslavia (A/C.3/SR.1008, para 14), Ceylon (A/C.3/SR.1010, para 9), Bulgaria (A/C.3/SR.1012, para 15) and Yugoslavia (A/C.3/SR.1013, paras 14–15, 17); see in this regard also the Report of the Canadian Commission of Inquiry on War Criminals (Deschenes Commission, 1986), 143.

[94]Statement of the State representative of Yugoslavia at the Third Committee, GAOR, 15th Session (1960), A/C.3/SR.1008, 135, as referred to by *W. N. Ferdinandusse*, Direct Application of International Criminal Law in National Courts (2006), 234.

[95]Statement of the State representative of Ghana at the Third Committee, GAOR, 15th Session (1960), A/C.3/SR.1010, 145, para 17 (Ghana). Similar references by the delegates of Czechoslovakia and Afghanistan and Romania (*id.*, 146–147). See *Ferdinandusse* (supra note 94), 234.

[96]*Ferdinandusse* (supra note 94), 224ff with further references to the jurisprudence of national and international courts.

[97]See *Ferdinandusse* (supra note 94), 229 referring to case law before East-Timor's Court of Appeal, the Senegalese court of Appeals and the Dutch Supreme Court.

[98]*Ferdinandusse* (supra note 94), 226ff referring to the case law before Argentinean Courts, the Colombian Constitutional Court, the Slovenian Constitutional Court, the Hungarian Constitutional Court, as well as explicit inclusion of the Nuremberg Clause in national law in the 1997 Polish Constitution, the Criminal Code of Bosnia and Herzegovina and the Canadian Constitution.

[99]Compare for the universal level Art. 15 ICCPR and Art. 7 ECHR for the regional level.

The European Court of Human Rights (ECtHR) was confronted with the question of application of *nullum crimen sine lege* (Art. 7 ECHR) in the case of *Naletilić v. Croatia*. The suspect, accused of international crimes, challenged his transfer to the ICTY in The Hague on the basis that he would face a heavier penalty before the ICTY than in Croatia. The ECtHR declared his complaint inadmissible: "As to the applicant's contention that he might receive a heavier punishment by the ICTY than he might have received by domestic courts if the latter exercised their jurisdiction to finalise the proceedings against him, the Court notes that, even assuming Article 7 of the Convention to apply to the present case, the specific provision that could be applicable to it would be paragraph 2 rather than paragraph 1 of Article 7 of the Convention. This means that the second sentence of Article 7 § 1 of the Convention invoked by the applicant could not apply."[100]

Thus the ECtHR made a distinction in the applicability of the *nullum crimen sine lege* principle in relation to "ordinary" domestic crimes and "international crimes". The latter are covered by paragraph 2 of Art. 7 of the Convention.

In conclusion it can be said that the NCSL principle now has a firm place in human rights documents, as well as in international humanitarian law conventions. This inclusion of the principle in binding international conventions ensures that it cannot be regarded merely as an unbinding principle of justice on the international plane anymore. However, the inclusion of the Nuremberg clause in human rights documents as interpreted in the subsequent practice of domestic and international (human rights) courts allows a different application of the principle in relation to the commission of international core crimes. Consequently, it needs to be considered what content is to be given to this "international" NCSL principle when concerned with international core crimes.

3.8 The Obligation of International Criminal Tribunals to Comply with *Nullum Crimen Sine Lege*

The development of the NCSL principle in human rights and humanitarian law instruments adds a further dimension to the discussion of international criminal law that did not exist at the time of the IMT Nuremberg, the IMTFE Tokyo and other post World War II tribunals. Indeed the claim that NCSL is solely an unbinding principle of justice or policy is hard to maintain, as it is firmly established in binding form in various human rights law and humanitarian law conventions. Despite this

---

[100]European Court of Human Rights, *Naletilić v. Croatia*, Application No. 51891/99, Admissibility Decision, 4 May 2000 (*Naletilić* Admissibility Decision), para 2.

development, the NCSL principle is nevertheless only occasionally grounded in the underlying statutes of international criminal tribunals.[101]

It is evident that these international conventions cannot bind the international criminal tribunals *per se*, since they bind State parties to the respective international treaties, establishing a relationship between the individual and the State.[102] However, the legal literature affirms the bindingness of NCSL for international criminal tribunals, varying only on the grounds: for some *nullum crimen sine lege* rests upon general principles,[103] others conceive it as a rule of customary law,[104] while others go as far as to claim that it is part of *ius cogens*.[105] While there are differences in relation to the underlying source, the universal application of NCSL is firmly established in the legal literature. These references affirm that while international organizations[106] cannot be bound directly by conventional instruments of which they are not parties, the obligation to adhere to *nullum crimen sine lege* requirements is established *via* other sources of international law.[107] However, the

---

[101] Indeed only the Rome Statute in Art. 22 and Section 12 of the Statute of the Special Panels in East Timor, UNTAWT Regulation No. 2000/15, 6 June 2000, contain a provision on NCSL, while the Extraordinary Chambers in the Courts of Cambodia cf. Law on the Establishment of the Extraordinary Chambers with Inclusion of Amendments as promulgated on 27 October 2004 (ECCC Statute) refers to Art. 15 ICCPR in its Art. 33. Neither the ICTY Statute, the ICTR Statute, nor the SCSL Statute has a provision on NCSL.

[102] See however the French delegate *Cassin*, who stated that NCSL shall "protect the individual from arbitrary actions even by international organizations", at the 5th Session of the Commission on Human Rights (1949), E/CN.4/SR.112, 8, as cited by *D. Weissbrodt*, The Right to a Fair Trial under the Universal Declaration of Human Rights and the International Covenant on Civil and Political Rights (2001), 80.

[103] *Cassese* (supra note 80), 32ff, establishes *nullum crimen singe lege* as a "principle of international criminal law", explaining that it may only "bear scant resemblance to those of municipal systems". See also *Bassiouni* (supra note 40) differentiating between the NCSL principle as derived from general principles from domestic systems (p. 127ff), and from general principles of international law (p. 140ff). Others establish it on basis of general principles deriving from national laws, cf. *O. Triffterer*, Preliminary Remarks: The Permanent International Criminal Court – Ideal and Reality, in Triffterer (ed.), Commentary on the Rome Statute of the International Criminal Court (2008), 22, RN 18; *O. Triffterer*, Dogmatische Untersuchungen zur Entwicklung des materiellen Völkerstrafrechts seit Nürnberg (1966), 126; *A. Eichhofer*, Die Rechtsquellen des Völkerstrafrechts, Kühner/Esser/Gerding (eds.), Völkerstrafrecht (2007), 9.

[104] *Lamb* (supra note 57), 734; *Gallant* (supra note 4), 352ff, 393; *G. Werle*, Völkerstrafrecht (2007), MN 100; *J.-M. Henckaerts*, Customary International Humanitarian Law (2005) (ICRC Custom Study), Volume I: Rules, Rule 101, 371.

[105] *Meron* attests that the "prohibition of retroactive penal measures is a fundamental principle of criminal justice and a customary, even peremptory, norm of international law that must be observed in all circumstances by national and international tribunals." *T. Meron*, War Crimes Law Comes of Age (1998), 244.

[106] The SCSL for example is an international organization in its own right, while the ICTY and ICTR are subsidiary organs of the UN Security Council.

[107] See generally on that issue *T. Kleinlein*, Konstitutionalisierung im Völkerrecht (2012), 598. See in relation to international criminal tribunals *C. J. M. Safferling* Towards an International Criminal Procedure (2001), 53ff.

bindingness can also derive from State obligations, albeit indirectly: as international organizations are founded by States, they cannot transfer more competences than they themselves possess (*nemo plus iuris transferre potest quam ipse habet*). That maxim would not lead to the direct bindingness of the conventional instruments on the international organization itself, but concerns the transferred competence to the international organization. Any act of the international organization contrary to pre-existing conventional obligations of its Member States would be considered void.[108] Furthermore, theoretically, international organizations could be bound by human rights merely by acceptance *via* a unilateral act.[109]

In addition to rooting the legally binding force of NCSL in the sources of international law, adherence to NCSL is warranted from the perspective of legitimacy of the trials. In order to adhere to NCSL the Secretary General linked the legality of the proceedings before the ICTY with customary international law as the basis of criminal convictions.[110] International criminal law has a dual nature: while it is a branch of public international law, its subject matter is criminal law, requiring that it also adheres to the appropriate fundamental principles.[111] Moreover, compliance with NCSL is also a practical matter: States should not be required to breach their own human rights obligations when executing a request for extradition/surrender[112] of suspects, and thus international criminal tribunals need to comply in order to ensure the willing co-operation of States.[113]

---

[108]With regard to the relationship between human rights protected under the ECHR and the competence of European Community, see *H. G. Schermers*, The European Communities bound by Fundamental Human Rights, 27 Common Market Law Review (1990), 252: "In transferring power to a newly established Community, the Member States could not grant the Community any possibility to infringe the rights guaranteed by the Convention [European Convention on Human Rights]. Any rules made by the Community contrary to the Convention are therefore void."

[109]*Kleinlein* (supra note 107), 564ff.

[110]See the references to the reports of the SG on the different tribunals (infra note 244).

[111]*Triffterer* (supra note 103), 124, 126. See also *Hauck* (supra note 8), 65:"Its [NCSL's] ethical background calls for a valid origin of the creation of criminal offences, binding to any civilized system of criminal justice."

[112]The Rome Statute in Art. 102 differentiates between the wordings 'surrender', *i.e.* the *sui generis* delivery up of a person by a State to the ICC and 'extradition', which according to the Rome Statute solely refers to the delivery up of a person by one State to another State. Cf. *W. Schabas*, The International Criminal Court. A Commentary on the Rome Statute (2010), Art. 102, 1058ff.

[113]See also *S. Zappalà*, Human Rights in International Criminal Proceedings (2007), 6.

3.9 *Nullum Crimen Sine Lege* in International Criminal Law: A *sui generis* Principle?

Despite shortcomings in their respective statutes,[114] all international criminal tribunals accept the applicability of the NCSL principle in their proceedings. The case law reveals that the accused individual can claim the violation of the NCSL principle as grounds to contest the jurisdiction of the tribunals, even without explicit manifestation in the underlying statutes.[115] The ICTY *Kordić* Trial Chamber declared that the NCSL principle should be relied on to assess the subject-matter jurisdiction of the ICTY.[116] The NCSL principle applies to both charges concerning the underlying criminal offences and the forms of liability.[117] While the general acceptance of the application of the principle to determine the jurisdiction of international criminal tribunals is firmly established, it remains to be seen what content is given to the NCSL principle when applied to international core crimes. As elaborated above, the practice of international and national courts demonstrates that the application of the NCSL principle between the domestic legal order primarily concerned with "ordinary" domestic crimes, and the international legal order concerned with international core crimes, may differ.[118] This debate in the context of international criminal tribunals was most intense at the ECCC: The defendants argued that the ECCC differed from other international criminal tribunals, most notably the UN *ad hoc* tribunals, as it was established within the existing court structure of Cambodia and as such was bound to respect Cambodian law. According to their argument, the ECCC was obliged to apply the domestic NCSL principle, which would bar a Cambodian court from prosecuting crimes on the basis of international law. The defendants stated that the ECCC would only be allowed to prosecute international crimes if they had been criminalized under domestic Cambodian law at the time of their commission, which for the period of

---

[114]See supra note 101.

[115]Compare further for the ICTY: *Tadić* Appeals Chamber Jurisdiction Decision, para 139; *Prosecutor v. Hadžihasanović*, Case No. IT-01-47-AR 72, Decision on Interlocutory Appeal Challenging Jurisdiction in Relation to Command Responsibility, Appeals Chamber, 16 July 2003, paras 10–36; Compare for the ICTR: *Prosecutor v. Akayesu*, Case No. ICTR-96-4-T, Trial Judgment, 2 September 1998, paras 611–17; *Prosecutor v. Kanyabashi*, Case No. ICTR-96-15-T, Decision on Defence Motion on Jurisdiction, Trial Chamber, 18 June 1997; Compare for the SCSL: *Prosecutor v. Norman*, Case No. SCSL-2004-14-AR72(E), Decision on Preliminary Motion Based on Lack of Jurisdiction (Child Recruitment), Appeals Chamber, 31 May 2004 (*Norman* Appeals Chamber Decision), para 8ff. See also *Gallant* (supra note 4), 311ff, who considers that NCSL before international criminal tribunals is applicable as a jurisdictional as well as a substantive issue.

[116]ICTY, *Prosecutor v. Kordić et al.*, IT-95-14/2-T, Trial Chamber, Judgment, 26 February 2001, para 20.

[117]See for example ECCC, *Prosecutor v. Kaing Guek Eav (Duch)*, Case No. 001/18-07-2007-ECCC/SC, Supreme Court Chamber, Appeals Judgment, para 91.

[118]See supra note 96–98 and accompanying text.

the ECCC's temporal jurisdiction had neither been the case for international crimes, such as genocide, crimes against humanity, war crimes, nor for international modes of liability, such as command responsibility.[119] The ECCC Pre-Trial Chamber in its response dismissed the defence appeals, stating that the ECCC law gave the Court jurisdiction over international crimes, and that in accordance with Art. 15 ICCCPR when international crimes are concerned the *international principle of legality* is applicable.[120] The international principle of legality allows recourse to the different sources of international law in order to establish international crimes and modes of liability.[121] Thus, even with respect to hybrid courts such as the ECCC, the case law establishes that the applicable version of the NCSL principle is the "international principle of legality". Legal scholars also argue that when international core crimes are being pursued at the international level, in contrast to the prosecution of ordinary domestic crimes, only the "core" of the NCSL principle shall find application.[122] One aim of this study is to fill this "core" of the NCSL principle with content. First, however, we must turn to the question of what justifies a differential application of the NCSL principle between ordinary domestic crimes and core international crimes.

From a normative perspective, it is clear that the "Nuremberg Clause"[123] has been used to justify a distinction between the application of the NCSL principle for "ordinary" domestic crimes on the one hand and core international crimes on the other hand.[124] Thus, the human rights treaties that established the *nullum crimen*

---

[119]ECCC, *Ieng Thirith* Defence Appeal from the Closing Order, Case No. 002/19-09-2007-ECCC/ OCIJ (PTC 145), 18 October 2010, paras 15, 24ff, 41ff, 67, 84; *Nuon Chea* Defence Appeal Against the Closing Order, Case No. 002/19-09-2007-ECCC/OCIJ (PTC 146), 18 October 2010, paras 6ff, 16ff, 26ff; *Ieng Sary's* Appeal Against the Closing Order, Case No. 002/19-09-2007-ECCC/OCIJ (PTC 75), 25 October 2010, paras 108ff.

[120]ECCC, Pre-Trial Chamber, Public Decision on *Ieng Sary's* Appeal Against the Closing Order, Case No. 002/19-09-2007-ECCC/OCIJ (PTC 75), 11 April 2011 (Pre-Trial Chamber Decision on *Ieng Sary*'s Appeal Against the Closing Order), para 213 (emphasis added); Pre-Trial Chamber, Public Decision on Appeals by *Nuon Chea* and *Ieng Thirith* against the Closing Order, Case No. 002/19-09-2007-ECCC/OCIJ (PTC 145 & 146), 15 February 2011, paras 95ff.

[121]*Ibid.*

[122]*O. Triffterer*, Bestandsaufnahme zum Völkerstrafrecht, in Hankel, Stuby (eds.), Strafgerichte gegen Menschheitsverbrechen (1995), 219: "Der Kerngehalt dieses Satzes, der sich zu einem Teilaspekt des Menschenrechts auf persönliche Freiheit entwickelt hat und durch dessen Verankerung im Völkerrecht bestätigt worden ist, beinhaltet, daß zur Beseitigung von Willkür jeder staatliche Eingriff in die Freiheitssphäre des Einzelnen an das Vorhandensein einer Norm gebunden sein muß; diese kann dem gesetzten oder dem ungesetzten Recht angehören. Sie muß bereits zur Tatzeit existent sein, ein näher bestimmtes Verhalten festlegen und durch den Hinweis auf dessen Strafbarkeit eine an den Einzelnen gerichtete generelle Strafdrohung enthalten"; *K. Ambos*, Remarks on the General Part of International Criminal Law, 4 Journal of International Criminal Justice (2006), 669, stating that the basic components of the NCSL principle in ICL are *lege praevia* and *lege certa*; *Heinsch* (supra note 7), 322; *Bassiouni* (supra note 40), 144.

[123]Paragraph 2 of Art. 15 ICCPR and Art. 7 ECHR.

[124]*Ferdinandusse* (supra note 94), 224ff *i.a.* referring to the case law of Argentina, the Colombian Constitutional Court, the French Court de Cassation in the *Barbie* Case, the Slovenian Constitutional Court, the Hungarian Constitutional Court and the ECtHR in its *Naletilić* Admissibility Decision, para 2.

sine lege principle in binding form on the international plane, can themselves be used to justify a differential treatment of the *nullum crimen sine lege* principle as applied to "ordinary" domestic crimes and international core crimes.

From a structural perspective, a differentiation between the principles as applied in the international legal order compared to the domestic legal sphere is also indicated. This is evident from the theoretical and philosophical foundations of the NCSL principle that cannot be transferred from the domestic to the international legal order.[125] The principle of separation of powers and the question of the democratic legitimacy are also discussed within the sphere of international criminal law[126]; however, international law does not know a permanent and representative international legislative authority that could fulfill such a democratic task.[127] The NCSL principle as "the citizen's bulwark against the State's omnipotence"[128] may at first sight appear to be ill-suited at the international level. As prosecutions before international criminal tribunals are generally conducted against individuals who "bear the greatest responsibility",[129] these individuals are—when committing atrocities—themselves in positions of authority in States or State-like entities committing crimes in weak, decentralized States or in the context of State collapse. However, even "powerful" individuals might be faced with arbitrary power when charges are brought against them by the "omnipotent" international community. Consequently, this foundation of the NCSL principle, best described in the international context as "the individual's bulwark against the international community's omnipotence", finds its application in international criminal law.[130] Furthermore, the principle of individual guilt as the underlying central idea of NCSL, holding individuals accountable because of their conscious "deviance from societal expectations",[131] is a valid foundation on the international plane. This was affirmed by

---

[125] See Sect. 3.4, Theoretical and Philosophical Foundations.

[126] *M. Glasius*, Do International Criminal Courts Require Democratic Legitimacy, 23 European Journal of International Law (2012), 43ff.

[127] See the US Military Tribunal, *Altstötter and Others Case*, 41: "International law is not the product of statute for the simple reason that there is as yet no world authority empowered to enact statutes of universal application." See also Opening Statement of US Chief Prosecutor *Jackson*, IMT Nuremberg Judgment, Vol. II, 147: "International law is not capable of development by the normal processes of legislation, for there is no continuing international legislative authority."

[128] *von Liszt* (supra note 9), 1009–1010.

[129] See the Report on Prosecutorial Strategy, Office of the Prosecutor of the ICC, 14. September 2006, available at: http://www.icc-cpi.int/NR/rdonlyres/D673DD8C-D427-4547-BC69-2D363E07274B/143708/ProsecutorialStrategy20060914_English.pdf (last visited: 2 December 2014); compare also Statue of the Special Court for Sierra Leone, Art. 1. The ECCC Statute speaks also of "senior leaders" in its Art. 1 and the IMT Nuremberg trial concerned the "major German war criminals".

[130] See in this regard ECCC *Duch* Appeals Judgment, para 90: "The Supreme Court finds that the restraining function of the international principle of legality is of particular importance in international criminal law as it prevents international or hybrid tribunals and courts from unilaterally exceeding their jurisdiction by providing clear limitations on what is criminal."

[131] *D. Robinson*, A Cosmopolitan Liberal Account of International Criminal Law, 26 Leiden Journal of International Law (2013), 134.

the ICTY *Tadić* Appeals Chamber stipulating that "[t]he basic assumption must be that in international law as much as in national systems, the foundation of criminal responsibility is the principle of personal culpability".[132] Consequently, the protection of the individual against arbitrary charges and the principle of individual guilt, key aspects of the theoretical foundations of the NCSL principle in the domestic legal sphere, are also valid theoretical foundations of the NCSL principle in international criminal law proceedings.

3.10 The Guarantees of the *Nullum Crimen Sine Lege* Principle in International Criminal Law: The Principle of *Nullum Crimen Sine Iure*

3.10.1 Preliminary Remarks

Treating the NCSL principle in relation to international criminal law as a *sui generis* principle, or the "international principle of legality", necessarily involves considering the structural differences between the domestic legal systems and the international legal order. Indeed, in the words of the US Military Tribunal in the Justice Case, to force international criminal tribunals to apply the same NCSL principle as in the domestic sphere would have "strangled" international criminal law at birth.[133] The question here is which curtailments of the NCSL principle are necessary due to a structural "deficit" of the international legal order in terms of the law formation process and the applicable sources of international criminal law. The specificity of international criminal law in relation to differences in its sources of law and its legislators when compared to the domestic legal order, means that the *nullum crimen sine lege* principle on the international plane must necessarily be construed differently.[134] On the same token, however, international criminal proceedings must nevertheless comply with the theoretical foundations of the protection of the individual against arbitrary charges and the principle of individual guilt.

---

[132]ICTY, *Tadić* Appeals Judgment, para 186 stating that this principle is *inter alia* laid down in the ICTY Statute in its Art. 7 (1). Note, however, that the Appeals Chamber was speaking generally about the principle of personal culpability and not specifically about the NCSL principle.

[133]US Military Tribunal, *Altstötter and Others Case*, 974–5.

[134]*Prosecutor v. Karemera*, Case No. ICTR-98-44-T, Trial Chamber, Decision on the Preliminary Motions By the Defence Challenging Jurisdiction in Relation to Joint Criminal Enterprise, 11 May 2004 (*Karemera* Trial Chamber Decision), para 43; see also *Boot* (supra note 10), 216; *Bassiouni* (supra note 40), 144, stating that the NCSL principle "must balance between the preservation of justice and fairness for the accused and the preservation of world order, taking into account the nature of international law, the absence of international legislative policies and standards, the *ad hoc* processes of technical drafting"; see also *M.C. Bassiouni* and *P. Manikas*, The Law of the International Criminal Tribunal for the Former Yugoslavia (1996), 265; compare also ICTY, *Prosecutor v. Delalić* (Čelebici), Case No. IT-96-21-T, Trial Chamber, Judgment, 16 November 1998, para 405.

On the basis of this theoretical foundation, this chapter will consider if and to what extent the four guarantees established above—*nullum crimen sine lege scripta, stricta, certa and praevia*[135]—find application in international criminal law proceedings and what these guarantees imply for the underlying sources of international law. These four guarantees should not be viewed in clinical isolation but should be complementary to one other in order to find a viable approach to the principle of *nullum crimen sine lege* in international criminal proceedings. Before addressing these issues, some general remarks on the applicable law in international criminal proceedings are indicated.

3.10.2 The Quest for Applicable Law

It is evident that international criminal tribunals are bound by their respective statutes, their "constituent instruments" and *raison d'être*. The legal basis of these statutes, however, differ considerably: whereas the Rome Statute of the International Criminal Court (Rome Statute) and the Statute for the Special Court for Sierra Leone (SCSL) are international conventions,[136] the International Criminal Tribunal for the Former Yugoslavia (ICTY) and the International Tribunal for Rwanda (ICTR) were established by a binding Chapter VII Security Council resolution.[137] The Statute of the Special Tribunal for Lebanon (STL) is caught between the two stools of an international agreement between the UN and Lebanon and a Security Council Resolution,[138] while the Extraordinary Chambers in the Courts of Cambodia (ECCC) are based on domestic legislation.[139]

It is indeed stunning to see that most of the statutes of international criminal tribunals do not comment on the applicable law the judges are expected to use. The only exception in this regard is the Rome Statute, which even declares a hierarchy of applicable norms within its Art 21[140]: The Rome Statute "in the first place"

---

[135]See Sect. 3.3, The Four Guarantees of *Nullum Crimen Sine Lege*.

[136]Rome Statute; Statue of the Special Court for Sierra Leone.

[137]ICTY Statute; ICTR Statute.

[138]While there exists an agreement between the United Nations and the Lebanese Republic on the establishment of a Special Tribunal, due to a political stalemate the Statute of the STL was established pursuant to UNSC Res 1757/(2007) (30 May 2007).

[139]ECCC Statute.

[140]Compare further *M. McAuliffe deGuzman*, Article 21, in Triffterer (ed.), Commentary on the Rome Statute of the International Criminal Court (2008), 701ff; *J. Verhoeven*, Article 21 of the Rome Statute and the Ambiguities of Applicable Law, 23 Netherlands Yearbook of International Law (2002), 11. Note however that no such hierarchy exists between the three main sources in Art. 38 ICJ Statute. Cf. *V.D. Degan*, On the Sources of International Criminal Law, 4 Chinese Journal of International Law (2005), 50. See also *W.A. Schabas*, The UN International Criminal Tribunals (2006), 75–76, who, however, declares in relation to Art. 38 ICJ Statute that "in reality the first two [*i.e.* treaty and customary norms] take precedence."

provides an exhaustive list of crimes within the jurisdiction of the ICC that is accompanied by elements of crimes as an aid to interpretation. Only "where appropriate" shall recourse be taken to international conventions and customary international law,[141] and failing that, general principles of law. The other statutes of international criminal tribunals cannot compare with the elaborated provisions of the Rome Statute. Arts. 1 and 2 of the ECCC Statute that determine the purpose and competence of the ECCC merely contain a reference to international humanitarian law and custom, as well as international conventions recognized by Cambodia. While the SCSL Statute is silent on the matter of applicable law, its Rules of Procedure and Evidence provide in Rule 72*bis* lit ii that "where appropriate, other applicable treaties and the principles and rules of international customary law" shall be considered applicable law. Neither the ICTY Statute nor the ICTR Statute has any provisions on applicable law whatsoever.[142]

Turning to the articles that define the subject-matter jurisdiction of the tribunals by enumerating the catalog of international crimes, they also enumerate some of the preconditions that make them punishable under international law. This does not necessarily mean, however, that these statutory specifications are the proper legal basis for the criminal convictions themselves. The reason for such a conclusion is plain and simple: most international criminal tribunals were established on an *ad hoc* basis. If the international criminal tribunals must decide over crimes that were committed before the tribunals were established, the offences enshrined in the statutes must necessarily reflect international law in force at the time the offence was committed. Hence, the criminal provisions contained in the respective statutes serve as a jurisdictional skeleton for the purpose of defining and limiting the subject-matter jurisdiction, while the legal basis for criminal convictions must lie elsewhere, in international conventions, customary international law or general principles. As such it is self evident that the international criminal tribunals take recourse to the classical sources of international law as listed in Art. 38 ICJ Statute. In the words of the ICTY *Kupreškić* Trial Chamber:

> Being international in nature and applying international law *principaliter*, the Tribunal cannot but rely upon the well-established sources of international law.[143]

---

[141]It is obvious that the term "rules" of international law used by the Rome Statute clearly encompasses customary law, cf. *McAuliffe de Guzman*, id, 708.

[142]Although most statutes refer to war crimes as violations of the "laws or customs of war" that is not to be equated with a provision concerning the applicable law.

[143]ICTY, *Kupreškić* Trial Judgment, para 540; The *Delalić* Appeals Chamber in its Judgment, referred to the "usual sources of international law", conventional and customary law and general principles. See also the reference to Art. 38 ICJ Statute as the authoritative list of the sources of international law by the *Delalić* Trial Chamber Judgment, para 414; *Prosecutor v. Aleksovski*, IT-95-14/1A, Appeals Chamber, Judgment, 24 March 2000, Declaration of Judge Hunt, footnote 1; *Prosecutor v. Erdemović*, IT-96-22-A, Appeals Chamber, Judgment, 7 October 1997, Joint Separate Opinion of Judge McDonald and Judge Vohrah, para 40 and para 4: a "proper interpretation of the Statute and the Rules involves a consideration of international law authorities". See also ECCC, *Duch* Appeals Judgment, para 92: "As for the applicable international law, the plane

As a branch of international law, international criminal law draws upon the same sources as public international law.[144] These sources are enshrined in Article 38 (1) of the Statute of the International Court of Justice, consisting of *"international conventions*, whether general or particular, establishing rules expressly recognized by the contesting states, *international custom*, as evidence of a general practice accepted as law and the *general principles of law* recognized by civilized nations."[145]

3.10.3   The scripta *Requirement and the Sources of International Law: International Conventions as the Sole Legal Basis for Individual Criminal Responsibility?*

If the *nullum crimen sine lege scripta* requirement (the requirement of written statutory provisions) would be applicable in international criminal proceedings, then the only possible underlying source of criminalization would consist of international conventions. The *scripta* requirement excludes the possibility of using unwritten sources of law, such as customary international law and general principles of law, as an adequate legal basis in international criminal proceedings.

With regards to the *scripta* requirement the Rome Statute takes an exceptional place among the statutes of international criminal tribunals. The Rome Statute as an international convention does not only create the jurisdictional frame for the ICC, but is in itself the source of substantial criminal norms binding on individuals of its State parties when it has jurisdiction over them.[146] In comparison to other statutes of international criminal tribunals, the Rome Statute has a strong articulation of the *nullum crimen sine lege* principle in its Art. 22. As such it seems that the Rome Statute upholds the *scripta* requirement.[147] Nevertheless, if the ICC encountered a situation involving nationals of non-State Parties in cases of SC referrals or *ad hoc* acceptance of jurisdiction by a non-State Party, it would be necessary to

---

of reference is broader, encompassing international conventions, customary international law and general principles of law recognised by the community of nations applicable at the relevant time."

[144]*Triffterer* (supra note 103), 128; *K. Ambos*, Der allgemeine Teil des Völkerstrafrechts (2002), 40ff; *D. Akande*, Sources of International Criminal Law, in *Cassese* (ed.), Oxford Companion to International Criminal Justice (2009), 41ff.

[145]Statute of the International Court of Justice, 26 June 1945, 33 UNTS 993, Art. 38 (emphasis added).

[146]*M. Milanovic*, Is the Rome Statute Binding on Individuals? (And Why We Should Care), 9 Journal of International Criminal Justice (2011), 25ff.

[147]Whereas *Ambos* (supra note 122), 670f claims that all four guarantees of NCSL including *lex scripta* are enshrined in Art 22 of the Rome Statute, he asks with reference to Art. 21 "whether the ICC could invoke norms outside the Statute to create or increase punishment."

demonstrate that the Rome Statute reflects customary international law. The Rome Statute as an international treaty does not bind non-State Parties and consequently in such cases customary international law is the proper legal source for establishing the criminal responsibility of the individual. Otherwise, in such instances the Rome Statute would have to be applied retroactively upon individuals of non-State parties.[148]

While the drafting of the Rome Statute has been effusively referred to as a "quasi-legislative event that produced a criminal code for the world",[149] one has to agree with *Cassese* that the ICC Statute is not a codification of international criminal law as such, but solely lays down definitions of crimes and the general part of international criminal law, which the ICC shall apply.[150] The statute *per se* is however of limited use for other tribunals, since they are not bound by it, unless it can be shown that as an international treaty it has developed into or reflects customary international law.[151] However, the utility of the Rome Statute for other international criminal tribunals depends on the exact moment of the commission of the crime, that is, whether or not the crime had been committed before or after the Rome Statute entered into force.[152]

As stated above, the statutes of most international criminal tribunals are, however, necessarily just jurisdictional in nature as they are established on an *ad hoc*

---

[148]According to *Broomhall* with regard to nationals of non-State Parties in case of SC referrals or *ad hoc* acceptance of jurisdiction by the non-State Party "the only legitimate basis for establishing the criminal responsibility of individuals would presumably [...] be that of customary law." See B. Broomhall, Art. 22, in Triffterer (ed.), Commentary on the Rome Statute of the International Criminal Court (2008), MN 14–22. See also *S. Bock* and *L. Preis*, Strafbarkeit nach Völkergewohnheitsrecht oder Verstoß gegen das Rückwirkungsverbot? – Drittstaatenangehörige vor dem IStGH, 20 Humanitäres Völkerrecht – Informationsschriften (Journal of International Law of Peace and Armed Conflict) (2007), 148ff. For a different opinion see *W. Schabas*, An Introduction to the International Criminal Court (2004), 71–2.

[149]*L. N. Sadat*, The International Criminal Court and the Transformation of International Law: Justice for the New Millennium (2002), 263.

[150]*Cassese* (supra note 80), 14; compare also *R. Cryer*, International Criminal law vs State Sovereignty: Another Round?, 16 European Journal of International Law (2006), 990ff.

[151]For the interplay of treaties and the development of customary law cf. ICJ, North Sea Continental Shelf Cases, paras 60–82; The ICC Statute has been referred to by the ICTY as both *opinio iuris* (ICTY, *Furundžija* Trial Judgment, para 227) and also as evidence of State practice (*Prosecutor v. Krnojelac*, IT-94-I-A, Appeals Chamber, Judgment, 17 September 2003, para 221). See also ICTY, *Furundžija* Trial Judgment, para 227 stating that "[d]epending on the matter at issue, the Rome Statute may be taken to restate, reflect or clarify customary rules or crystallize them, whereas in some areas it creates new law or modifies existing law." See also *Kupreškić* Trial Judgment, para 580, stipulating that although the Rome Statute may be indicative of *opinio iuris*, in relation to the crime against humanity of persecution, requiring a nexus to another crime it would not reflect customary international law. See further Sect. 7.5.3.3, Rome Statute.

[152]In some cases it was held that while the Rome Statute post-dates the commission of the crimes that were adjudicated before the tribunals, the Statute could nevertheless be treated as a useful key to the *opinio iuris* of States, cf. ICTY, *Prosecutor v. Krstić*, IT-98-33-T, Trial Chamber, Judgment, 2 August 2001, para 541; see also SCSL, *Prosecutor v. Fofana* et al, Case No. SCSL-04-14-A, Appeals Chamber, Judgment, 28 May 2008, para 403.

basis. The legal basis for criminal convictions must lie elsewhere in the sources of international law. Reliance on international conventions as a legal basis for individual criminal convictions stands to reason as different conventional instruments find their replication in the statutes of international criminal tribunals. For example, the ICTY Statute incorporates various conventional provisions: Art. 2 ICTY Statute contains the grave breaches regime of the 1949 Geneva Conventions, Art. 3 ICTY Statute employs Arts. 23 (a), 23 (g), 25, 27 and 47 of the Annex to the 1907 Hague Convention IV, Art. 4 ICTY Statute is the *verbatim* adoption of Arts. II and III of the Genocide Convention, and Art. 5 ICTY Statute relies on the formulation of Art. 6 (c) IMT Nuremberg Charter. Such an overlap of the jurisdictional provisions of the statutes of international criminal tribunals and certain norms of international (humanitarian) law conventions may well prompt the conclusion that the proper source of individual criminal responsibility lies within conventional norms, which also fulfill the *scripta* requirement. However, international criminal tribunals have not leapt to that conclusion. As will be seen below, taking recourse to other sources of international law, in particular customary international law, was necessary in order to uphold the *praevia* requirement of the *nullum crimen sine lege* principle, since generally international conventions are not drafted as criminal norms.[153]

The demand for a codification of international criminal norms has been postulated for years[154] and the advantages of such an approach are evident with regard to the foreseeability and calculability of the criminality of individual conduct. However, if the *nullum crimen sine lege scripta* requirement had been upheld in international criminal proceedings before post World War II and modern international criminal tribunals, international criminal law, as we know it today, would not exist. It would have made the pre-existence of an international criminal code a *condition sine qua non* for the existence of individual criminal responsibility at the international level, that is to say, conventional criminal norms that directly bind individuals. For decades the world's leaders have failed to convene a conference to draw up a universal convention on international crimes.[155] This lack of conventional international criminal norms has not prevented the development of international criminal law. The IMT Nuremberg took recourse to customary international law as a legal basis for individual criminal responsibility,[156] and modern international criminal tribunals have also not made criminal convictions dependent on the

---

[153]See Sect. 3.10.5, The *praevia* Requirement and the Sources of International Law.

[154]*Bassiouni* (supra note 40), 144.

[155]In 1996 the ILC finalized the "Draft Code of Crimes against Peace and Security of Mankind" and considered that it could take the form of an international convention, see International Law Commission, Draft Code of Crimes against the Peace and Security of Mankind with commentaries, Yearbook of the International Law Commission (1996), Vol. II, Part 2, p. 17, para 47. However, such a convention has never been drafted. To some extent the international community has met these demands with the creation of the Rome Statute. See, however, supra note 149ff and accompanying text.

[156]See IMT Nuremberg Judgment, Vol. 1, 221.

existence of conventional international criminal norms.[157] That development has left its mark on the *nullum crimen sine lege* provisions in international human rights conventions, which in relation to the applicable law are rather flexible. The drafting history of the *nullum crimen sine lege* provisions as contained in the UDHR and the ICCPR reveals that all the sources of international law could function as the underlying source for individual criminal responsibility.[158] This variety in the underlying sources means that in this context the legality principle is best described as *nullum crimen sine iure* (NCSI).[159] The Roman word *iure* better reflects the applicable sources of international law that not only consists of written law in the form of conventions, but also unwritten norms such as customary international law and general principles of law.[160] In the following, this study will use the terminology *nullum crimen sine iure* when elaborating on the application of this principle before international criminal tribunals.

While thus the *scripta* requirement has not been upheld in international criminal proceedings, it should be noted that a codification of international criminal norms would simultaneously benefit the *certa* requirement, making the existence of individual criminal responsibility tangible to the individual.[161] As such any codification of international criminal law aids individuals by providing protection against arbitrary charges, and informing them of criminal accountability for acts listed in conventions on international crimes.[162] A codification of international criminal law would be a valuable endeavor for the future of international criminal law.

3.10.4   The stricta *Requirement and the Sources of International Law*

Concerning the requirement of *nullum crimen sine iure stricta*, there are diverging views in the literature as to whether it also applies in the context of international criminal law.[163] In relation to written norms such as conventional international

---

[157]See Sect. 3.10.5, The *praevia* Requirement and the Sources of International Law.

[158]See above supra note 81 and accompanying text.

[159]*Bassiouni* (supra note 40), 144; see also *Bassiouni, Manikas* (supra note 134), 265.

[160]Other writers however adhere to the traditional wording *nullum crimen sine lege* and claim that *lege* does not exclude unwritten norms, see *Ferdinandusse* (supra note 94), 232f.

[161]See also *Dana* (supra note 108), 864, considering that as "to the quality of law, *lex scripta* and *lex certa* work in tandem".

[162]See, however, *Kress* (supra note 11), MN 3, who considers that the *lege scripta* requirement cannot be based on the theoretical foundations of protection of the individual against arbitrary charges. See further Sect. 3.4, Theoretical and Philosophical Foundations.

[163]*Ambos* (supra note 122), 669 stating that whether the *lex stricta* requirement is applicable to ICL is not clear; *Bassiouni* (supra note 40), 144 claims that the "minimum standard of legality permits the resort to the rule *ejusdem generis* with respect to analogous conduct"; *Gallant* (supra note 4), 362, claims that narrow interpretation is not a requirement of NCSL under current customary international law.

criminal norms, the question arises as to whether these could be ascribed to conduct that they do not clearly proscribe. The Rome Statute contains a *nullum crimen sine iure stricta* provision in its Art. 22 (2), requiring that the definitions of crimes are narrowly construed.[164] However, the Rome Statute also makes exceptions to this rule. For example Art. 7 (1) (k) ICC Statute contains the residual crime against humanity of "other inhumane acts of a similar character". This crime necessarily allows taking recourse to the *ejusdem generis* (of the same kind) analogy.[165] Indeed, the possibility to use an *ejusdem generis* analogy is inherent to certain crimes under international law.[166] Nevertheless, apart from these special cases *nullum crimen sine iure stricta* is firmly established in case of the ICC in order to protect the individual from retrospective crime creation and to put the individual on fair notice of the criminality of the underlying conduct.[167] It has been argued that this firm prohibition of analogy within the Rome Statute is the critical reaction to the liberal use of analogies by modern international criminal tribunals, most notably by the judges of the ICTY.[168] Such a reaction would indicate that judges adjudicating upon unwritten international criminal norms[169] would not be bound by the principle of *nullum crimen sine iure stricta*. *Cassese*, however, argues that the prohibition of analogy applies to both international criminal law based upon treaty law as well as customary law,[170] a view, which is to be concurred. The critique that judges of international criminal tribunals applying customary international law as a legal basis adhere to an analogous law creation does not pass closer examination. Admittedly, there are certain crimes that inherently make it possible to take recourse to *ejusdem generis* analogy: for example, the crimes against humanity of

---

[164]Rome Statute, Art. 22 (2).

[165]*Ambos* (supra note 122), 670; *Broomhall* (supra note 148), MN 45; *Cassese* (supra note 80), 49. See, also ICTY, *Kupreškić* Trial Judgment, paras 563ff. When the *Stakić* Trial Chamber declined to enter a conviction of 'other inhumane acts' on basis of forcible transfers because "[t]he crime of 'other inhumane acts' subsumes a potentially broad range of criminal behavior and may well be considered to lack sufficient clarity, precision and definiteness it might violate the fundamental criminal law principle *nullum crimen sine lege certa*", it was nevertheless overruled by its Appeals Chamber. See, ICTY, *Prosecutor v. Stakić*, IT-97-24-T, Trial Chamber, Judgment, 31 July 2003, paras 719ff, and ICTY, *Prosecutor v. Stakić*, IT-97-24-A, Appeals Chamber, Judgment, 22 March 2006, paras 313ff.

[166]See also Art. 7 (1) (g) Rome Statute "any other form of sexual violence of comparable gravity", *Broomhall* (supra note 148), MN 45 (footnote 67).

[167]*Broomhall* (supra note 148), MN 41. For a different view see *K. Ambos*, Treatise on International Criminal Law, Volume 1 (2013), 91, who considers that in practice judges at the ICC might arguably violate the prohibition of analogy through their interpretations.

[168]*Schabas* (supra note 112), Art. 22, 410; *Broomhall* (supra note 148), MN 43.

[169]Generally customary international criminal law has been the legal basis for individual criminal responsibility before international criminal tribunals, see Sect. 3.10.5.4, The *praevia* Requirement and Customary International Law.

[170]*Cassese* (supra note 80), 48.

persecution[171] or "other inhumane acts."[172] However, it would be overstating the point to suggest that apart from these specific instances there is a general approach by international criminal tribunals detectable in that regard. For example, it has been argued in the legal literature that the ICTY *Tadić* Appeals Chamber Decision violated the prohibition of constitutive crime analogy by expanding the scope of war crimes, traditionally restricted in its scope of application to international armed conflicts, to include crimes committed in non-international armed conflicts.[173] The language of the ICTY *Tadić* Appeals Chamber might warrant such a conclusion by stipulating that "[w]hat is inhumane, and consequently proscribed, in international wars, cannot but be inhumane and inadmissible in civil strife."[174] However, on a closer look it is evident that the ICTY *Tadić* Appeals Chamber does not simply expand the scope of application of individual criminal responsibility for war crimes committed in international armed conflict to cover non-international armed conflicts. It determined that customary international criminal law specifically covers war crimes committed in internal armed conflicts. The Appeals Chamber conducted an independent analysis as to whether customary international law provided for individual criminal responsibility in internal armed conflicts.[175] Whereas one might criticize how customary law is found and determined by international criminal tribunals, this issue is fundamentally different from the question of law creation by analogy. Thus, when customary international criminal norms are concerned, the question is whether certain conduct falls within the scope of application of a customary rule, which must be distinguished from crime expansion by analogy. For example, on the issue of command responsibility under customary international law, the ICTY *Hadžihasanović* Appeals Chamber decided that "no practice can be found, nor is there any evidence of *opinio juris* that would sustain the proposition that a commander can be held responsible for crimes committed by a subordinate prior to the commander's assumption of command over that subordinate."[176] In their dissenting opinion to this decision Judges *Shahabuddeen* and *Hunt* argued that the concept of command responsibility under customary international law was

---

[171] See for example ICTY, *Kupreškić* Trial Judgment, paras 620ff; ECCC, *Duch* Appeals Judgment, paras 241ff.

[172] See the references to the jurisprudence in supra note 165.

[173] *Schabas* (supra note 112), Art. 33, 410–11; W. *Schabas*, An Introduction to the International Criminal Court (2004), 94; see also C. *Kress*, War Crimes Committed in Non-international Armed Conflict and the Emerging System of International Criminal Justice, 30 Israel Yearbook on Human Rights (2001), 104ff, discussing an "assimilation" of the law of non-international armed conflict to the law of international armed conflict, although still acknowledging that the Appeals Chamber was searching for customary criminal rules in the law of NIACs.

[174] ICTY, *Tadić* Appeals Chamber Jurisdiction Decision, para 119.

[175] ICTY, *Tadić* Appeals Chamber Jurisdiction Decision, paras 128ff. See also A. *Cassese*, International Criminal Law (2013), 32, while referring to a process of "adaptation", however clearly states that the Appeals Chamber "unanimously held that some customary rules of international law criminalized certain categories of conduct in non-international armed conflict."

[176] ICTY, *Hadžihasanović* Appeals Chamber Decision, para 45.

broad enough to cover this situation.[177] The majority of the ICTY *Hadžihasanović* Appeals Chamber disagreed with the dissenting opinions, viewing their proposals as a form of crime expansion per analogy, since they stretched the concept of command responsibility as it existed under customary international law.[178] As shown by the dissenting opinions there might be different understandings of the scope of application of customary international criminal law. However, the judges themselves did not argue that command responsibility should be expanded in order to cover analogous conduct that was not within the scope of application under the customary norm in question.[179] Consequently, one has to agree with *Hauck* that the application of customary international criminal law *per se* cannot expand criminal liability by analogy.[180] State practice and *opinio iuris* either warrant the conclusion that customary international criminal law covers the conduct in question, or that it does not. Either customary international criminal law exists or it does not.

With regards to general principles of law, this source of law is particularly worrisome from the perspective of *nullum crimen sine iure stricta*. According to some authors general principles of law are used in the doctrine of sources of international law subsidiarily to conventional and customary rules in order to close existing gaps.[181] Using general principles of law as gap-fillers evidentially conflicts with the prohibition of creating crimes per analogy.

3.10.5   The praevia *Requirement and the Sources of International Law*

3.10.5.1   The Shift from Substantive Justice to Strict Legality

Historically, there have been doubts as to whether international law could fulfill the *nullum crimen sine iure praevia* requirements. *Kelsen* argued that the NCSI principle "does not apply to customary law and to law created by a precedent, for such

---

[177]ICTY, *Hadžihasanović* Appeals Chamber Decision, Partial Dissenting Opinion of Judge Shahabuddeen, paras 8ff; ICTY, *Hadžihasanović* Appeals Chamber Decision, Separate and Partially Dissenting Opinion of Judge Hunt, para 8.

[178]ICTY, *Hadžihasanović* Appeals Chamber Decision, para 52.

[179]At the ICTY this restricted understanding of the scope of application for command responsibility did not alter and has not led to a change in the jurisprudence; in contrast the SCSL, *Prosecutor v. Sesay*, Case No. SCSL-04-15-T, Trial Chamber, Judgment, 2 March 2009, para 296, determined that command responsibility for subordinates' conduct prior to the commander's assumption of command over that subordinate "reasonably fall[s] within the application of the principle of superior command responsibility as it exists at customary international law".

[180]*Hauck* (supra note 8), 64. The issue is, however, different to certain crimes such as 'other inhumane acts' or 'persecution' as established above that inherently allow for a *ejusdem generis* analogy.

[181]See for example *M.N. Shaw*, International Law (2003), 93.

law is *necessarily retroactive* in respect to the first case to which it is applied."[182] However, it seems that such a position is outdated. There is general agreement among legal scholars that one of the core requirements applicable in international criminal law proceedings is *nullum crimen sine iure praevia*: a crime must have been established by a written or unwritten rule before its commission, thereby excluding the possibility of *ex post facto* criminal law creation.[183] International criminal tribunals accept that they are bound by *nullum crimen sine iure praevia* and as such can only enter criminal convictions if at the time of its commission an international criminal norm has been established.[184] It is precisely the development of human rights that bars international criminal tribunals from brushing aside the NCSI principle as an unbinding principle of justice, as may have been done by certain post World War II tribunals.[185] This development evinces the shift, as stated by *Cassese*, from substantive justice to the doctrine of strict legality.[186] The requirement of the existence of positivistic, pre-established criminal norms might stand in contrast to our moral intuition when horrendous acts have occurred. The immorality of the underlying acts might be considered to be an adequate basis for the justification of criminal punishment.[187] The argument of *malum in se*, as a re-invocation of natural law doctrines,[188] looking solely at the abhorrent nature of the individual's conduct or the consequences thereof is a powerful tool to suggest that moral wrongdoing is to be equated with individual criminal responsibility. Under such a conception the role of the NCSI principle would be reduced to one that only protects legitimate confidence.[189] On grounds of moral considerations the accused would be trapped within the international criminal law wonderland and the Queen of Hearts of the international community would order: "Off with his head"[190]! However, as we have been reminded by Judge *Robert* in his dissenting

---

[182]*Kelsen* (supra note 48), 165 (emphasis added).

[183]*Cassese* (supra note 80), 44; *Gallant* (supra note 4), 357ff; *Heinsch* (supra note 7), 322; *Ferdinandusse* (supra note 94), 223; *Triffterer* (supra note 103), 124–128; *Bassiouni* (supra note 40), 144.

[184]Generally international criminal tribunals consider that the authority to convict individuals depends on the existence of crimes and modes of liability under customary international law. See the reference to the jurisprudence in supra note 247ff.

[185]See Sect. 3.5, *Nullum Crimen Sine Lege* and the IMT Nuremberg and the IMTFE Tokyo and Sect. 3.6, *Nullum Crimen Sine Lege* and Post World War II US Military Tribunals.

[186]*Cassese* (supra note 80), 36ff.

[187]*I. Tallgreen*, The Sensibility and Sense of International Criminal Law, 13 European Journal of International Law (2002), 564.

[188]*van Schaack* (supra note 49), 155ff, who sees in the equation of the morally wrong and the legally criminal an invocation of natural law doctrines.

[189]*C. Tomuschat*, The Legacy of Nuremberg, 4 Journal of International Criminal Justice (2006), 830. See also ICTY, *Prosecutor v. Delalić* (Čelebici), IT-96-21-A, Appeals Chamber, Judgment, 20 February 2001, para 179: "The purpose of this principle is to prevent the prosecution and punishment of an individual for acts which he reasonably believed to be lawful at the time of their commission."

[190]*L. Carroll*, Alice's Adventures in Wonderland (1869), 104.

opinion to the *Norman* Decision before the SCSL, "it is precisely when the acts are abhorrent and deeply shocking that the principle of legality must be most stringently applied, to ensure that a defendant is not convicted out of disgust rather than evidence, or of a non-existent crime. *Nullum crimen* may not be a household phrase, but it serves as some protection against the lynch mob."[191] *Schabas* argued that the UN tribunals merely adhere to the *nullum crimen* principle formally, and that in reality modern international criminal judges have not given due consideration to its requirements, like their predecessors at Nuremberg.[192] However, it is precisely the firm establishment of the *nullum crimen sine lege* principle in human rights instruments that bars international criminal tribunals from neglecting its requirements when determining applicable international criminal law. Reference to the NCSI *praevia* principle in international criminal trials cannot be just empty rhetoric on part of the judges, but must be filled with content: One cannot simply ignore the word *crimen* in the principle requiring a pre-existing international criminal norm as a legal basis for individual criminal convictions. The ICTY *Hadžihasanović* Appeals Chamber affirmed that the "immorality or appalling character of an act is not a sufficient factor to warrant its criminalization".[193] It is thus clear that international criminal tribunals are bound by the *nullum crimen sine iure praevia* requirement. However, the question remains whether all sources of international law are adequate in that regard.

3.10.5.2 The *praevia* Requirement and International Conventions

At the very start of the ICTY, the *Tadić* Appeals Chamber in its Jurisdiction Decision established the four *Tadić* conditions in relation to the application of Art. 3 ICTY Statute "Violations of the laws or customs of war".[194] It opened the door for "agreements which have not turned into customary international law" as a possible legal basis for criminal convictions.[195] This assessment of the *Tadić* Appeals Chamber stood in contrast to the report on the ICTY of the Secretary General, who linked the legality of the proceedings with individual criminal

---

[191] SCSL, *Norman* Appeals Chamber Decision, Dissenting Opinion Judge Robertson, para 12.

[192] *Schabas* (supra note 140), 63.

[193] ICTY, *Hadžihasanović* Appeals Chamber Decision, para 41.

[194] ICTY, *Tadić* Appeals Chamber Jurisdiction Decision, para 94, establishing the conditions that must be fulfilled for a violation of IHL to be caught by Art. 3 ICTY Statute: 1. violation of a rule of IHL; 2. that rule must be customary in nature or if part of treaty law subject to conditions under para 143; 3. the violation must be "serious"; and 4. the violation must entail individual criminal responsibility.

[195] ICTY, *Tadić* Appeals Chamber Jurisdiction Decision, paras 89 and 94 further referring to para 143: "It follows that the International Tribunal is authorized to apply, in addition to customary international law, any treaty which: (i) was unquestionably binding on the parties at the time of the alleged offence; and (ii) was not in conflict with or derogating from peremptory norms of international law, as are most customary rules of international humanitarian law."

convictions on basis of customary international law that had to be established beyond any doubt.[196] The report of the Secretary General has been equated with the *travaux préparatoires* for the interpretation of the ICTY Statute.[197] However, it seems that part of the reasoning of the Secretary General for a restricted approach to use conventional norms as a legal basis for individual criminal convictions was owed to the dissolution of Yugoslavia "so that the problem of adherence of some but not all States to specific conventions does not arise."[198] Thus, it seems that in only inner-State conflicts such as Rwanda and Cambodia, the ICTR and ECCC would not have been confronted with uncertainty concerning the applicability of treaty norms that are undoubtedly binding on the ratifying State parties.

Despite the Secretary General's restrictive position with regard to the ICTY, the *Kordić* Appeals Chamber considered that conventional norms, irrespective of whether they reflect customary international law or not, can also fulfill the *nullum crime sine iure* requirements.[199] The ICTY *Galić* Trial Chamber assessed individual responsibility for the crime of "inflicting terror upon civilians" under Art. 3 ICTY Statute exclusively on a treaty basis, referring to Art. 51 (2) Additional Protocol I (AP I) and Art. 13 (2) Additional Protocol II (AP II).[200] The ICTY *Galić* Trial Chamber was satisfied that these conventional norms provide an adequate legal basis for individual criminal responsibility and did not consider it necessary to elaborate whether the crime of terror also has a foundation under customary international law.[201] The Trial Chamber found that the conventional basis it referred to adequately establishes individual criminal responsibility for this crime as "is evident from the content and context of Additional Protocol I."[202] On appeal the defendant raised the objection that the Trial Chamber falsely considered treaty law to be a valid basis for the ICTY's jurisdiction. While the ICTY *Galić* Appeals Chamber formally rejected the grounds of appeal raised by the defendant, determining that conventional law may constitute the legal basis for its subject matter jurisdiction under Article 3 ICTY Statue, it nevertheless stated that it has been the

---

[196]See Report of the Secretary-General Pursuant to Paragraph 2 of Security Council Resolution 808 (1993), 3 May 1993, UN Doc S/25704), para 34 (SG Report on ICTY).

[197]See *Degan* (supra note 140), 63; *Schabas* (supra note 140), 82.

[198]SG Report on ICTY (supra note 196), para 34.

[199]ICTY, *Prosecutor v. Kordić*, IT-95-14/2-A, Appeals Chamber, Judgment, 17 December 2004, para 44, referring to the ratification of the two additional protocols to the 1949 Geneva Conventions by the SFRY and the declarations of successions of Croatia and Bosnia and Herzegovina. Also the ECCC Trial Chamber adopted this approach, see ECCC, *Prosecutor v. Kaing alias Duch*, Case No. 001/18-07-2007/ECCC/TC, Trial Chamber, Judgment, 26 July 2010, para 404.

[200]Additional Protocol I; Protocol Additional to the Geneva Conventions of 12 August 1949 and Relating to the Protection of Victims of Non-International Armed Conflicts (Protocol II), 8 June 1977, 1125 UNTS 609.

[201]ICTY, *Prosecutor v. Galić*, IT-98-29-T, Trial Chamber, Judgment, 5 December 2003, para 138.

[202]*Ibid*, para 127.

consistent approach of the tribunal to satisfy itself that the crimes under its jurisdiction were also criminal under customary international law.[203]

When determining whether conventional norms can be used as a legal basis for individual criminal responsibility, first of all, it must be stressed that according to the fourth *Tadić* condition, it is crucial that "violation of the rule must entail, under customary or conventional law, the individual criminal responsibility of the person breaching the rule."[204] As has rightly been pointed out by the ICTY *Galić* Appeals Chamber, conventional norms generally only provide for the "prohibition of a certain conduct, not for its criminalization".[205] Thereby, it highlighted that conventional norms can hardly pass the *nullum crimen sine iure praevia* requirement. While the respective statutes of international criminal tribunals "borrow" from conventional humanitarian law instruments to determine their subject-matter jurisdiction, it is evident that these conventions were generally created to stipulate inter-State obligations and were not intended to provide for individual criminalization.[206] The breaches of these obligations entail State responsibility, but they do not necessarily trigger individual criminal responsibility. Illegality under public international law is thus not to be equated with criminality under international criminal law.[207] The reason for a restricted approach to using conventional norms as the legal basis for individual criminal responsibility, is the fact that while theoretically it is possible that international conventions can form the legal basis for individual criminal convictions, in practice the drafters of international conventional law refrain from creating international conventions as criminal codes or norms. Therefore, barring exceptional cases, international criminal tribunals were encouraged to show that the conventional humanitarian law instruments were applicable on the

---

[203]ICTY, *Prosecutor v. Galić*, IT-98-29-A, Appeals Chamber, Judgment, 30 November 2006, para 83.

[204]ICTY, *Tadić* Appeals Chamber Jurisdiction Decision, para 94.

[205]ICTY, *Galić* Appeal Judgment, 83 (emphasis added).

[206]See ICTY, *Galić* Appeal Judgment, para 83: "treaty provisions will only provide for the prohibition of a certain conduct not its criminalisation, or the treaty provision itself will not sufficiently define the elements of the prohibition they criminalise". See also G. *Mettraux*, International Crimes and the *ad hoc* Tribunals (2005), 8.

[207]There are, however, sparse examples detectable in the jurisprudence that would equate State responsibility with individual criminal responsibility, see for example the Separate Opinion of Judge Shahabuddeen in ICTY, *Galić* Appeal Judgment, para 5, referring to *Oppenheim's* International Law claiming that "it is an established principle of customary international law that individual members of armed forces of the belligerents – as well as individuals generally – are directly subject to the law of war and may be punished for violating its rules." For the ICTR see *Prosecutor v. Kayishema*, ICTR-95-1-T, Trial Chamber, Judgment, 21 May 1999, para 55f which has applied treaty norms (Common Article 3 and AP II) as a legal basis for individual criminal responsibility and did not inquire whether those reflect a customary norm. It stated: "In the present case, such an analysis seems superfluous because the situation is rather clear. Rwanda became a party to the Conventions of 1949 on 5 May 1964 and to Protocol II on 19 November 1984. These instruments, therefore, were in force in the territory of Rwanda at the time when the tragic events took place within its borders."

basis of both treaty law *and* customary law, which entails individual criminal responsibility.[208]

The position that conventional humanitarian law instruments do not entail individual criminal responsibility also holds true, according to *Simma* and *Paulus*, for the grave breaches regime. They claim on basis of the principle of *aut dedere aut iudicare*, the obligation of State parties to the Geneva Convention to either try or extradite alleged war criminals, that one cannot qualify grave breaches as "crimes of a truly international character".[209] Other authors took a different position, arguing that grave breaches indisputably provide for individual criminal responsibility.[210] The relationship between grave breaches and war crimes, in particular whether grave breaches are to be equated with war crimes, seems dubious. The 1949 Geneva Conventions do not use the term "war crimes" and the *travaux pré paratoires* also reveal that the drafters did not intend to create a penal code.[211] However, other international instruments, whether intentionally or not, explicitly construe grave breaches as war crimes.[212] When the additional protocols were drafted, despite debates at the Diplomatic Conference, Article 85 para 5 Additional Protocol I states that "grave breaches (...) shall be regarded as war crimes".[213] According to *Öberg*, by "deciding that grave breaches constituted war crimes, the drafters gave the former a new additional meaning, providing them with criminal consequences in international law."[214] While most international conventions were not drafted as international penal codes *per se*, an evolutionary interpretation,

---

[208] See for the ICTR: *Prosecutor v. Musema*, ICTR-96-13-T, Trial Chamber, Judgment, 27 January 2000, para 240; *Prosecutor v. Semanza*, ICTR-97-20-T, Trial Chamber, Judgment, 15 May 2003, para 353; *Akayesu* Trial Judgment, paras 608–617; see for the ICTY, *Galić* Appeal Judgment, para 85; see for the ECCC, *Prosecutor v. Kaing alias Duch*, Case No. 001/18-07-2007/ECCC/TC, Trial Chamber, Judgment, 26 July 2010, para 33.

[209] *B. Simma* and *A.L. Paulus*, The Responsibility of Individuals for Human Rights Abuses in Internal Conflicts: A Positivist View, in 93 American Journal of International Law (1999), 310–311.

[210] Cf. *T. Meron*, The Humanization of International Law (2006), 102. See also *G. Werle*, Principles of International Criminal Law (2009), 357 (footnote 97) and 359.

[211] *M. D. Öberg*, The absorption of grave breaches into war crimes, International Review of the Red Cross, Volume 91, Number 873 (2009), 166, referring to the Dutch delegate stating that "the aim was not to produce a penal code, but to make it obligatory for the Contracting Parties to include certain provisions in their own codes"; See also *H. Fischer*, Grave Breaches of the 1949 Geneva Conventions, in McDonald, Swaak-Goldman (eds.), Substantive and Procedural Aspects of International Criminal Law (2000), Vol. I, 70; *Mettraux* (supra note 206), 8, referring to the Fourth Report drawn up by the Special Committee of the Joint Committee, 12 July 1949, Final Record of Diplomatic Conference II, Section B, 115: "an act only becomes a crime when this act is made punishable by a penal law. The conference is not making international penal law but is undertaking to insert in the national penal laws certain acts enumerated as grave breaches of the Convention, which will become crimes when they have been inserted in the national penal laws."

[212] See Convention on the non-applicability of statutory limitations to war crimes and crimes against humanity, 26 November 1968, 754 UNTS 73, Art. I.

[213] Additional Protocol I, Art. 85 (5).

[214] *Öberg* (supra note 211), 167.

taking into account subsequent treaty practice, could result in certain treaty norms also foreseeing their criminalization from a modern perspective.[215] When the plain language it is not clear as to whether a treaty norm was intended to set out a crime, following the statement of the ICTY *Kordić* Appeals Chamber, the "criminalization as a matter of international law depends on the practice of the Contracting States."[216] Methodologically speaking the criminalization of a treaty norm that was not drafted as a penal norm as such can be established on two grounds: firstly, it could be established by interpretation taking into account the subsequent practice of the State parties (Art. 31 (3) (b) Vienna Convention on the Law of Treaties (VCLT))[217]; or secondly, on the basis of the existence of a customary norm that mirrors the treaty norm *plus* its criminalization. The ICTY jurisprudence seems to favor the latter approach, applying grave breaches that *qua* custom entail individual criminal responsibility.[218]

The 1948 Genocide Convention takes an exceptional position among international conventions, since Article VI allows for trials against individuals on the international as well as the domestic legal plane and the convention defines the elements of the crime of genocide precisely. According to *Simma* and *Paulus*, the Genocide Convention itself thus establishes the "truly *international* legal character of the crime",[219] providing not only for its inter-State prohibition but also for the criminalization of genocide applicable to individuals. It affirms in Art. I that genocide is a crime under international law, gives a definition of genocide in Art. II, and in Art. III lists other acts than perpetration that are also criminal: conspiracy to commit genocide, direct and public incitement to commit genocide, attempt to commit genocide, and complicity in genocide.[220]

For the final category of international "core" crimes, crimes against humanity, it is evident that there cannot be a conventional legal basis for individual criminal responsibility for the simple reason that crimes against humanity have not yet been made the subject of a specific international convention. Although there have been efforts to forge a convention on crimes against humanity,[221] regrettably to date those efforts have failed.

---

[215] See also *I. Bantekas*, Reflections on Some Sources and Methods of International Criminal and Humanitarian Law, 6 International Criminal Law Review (2006), 121ff.

[216] ICTY, *Kordić* Appeals Judgment, paras 65–66.

[217] Vienna Convention on the Law of Treaties, 23 May 1969, 1155 UNTS 331, Art. 31 (3) (b); for interpretation through subsequent practice cf. *O. Dörr*, Article 31, in Dörr/Schmalenbach (eds.), Vienna Convention on the Law of Treaties. A Commentary (2012), MN 76ff.

[218] See e.g. the ICTY; *Kordić* Appeals Judgment, para 75, holding that if a crime constitutes a grave breach of the Geneva Conventions it constitutes a crime *qua custom*. Compare also *Mettraux* (supra note 206), 9.

[219] *Simma, Paulus* (supra note 209), at 308 (emphasis in original). Art. VI Genocide Convention stipulating that persons charged with genocide shall be tried *inter alia* by an international penal tribunal; compare also *Mettraux* (supra note 206), 8.

[220] Genocide Convention, Arts. I-III.

[221] Cf. *M. C. Bassiouni*, "Crimes against Humanity:" The Need for a Specialized Convention, 31 Columbia Journal of Transnational Law (1994), 457ff; see also L. N. Sadat (ed.), Forging a Convention for Crimes against Humanity (2013).

In conclusion, it can be said that in theory conventional law can form the basis for individual criminal responsibility. However, international conventions—with the exception of the Genocide Convention—generally stipulate State obligations and are not drafted as criminal norms applicable to individuals. They therefore cannot serve as the legal basis for individual criminal responsibility, because they lack the *nullum crimen sine iure praevia* requirement.

3.10.5.3   The *praevia* Requirement and General Principles of Law

Theoretically, the NCSI principle does not exclude general principles of law as a legal basis for individual criminal responsibility as such, as they were expressly referred to in the Nuremberg Clause ("general principles of law recognized by the community of nations") and are also contained in the notion of "criminal offence under international law" under paragraph 1 of the *nullum crimen sine lege* provisions as contained in human rights conventions.[222]

Nevertheless, it has been argued that the required level of certainty, the *nullum crimen sine iure certa* requirement, excludes general principles as a legal basis for individual criminal responsibility. The International Law Commission (ILC), when drafting the Code of Crimes against the Peace and Security of Mankind, stressed the argument that general principles of law are not precise enough to describe criminal conduct.[223] This view is also widely supported in the legal literature.[224] Thus, general principles of law are mainly excluded as a legal basis for international crimes on basis of the *nullum crimen sine iure certa* requirement. However, as has rightly been put forward by *Ashworth*, there are no strict divisions between the *certa*

---

[222]See Sect. 3.7, Changing the Picture? *Nullum Crimen Sine Lege* and Its Inclusion in Human Rights Law and Humanitarian Law Conventions.

[223]See the 1996 ILC Draft Code, Article 13 (Non-retroactivity), p. 39 (para 5), referring to the possibility of conventional and customary law as a legal basis for criminal prosecution, although further stating that the ILC did not seek a "wider possibility to be used with such flexibility that it might give rise to prosecution on legal grounds that are too vague. For this reason it preferred to use in paragraph 2 the expression 'in accordance with international law' rather than less concrete expressions such as 'in accordance with the general principles of international law'."

[224]Cf. *Boot* (supra note 10), 140, 328; *van Schaack* (supra note 49), 167; *M. C. Bassiouni*, The Sources and Content of International Criminal Law: A Theoretical Framework, in: Bassiouni (ed.), International Criminal Law, Vol. I (1999), 33; see also *O. Triffterer*, Der ständige Internationale Strafgerichtshof – Anspruch und Wirklichkeit, in Gössel/Triffterer (eds.), Festschrift Zipf (1999), 505: "weil sich durch Grundsätze keine konkreten Umschreibungen strafbarer Verhaltensweisen festlegen lassen."; *O. Triffterer*, Preliminary Remarks: the permanent ICC – Ideal and Reality, in Triffterer (ed), Commentary on the Rome Statute of the International Criminal Court (2008), 23 (MN 19): "because *principles* cannot describe with sufficient precision a behavior that can and should be punished." (emphasis in original).

and the *praevia* requirements.[225] The *certa* and the *praevia* requirements are necessarily intertwined, and this particular link will be discussed here in relation to general principles of law. The reason for a restricted role of general principles as the underlying source of individual criminal responsibility lies in the fact that these principles—either conceived as general principles deriving from the domestic legal order (general principles in *foro domestico*) or general principles of international (criminal) law[226]—generally contain overarching, guiding, basic legal principles.[227] These *basic principles* cannot be used to transpose detailed domestic criminal norms from the domestic legal sphere to the international legal order.[228] For this reason general principles play a more important role in relation to the general part of international criminal law, such as grounds for excluding criminal responsibility (self-defence, necessity and duress, mistake of fact, mistake of law), *ne bis in idem*, and so forth.[229]

Despite this predominant role in relation to international criminal law, general principles have on rare occasions played a role in the interpretation and even identification of elements of crimes.[230] A well-known, as although widely

---

[225]*A. Ashworth*, Principles of Criminal Law (2006), 74: "a vague law may in practice operate retroactively, since no one is quite sure whether given conduct is within or outside the rule."; see also *Hauck* (supra note 8), 65, discussing the close relationship between *lex certa* and *lex praevia* by an analysis of English criminal law.

[226]There has been the proposition that within the system of ICL one should distinguish between three different sets of general principles: general principles of international criminal law, general principles of international law and general principles recognized by the community of nations. ICTY, *Kupreškić* Trial Judgment, para 591; ICTY, *Furundžija* Trial Judgment, para 177; the most prominent proponent in the legal literature for these three sets of general principles is *Cassese*, who "coincidentally" also sat in the *Kupreškić* and *Furundžija* Trial Chambers, see *Cassese* (supra note 80), 20–25.

[227]*M.N. Shaw*, International Law (2008), 98ff referring to *res judicata, pacta sunt servanda*, the principle of good faith and *ex injuria jus non oritur*; see also *I. Brownlie*, Principles of Public International Law (2008), 16ff listing *inter alia* as general principles of international law the principles of consent, reciprocity, equality of states, good faith.

[228]See for example ICTY, *Prosecutor v. Kunarac*, IT-96-23-T & IT-96-23/1-T, Trial Chamber, Judgment, 22 February 2001, para 439: In considering general principles of law "the Trial Chamber does not conduct a survey of the major legal systems of the world in order to identify a specific legal provision which is adopted by a majority of legal systems but to consider, from an examination of national systems generally, whether it is possible to identify certain basic principles".

[229]*Triffterer* (supra note 224), 23; *G. Werle*, General Principles of International Criminal Law, in Cassese (ed.), The Oxford Companion to International Criminal Justice (2009), 54ff. See also SG Report on ICTY (supra note 196), para 58: "The International Tribunal itself will have to decide on various personal defences which may relieve a person of individual criminal responsibility, such as minimum age or mental incapacity, drawing upon *general principles of law recognized by all nations*." (emphasis added); see also Art. 14 of the 1996 ILC Draft Code: "The competent court shall determine the admissibility of defences in accordance with the *general principles of law*, in light of the character of each crime." (emphasis added).

[230]See for example ICTY, *Prosecutor v. Blaškić*, IT-95-14-A, Appeals Chamber, Judgment, 29 July 2004, paras 34ff referring to national jurisdictions in order to establish the standard of *mens rea* for ordering under Art. 7 (1) ICTY Statute.

criticized, example is the ICTY *Furundžija* Trial Chamber Judgment, which had to determine whether forced oral penetration was covered by the *actus reus* of the crime of rape. Since it could not find an answer in treaty law or customary law the Trial Chamber consequently referred to general principles in a subsidiary manner in order to fill the legal gap.[231] Its analysis of general principles of domestic criminal law displayed major discrepancies with some domestic legal systems treating forced oral penetration as the crime of rape, while others treated it as sexual assault. Despite this apparent deadlock on the national level, the ICTY Trial Chamber did not stop there. It stated that faced with such inconsistency in the domestic legal systems, it could resort to *general principles of international criminal law*, or, failing that to *general principles of international law*.[232] It found on basis of the international "general principle of respect for human dignity" that forced oral penetration was to be classified as rape and not as "minor" sexual assault. Astonishingly, the *Furundžija* Trial Chamber found no contradiction with the NCSI principle in such an approach, as forced oral penetration was criminal no matter what, and the accused could only argue a harsher "stigmatization" as a convicted rapist in comparison to the "minor" offense of sexual assault. Furthermore, the chamber argued that the NCSI principle had to bow to the higher principle as "any such concern is amply outweighed by the fundamental principle of protecting human dignity, a principle which favours broadening the definition of rape."[233] That example from the jurisprudence shows that apart from the general aspect of international criminal law, general principles in rare cases have been used to function as an interpretive tool when interpreting specific definitions of crimes.[234] However, it is precisely this value-oriented interpretation on the basis of vague general principles such as "human dignity" that has been criticized by various writers as being in conflict with fundamental liberal principles of criminal law.[235] Furthermore, if these general principles of international (criminal) law do not derive from domestic criminal law systems, what then is their source of origin? *Akande* rightly criticized this approach, stating that "human dignity" is "hardly a general principle of law but more appropriately a value which rules of law seek to promote."[236] It seems that in that regard "general principles" have been used to

---

[231]ICTY, *Furundžija* Trial Judgment, para 177; with regard to the subsidiarity of general principles see also F. O. *Raimondo*, General Principles of Law in the Decisions of International Criminal Tribunals (2008), 171, referring also to the Rome Statute, Art. 21 (1) (c) that declares general principles to be applicable only after other sources have been used.

[232]ICTY, *Furundžija* Trial Judgment, para 182.

[233]ICTY, *Furundžija* Trial Judgment, paras 183–4.

[234]Cf. *Triffterer* (supra note 224), 23.

[235]That would correspond to the second stage of reaction to ICL according to *Robinson*, see D. *Robinson*, A Cosmopolitan Liberal Account of International Criminal Law, 26 Leiden Journal of International Law (2013), 134ff.

[236]*Akande* (supra note 144), 52; see also the critique of *Raimondo* (supra note 231), 170.

conceal judicial law making, which is in conflict with the *nullum crimen sine iure praevia* requirement.[237]

Despite this just criticism, when taking recourse to general principles of law in the realm of international criminal law, some authors nevertheless seek to give general principles of law a more prominent role in international criminal proceedings. *Ambos* proposes that general principles understood in the traditional way as being derived from the domestic legal orders should be used to verify customary international criminal law in *statu nascendi*.[238] While admittedly innovative, this approach seems doctrinally questionable and international criminal tribunals have generally avoided such an approach.[239] Furthermore, he suggests that international general principles understood as "opinio iuris without concordant state practice" should play a greater role as a legal basis in international criminal proceedings due to the rudimentary state of international criminal law.[240] However, it should be noted that according to the predominant view in the legal literature, methodologically speaking, an "opinio iuris without concordant state practice" is a method to determine customary international law on basis of a modern understanding.[241] International criminal tribunals have also sought to establish customary international law on that basis, but did not use it to establish general principles of law.[242]

3.10.5.4   The *praevia* Requirement and Customary International Law

Historically, taking recourse to customary international law has a long tradition in international criminal proceedings. The IMT Nuremberg stated:

> The law of war is to be found not only in treaties, but in the customs and practices of states which gradually obtained universal recognition [. . .]. This law is not static, but by continual adaptation follows the needs of a changing world.[243]

In the modern era of international criminal law, starting with the UN *ad hoc* tribunals, the predominant role of customary international law as the legal basis for international criminal convictions has been highlighted by the reports of the

---

[237] *F.O. Raimondo*, General Principles of Law, Judicial Creativity, and the Development of International Criminal Law, in Darcy, Powderly (eds.), Judicial Creativity at the International Criminal Tribunals (2010), 59.

[238] *Ambos* (supra note 144), 40ff.

[239] See also *Raimondo* (supra note 231), 167.

[240] *Ambos* (supra note 144), 43f, citing *B. Simma*, International Human Rights and General International Law, in collected Courses of the Academy of European Law, Volume IV (1995), 225; compare also *M.C. Bassiouni*, A Functional Approach to General Principles of International Law, 11 Michigan Journal of International Law (1990), 768ff.

[241] See further Sect. 4.3.2, The Procedural Aspect of Modern Customary International Law.

[242] See for example ICTY, *Kupreškić* Trial Judgment, para 525; ECCC, *Duch* Appeals Judgment, para 93.

[243] IMT Nuremberg Judgment, Vol. 1, 221.

Secretary General on the international criminal tribunals. He linked the legality of the proceedings before international criminal tribunals to customary international law, in order to adhere to the *nullum crimen sine iure* principle.[244] In relation to the ICTY, he explicitly listed international conventions as evidence of applicable customary norms: the 1949 Geneva Conventions, the 1907 Hague Convention IV, the Genocide Convention and the IMT Nuremberg Charter.[245] While not all chambers excluded treaty norms as a legal basis for criminal convictions, in most cases they have shown that the treaty norms were also applicable on a customary law basis.[246]

The ICTY determined that its mandate obliged it to apply legal principles that are "beyond doubt part of customary international law" and thus made criminal convictions dependent on the existence of customary international criminal norms.[247] In the wording of the ICTY *Milutinović* Appeals Chamber:

> The Tribunal only has jurisdiction over a listed crime if that crime was recognized as such under customary international law at the time it was allegedly committed. The scope of the Tribunal's jurisdiction *ratione materiae* may therefore be said to be determined both by the Statute, insofar as it sets out the jurisdictional framework of the International Tribunal, and

---

[244]SG Report on ICTY (supra note 196), para 34. Similarly in relation to the SCSL the SG required the existence of international crimes *qua* custom to adhere to *nullum crimen sine lege*, see Report of the Secretary-General on the establishment of a Special Court for Sierra Leone, 4 October 2000, UN Doc. S/2000/915 (SG Report on the SCSL), para 12; for the criticism on the drafting of the ICTR Statute leaving the boundaries of customary law see Report of the Secretary-General Pursuant to Paragraph 5 of Security Council Resolution 955 (1994), 13 February 1995, UN Doc S/1995/134 para 12 (SG Report on ICTR), para 12 stating that "the Security Council has elected to take a more expansive approach to the choice of the applicable law than the one underlying the statute of the Yugoslav Tribunal, and included within the subject-matter jurisdiction of the Rwanda Tribunal international instruments regardless of whether they were considered part of customary international law or whether they have customarily entailed individual criminal responsibility of the perpetrator of the crime."

[245]SG Report on ICTY (supra note 196), para 35.

[246]Barring exceptional cases, international criminal tribunals at least showed that the conventional instruments were applicable on the basis of both treaty law and customary law, see for the ICTR: *Musema* Trial Judgment, para 240; *Semanza* Trial Judgment, para 353; *Akayesu* Trial Judgment, paras 608–17; see for the ICTY, *Galić* Appeal Judgment, para 85; see for the ECCC, *Duch* Trial Judgment, para 33.

[247]See for example ICTY, *Hadžihasanović* Appeals Chamber Decision, para 44; *Blaškić* Appeals Judgment, paras 139–141: "while the Statute of the International Tribunal lists offences over which the International Tribunal has jurisdiction, the Tribunal may enter convictions only where it is satisfied that the offence is proscribed under customary international law at the time of its commission."; *Prosecutor v. Strugar*, IT-01-42-AR72, Appeals Chamber, Decision on Interlocutory Appeal, 22 November 2002, paras 10–14; see also Separate and Partially Dissenting Opinion of Judge Schomburg to the *Galić* Appeal Judgment, para 21: the "Tribunal is not acting as a legislator; it is under an obligation to apply only customary international law applicable at the time of the criminal conduct. . . the International Tribunal is required to adhere strictly to the principle of *nullum crimen sine lege praevia* and must ascertain that a crime was 'beyond any doubt part of customary law'." See also *Kordić* Trial Judgment, para 20: "[T]he International Tribunal only has jurisdiction over offences that constituted crimes under customary international law at the time the alleged offences were committed."

by customary international law, insofar as the Tribunal's power to convict an accused of any crime listed in the Statute depends on its existence *qua* custom at the time this crime was allegedly committed.[248]

Other international criminal tribunals followed suit, determining that the legal basis for convictions for breaches of international crimes before them generally must be found in customary international law.[249]

While in practice chambers might be tempted to take the shortcut by simply arguing that a treaty provision constitutes a crime *qua* custom,[250] as has been stated before, conventional norms generally will only provide for the prohibition of a certain conduct, but not for its criminalization.[251] A proper understanding of customary international law as a legally valid basis for individual criminal responsibility would thus require that the customary crime is not "solely" congruent with treaty provisions under, for example, international humanitarian law. Customary international law, while possibly mirroring the relevant treaty provisions, adds to that mirror a transformation of norms containing State obligations into criminal provisions that are directly binding upon individuals. The advantage of the reliance on customary international law as a legal basis of international criminal law lies in the fact that it potentially bypasses the defects of conventional inter-State norms: the customary norm expressly criminalizes conduct as a customary international criminal norm.[252]

At the outset, however, there appears to be a clear contradiction between the demand that international criminal tribunals should only apply criminal norms that are beyond any doubt part of customary law,[253] and the appraisal of the judges of international criminal tribunals in the legal literature for their "judicial creativity" or "judicial activism"[254] when determining customary international criminal law. Indeed, doubts have been expressed whether the way customary international law has been found and determined by international criminal tribunals could be

---

[248]ICTY, *Prosecutor v. Milutinović* et al, IT-99-37-AR72, Appeals Chamber, Decision on Dragolub Ojdanić's Motion Challenging Jurisdiction – Joint Criminal Enterprise, 21 May 2003 (*Ojdanić* Appeals Chamber Decision), paras 9–10.

[249]See. for the ICTR, *Akayesu* Trial Judgment, para 611ff; See for the SCSL: *Prosecutor v. Fofana*, Case No. SCSL-04-14-T, Trial Chamber, Judgment, 2 August 2007, para 94; *Prosecutor v. Brima* et al, Case No. SCSL-04-16-T, Trial Chamber, Judgment, 20 June 2007, paras 636ff.

[250]The ICTY Appeals Chamber in *Kordić* held that if a war crime constitutes a grave breach of the Geneva Conventions it constitutes a crime *qua custom*, see *Kordić* Appeals Judgment, para 75.

[251]ICTY, *Galić* Appeal Judgment, para 83.

[252]ICTY, *Galić* Appeal Judgment, para 83. See also ICTY, *Vasiljević* Trial Judgment, para 199, determining that for the existence of an international crime it does not suffice that the act in question was merely illegal under international law resulting in State responsibility or solely a crime under the domestic legal system of the perpetrator.

[253]See SG Report on ICTY (supra note 196), para 34.

[254]M. *Shahabuddeen*, Judicial Creativity and Joint Criminal Enterprise, in Darcy, Powderly (eds.), Judicial Creativity at the International Criminal Tribunals (2010), 184ff. See also the other contributions in Darcy, Powderly (eds.), Judicial Creativity at the International Criminal Tribunals (2010).

reconcilable with the *nullum crimen sine iure praevia* principle. The methods judges have applied when identifying customary international criminal law have been the point of considerable criticism in the legal literature. Judges at international criminal tribunals have been criticized for their selectivity,[255] and for making generalizations on the basis of a handful of cases.[256] It has been argued that the way customary law has been applied by the tribunals provided a "convenient licence for judicial law-making"[257] or as stretching, according to *Noellkaemper*, "the procedural requirements for the identification of customary international law, and thereby the requirements for procedural legitimacy, to its breaking point."[258]

However, despite such critique, the critical voices in the legal literature rarely go into greater depth concerning the concrete requirements of the *nullum crimen sine iure* principle in relation to international criminal proceedings. Despite frequent reference in the legal literature that in contrast to the *nullum crimen sine lege* principle applicable at the domestic level, only its "core"[259] as the "international principle of legality" is applicable to international crimes, the clear content of this "core" and its consequences for the determination of customary international criminal law are ignored. To answer the question whether the methods international criminal tribunals have applied for determining customary international criminal law potentially violate the *nullum crimen sine iure* principle, one must consider the level of requirement imposed on international criminal tribunals by the guarantees of *nullum crimen sine iure*. The theoretical basis and methodological difficulties of determining customary international law will be discussed in detail in a later chapter.[260] However, at this point some general remarks on the relation between *nullum crimen sine lege praevia* and customary international law, and its consequences for methodological approaches when identifying customary international law are necessary. If strict requirements for *nullum crimen sine iure praevia* are applied, customary international criminal law could only be established on the basis of the traditional method for the determination of customary international law: it could only be proven to exist by establishing consistent, general and enduring State practice coupled with *opinio iuris*, the subjective conviction of States that their acts (*i.e.* State practice) are required by an already existing rule of international law.[261]

---

[255]W. *Schabas*, Customary Law or "Judge-Made" Law: Judicial Creativity at the UN Criminal Tribunals, in Doria (ed.), The Legal Regime of the International Criminal Court (2009), 86; *Bantekas* (supra note 215), 130.

[256]A. *Zahar*, G. *Sluiter*, International Criminal Law (2008), 105; A. *Nollkaemper*, The Legitimacy of International Law in the Case Law of the International Criminal Tribunal for the Former Yugoslavia, in Vandamme/Reestman (eds.), Ambiguity in the Rule of Law (2001), 17.

[257]*Schabas* (supra note 255), 100.

[258]*Nollkaemper* (supra note 256), 18.

[259]See the references to the legal literature in supra note 122.

[260]See Chap. 4, The Formation of Customary International Law and Its Methodological Challenges.

[261]See Sect. 4.2.1, State Practice Under a Traditional and Sect. 4.2.2, Opinio Iuris Under a Traditional Interpretation.

Other methodological approaches[262] to customary international law beyond this traditional method used in international criminal proceedings would necessarily violate the *nullum crimen sine iure praevia* requirement. Some prominent proponents, most notably the ILC, consider that there is a common approach to the identification of customary international law.[263] In contrast, *Verdross* has suggested that a range of differing approaches and theories may be more suitable.[264] If still one was to argue that international criminal tribunals applying different approaches to customary international criminal law all act in conformity with the *nullum crimen sine iure praevia* requirement, then the principle must be flexible enough to accept that there are a multitude of different approaches apart from the traditional method. However, should one accept such a variety of approaches then it appears doubtful if the *nullum crimen sine iure praevia* requirement could have any meaningful implication. If customary international criminal can be based on different methods, including progressive methodological approaches, it is hard to imagine how the *praevia* requirement could ever be violated: If customary international law is a "dance floor where (almost) anything goes",[265] there is no limit for the ascertainment of customary international law. Under such difficult methodological conditions in international criminal proceedings, any crime or mode of liability could also be claimed as part of customary international criminal law, rendering *nullum crimen sine iure praevia* a meaningless, empty Roman phrase. The doctrinal confusion surrounding customary international law—there being neither a generally accepted unified theory concerning the constituent elements to customary international law, nor agreement on the possible evidences for the identification of these elements[266]—makes it a problematic source for establishing individual criminal responsibility. By accepting a variety of different methodological approaches for its determination, the central issue with regard to the *nullum crimen sine iure* guarantees no longer concerns the *praevia* requirement. Rather we face the problem of how to arrange customary international law as a legal basis for criminal convictions with the requirements of accessibility of the international

---

[262]These other approaches to customary international law are discussed in Sect. 4.3, Modern Customary International Law.

[263]See further Sect. 4.4, The Identification of Customary International Law: The Challenge Ahead.

[264]A. *Verdross*, Entstehungsweisen und Geltungsgrund des universellen völkerrechtlichen Gewohnheitsrechts, 29 Zeitschrift für ausländisches öffentliches Recht und Völkerrecht (1969), 636.

[265]*d'Aspremont* in a contemporary formulation has compared "customary international law with a dance floor where (almost) anything goes", see http://www.ejiltalk.org/customary-international-law-as-a-dance-floor-part-i/#more-10650 (last visited 16 June 2017).

[266]See Chap. 4, The Formation of Customary International Law and Its Methodological Challenges. The present author has tried to shed some light on the classification of the evidence used by international criminal tribunals when identifying customary international law as relevant material for the law-creating process of State practice and *opinio iuris* or as a law-determining agency, that is subsidiary means for the determination of customary international law. See Chap. 7, Relevant Material for Proving the Existence of Customary International Criminal Law.

criminal norm and foreseeability of criminal punishment as demanded by the
nullum crimen sine iure certa guarantee.

3.10.6 The certa *Requirement and the Sources of International Law*

3.10.6.1   The Two Facets of the *certa* Requirement

The *nullum crimen sine iure certa* requirement consists of two different facets:
Firstly, it is directed at the legislator as an "imperative for improvement"[267] to draft
adequate penal norms. Secondly, it is a safeguard requirement for the individual and
as such closely connected to the two philosophical foundations of the NCSI principle in international criminal law: the protection of the individual against arbitrary
charges and the principle of individual guilt.

3.10.6.2   The *certa* Requirement as an Imperative for Improvement

The *nullum crimen sine iure certa* requirement as an "imperative for improvement"
as derived from domestic criminal law addresses the legislator, who is required to
define *ex ante* criminal norms with adequate precision.[268] The question is whether
this facet of the *certa* requirement can be transposed to the international legal order.
The legislative process on the international plane is more complex: We lack one
single body with law-creating authority, finding instead a decentralized legal
system in which multiple actors, primarily the 194 States, are positioned in a
horizontal relationship possessing equal law-setting capacities. Similar to the
above quoted *Justice* Case before the US Military Tribunal, the ICTY *Delalić*
Trial Chamber, in one the ICTY's early cases, highlighted the difference of
criminalisation at the international level:

> Whereas the criminalisation process in a national criminal justice system depends upon
> legislation which dictates the time when conduct is prohibited and the content of such
> prohibition, the international criminal justice system attains the same objective through
> treaties or conventions, or after a customary practice of the unilateral enforcement of a
> prohibition by States.[269]

Applying a strict *nullum crimen sine iure certa* requirement on the international
plane understood as a demand on the legislators, that is the States, as an "imperative
for improvement" would mean that the States would be required *ex ante* to draft

---

[267]*Hauck* (supra note 8), 61.

[268]*Hauck* (supra note 8), 61, referring to criminal law textbooks from civil law and common law
jurisdictions.

[269]ICTY, *Delalić* Trial Chamber Judgment, para 404.

precise international criminal norms. This could only be achieved by means of an international convention as an international criminal code, which to date has not been established.[270] The creation of unwritten norms such as customary international law is uncoordinated, taking time and lacking precision concerning its content and the exact point of time when a customary international norm comes into existence.[271] For this reason the domestic law analogy of the *certa* requirement as an "imperative for improvement" to the legislators is hardly applicable to all sources of international law, since such precision cannot be achieved within the uncoordinated way customary international law comes into existence.[272] This facet can still be used to appeal to the States as the legislators on the international plane to take positive action by drafting and ratifying international conventions containing international criminal law.[273] It could also be used to promote a more conscious approach of using customary international law as a law-making tool in order that States clearly reveal and take position on their State acts so that the identification of customary international law becomes a more tangible endeavor.

3.10.6.3   The *certa* Requirement as a Safeguard Requirement for the Individual

The second facet of the NCSI *certa* requirement is a safeguard for the individual and as such closely connected to the two philosophical foundations of the NCSI principle in international criminal law: the protection of the individual against arbitrary charges and the principle of individual guilt. It demands accessibility, meaning that the criminal norm is accessible to the individual, and foreseeability, meaning that the breach of that criminal norm makes criminal prosecution a foreseeable consequence.[274] The requirements of accessibility and foreseeability

---

[270]See above Sect. 3.10.3, The *scripta* Requirement and the Sources of International Law: International Conventions as the Sole Legal Basis for Individual Criminal Responsibility?.

[271]See Chap. 4, The Formation of Customary International Law and Its Methodological Challenges.

[272]*Hauck* (supra note 8), 62.

[273]See the Dissenting Opinion of Judge Robertson to the SCSL *Norman* Appeals Chamber Decision, para 14, determining that the NCSI principle impels the international community "to take positive action against abhorrent behavior, or else that behavior will go unpunished. It thus provides the rationale for (...) treaties and Conventions".

[274]See on the requirements of accessibility and foreseeability before international criminal tribunals: ICTY *Prosecutor v. Hadžihasanović*, Appeals Chamber Decision on Command Responsibility, para 34; ICTY, *Vasiljević* Trial Judgment, para 201; ICTY, *Ojdanić* Appeals Chamber Decision, para 37; ICTR, *Karemera* Trial Chamber Decision, para 43; SCSL, *Prosecutor v. Sesay*, Case No. SCSL-04-15-A, Appeals Chamber, Judgment, 26 October 2009, para 891; ECCC, *Prosecutor v. Ieng*, Case No 002/19-09-2007-ECCC/OCIJ (PTC38), Pre-Trial Chamber, Public Decision on the Appeals Against the Co-Investigative Judges Order on Joint Criminal Enterprise (JCE), 20 May 2010 (Pre-Trial Chamber Public Decision on the JCE Appeals), para 45; ECCC, *Duch* Appeals Judgment, para 96; see on the requirements of accessibility and foreseeability in the

do not postulate a proof of subjective knowledge, that the individual is informed about the content of the criminal norm and the consequences of its breach. What is required is an abstract possibility to know, including if need be, with the aid of legal counseling or by taking into consideration pre-existing judicial interpretation of the law.[275] The jurisprudence of international criminal tribunals in relation to these requirements reveals different approaches that are applied simultaneously: the first approach systematically sweeps away objections in relation to accessibility and foreseeability on basis of moral blameworthiness. The second approach assesses accessibility and foreseeability from the viewpoint of whether the underlying conduct is criminal in a general sense. In contrast, the third approach assesses them from the viewpoint of the concrete international criminal norm.

3.10.6.3.1   The *certa* Requirement and the Moral Blameworthiness

With regard to the first approach, concerns in relation to accessibility of the law and foreseeability of punishment have been sweepingly denied.[276] Considering morality concepts, the ICTY *Milutinović* Appeals Chamber considered that there is a difference in scope between the guarantees of NCSI *praevia* and NCSI *certa*:

> Although the *immorality* or appalling character of an act *is not a sufficient factor to warrant its criminalisation* under customary international law, it may in fact play a role in that respect, insofar as *it may refute any claim by the Defence that it did not know of the criminal nature of the acts.*[277]

However, such a view is not very convincing. As stated before, the *certa* and *praevia* requirement are necessarily intertwined.[278] It would amount to a sheer absurdity to claim that with regard to *nullum crimen sine iure praevia* morality and

---

legal literature: *Gallant* (supra note 4), 359ff; *Ferdinandusse* (supra note 94), 236ff *inter alia* referring to ECHR, *C.R. v. the United Kingdom*, Application No. 20190/92, 21 October 1995, para 33 stipulating that law under the NCSL principle "comprises written as well as unwritten law and implies qualitative requirements, notably those of accessibility and foreseeability".

[275] *Kress* (supra note 11), MN 29 referring to the jurisprudence of the European Court of Human Rights; *Krivec* (supra note 12), 12.

[276] For example, ICTY, *Delalić* Trial Judgment, para 313: "The purpose of this principle is to prevent the prosecution and punishment of an individual for acts which he reasonably believed to be lawful at the time of their commission. It strains credibility to contend that the accused would not recognize the criminal nature of the acts alleged in the Indictment." This conception was accepted and fully shared by the *Delalić* Appeals Chamber Judgment, paras 179–180; see also *Ferdinandusse* (supra note 94), 241 with further references to the legal literature and national case law.

[277] ICTY, *Ojdanić* Appeals Chamber Decision, para 42 (emphasis added). This position has been fully endorsed by the ECCC, see ECCC, *Prosecutor v. Kaing alias Duch*, Case No. 001/18-07-2007/ECCC/TC, Trial Chamber, Judgment, 26 July 2010, para 32 and endorsed by ECCC, *Duch* Appeals Judgment, para 212.

[278] *Ashworth* (supra note 225), 74: "a vague law may in practice operate retroactively."

criminality are strictly to be separated but with regard to *nullum crimen sine iure certa* a mere understanding of moral taste is adequate to establish foreseeability and accessibility. This is especially absurd in regard to the two philosophical foundations of the protection of the individual against arbitrary charges and the principle of individual guilt. Rather than equating immorality with foreseeability/accessibility of criminality, international criminal tribunals are best advised to establish whether the criminality of the underlying punishable conduct was accessible and whether the consequences, criminal prosecution were foreseeable in case of its breach.

3.10.6.3.2   The *certa* Requirement and the General Sense of the Underlying Criminality

Another approach apparent in the jurisprudence accepts the existence of a pre-established international criminal norm—be it based on customary international law, treaty law or general principles of law—for the fulfillment of the *praevia* requirement. However, with regard to the *certa* requirements of accessibility and foreseeability, it places its focus on whether the underlying *conduct* was in some way criminal. In that regard the ICTY *Hadžihasanović* Trial Chamber was particularly lenient in relation to the foreseeability of punishment, stating that "whether the conduct may lead to criminal responsibility, disciplinary responsibility or other sanctions is not of material importance."[279] The Trial Chamber was, however, eventually overruled by the Appeals Chamber requiring that "[a]s to foreseeability, the conduct in question is the concrete conduct of the accused; he must be able to appreciate that the conduct is *criminal in the sense generally understood*, without reference to any specific provision."[280] Whereas the ICTY *Hadžihasanović* Appeals Chamber required that criminal responsibility was foreseeable, it focused generally on the underlying criminal conduct and not on the concrete underlying international criminal norm that was charged. Under such a perception of accessibility/foreseeability, the individual's appreciation that his conduct is criminal in a general sense does not require that the concrete contours of the international crime are accessible. Consequently, the criminalization of the underlying conduct as "ordinary" domestic crimes could be used to dismiss doubts of accessibility and foreseeability. In this case, the domestic criminal law of the country of residence or origin of the accused could be of particular importance.[281] For example, the ICTY *Ojdanić* Appeals

---

[279] See for the ICTY, *Prosecutor v. Hadžihasanović*, IT-01-47-PT, Trial Chamber, Decision on Joint Challenge to Jurisdiction, 12 November 2002, para 62. In the same vein SCSL. *Norman* Appeals Chamber Decision, para 25.

[280] ICTY *Hadžihasanović* Appeals Chamber Decision, para 34 (emphasis added); see also SCSL, *Norman* Appeals Chamber Decision, paras 25 and 51; *Gallant* (supra note 4), 322.

[281] See for example ICTY, *Delalić* Appeals Judgment, paras 179 with reference to the Criminal Code of the SFRY as being in line with the NCSL principle. See also ECCC, Case No 002 - Pre-Trial Chamber Public Decision on the JCE Appeals, para 72 stating that modes of liability of

Chamber held that "this Tribunal does not apply the law of the former Yugoslavia to the definition of the crimes and forms of liability within its jurisdiction. It does, as pointed out above, apply customary international law in relation to its jurisdiction *ratione materiae*. It may, however, have recourse to domestic law for the purpose of establishing that the accused could reasonably have known that the offence in question or the offence committed in the way charged in the indictment was prohibited and punishable."[282]

Under such a perception of accessibility/foreseeability an individual will not be successful in claiming non-accessibility to the international criminal norm or non-foreseeability of punishment as a defence in international criminal proceedings, if his/her conduct is considered criminal in his/her own legal order, even if the domestic crime or mode of liability is expressed in different terms and "only" the enforcement as an international crime takes place before an international criminal tribunal.[283]

3.10.6.3.3 The *certa* Requirement and the Concrete Underlying International Criminal Norm

The final approach in relation to the *certa* requirement in the jurisprudence of international criminal tribunals places its focus on the analysis of accessibility/ foreseeability of the concrete underlying international criminal norm or form of liability, that is whether or not the concrete customary international criminal norm was accessible to the individual and whether criminal liability was a foreseeable consequence of the breach of this international criminal norm.[284] The ICTY *Hadžihasanović* Appeals Chamber stated that "accessibility does not exclude

JCE I and II as recognized by the ICTY under customary international law also "have an underpinning in the Cambodian law concept of co-authorship applicable at the time, the Pre-Trial Chamber has no doubt that liability based on a common purpose, design or plan was sufficiently accessible and foreseeable to the defendants."

[282]ICTY, *Ojdanić* Appeals Chamber Decision, para 40.

[283]See *Gallant* (supra note 4), 320ff speaking in that regard of "retroactive re-characterization"; *T. Meron*, International Criminalization of Internal Atrocities, 89 American Journal of International Law (1995), 566, who in relation to the inclusion of Common Article 3 within the Jurisdiction of the ICTR Statute stated: "In arguing against any challenge on *ex post facto* grounds, one must emphasize that common Article 3 and Additional Protocol II are treaty obligations binding on Rwanda, that they clearly proscribe certain acts, and that those acts are *also prohibited by the criminal law of Rwanda, albeit in different terms*" (emphasis added).

[284]See for example ICTY, *Vasiljević* Trial Judgment, para 193: "From the perspective of the *nullum crimen sine lege* principle, it would be wholly unacceptable for a Trial Chamber to convict an accused person on the basis of a prohibition which, taking into account the specificity of customary international law and allowing for the gradual clarification of the rules of criminal law, is either insufficiently precise to determine conduct and distinguish the criminal from the permissible, or was not sufficiently accessible at the relevant time. A criminal conviction should indeed never be based upon a norm which an accused could not reasonably have been aware of at the time

reliance being placed on a law which is based on custom".[285] The ICTY *Milutinović* Appeals Chamber held that "[t]his Tribunal must therefore be satisfied that the crime or the form of liability with which an accused is charged was sufficiently foreseeable and that the law providing for such liability must be sufficiently accessible at the relevant time, taking into account the specificity of international law when making that assessment."[286] Judge *Nieto-Navia* in his separate and partially dissenting opinion of the ICTY *Galić* Trial Judgment held that "[o]nce it is satisfied that a certain act or set of acts is indeed criminal under customary international law, a Trial Chamber must finally confirm that this offence was defined with sufficient clarity under international customary law for its general nature, its criminal character and its approximate gravity to have been sufficiently foreseeable and accessible."[287] The same approach is detectable at the SCSL where the *Sesay* Appeals Chamber noted "that a determination of 'foreseeability' and 'accessibility' with the principle of *nullum crimen sine lege* must take into account the 'specificity of international law'."[288] Furthermore, the ECCC the *Duch* Appeals Judgment also referred to "the protective function of the principle of legality" and analyzed the accessibility criterion on the basis of the international criminal norm with the existence of an applicable international treaty or customary international law.[289] The common denominator of these examples is that the *nullum crimen sine iure certa* requirements of accessibility and foreseeability can be established on the basis of the concrete underlying legal basis of individual responsibility on the international plane, that is, the international criminal norm.

3.10.6.3.4 Legal Assessment of These Three Approaches to Establish the *certa* Requirement

In the prosecution of core crimes under international law, defendants have not been successful in raising issues of *nullum crimen sine iure certa*. Even human rights courts have not been overly positivistic when international core crimes are at stake.[290] It thus can be stated that the consistency of the application and development of customary international criminal law with the fundamental criminal

---

of the acts, and this norm must make it sufficiently clear what act or omission could engage his criminal responsibility."

[285] ICTY, *Hadžihasanović* Appeals Chamber Decision, para 34.

[286] ICTY, *Ojdanić* Appeals Chamber Decision, para 38.

[287] ICTY, Separate and Partially Dissenting Opinion of Judge *Nieto-Navia* in ICTY, *Prosecutor v. Galić*, IT-98-29-T, Trial Chamber, Judgment, 5 December 2003, para 111.

[288] SCSL, *Sesay* Appeals Judgment, para 891.

[289] ECCC, *Duch* Appeals Judgment, paras 97, 160, 162, 280.

[290] *Schabas* (supra note 112), Art. 22, 404 stating that human rights courts in relation to international crimes "have also eschewed an excessive positivism, accepting that the principle *nullum crimen* is respected even by unwritten or judge-made rules".

principle of *nullum crimen sine iure* has not been the subject of a rigid examination. Indeed, the three approaches identified above reveal that international criminal tribunals are rather flexible when establishing the *certa* requirement. It is safe to argue that in international criminal proceedings one does not encounter stringent *nullum crimen sine iure certa* requirements. From the jurisprudence alone one cannot see a preference for one of the approaches over the other, since they are generally referred to in parallel. The case law seems to indicate that in order to determine accessibility and foreseeability the three different approaches can be used as alternatives.[291]

However, it is problematic that the immorality of the underlying act can be used to consider accessibility and foreseeability of criminal punishment under customary international law, particularly if the *nullum crimen sine iure praevia* requirement would not require that the customary international criminal norm is established on basis of the traditional method, that is consistent, general and enduring State practice coupled with *opinio iuris*. If customary international criminal law could be established on the basis of a deductive approach or a prevailing *opinio iuris sive necessitatis*, and its accessibility and foreseeability was merely established on basis of moral considerations, than it seems that there is no limit to the "creativity" or "activism" of judges when determining customary international criminal law. For these reasons one has to oppose that *nullum crimen sine iure certa* can be established by taking recourse merely to an understanding of moral taste.[292]

There are also reasons why taking recourse to domestic criminal law in order to establish the *nullum crimen sine iure certa* requirements of accessibility and foreseeability should be applied cautiously: Certain crimes or modes of liability under international criminal law are so specific that the domestic analogy to a national penal code would either not work at all, or would not grasp the concept

---

[291] See for example ICTY, *Ojdanić* Appeals Chamber Decision with regard to foreseeability and accessibility to JCE, para 43. The simultaneous application of the different approaches is particularly evident in the case law of the ECCC: see ECCC, Co-Investigating Judges, Order on the Application at the ECCC of the Form of Liability Known as Joint Criminal Enterprise, Case File No: 002/19-09-2007-ECCC-OCIJ, 8 December 2009, para 20: the "test of foreseeability and accessibility can be satisfied when the alleged activity was criminalised under national law *or* under international law at the particular time period." ECCC, Case No 002 Pre-Trial Chamber Public Decision on the JCE Appeals, para 45: "contrary to what some of the Appellants assert, the question of whether JCE is a form of responsibility recognized in domestic law may be relevant when determining whether it was foreseeable to the Charged Person that his/her alleged conduct may entail criminal responsibility. However, it is not necessary that JCE also be punishable in domestic law in addition to being a recognized form of liability under customary international law for it to apply before the ECCC." See also Pre-Trial Chamber Decision on *Ieng Sary*'s Appeal Against the Closing Order, para 238: "The Pre-Trial Chamber finds that for the standard of the principle of legality to be met in the ECCC the requirement for existence of the crime in domestic law is not absolute, it is rather optional. It is sufficient to find that the crime or mode of liability existed in one of the other bodies of law"; see also ECCC, *Duch* Appeals Judgment, para 91.

[292] See Sect. 3.10.6.3.1, The *certa* Requirement and the Moral Blameworthiness.

properly.[293] In the words of the ICTY *Furundžija* Trial Chamber: "account must be taken of the specificity of international criminal proceedings when utilizing national law notions. In this way a mechanical importation or transposition from national law into international criminal proceedings is avoided, as well as the attendant distortions of the unique traits of such proceedings."[294] Although this statement relates seeking a definition for rape as found in the domestic legal systems of the world—that is on the basis of a general principle—the logic behind the reasoning also applies to the accessibility/foreseeability requirements. Also in that regard the specificity of international criminal proceedings have to be taken into consideration. The case law of the ECCC is instructive on this point. The ECCC Pre-Trial Chamber highlighted that the elements of crime in the domestic and the international contexts are not necessarily congruent with one other: In the *Duch* Case the Pre-Trial Chamber stated that while the domestic definition of torture required two alternative subjective elements of the crime, namely torturing for the purpose of "inflict[ing] acts of torture to obtain, under pain, information for the commission of a felony or misdemeanor" or "inflict[ing] acts of torture out of barbarity", these were not applicable to the "international definition" of torture.[295] The ECCC Pre-Trial Chamber further held that "murder" as an international crime committed as a crime against humanity or war crime does not require the specific subjective element of premeditation, which is required under domestic Cambodian criminal law.[296] Consequently, the Pre-Trial Chamber in its Appeal Decision against *Chea* and *Thirith* held "that where the constitutive elements are not identical, domestic and international crimes are to be treated as distinct crimes,"[297] a position that has been affirmed by the ECCC Supreme Court Chamber.[298] A cautious use of concepts of criminal law derived from the domestic legal sphere would maintain the specificity of international criminal proceedings. This argument is supported by the fact that international crimes necessarily contain chapeau

---

[293] For example: the war crimes of conscripting or enlisting children, compelling a prisoner of war or a civilian to serve in the forces of a hostile power, extensive destruction and appropriation of property not justified by military necessity and carried out unlawfully and wantonly, or the mode of liability of command responsibility. These are crimes or modes of liability that generally did not find a counterpart in "ordinary" domestic penal codes. Obviously, the ratification of the Rome Statute has also sparked a trend of domestic implementation of international criminal law within the domestic sphere. That development, however, generally took place after the crimes charged before the ICTY, ICTR, SCSL and ECCC have been committed.

[294] ICTY, *Furundžija* Trial Judgment, para 178.

[295] ECCC, Pre-Trial Chamber, Public Decision on Appeal against Closing Order indicting Kaing Guek Eav alias Duch, Case File No. 001/18-07-2007-ECCC/OCIJ (PTC 02), 5 December 2008, para 72 referring to the 1956 Penal Code.

[296] *Id.*, para 84.

[297] ECCC, Pre-Trial Chamber Decision on *Ieng Sary*'s Appeal Against the Closing Order, para 153.

[298] The Pre-Trial Chamber's position has been affirmed by the Supreme Court Chamber in the ECCC *Duch* Appeals Judgment, para 182. The Supreme Court Chamber determined that rape was not a distinct crime against humanity under the temporal jurisdiction of the ECCC.

elements,[299] which are lacking in the domestic context.[300] While "ordinary" domestic penal norms might establish foreseeability/accessibility of the criminality of the underlying conduct, they do not create foreseeability/accessibility for the wider context of international criminal norms, namely the chapeau requirements. ICTY jurisprudence confirms that the chapeau requirements for the prosecution of international crimes are both a jurisdictional prerequisite—since only then the crimes fall within the subject matter jurisdiction of international criminal tribunals—as well as a substantive element of the crime—requiring knowledge in order to hold individuals criminally responsible.[301] In the words of the *Tadić* Appeals Chamber with regard to crimes against humanity, "crimes which are unrelated to widespread or systematic attacks on civilian population *should not be prosecuted as crimes against humanity*. Crimes against humanity are crimes of a special nature to which a greater degree of moral turpitude attaches than to an ordinary crime. Thus to convict an accused of crimes against humanity, it must be proved that the crimes were related to the attack on a civilian population (occurring during an armed conflict) and that the accused *knew* that his crimes were so related."[302]

An approach that takes due account of the specificity of international criminal proceedings draws on the chapeau requirements not only as a necessary jurisdictional criterion and as part of the *mens rea* component of the elements of the crime—that is, establishing knowledge of the wider context of the crime so that

---

[299]Chapeau requirements are contextual elements that elevate ordinary crimes to the international level and redefine them as international crimes. For instance, crimes against humanity require that the act is committed as part of a widespread, systematic attack directed against a civilian population.

[300]One example in that regard from ECCC jurisprudence concerns the crime of rape as a distinct crime against humanity. Whereas the Co-Prosecutors argued that since rape was enshrined in the domestic penal code it would have been foreseeable to the accused *Thirith* that rape constituted a crime against humanity, the Pre-trial Chamber rejected that argument. It stated "Rape as it is defined under domestic criminal codes does not contain such [chapeau] elements. As such, the facts evidencing rape as a crime against humanity may also support a charge of rape under domestic law, but the same may not be true in reverse, given that an isolated event unconnected to a broader attack does not amount to a crime against humanity." See ECCC, Pre-Trial Chamber, Public Decision on Appeals by *Nuon Chea* and *Ieng Thirith* against the Closing Order, para 153; the Pre-Trial Chamber, however, left open the possibility that rape may be charged under 'other inhumane acts' as a crime against humanity, but determined that this is not a jurisdictional issue it had to solve, but left is to the Trial Chamber, see paras 165f. See also *N. Hayes*, Creating a Definition of Rape in International Law: The Contribution of the International Criminal Tribunals, in Darcy, Powderly (eds.), Judicial Creativity at the International Criminal Tribunals (2010), 149–150, stating that "it is questionable whether the domestic crime of rape is even the correct paradigm from which to interpret a definition for the international crime of rape", with further references.

[301]See e.g., ICTY, *Prosecutor v. Naletilić*, IT-98-34-A, Appeals Chamber, Judgment, 3 May 2006, para 116.

[302]ICTY, *Tadić* Appeals Chamber Judgment, para 271 (emphasis added). It needs to be added that the correct legal characterization of the chapeau requirements is not required by the perpetrator but an awareness of the factual circumstances of the chapeau requirements must be shown, see ICTY, *Naletilić* Appeals Judgment, paras 119ff.

an individual can be convicted of an international crime—but also when establishing the NCSI *certa* requirements of accessibility/foreseeability. Therefore, the specificity of international criminal law should be taken into account when elaborating on the NCSI *certa* requirements of accessibility/foreseeability, reducing the possibility of recourse to "ordinary" domestic criminal law. Consequently, the requirements of foreseeability and accessibility are best established on basis of the concrete, underlying international criminal norm.

3.10.6.4   The *certa* Requirement and Customary International Criminal Law

The specificity of international criminal law should be taken into account when elaborating on *nullum crimen sine iure certa*. Therefore, the requirements of accessibility/foreseeability should be established on basis of the concrete, underlying international criminal norm. As mentioned, international criminal tribunals have generally based their convictions on the pre-existence of a crime under customary international law in order to fulfill the *nullum crimen sine iure praevia* requirement.[303] It is, however, another question how precise we can afford that *crimen* to be. Looking at the underlying unwritten sources of international criminal law, such as customary international law, in relation to the *certa* requirement, the *nullum crimen sine iure* principle is put to the test.[304]

   When referring to customary international law as the underlying legal basis of individual criminal responsibility, international criminal tribunals generally use broad language, such as "accessibility does not exclude reliance being placed on a law which is based on custom".[305] Other chambers diminish the role of the *certa* requirement by simply arguing that the accessibility of customary international criminal law may "not be straightforward".[306] In contrast, when considering the requirements of accessibility to the customary international criminal norm and foreseeability of punishment in case of its breach for the individual, the ICTY *Vasiljević* Trial Chamber used rather strong terms:

> If customary international law does not provide for a sufficiently precise definition of a crime listed in the Statute, the Trial Chamber would have no choice but to refrain from exercising jurisdiction over it, regardless of the fact that the crime is listed as a punishable offence in the Statute.[307]

---

[303] See the references in supra note 247ff.

[304] Some authors go as far as to deny that the *certa* requirement finds application in international criminal proceedings, see for example *Heinsch* (supra note 7), 322.

[305] See for example ICTY, *Hadžihasanović* Appeals Chamber Decision, para 34.

[306] ICTY, *Ojdanić* Appeals Chamber Decision, para 41; SCSL, Sesay Appeals Judgment, para 891; ICTR, *Karemera* Trial Chamber Decision, para 43.

[307] ICTY, *Vasiljević* Trial Judgment, para 202 further stating: "This is so because, to borrow the language of a US military tribunal [the Hostage Case] in Nuremberg, anything contained in the statute of the court in excess of existing customary international law would be a utilisation of

Despite this warning, an analysis of the jurisprudence of the ICTY, the ICTR and the SCSL reveals that the question of how accessibility and foreseeability with regard to the concrete underlying customary international criminal norm can be established has attracted little attention. There is only one case before the ICTY and one before the ICTR, in which the respective chambers held that accessibility to the concrete customary international criminal norm was given due to "a long and consistent stream of judicial decisions, international instruments and domestic legislation".[308] However, without even referring to one explicit single instance in that regard, even these two cases of the UN *ad hoc* tribunals display a half-hearted handling of the *certa* requirement. Generally, it seems as if international criminal tribunals avoid the task of establishing whether accessibility and foreseeability to the concrete international criminal norm has been given in particular cases. The jurisprudence of the UN *ad hoc* tribunals implies that if criminal responsibility is given under customary international law, the criteria of accessibility and foreseeability can be assumed.[309] A customary criminal norm is based on a plurality of sources from the international and various national legal orders: State practice in the form of physical and verbal acts and paper practice, such as policy statements and press releases as well as the conduct of States in international organizations including the resolutions they vote for[310]; domestic law, military manuals, and national and international case law. It seems dubious, therefore how a customary criminal norm

---

power not of law." See also at para 193 by reference to the case law of the ECtHR: "From the perspective of the *nullum crimen sine lege* principle, it would be wholly unacceptable for a Trial Chamber to convict an accused person on the basis of a prohibition which, taking into account the specificity of customary international law and allowing for the gradual clarification of the rules of criminal law, is either insufficiently precise to determine conduct and distinguish the criminal from the permissible, or was not sufficiently accessible at the relevant time. A criminal conviction should indeed never be based upon a norm which an accused could not reasonably have been aware of at the time of the acts, and this norm must make it sufficiently clear what act or omission could engage his criminal responsibility."

[308]ICTY, *Ojdanić* Appeals Chamber Decision, para 41; however in para 43 the Appeals Chamber implies that NCSI *certa* is given due to FRY domestic criminal law, other domestic jurisdictions that "run parallel to custom", and the "egregious nature" of the charged crimes. This example shows that the three approaches to the *certa* requirement are used as alternatives; for the ICTR, see *Karemera* Trial Chamber Decision, para 44.

[309]See for example ICTY, *Stakić* Appeals Judgment, para 101; this critique in relation to ICTY case law has been raised by the ECCC, Case No 002 Pre-Trial Chamber Public Decision on the JCE Appeals, para 45.

[310]Compare Sect. 4.3.2. The Procedural Aspect of Modern Customary International Law and all the possible sources for State practice under a modern understanding of customary international law. *I. Brownlie*, Principles of Public International Law (2008), 6; *International Law Association*, London Conference (2000), Committee on Formation of Customary (General) International Law, Final Report of the Committee, Statement of Principles Applicable to the Formation of General Customary International Law, Part II: The Objective Element: State Practice, pp. 13–20. See also the material referred to by the international criminal tribunals in Chap. 7, Relevant Material for Proving the Existence of Customary International Criminal Law.

can ever be accessible and its punishment be foreseeable.[311] When the knowledge of criminal statutes by individuals on the domestic level is a legal fiction, it follows that the knowledge of customary international criminal law is a fiction of a legal fiction.

The argument against stringent requirements in relation to accessibility and foreseeability generally focuses on the nature of international law and the lack of a central legislator in particular.[312] Therefore, due to uncertain factors in the creation and determination of customary law it is suggested that the requirements of accessibility and foreseeability need to be loosened. Critics, however, argue that instead it is the relativization of the NCSI principle that comes at the expense of precision when determining customary international criminal law.[313] Taking the requirements of accessibility and foreseeability seriously would in turn secure that customary international law as a source of international criminal law can meet the standard of specificity equivalent to written law.[314] Yet one must ask how such an ambitious goal can be achieved.

It should be stressed that the NCSI *certa* requirement is an objective requirement that does not require concrete, subjective, individual knowledge of the law, but is fulfilled if there is a possibility to know, that is to say, whether accessibility to the international criminal norm and foreseeability of its punishment can be established objectively.[315] In that regard subsidiary sources may be of particular importance: The case law of the ECtHR reveals that Art. 7 of the European Convention on Human Rights, its *nullum crimen sine lege* provision, is not violated if accessibility and foreseeability of statutory law can only be established by "appropriate legal advice"[316] or "in the light of the accompanying interpretive case-law".[317]

---

[311]*Ferdinandusse* (supra note 94), 239. See also *Verhoeven* (supra note 140), 22, asking how could an individual "be satisfactorily informed of the existence or exact content of a customary international rule [. . .], which the states themselves very often remain largely ignorant of". Similarly *Lamb* (supra note 57), 743, stating that the NCSL principle, which "is based explicitly upon the value of legal certainty, sits uneasily with the very nature of customary international law, which is unwritten and frequently difficult to define with precision."

[312]See the US Military Tribunal, *Altstötter and Others Case*, 41. See also Opening Statement of US Chief Prosecutor *Jackson*, IMT Nuremberg Judgment, Vol. II, 147: "International law is not capable of development by the normal processes of legislation, for there is no continuing international legislative authority."

[313]See *Hauck* (supra note 8), 59.

[314]*M. C. Bassiouni*, Universal Jurisdiction for International Crimes, 42 Virginia Journal of International law (2001–2002), 105, who considers that customary international law as a source of substantive international criminal law should meet "the standard of specificity equivalent to that of conventional international law."

[315]*Cassese* (supra note 175), 52: "International law, like most national systems, does not require awareness of the illegality of an act for the act to be regarded as an international crime."

[316]ECtHR, Case of *Cantoni v. France*, Application No. 17862/91, Judgment, 11 November 1996, para 35; Case of *Tolstoy Miloslavsky v. The United Kingdom*, Application No. 18139/91, Judgment, 13 July 1995, para 37.

[317]ECtHR, Case of *Cantoni v. France*, Application No. 17862/91, Judgment, 11 November 1996, para 32. See also *Lauterpacht* considering the role of judicial precedent stating that "judicial decisions, particularly when published, become part and parcel of the legal sense of the community",

Consequently, the ECtHR held that in relation to unclear or vague statutes, the body of a settled jurisprudence could be used to "flesh out the content".[318] Applied to customary international criminal norms, accessibility to the concrete international criminal norm and foreseeability of punishment could be established *via* subsidiary sources since they make customary international criminal law tangible to individuals. Previous judgments of international criminal tribunals are useful in establishing accessibility to the international criminal norm and foreseeability of its punishment, because in these proceedings individuals have already been convicted on basis of the concrete underlying international criminal norm. One might agree with the ECtHR that international criminal law case law "fleshes out the content" of customary international criminal law. The ECCC jurisprudence pays particular attention to the NCSI requirements of accessibility and foreseeability,[319] and it is therefore instructive on the use of previous international criminal judgments to establish foreseeability of punishment and accessibility to customary international criminal norms. The Co-Investigating Judges[320] stated in their closing order that "[w]ith respect to crimes against humanity, their prohibition under customary law is considered to have been sufficiently accessible to the Charged Persons, with particular regard to the World War II trials held in Nuremberg and Tokyo" and that modes of liability, including joint criminal enterprise or superior responsibility "were also set out under international law through sources such as the trials following World War II and as such can be considered sufficiently accessible

---

H. Lauterpacht, International Law – Being the Collected Papers of Hersch Lauterpacht (ed., E. Lauterpacht), Volume 2, The Law of Peace (1975), 473–474.

[318]ECtHR, Case of *Association Ekin v. France*, Application No. 39288/98, Judgment, 17 July 2001, para 46; Case of *Kokkinakis* v. Greece, Application No. 14307/88, Judgment, 25 May 1993, para 40; strictly speaking these two cases do not concern Art. 7 of the ECHR (*nullum crimen sine lege*), however, the Court has applied a holistic approach to the requirements of "accessibility" and "foreseeability" which also concerns the question of whether certain infringements of other conventional rights are "prescribed by law", see for example ECtHR, *CR v. the United Kingdom*, para 33: "The Court thus indicated that when speaking of 'law' Article 7 alludes to the very same concept as that to which the Convention refers elsewhere when using that term, a concept which comprises written as well as unwritten law and implies qualitative requirements, notably those of accessibility and foreseeability".

[319]The ECCC Supreme Court Chamber rebukes its Trial Chamber if they do not sufficiently elaborate on the NCSI *certa* requirements, see ECCC, *Duch* Appeals Judgment, para 159: "the Supreme Court Chamber now addresses the additional requirement under the principle of legality that charged offences were sufficiently foreseeable and the law providing for such liability was sufficiently accessible to the Accused at the relevant time. Although the Trial Chamber properly identified this requirement, it was not followed with sufficient analysis".

[320]The court structure at the ECCC is different to that of other international criminal tribunals, especially when it comes to the investigative stage. The ECCC has Co-Investigating Judges, a concept derived from the French legal system, that consist of one international and one national judge. They carry out the investigations prior to the trial phase. Their investigations are concluded by a closing order leading to either the indictment of the person charged or the dismissal of the case. The closing order is open to appeal by the Pre-Trial Chamber.

to the Charged Persons."[321] The *Ieng Sary* defence argued in its appeal against the closing order that "[t]hese crimes and forms of liability would also not have been accessible to him simply because they may have existed in some post-World War II jurisprudence",[322] but the Pre-Trial Chamber dismissed the appeal, backing the findings of the co-investigating judges.[323] Consequently, according to ECCC jurisprudence the NCSI *certa* requirements of accessibility to the customary international criminal norm and foreseeability of its punishment can be fulfilled by reference to previous judgments that have applied international criminal law.[324] An individual could thus not simply ignore the findings of pre-established international criminal case law. With regard to customary international law as the underlying legal basis for international criminal law convictions, it would not be necessary for the individual to comprehend the method previous international criminal tribunals have used to establish customary international criminal law. Even if the methods applied by various international criminal tribunals are not visible to the individual or even differ, but the final result,—the existence of customary international criminal law—is firmly established by the jurisprudence, these judgments could function as a valid source to establish accessibility to the international criminal norm and foreseeability of its criminal punishment. Under the NCSI *certa* requirements, the individual must only comprehend the *consequences* of the customary law determination of international criminal tribunals: There exists an international criminal norm to which individual criminal responsibility is attached in case of its breach. An individual does not have to comprehend the underlying method as to how these tribunals arrived at their findings. Consequently, even if the determination of a customary international criminal norm is based on diverging methodological approaches, individuals could not successfully claim that they have not been put on notice of the criminality of their actions or omissions. The foreseeability/accessibility requirements only foresee that the consequences of criminal prosecution for the individual are comprehensible.

Such an approach to establish accessibility/foreseeability *via* pre-existing international criminal law jurisprudence appears to be acceptable when the jurisprudence is uniform in its application. However, the issue is more complicated in cases where conflicting jurisprudence exists, where some judgments affirm the existence

---

[321]ECCC, Co-investigating Judges, Case File No. 002/19-19-2007-ECCC-OCIJ, Closing Order, 15 September 2010, paras 106–7.

[322]ECCC, *Ieng Sary's* Appeal Against the Closing Order, para 131.

[323]See ECCC, Pre-Trial Chamber Decision on *Ieng Sary's* Appeal Against the Closing Order, para 210, in paras 413–460 it established accessibility and foreseeability for superior responsibility under customary international law exclusively on the basis of post-World War II jurisprudence.

[324]See also ECCC, Pre-Trial Chamber, Public Decision on Appeals by *Nuon Chea* and *Ieng Thirith* against the Closing Order, paras 130ff, on whether the count of 'other inhumane acts' as a crime against humanity was accessible and foreseeable see paras 162, for superior responsibility see para 231; see also ECCC, *Duch* Appeals Judgment, para 161 considering that forced labour was punishable as enslavement as a crime against humanity, para 211 for torture as a crime against humanity and para 280 for persecution as a crime against humanity.

of a customary international criminal norm and others reject it.[325] Such an ambiguity in the jurisprudence could impede the usefulness of the diverging judgments
to create certainty with regard to the existence of a customary international criminal
norm. This is all the more true, since the different international criminal tribunals do
not share a common appeals chamber—a court of last instance—that could clearly
settle conflicting jurisprudence.[326] The jurisprudence of the ECtHR appears to
imply that the use of previous jurisprudence to make domestic law accessible and
foreseeable is dependent on the existence of a "settled line of consistent, clear and
precise decisions"[327] or "settled national case law"[328] on the issue. Transposed to
the determination of customary international criminal law, any ambiguity in the
case law of the different international criminal tribunals creates uncertainty to the
exact content of the law. Thus, conflicting jurisprudence on international criminal
law issues could prevent the use of case law as means to establish the *nullum crimen
sine iure certa* requirements.[329] Any uncertainty within conflicting jurisprudence
could not be used to create certainty with regard to the *nullum crimen sine iure certa*
requirements. By adhering to the principle *in dubio pro reo*,[330] the accused is given
the benefit of the doubt on the existence and scope of customary international
criminal law.

---

[325]There are different views on the existence or non-existence of customary international law
detectable among international criminal tribunals: for example the ICTY, *Prosecutor v. Perišić*,
Appeals Chamber, Judgment, 28 February 2013, paras 25ff, determined that specific direction was
a component of the *actus reus* of aiding and abetting liability under customary international law,
while the *Prosecutor v. Taylor*, Case No. SCSL-03-01-A, Appeals Chamber, Judgment,
26 September 2013 at para 486 stated "that 'specific direction' is not an element of the *actus
reus* of aiding and abetting liability [. . .] under customary international law." The ICTY Appeals
Chamber, *Prosecutor v. Šainović*, IT-05-87-A, Appeals Chamber, Judgment, 23 January 2014,
paras 1617ff followed the conception of the SCSL Appeals Chamber. The ECCC Trial Chamber
also adhered to that conception, see *Prosecutor v. Nuon*, Case File No. 002/19-09-2007/ECCC/TC,
Trial Chamber, Judgment, 7 August 2014, paras 707ff. Another example concerns the JCE
doctrine, where the ECCC Pre-Trial Chamber openly challenged the customary law finding of
the ICTY Appeals Chamber in its *Tadić* Judgment concerning the third form or "extended form" of
joint criminal enterprise, as it did not deliver consistent and widespread State practice and *opinio
iuris* at the time relevant to the temporal jurisdiction of the ECCC. See ECCC, Case No 002 -
Pre-Trial Chamber Public Decision on the JCE Appeals, para 77. Consequently, the third form of
JCE has found no application in ECCC jurisprudence.

[326]As noted by *Koskenniemi*, fragmentation of law can be caused by conflicting interpretations of
different international courts; see Report of the Study Group of the International Law Commission,
Fragmentation of International Law: Difficulties Arising from the Diversification and Expansion
of International Law, UN Doc. A/CN.4/L.682 (13 April 2006), paras 49–52.

[327]ECtHR, *Ekin Association* Case, para 46.

[328]ECtHR, *Kokkinakis* Case, para 40.

[329]See also *Ferdinandusse* (supra note 94), 240; see also ICTY *Delalić* Appeals Judgment, para
260: "No force of precedent can be ascribed to a proposition that is interpreted differently by
equally competent courts".

[330]See Sect. 5.2, The Role of Judges: Determining, Developing or Creating Customary International Criminal Law?.

Such a restrictive approach imposes strict requirements whereby accessibility/ foreseeability on the basis of previous case law could only be achieved by a uniform jurisprudence, which maintains a high standard of certainty of the scope and applicability of customary international criminal law. Nevertheless, what if, "certainty" is not the striven goal? The requirements of foreseeability/accessibility might be understood as "merely" putting the individual on notice that criminal prosecution is a *possible consequence*. Despite diverging case law, the individual could then reasonably foresee that certain courts have considered that an international criminal norm existed, or have interpreted it either restrictively or expansively. Nevertheless, criminal prosecution would be one possible foreseeable consequence. Such less stringent requirement on *nullum crimen sine iure certa* would grant the judges at international criminal tribunals some discretion in the interpretation of customary international criminal law.[331] It seems, however, questionable if such a wide approach would comply with fundamental criminal law principles. It seems to turn the *in dubio pro reo* principle upside down, turning it into *in dubio contra reum*.

Thus far the focus to establish the requirements of accessibility and foreseeability has been placed on pre-existing international criminal case law. However, it should be stated that the existence of pre-existing jurisprudence is not a *sine qua non* requirement to establish the *nullum crimen sine iure certa* requirements. As has rightly been put forward by Judge *Robertson*, "[t]he requisite clarity will not necessarily be found in there having been previous successful prosecutions in respect of similar conduct, since there has to be a first prosecution for every crime and we are in the early stages of international criminal law enforcement."[332] Lacking jurisprudence, how could the requirements of accessibility and foreseeability then be established?

If one was to impose stringent demands on the requirements of accessibility to and foreseeability of customary international criminal law, one would apply—in the words of *Meron*—a "methodological conservatism".[333] Methodological conservatism is the proof of both elements of customary international law by a traditional approach on the basis of enduring, widespread and consistent State practice supported by a corresponding *opinio iuris*. It is thus clear that under such

---

[331]The ECtHR was concerned with a similar situation in the Case of *Kazakov v. Russia*, Application No. 1758/02, Judgment, 18 December 2008, para 24, where the Court held that despite pre-existing divergent case-law of Russian courts on the question whether the obligation to publish an apology was prescribed under Russian law, "the courts were reasonably inclined to interpret the notions of refutation or rectification as possibly including an apology." The ECtHR determined that foreseeability and accessibility was thus given in that case. It was only later that the Plenary Supreme Court authoritatively settled the issue by holding that an apology was not prescribed under Russian law.

[332]Dissenting Opinion Judge Robertson to the SCSL, *Norman* Appeals Chamber Decision, para 13.

[333]Cf. *T. Meron*, Editorial Comment, Revival of Customary Humanitarian Law, 99 American Journal of International Law (2005), 821f. It must be noted that *Meron* stated that "there is no inherent reason that such a requirement is compelled by the legality principle", id., 823.

a "methodological conservatism", accessibility/foreseeability is not established *via* international criminal law jurisprudence as an aid, a subsidiary mean, to make customary international norms tangible to individuals, but by establishing an objective accessibility/foreseeability to the underlying customary international criminal norm itself. Thus, under a "methodological conservatism" the *nullum crimen sine iure certa* and *praevia* requirements overlap. The *nullum crimen sine iure* principle might function as a legal restraint on the judge's ability to choose freely between different methods of determining customary law, requiring them to apply the traditional method.[334] Consequently, the judges would be required to prove lasting, widespread and consistent State practice supported by a corresponding *opinio iuris*, therewith the individual is adequately informed about the existence and content of customary international criminal norms. The traditional method to determine customary international criminal law could create a high level of certainty with regard to the *nullum crimen sine iure certa* requirements of accessibility and foreseeability. Such a restrictive and very positivistic approach would bar the judges from applying other, modern, progressive approaches to customary international law. However, in human rights jurisprudence the ECtHR case law reveals that the court has "eschewed an excessive positivism"[335] in the few cases were it had to elaborate on the questions of foreseeability and accessibility under Art. 7 ECHR in relation to the commission of international crimes. Rather, the ECtHR took the "flagrantly unlawful nature of the ill-treatment" into consideration.[336] Furthermore, as it seems the ECtHR is determined that the accessibility/foreseeability requirements need not establish absolute certainty of criminal punishment, but that the *nullum crimen sine iure certa* requirements are fulfilled if the individual could foresee *a risk of being prosecuted*.[337] In that regard the ECtHR only considers whether there was some international legal instrument generally available that could have placed the individual on notice of such a risk.[338] Astonishingly, the ECtHR held that foreseeability of a risk of being charged for an

---

[334]See also *T. Hoffmann*, The Gentle Civilizer of Humanitarian Law, in Stahn/van den Herik (eds.), Future Perspectives on International Criminal Justice (2010), 67, who determines that the SG Report on ICTY (supra note 196), demanding the ICTY to apply norms that are "beyond any doubt part of customary law" results in the "inescapable conclusion" that the ICTY "was obliged to use only the most conservative positivist methodology in finding the applicable law".

[335]*Schabas* (supra note 112), Art. 22, 404.

[336]ECtHR, *Kononov v. Latvia*, para 238; see also *Jorgić v. Germany*, Application No. 74613/01, Judgment, 12 July 2007, para 113 referring to "acts of a considerable severity".

[337]ECtHR, *Kononov v. Latvia*, para 238; *Ould Dah v. France*, Application No. 13113/03, Decision on Admissibility, 17 March 2009, p. 19.

[338]ECtHR, *Kolk and Kislyiy v. Estonia*, p. 9, stating that since the Soviet Union was a member State of the UN the "Soviet authorities" could not claim that they did not know about the development of crimes against humanity under international law by the development of the London Agreement and the General Assembly affirmation of the Nuremberg Principles. Official publication is not required according to the ECtHR: see ECtHR, *Kononov v. Latvia*, para 237 determined that it is irrelevant "that those international laws and customs were not formally published in the USSR or in the Latvian SSR".

international crime could even be established on basis of a progressive interpretation of the law by the court of a State party, even when the majority of legal writers and the practice of international criminal tribunals have favored a more restrictive application. In the *Jorgić* Case the ECtHR held in 2007 that the progressive interpretation of the crime of genocide by the German courts did not violate Art. 7 ECHR. The German courts did not consider the biological-physical destruction of a group to be a necessary element of the crime of genocide but instead relied on the social destruction of the group. According to the ECtHR the individual could foresee the risk of being prosecuted on basis of a minority opinion in the legal literature and the non-binding General Assembly Resolution 47/121 of 18 December 1992.[339] That result came as a surprise since the ICTY *Krstić* Trial Chamber previously held that in order to comply with the NCSI principle "despite recent developments [specifically referring to the German *Jorgić* Case], customary international law limits the definition of genocide to those acts seeking the physical or biological destruction of all or part of the group."[340] Nevertheless, the ECtHR came to the conclusion that the German courts' wide "interpretation of the crime of genocide could reasonably be regarded as consistent with the essence of that offence and could reasonably be foreseen by the applicant at the material time."[341] One needs to highlight the fact that in place of an expansive interpretation of the crime of genocide, it would have been possible to convict *Jorgić* under crimes against humanity, which would not have been problematic from the standpoint of the *nullum crimen sine iure* principle. Furthermore, German legal scholars consider that in light of the jurisprudence of international criminal tribunals, it seems questionable whether the German courts will adhere to their wide interpretation of genocide.[342] Nevertheless, it has to be noted that the ECtHR considers that the *nullum crimen sine iure certa* requirements are upheld if there is merely some material available that potentially places the individual on notice of a risk of prosecution.

In conclusion, it can be said that a determination of whether or not international criminal tribunals have potentially violated the *nullum crimen sine iure certa* in relation to the concrete underlying customary international criminal norm, depends on the level of certainty the principle shall protect. A high level of certainty of accessibility to the customary international criminal norm and foreseeability of criminal punishment could be established by the requirement of consistent pre-existing international criminal case law being used as subsidiary means that make customary international law tangible to individuals, or by a methodological

---

[339]ECtHR, *Jorgić v. Germany*, paras 103ff; the General Assembly in Res. 47/121 (1992) considered that "the abhorrent policy of 'ethnic cleansing' [...] is a form of genocide".

[340]ICTY, *Krstić* Trial Judgment, para 580.

[341]ECtHR, *Jorgić v. Germany*, para 114.

[342]See C. *Safferling* and S. *Kirsch*, Zehn Jahre Völkerstrafgesetzbuch, 44 Juristische Arbeitsblätter (2012), 483, who consider that instead German courts might enter convictions for crimes against humanity.

conservatism in relation to the determination of customary international criminal law. Furthermore a "methodological conservatism" could function as a legal restraint to the judge's ability to choose freely between different methods of customary law determination (*inter alia* by relying on modern approaches) and would require the judges to adhere to the traditional method when determining the existence and scope of customary international criminal law. On the other hand, the case law of the ECtHR seems to indicate that a lesser level of certainty might still be considered adequate to establish the criteria of accessibility and foreseeability. Indeed, if it suffices merely to establish a risk of a possible criminal prosecution, it seems that even progressive developments of international criminal law could be considered foreseeable, as long as there was theoretically some material available that placed the individual on notice. In that regard individuals have to anticipate any possible arguable interpretation of the scope of customary international criminal law, including "exotic" interpretations. Such a lesser level of certainty would consequently give judges considerable discretionary powers in determining whether the *nullum crimen sine iure certa* requirements have been violated in specific cases.

3.11   Concluding Remarks on the Principle of *Nullum Crimen Sine Iure*

In conclusion it can be said that the NCSL principle as applied in international criminal proceedings has been subjected to many changes. While in the post World War II era international criminal tribunals were in a position to treat it as an unbinding principle of justice, the firm inclusion of the NCSL principle in international human rights and humanitarian law treaties resulted in a changing treatment of the principle in recent years. Nevertheless, the theoretical and philosophical foundations that cannot be transposed from the domestic legal order to the international legal sphere, and the "Nuremberg Clause" in human rights treaties ensure, that in international criminal proceedings NCSL is a *sui generis* principle and is best referred to as the *nullum crimen sine iure* principle. This terminology secures that the sources of international criminal law also consist of unwritten sources. The guarantee of *nullum crimen sine iure scripta* is thus not legally required in international criminal law proceedings. The ICC, when applying the Rome Statute as the source of its criminal convictions, is generally bound by the *nullum crimen sine iure stricta*. However, it is argued that generally customary international criminal law *per se* cannot be applied analogously to expand criminal liability. Customary international criminal law either warrants the conclusion that the conduct in question is covered by the customary norm or it does not. There are different approaches in the jurisprudence of international criminal tribunals in relation to the *nullum crimen sine iure certa* requirements of accessibility and foreseeability: one approach systematically sweeps away objections in relation to accessibility and foreseeability, another is based on the concrete international criminal norm, while the final one is based on the criminality of the underlying conduct by taking recourse to domestic criminal law. For the reasons stated above, the present author considers it most suitable to establish accessibility to the concrete international criminal norm and foreseeability of its criminal punishment, while taking into account the nature and structure of international law.

Furthermore, *nullum crimen sine iure praevia* requires the existence of pre-established criminal norms on basis of the sources of public international law, such as international conventions, customary international law or general principles of law. However, that does not mean that all sources of public international law are to be considered adequate sources for the legal basis of individual criminal responsibility. International conventions generally stipulate inter-State obligations and are not drafted as penal provisions. As such they generally could not fulfill the *nullum crimen sine iure praevia* requirement. The vague nature of general principles of law precludes them from being an adequate legal basis for criminal convictions, as they fail to fulfill the *nullum crimen sine iure certa* requirement. Due to these shortcomings it was only natural that international criminal tribunals would focus on customary international criminal norms. Taking recourse to customary international law has a long tradition in international criminal proceedings. The IMT Nuremberg based its conviction on this source of law. The ICTY determined that its mandate obliged it to apply legal principles that are "beyond doubt part of customary international law" and has made criminal convictions dependent on the existence of customary international criminal norms, a view which has been adopted by other international criminal tribunals.[343]

However, international criminal tribunals should have been more specific in their elaboration of the *nullum crimen sine iure* requirements when the underlying source of criminalization was customary international criminal law. Before elaborating on the formation and determination of customary international law in public international law in general and in international criminal proceedings in particular, we must address some issues of the *nullum crimen sine iure* principle in relation to that particular source of international criminal law. The *nullum crimen sine iure praevia* requirement must be flexible to accept the different methodological approaches to customary international criminal law beyond the traditional method. Otherwise international criminal tribunals would have been obliged to establish proof of consistent, general and enduring State practice coupled with *opinio iuris* for each and every concrete crime and mode of liability within their jurisdiction. Thus, the acceptance of a flexible *nullum crimen sine iure praevia* requirement is a precondition to accept different methodological approaches. The *nullum crimen sine iure certa* requirements of accessibility and foreseeability gain all the more importance with the acceptance of a variety of methods. Regrettably, it is safe to say that the issues of accessibility to the concrete underlying customary international criminal norm and foreseeability of its criminal punishment, except in the case law

---

[343] See the references to the jurisprudence in supra note 247ff.

of the ECCC, have attracted little attention in the jurisprudence of international criminal tribunals. It is quite possible that because of the difficulty of establishing certainty when the legal basis is an unwritten source of law, international criminal tribunals have focused on the immorality of the underlying conduct or whether the conduct was criminal in a sense generally understood on basis of domestic criminal law or general principles of law.[344] Nevertheless, as argued in the previous chapter, the *certa* requirement shall be established on basis of the concrete underlying basis of criminalization, the customary international criminal norm. Whether or not the way customary international criminal law has been found by international criminal tribunals violates the *nullum crimen sine iure certa* requirement, however, depends on the level of certainty the principle shall protect.[345]

---

[344]See Sect. 3.10.6.3.1, The *certa* Requirement and the Moral Blameworthiness.

[345]See Sect. 3.10.6.4, The *certa* Requirement and Customary International Criminal Law.

Chapter 4
The Formation of Customary International Law and Its Methodological Challenges

4.1 Preliminary Remarks

Developing a methodological underpinning for customary international law has been a constant challenge. Indeed, customary law has become an inspiring source for innovative legal theories. Lacking a coherent theoretical basis, critics have suggested that customary international law has an "identity crisis",[1] or is "situated in a theoretical minefield."[2] Indeed, there appears to be no common consensus, on either a catalogue of specific rules that have attained the status of customary law, or on the doctrinal and methodological approaches required to establish and determine customary international law as a source of law. When discussing customary international law as a source of international law three levels have to be distinguished: (1) the nature of customary international law, (2) the constitutive elements necessary for the formation of customary international law and (3) the evidence for the identification of customary international law.[3]

The lack of any unifying approach to customary international law originates in the differing theories about the nature or basis of custom in schools of thought, such as natural law or positive law (*inter alia* being based on consent[4] or

---

[1]*B. Simma* and *P. Alston*, The Sources of Human Rights Law: Custom, Jus Cogens, and General Principles, 12 Australian Yearbook of International Law (1988–1989), 88. See also *J. P. Kelly*, The Twilight of Customary International Law, 40 Vanderbilt Journal of International Law (2000), 450: "[T]here is neither a common understanding of how customary international legal norms are formed, nor agreement on the content of those norms."

[2]*M. Koskenniemi*, The Pull of the Mainstream, 88 Michigan Law Review (1990), 1947.

[3]See also *L. Blutman*, Conceptual Confusion and Methodological Deficiencies: Some Ways that Theories on Customary International Law Fail, 25 European Journal of International Law (2014), 536.

[4]*C. L. Lim, O. Elias*, Withdrawing From Custom and the Paradox of Consensualism in International Law, 21 Duke Journal of Comparative & International law (2010), 143ff. See also *C. L. Lim, O. Elias*, The Paradox of Consensualism in International Law (1998).

© Springer International Publishing AG 2017
T. Rauter, *Judicial Practice, Customary International Criminal Law and* Nullum Crimen Sine Lege, DOI 10.1007/978-3-319-64477-6_4

belief[5]). These consequently influence the way customary international law is created, found or determined. Focusing on the classical distinction between positivism and naturalism, in natural law doctrine law is not created by humankind but is deduced from nature, the divine, reason, morality or justice.[6] The classics of international law theorists, such as *Francisco de Vitoria, Francisco Suarez, Hugo Grotius, Emerich de Vattel*, all shared the belief that customary international law could be based on human reason.[7] In natural law doctrines customary law is based on some form of declaratory evidence; it does not have constitutive elements, as customary law is not created, but is found and deduced from some higher "law". Over the course of the nineteenth century, natural law doctrine was gradually replaced by positivism.[8] Positivism separated law from nature or morality and determined that "law exists by *position*" being "set by men to men".[9] Positivism upholds a strictly normative and value-free concept of law. It is evident that customary law, being set by men, necessarily is created and thus requires constitutive elements.

But where are the elements, either constitutive or declarative, of customary international law to be found? Every theory of international customary law, be it traditional or modern, restrictive or progressive, starts with Art. 38 para 1 lit. b of the Statute of the International Court of Justice (ICJ Statute),[10] which describes international custom "as evidence of a general practice accepted as law". The wording suggests that customary law consists of two distinctive elements: State

---

[5]*B. D. Lepard*, Customary International Law – A New Theory with Practical Applications (2010), 8: "A customary international norm arises when states generally believe that it is desirable now or in the near future to have an authoritative legal principle or rule prescribing, permitting, or prohibiting certain conduct. This belief constitutes *opinio juris*, and it is sufficient to create a customary law norm."

[6]*A. Orakhelashvili*, Natural Law and Customary Law, 68 Zeitschrift für ausländisches, öffentliches Recht und Völkerrecht (2008), 71.

[7]See *H. G. Cohen*, Finding International Law: Rethinking the Doctrine of Sources, 93 Iowa Law Review (2007), 79ff with further references.

[8]In the wording of the Mexico-United States General Claims Commission, North American Dredging Company of Texas (USA) v. Mexico, March 1926, 4 Reports of International Arbitral Awards, 29f: "The law of nature may have been helpful, some three centuries ago, to build up a new law of nations, and the conception of inalienable rights of men and nations may have exercised a salutary influence, some one hundred and fifty years ago, on the development of modern democracy on both sides of the ocean; but they have failed as durable foundation of either municipal or international law and cannot be used in the present day as substitutes for positive municipal law, on the one hand, and for positive international law, as recognized by nations and governments through their acts and statements, on the other hand."

[9]*J. Austin*, The Province of Jurisprudence Determined (1832), 130. Compare also *S. Hall*, The Persistent Spectre: Natural Law, International Order and the Limits of Legal Positivism, 12 - European Journal of International Law (2001), 279.

[10]ICJ Statute, Art. 38.

practice as a material element and *opinio iuris* as a psychological element.[11] In the wording of the ICJ:

> [T]wo conditions must be fulfilled. Not only must the acts concerned amount to a settled practice, but they must also be such, or be carried out in such a way, as to be evidence of a belief that this practice is rendered obligatory by the existence of a rule of law requiring it. The need for such a belief, *i.e.* the existence of a subjective element, is implicit in the very notion of the *opinio juris sive necessitatis.* The states concerned must therefore feel that they are conforming to what amounts to a legal obligation.[12]

The importance of both elements, State practice and *opinio iuris*, for the determination of the existence of customary international law has been repeatedly highlighted in the jurisprudence of the ICJ.[13]

However, technically speaking, Art. 38 ICJ Statute is not an abstract determination of what the sources[14] of law are, but merely determines which law the ICJ has to apply when cases come before it.[15] This conclusion holds true even though widespread State practice uses the article as the authoritative enumeration of

---

[11] The publications on theories to custom or respectively on its elements are extensive, compare for example: *A. T. Guzman*, Saving Customary International Law, 27 Michigan Journal of International Law (2005), 115ff; *J. Kammerhofer*, Uncertainty in the Formal Sources of International Law: Customary International Law and Some of its Problems, 15 European Journal of International Law (2004), 523ff; *R. Kolb*, Selected Problems in the Theory of Customary International Law, 50 Netherlands International Law Review (2003), 119ff; *J. L. Slama*, Opinio Juris in Customary International Law, 15 Oklahoma City University Law Review (1990), 603ff; *F. L. Kirgis*, Custom on a Sliding Scale, 81 American Journal of International Law (1987), 146ff; *R. M. Walden*, The Subjective Element in the Formation of Customary International Law, 12 Israel Law Review (1977), 344ff; *A. Verdross*, Entstehungsweisen und Geltungsgrund des universellen völkerrechtlichen Gewohnheitsrechts, 29 Zeitschrift für ausländisches öffentliches Recht und Völkerrecht (1969), 635ff.

[12] ICJ, North Sea Continental Shelf Cases, para 77. This quotation refers to the current state of customary international law, while historically customary international law has been seen as "a manifestation of pre-existing law." For further discussion see *J. Kammerhofer*, Uncertainty in International Law – A Kelsenian Perspective (2011), 78 (footnote 92), with further references.

[13] ICJ, Continental Shelf Case (Libya v. Malta), Judgment, 3 June 1985, ICJ Reports (1985), para 27; Right of Passage over Indian Territory (Portugal v. India), Judgment, 12 April 1960, ICJ Reports (1960), 40; Asylum Case (Colombia v. Peru), Judgment, 20 November 1950, ICJ Reports (1959), 276.

[14] For a discussion on the meaning of the term 'source' see *G. J. H. van Hoof*, Rethinking the Sources of International Law (1983), 57.

[15] *L. Kirchmair*, Die Theorie des Rechtserzeugerkreises – Eine rechtstheoretische Untersuchung des Verhältnisses von Völkerrecht zu Staatsrecht am Beispiel der österreichischen Rechtsordnung (2013), 186, referring to *G. G. Fitzmaurice*, Some Problems Regarding the Formal Sources of International Law, in Koskenniemi (ed.), Sources of International Law (2000), 77 and *M. H. Mendelson*, The Subjective Element in Customary International Law, 66 British Yearbook of International Law (1995), 179 (footnote 9), who uses the metaphor that the court decides whether the fruit is ripe and does not describe its ripening process. Accepting Art. 38 ICJ Statute as the formal source of the sources of international law results, in the words of *Escorihuela*, in the "paradoxical exposition of the sources of law in a norm the very authority of which the sources are supposed to explain." See *A. L. Escorihuela*, Alf Ross: Towards a Realist Critique and Reconstruction of International Law, 14 European Journal of International Law (2003), 730.

sources of international law,[16] or even as the authoritative statement of the formal source of the sources of international law.[17]

A formal source of law is a norm on norm-creation, which clearly focuses on the procedural aspect of a source that denotes the processes of how rules of law are created or determined.[18] Thus, with regard to this procedural aspect of formal sources of law, a differentiation must be made between the term 'source'—used to stipulate the constitutive element(s) for rules of international law[19]—and the term 'source'—used to lay down the evidentiary manifestations[20] of these constitutive element(s).[21] If Art. 38 ICJ Statute were such a formal source of law in the former sense, this would infer that both State practice and *opinio iuris* are necessarily constitutive elements for customary law creation. Traditional and modern theories, however, differ on the relative importance of the two elements, with some approaches going so far as to deny the necessity to prove the other element altogether. Such approaches presuppose that the two elements are merely evidentiary and that the constitutive element(s) for customary law creation must then necessarily lie elsewhere, beyond the realm of Art. 38 ICJ Statute. Some authors have argued that the constitutive element(s) for customary law are to be found in what has been described by *Kammerhofer* as a "meta-norm",[22] or by others following

---

[16]*G. M. Danilenko*, Law-Making in the International Community (1993), 33ff with further references.

[17]*de Aréchaga* argues that Art. 38 ICJ Statute is "a rule about rules", *J. de Aréchaga*, Custom and Treaties, in Change and Stability in International Law-Making (1988), Cassese, Weiler (eds.), 1; see also *Kammerhofer* (supra note 11), 541(footnote 93) with further references.

[18]*International Law Association*, London Conference (2000), Committee on Formation of Customary (General) International Law, Final Report of the Committee, Statement of Principles Applicable to the Formation of General Customary International Law, Part I, Definitions, Use of terms (viii), 12. For a distinction of the formal and material sources of law, see *Fitzmaurice* (supra note 15), 57f, who describes material, historical and indirect sources of law as those that inspire and form "the content of the law", and formal, legal, and direct sources of law as the method by which content "is clothed with legal validity and obligatory force". The present thesis adheres to that distinction and thus uses a different conception of the terms "formal" and "material" sources than *I. Brownlie*, Principles of Public International Law (2008), 1, who understands material sources as providing "evidence of the existence of rules". *Kammerhofer* (supra note 11), 541, describes a formal source of law as the source of both the validity and origin of norms. *Van Hoof* (supra note 14), 59, distinguishes between three layers, similar to those established above: the first being the basis of the binding force of international law, which he understands in the sense of *Kelsen's* Grundnorm and which he claims to be that "State ought to behave as they have customarily behaved"; the second being the constitutive element of rules of international law, which he regards as being consent (76ff); and the third being "the relevant manifestations on the basis of which the presence or absence of the constitutive element" can be established.

[19]That would correspond to layer (2) as identified above.

[20]That would correspond to layer (3) as identified above.

[21]*van Hoof* (supra note 14), 59–60.

[22]*Kammerhofer* (supra note 11), 538ff.

Hart's terminology in a "secondary rule of recognition".[23] *Hart's* concept of law differentiates between primary and secondary rules. Primary rules regulate conduct stipulating what individuals must or must not do and are law simply because the rules are accepted as such. Secondary rules are an indication of a more developed legal system, which have been recognized by the members of the society. Secondary rules of recognition are procedural in character and "specify the ways in which the primary rules may be conclusively ascertained, introduced, eliminated, varied, and the fact of their violation conclusively determined."[24] *Hart* himself has excluded the possibility of secondary rules of recognition for the sphere of international law, deeming rules of international law binding as primary rules simply because "they are accepted and function as such".[25] Other writers, however, have adapted his doctrine of secondary rules of recognition for the creation process of international law in general and customary international law in particular.[26] Yet the nature of such a meta-norm or secondary rule remains uncertain. It has been argued that secondary rules on the creation of law are themselves based on customary law, that they are part of a constitutional, superior meta-law, that there is no uniform basis but a plurality of ways by which custom can be created, or that these norms themselves are not contained within sources of law but merely are the result of a formless consensus.[27] *Hart* himself has argued that the origin of a secondary rule is

---

[23] *van Hoof* (supra note 14), 60, states that the constitutive elements come close to what *Hart* describes secondary rule of recognition; see also *A. A. D'Amato*, The Concept of Custom in International Law (1971), 41–44; *R. M. Walden*, Customary International Law: A Jurisprudential Analysis, 13 Israel Law Review (1978), 87.

[24] *H. L. A. Hart*, The Concept of Law (1961), 92.

[25] *Hart* (supra note 24), 209; see also *H. Mosler*, Völkerrecht als Rechtsordnung, 36 Zeitschrift für ausländische, öffentliches Recht und Völkerrecht (1976), 32: "So rudimentär die Prozeduren der Bildung und Änderung von Recht sein mögen, sie müssen notwendigerweise existieren. Fehlt eine Institution, die von den Rechtsgenossen zur Gestaltung der Rechtsordnung gebildet ist, wie es beispielsweise innerhalb des Staates in der Regel die Volksvertretung zu sein pflegt, so ist es die Gesamtheit der Mitglieder, welche die Regeln des Zusammenlebens aufstellt. Das ist die Grundregel, die aus der internationalen Gesellschaft eine Rechtsgesellschaft macht."

[26] *D'Amato* (supra note 23), 41–44; *van Hoof* (supra note 14), 53–55.

[27] *Kammerhofer* (supra note 11), 539–40 referring *inter alia* to *A. Verdross*, Die Quellen des universellen Völkerrechts (1973), 20, *H. Mosler*, The International Society as a Legal Community (1980), 16, as well as to *G. M. Danilenko*, The Theory of International Customary Law, 31 German Yearbook of International Law (1988), 17: "[T]he recognition of custom by States as a source of international law [. . .] is determined by *objective extralegal factors inherent in the structure of the international community*." (emphasis added); on the other hand, *Danilenko* (supra note 16), 27, with reference to *Fitzmaurice* (supra note 15) argues that the "ultimate formal source of law" does not "derive from ordinary sources: these are rules of natural law"; *Kammerhofer* (supra note 12), 202, is particularly critical concerning the approach to explain a meta norm of customary law creation by a customary norm itself, referring to *A. Ross*, A Textbook of International Law (1947), 83: "[T]he doctrine of the sources can never in principle rest on precepts contained in one among the legal sources the existence of which the doctrine itself was meant to prove." Often scholars have invoked such a secondary rule by inferred or general consensus from States, see *M. Byers*, Custom, Power and the Power of Rules (1999), 143ff with further references.

based on facts rather than on a normative sense of a norm.[28] *Kammerhofer* rejects this approach. For his "meta-norm" he follows *Kelsen*, who insists that norms can only be created on basis of norms and not on basis of facts, keeping a clear distinction between the "Ought" and the "Is". However, *Kelsen's* Grundnorm, as the basis of a positivistic legal order, would itself not be a positive norm but a feigned norm, which is neither set nor has a content.[29] Following *Kelsen* the origin of the meta-norm is, according to *Kammerhofer*, not factual but "laid in an assumption of logic."[30]

Whatever the basis of such a meta-norm or secondary rule of recognition, it is evident that its presumed existence is also necessary for the existence of different theories of customary international law. Such a presumption can indeed be used to circumvent the necessity of both State practice and *opinio iuris* as the traditional constitutive elements for the creation of customary international law as enshrined in Art. 38 ICJ Statute. The assumption of a meta-norm or secondary rule of recognition would thus be necessary to accept one-element approaches to customary international law doctrinally, in which one element takes precedent over the other. Alternatively it could be used to determine that consent is the constitutive element of rules of international law, whereas the role of the two elements of custom, State practice and *opinio iuris*, would be restricted to the evidentiary role of making that consent visible.[31] *Cheng's* approach of instant customary international law being based on *opinio iuris*, allows that in practice the two elements would not necessarily

---

[28]*Hart* (supra note 24), 107: "The assertion that it [the secondary rule] exists can only be an external statement of fact. [. . .] Its existence is a matter of fact." See also *N. Petersen*, Customary Law without Custom? Rules, Principles, and the Role of State Practice in International Norm Creation, 23 American University Law Review (2008), 300: "It [Hart's secondary rule] has to be understood as empirical recognition rather than in the normative sense of a basic norm." See also ILA (supra note 18), Introduction, para 6, arguing that "rules about the sources of international law, and specifically this source [customary international law], are to be found in the practice of States." Critically *Kammerhofer* (supra note 11), 544, in relation to *Hart's* concept: "We are, in effect, asked to study which rules are in *fact* seen as creating rules; aptly exemplified by the English constitution where, so Hart thinks, Parliament and the courts are simply *recognized* as law-givers which *makes* them the valid law-givers" (emphasis in original).

[29]*Kammerhofer* (supra note 11), 544 referring to *H. Kelsen*, Allgemeine Theorie der Normen (1979), 206: "Nur eine Norm kann der Geltungsgrund einer anderen Norm sein." Furthermore: "Die Grundnorm einer positiven Moral-oder Rechtsordnung ist . . . keine positive, sondern eine bloß gedachte, und das heißt eine fingierte Norm . . . Nur wenn sie vorausgesetzt wird . . . können diese Sinngehalte als verbindliche Moral- oder Rechtsnormen gedeutet werden."

[30]*Kammerhofer* (supra note 11), 545. Just as the Grundnorm in *Kelsen's* theory is a legal fiction that lies above the entire legal system and cannot be verified or proven, so it seems the meta-norm of customary international law as a fiction must be logically assumed.

[31]Indeed as *van Hoof* stipulates that the constitutive element of rules of international law is 'consent' then the two elements of customary international law necessarily are not constitutive elements but merely give evidence of that consent, whereby it cannot be excluded that 'consent' could not be established on basis of one evidentiary element alone; see *van Hoof* (supra note 14), 76.

vanish. Rather, customary law would consist of only one constitutive element, while the second would serve as the evidentiary manifestation of the first.[32]

To explain the existence of different approaches to customary international law, other writers have not engaged in theoretical discussion, but cited the actual changes in the structure of international relations influencing the sources of international law and the that way they are determined, found or created.[33]

We are faced, therefore with a confusion of various theories and methodological approaches to customary international law. *Thirlway* is right to remark that "the view one takes of customary law, and particularly of the way it comes into existence, necessarily affects the view taken of the present and future part to be played by custom in developing the law."[34] However, one must remember that one-element approaches to customary international law are exceptional and by no means the generally accepted method of how customary rules come into existence or are found. Indeed, the prevailing view in legal literature and international jurisprudence remains the idea that customary international law is based on two elements, State practice and *opinio iuris*. It is still generally argued that one cannot simply bypass the requirements laid down in Art. 38 ICJ Statute.[35] Nevertheless, legal doctrine has elaborated different approaches to customary international law, which have been classified into so-called "traditional" and "modern" approaches.[36] This thesis will adhere to this classification. The following will provide an overview of both traditional and modern theories to customary international law, and consider their implications for the constitutive or evidentiary purposes of State practice and *opinio iuris*.

---

[32]*B. Cheng*, United Nations Resolutions on Outer Space: "Instant" International Customary Law, in Cheng (ed.), International law: Teaching and Practice (1982), 251: "[T]he role of usage in the establishment of rules of international customary law is purely evidentiary: it provides evidence on the one hand of the contents of the rule in question and on the other hand of the *opinio juris* of the States concerned. Not only is it unnecessary that the usage should be prolonged, but there need also be no usage at all in the sense of repeated practice, provided that the *opinio juris* of the States concerned can be clearly established. Consequently, international customary law has in reality only one constitutive element, the *opinio juris*."

[33]*R.B. Baker*, Customary International Law in the 21st Century: Old Challenges and New Debates, 21 European Journal of international Law (2010), 173: "[T]he debate over whether consistent state practice and opinio juris are the only building blocks of customary international law is over, because clearly, for better or for worse, they no longer are." *C. Tomuschat*, International Law: Ensuring the Survival of mankind on the Eve of a New Century, 281 Recueil des Cours (1999), 86.

[34]*H.W.A. Thirlway*, International Customary Law and Codification (1972), 46.

[35]*van Hoof* (supra note 14), 82. See in that regard in particular the position of the ILC in Sect. 4.4, The Identification of Customary International Law: The Challenge Ahead.

[36]*A. E. Roberts*, Traditional and Modern Approaches to Customary International Law: A Reconciliation, 95 American Journal of International Law (2001), 757ff; *Simma, Alston* (supra note 1), 88.

4.2   Traditional Customary International Law

4.2.1   *State Practice Under a Traditional Interpretation*

State practice is generally seen as the key element of customary international law according to the traditional line of thinking. *Schwarzenberger*, for example, describes custom as a "superstructure of a comparative analysis of State practice".[37] This argument follows an inductive approach by proving the existence of a customary norm on repetitive instances of State practice[38] with a clear focus on positive State actions,[39] while purely verbal claims by States do not suffice.[40] Customary international law thus crystallizes through a pattern of State practice by an abstraction from facts.[41] State practice is evaluated by its duration, consistency (uniformity) and generality,[42] making customary international law detectable through empirical analysis. However, there are no clear criteria to establish whether a practice is uniform, general and lasting.[43] Furthermore, the ICJ raised the possibility that one element may make up for the weakness of the others in the *North Sea Continental Shelf Cases.*[44]

Nevertheless, the ICJ considers the lack of sufficient State practice or conflicting State practice as detrimental to "the authority of a general rule of international

---

[37]*G. Schwarzenberger*, The Inductive Approach to International Law (1965), 35. According to *Schwarzenberger* "[i]n any field, the use of the inductive method presupposes the existence of a fair amount of case material from which plausible generalizations may be attempted", see *G. Schwarzenberger*, The Inductive Approach to International Law, 60 Harvard Law Review (1947), 541.

[38]In the words of Judge *Koretsky* in his Dissenting Opinion to the North Sea Continental Shelf Cases, 156: "customary international law turns its face to the past".

[39]Cf. *Roberts* (supra note 36), 758; *Simma, Alston* (supra note 1), 88.

[40]*D'Amato* (supra note 23), 88ff. See also the dissenting opinion of Judge Read in the ICJ Fisheries Case (United Kingdom v. Norway), Judgment, 18 December 1951, ICJ Reports (1951), 191: "Customary international law is the generalization of the practice of States. This cannot be established by citing cases where coastal States have made extensive claims, but have not maintained their claims by the actual assertion of sovereignty over trespassing foreign ships. [. . .] The only convincing evidence of State practice is to be found in seizures, where the coastal State asserts its sovereignty over the waters in question by arresting a foreign ship." See also *Thirlway* (supra note 34), 51.

[41]*Petersen* (supra note 28), 301.

[42]*A. Pellet*, Article 38, in Zimmerman et al (eds.), The Statute of the International Court of Justice – A Commentary (2012), 817–818, MN 221.

[43]Compare *Kolb* (supra note 11), 133ff; *Kammerhofer* (supra note 11), 530.

[44]ICJ, North Sea Continental Shelf Cases, para 74: "Although the passage of only a short period of time is not necessarily, or of itself, a bar to the formation of a new rule of customary international law on the basis of what was originally a purely conventional rule, an indispensable requirement would be that within the period in question, short though it might be, State practice, including that of States whose interests are specially affected, should have been both extensive and virtually uniform in the sense of the provision invoked."

law."[45] Technically speaking, uncertainty, contradiction, fluctuation or discrepancy in State practice prevents a customary norm from being established.[46] In contrast *D'Amato* considers that a theory of customary international law should always be "claim-oriented". In situations concerning competing claims, the claim that creates a relative superiority of persuasiveness wins.[47] His approach departs from the classical evaluation of State practice in terms of duration, consistency (uniformity) and generality, to one in which the prevailing number of precedents creates relative persuasiveness.[48]

4.2.2 Opinio Iuris Under a Traditional Interpretation

Within the traditional approach to customary international law the second element of customary international law, the *opinio iuris*, has been characterized quite differently:

Firstly, in what *D'Amato* considers the "traditional view" on *opinio iuris*, it represents the subjective conviction of States that their acts (*i.e.* State practice) are required by an existing rule of international law. In other words States believe in the legality of their State practice.[49] This traditional view on *opinio iuris* is useful in identifying existing customary international law. However, it cannot explain the creation of new customary law.[50] The so called paradox of *opinio iuris* has been dealt with extensively in the legal literature: For establishing new customary international law States need to believe that their State practice already conforms

---

[45]ICJ, Fisheries Case, 131. However, in the Nicaragua Case the court backpedaled from this position stating that it is deemed "sufficient that the conduct of states should, in general, be consistent with such rules and that instances of state conduct inconsistent with a given rule should generally have been treated as breaches of that rule, not as indications of the recognition of a new rule." See ICJ, Nicaragua Case, 98.

[46]ICJ, Asylum Case, 277.

[47]*D'Amato* (supra note 23), 18.

[48]*D'Amato* (supra note 23), 91: "There is no metaphysically precise (such as 'seventeen repetitions') or vague (such as 'in the Court's discretion') answer possible. States simply do not organize their behavior along absolute lines. There is no international 'constitution' specifying when acts become law. Rather, states resort to international law in claim-conflict situations. In such instances, counsel for either side will attempt to cite as many acts as possible. Thus we may say that persuasiveness in part depends upon the number of precedents."

[49]*D'Amato* (supra note 23), 73; *Thirlway* (supra note 34), 54, goes further claiming that *opinio iuris* could also include "that if the practice in question was not required by the law, it was in the process of becoming so", referring to the Dissenting Opinion of Judge Lachs to the ICJ, North Sea Continental Shelf Cases, 230–231: "[Other States] may also have been convinced that the instrument ... was intended to become and would in due course become general law (the teleological element is of no small importance in the formation of law)".

[50]*Slama* (supra note 11), 605.

to a legal norm which they are about to establish.[51] It is unclear how, under this condition, a new customary rule emerges, unless we assume that at first States acted in legal error when establishing the customary norm.[52] It is difficult to conceive of an erroneous belief as an adequate basis for a legal norm.[53] The only way to maintain the traditional view on *opinio iuris* in relation to the creation of new customary norms would be to drop the requirement of simultaneousness of State practice and *opinio iuris*.[54] For such a creation of customary international law it is best to view the creation of customary international law as an evolving process. At first some States initiated the first practice, and with evolving generality, uniformity and duration that State practice was gradually joined by *opinio iuris*.[55] In the words of the ICJ in the North Sea Continental Shelf Cases:

> Some States have at first probably accepted the rules in question, as States usually do, because they found them convenient and useful, the best possible solution for the problems involved. Others may also have been convinced that the instrument elaborated [. . .] was to become and would in due course become general law. [. . .] Many States have followed suit under the conviction that it was law. [. . .].[56]

Secondly, some authors have argued that *opinio iuris* could be left aside altogether, rejecting any need to provide a separate analysis of the psychological element in the creation of customary international law.[57] Such a perception imagines customary international law as a source of law that follows a pattern of historical behavior. This is reflected in *Kelsen's* postulate that "states ought to behave as they have customarily behaved".[58] Various authors have argued that *Kelsen's* approach to customary international law, in which *opinio iuris* would not need to be shown separately from State practice, as deviating from the positivistic understanding that law emerges from State will. Based only on a historical pattern of State practice, it seems that customary international law results not from an

---

[51]See for example: *D'Amato* (supra note 23), 66; *Kammerhofer* (supra note 12), 78.

[52]*H. Kelsen*, Théorie du droit international coutumier, 1 Revue internationale de la théorie du droit (1939), 263; see also *Cheng* (supra note 32), 259; *van Hoof* (supra note 14), 87 (footnote 318) with further references.

[53]*O. Elias*, The Nature of the Subjective Element in Customary International Law, 33 International and Comparative Law Quarterly (1995), 503; *D'Amato* (supra note 23), 66: "it is the difficulty of imagining that all states participating in custom-formation were erroneously advised by their legal counsel as to the requirements of prior international law." *Kelsen* (supra note 52), 263.

[54]*van Hoof* (supra note 14), 91ff; see also *Elias* (supra note 53), 508.

[55]*Simma, Alston* (supra note 1), 88.

[56]ICJ, North Sea Continental Shelf Cases, para 78.

[57]*Kolb* (supra note 11), 121 referring to *P. Guggenheim*, Les deux éléments de la coutume en droit international, La technique et les principes du droit public: Etudes en l'honneur de Georges Scelle, Vol. 1 (1959), 275; *M. H. Mendelson*, The Formation of Customary International Law, 272 Recueil des Cours (1998), 289ff; *Kelsen* (supra note 52), 253ff who considered that *opinio iuris* solely disguised the law creating power of judges in the formation of customary international law; see also *I. Brownlie*, Principles of Public International Law (2008), 8. ILA (supra note 18), Part III: the Subjective Element, 29ff.

[58]*H. Kelsen*, Principles of International Law (1952), 418.

element of legislative State will, but from unintentional State acts.[59] *Kammerhofer* comes to *Kelsen's* defense, arguing that for the Austrian jurist the factual acts contained an element of will. This will of States manifests itself in *Kelsen's* postulate that "States ought to observe the behavioral regularity". Although it does not form a legislative will for individual customary norms, the postulate nevertheless includes a will element on the basis of a collective will to observe customary regularity.[60]

The most serious criticism against a dismissal of the role of *opinio iuris* is that State practice is value-free. Without some further element the practice alone can only be descriptive and not prescriptive.[61] Not every State act is envisaged to contribute or conform to a customary rule. The addition of *opinio iuris* serves as a means to distinguish acts based on legal obligations from acts of good will, habit or courtesy.[62] The PCIJ[63] and the ICJ[64] favour the inductive approach, which proves the existence of a customary norm on repetitive instances of State practice with the addition of *opinio iuris* as a necessary element to determine customary international law. In practice, however, the case law of the ICJ reveals a hesitation to delve into a search for the psychological element, revealing what *Koskenniemi* terms a "lack of a specific method for ascertaining the *opinio juris*".[65] It seems that even in the case law of the ICJ, the existence of *opinio iuris* as a means to distinguish legal obligations from non-binding usage is assumed when there is evidence of general State practice.[66]

---

[59]*Kammerhofer* (supra note 11), 546, referring to the criticism of *J. Raz*, The Concept of a Legal System (1980), 67 and *H. Günther*, Zur Entstehung von Völkergewohnheitsrecht (1970), 81–83.

[60]*Kammerhofer* (supra note 11), 547.

[61]*Kammerhofer* (supra note 11), 61.

[62]ICJ, Right of Passage over Indian Territory, 42–43; Asylum Case, 276–277; Jurisdictional Immunities of the State (Germany v. Italy: Greece Intervening), Judgment, 3 February 2012, ICJ Reports (2012) (Jurisdictional Immunities Case), para 55.

[63]PCIJ, Lotus Case.

[64]See the references to the jurisprudence in supra note 13.

[65]*M. Koskenniemi*, From Apology to Utopia (2005), 427ff, referring to the PCIJ's Lotus Case, the ICJ's Asylum Case, Fisheries Jurisdiction Cases, North Sea Continental Shelf Cases and US Military and Paramilitary Activities Case. The ILA (supra note 18), Section 19, p. 41 comes to a similar conclusion.

[66]See in this regard ICJ, North Sea Continental Shelf Cases, para 78: "[T]he general practice of States should be recognized as prima facie evidence that it is accepted as law"; Nicaragua Case, para 202: "existence in the *opinio juris* of States of the principle on non-intervention is backed by established and substantial practice"; cf. *I. Brownlie*, Principles of Public International Law (2008), 8; *R. Heinsch*, Die Weiterentwicklung des humanitären Völkerrechts durch die Strafgerichtshöfe für das ehemalige Jugoslawien und Ruanda (2007), 298–299; *Koskenniemi, id,* 427ff referring to a hypothesis of *opinio iuris* based on State practice. *Mendelson* (supra note 57), 283–293; *J.-M. Henckaerts*, Customary International Humanitarian Law (2005) (ICRC Custom Study), Vol. I: Rules, xlvi. In other instances the ICJ as well as the PCIJ explicitly referred to *opinio iuris*, however, mostly when negating the existence of customary international law, see e.g. ICJ, North Sea Continental Shelf Cases, paras 74–78; PCIJ, Lotus Case, 15–19.

Thirdly, others, most prominently *Kelsen*, departed from the conception of *opinio iuris* as acting in conformity with a legal norm but also included extra-legal features, such as a "sentiment of morality, equity, or justice".[67] While the modern doctrine of public international law reproduces the subjective element of customary international law in an abbreviated form as *opinio iuris* requiring a legal conviction, historically the phrase as a whole reads *opinio iuris sive necessitatis* ("an opinion of law or necessity"). Consequently, it has been argued that the psychological element could also include a conviction of the social, moral or political necessity and could thus include extra-legal convictions.[68] However, a strict positivistic understanding of law presupposes a legal rule and as such *opinio iuris* should be based on a legal conviction: "an alleged rule is not law just because it is (alleged to be) socially necessary."[69]

Finally, another theory would equate *opinio juris* with consent or acquiescence, thus requiring some form of State consent, either directly or implicitly.[70] This is the reason why the idea of a legislative will element by States has also been put forward under the concept of *opinio iuris*.[71] To adhere to the perception that international law is consensual in nature, various writers do not perceive *opinio iuris* as a belief that the State practice is required by law but understand custom as a "tacit agreement", rather than an agreement in written form, that places State consent at the centre of attention.[72] This voluntaristic conception that State consent is required to create law has the advantage of solving the *opinio iuris* paradox, because it recognizes the legislative will of States and thus the constitutive nature of custom.[73]

---

[67]*D'Amato* (supra note 23), *67 inter alia* referring to *Kelsen* (supra note 52), 263; compare also *Kammerhofer* (supra note 12), 79.

[68]For a more recent proposition to use an *opinio necessitatis* for establishing a customary rule of humanitarian intervention see *A. Cassese*, A Follow-Up: Forcible Humanitarian Countermeasures and Opinio Necessitatis, 10 European Journal of International Law (1999), 797ff.

[69]*Mendelson* (supra note 57), 271. *Hilpold* heavily criticized the approach taken by *Cassese* (supra note 68) in the following volume of the European Journal of International Law stating that an *opinio necessitatis* approach "is very dangerous for a consensus-oriented order as it introduces a unilateral element disguised as a constitutional norm, a higher ranking provision which allows no further discussion, thereby implying that the values on which this norm rests are commonly shared." See *P. Hilpold*, Humanitarian Intervention: Is there a Need for a Legal Reappraisal?, 12 European Journal of International Law (2001), 461–462.

[70]*D'Amato* (supra note 23), 68.

[71]Most famously pronounced by the PCIJ in the Lotus Case, para 44: "International law governs relations between independent States. The rules of law binding upon States therefore emanate from their own free will as expressed in conventions or by usages generally accepted as expressing principles of law and established in order to regulate the relations between these co-existing independent communities or with a view to the achievement of common aims. Restrictions upon the independence of States cannot therefore be presumed." See also ICJ, Nicaragua Case, para 135: "in international law there are no rules, other than such rules as may be accepted by the State concerned, by treaty or otherwise."

[72]Most prominently *G.I. Tunkin*, Co-Existence and International Law, 95 Recueil des Cours (1958), 13.

[73]*Walden* (supra note 11), 344ff with further references and 355; *Verdross* (supra note 11), 636–637 with further references. *Elias* (surpa note 53), 501; *Kammerhofer* (supra note 12), 77.

The consensual nature of custom is explained by some authors with reference to the persistent objector rule: During the formation of customary international law a State can prevent the applicability of that customary rule through consistent and repeated objection. Thus, in theory a State cannot be bound against its free will.[74]

On basis of the theory of customary international law being based on individual State consent, various authors have adopted a different understanding of "consent". This not only comprises explicit consent, but includes forms of inferred or implied consent. Customary international law is thus perceived as "a continuous process of raising mutual claims and the adoption of an attitude to such claims"[75] by either accepting them (not only through active participation but also by tacit agreement, *i.e.* acquiescence) or by rejecting them *via* protest (the persistent objector).[76] While treaty law is based on explicit consent as an opt-in system, customary international law, being based on inferred consent, is an opt-out system by the persistent objector doctrine.[77] There are, however, some protective measures, suggested for individual States: *Danilenko* claims that only States whose interests are specifically affected and that had knowledge of the newly establishing customary international law could be said to have acquiesced to its formation.[78] Nevertheless, generally it is argued that a tacit or inferred consent theory fails to explain why new States that never had the opportunity to object to customary international law are bound by it,[79] or why customary international law should bind States that only become affected after the customary international law norm has already been created.[80] More fundamentally it has been rightly questioned, if "silence does in fact equal consent."[81] Other writers,

---

[74]*J. I. Charney*, The Persistent Objector Rule and the Development of Customary International Law, 56 British Yearbook of International Law (1985), 16: "It is difficult to see how the acceptance of the [persistent objector] rule does not reflect an acceptance of the consent theory of international law. If a mere objection to an evolving rule of law can prevent application of that rule to the State, then each State has the unilateral power to decide whether or not to be bound by the rule." Contrary to that view, *Kolb* (supra note 11), 144: "If customary law were really voluntary, the whole doctrine of the persistent objector would be useless. For in not acquiescing in an emerging rule of international law, a state would automatically not be bound by this new rule."

[75]*K. Wolfke*, Custom in Present International Law (1964), 56.

[76]*Byers* (supra note 27), 142–146 states that customary international law does not depend on explicit consent but is based on "inferred consent"; see also *M. Akehurst*, Custom as a Source of International Law, 47 British Yearbook of International Law (1977), 38–42.

[77]*N. Petersen*, The Role of Consent and Uncertainty in the Formation of Customary International Law, in Lepard (ed.), Reexamining Customary International Law, available at: www.coll.mpg.de/pdf_dat/2011_04online.pdf (last visited 16 June 2017), 2.

[78]See *Danilenko* (supra note 16), 108.

[79]*Guzman* (supra note 11), 144 (footnote 125); *Byers* (supra note 27), 145; *I. M. L. de Souza*, The Role of State Consent in the Customary Process, 44 The International and Comparative Law Quarterly (1995), 533–534.

[80]*Kelsen* uses the example of a State that has just gained access to the sea but finds itself already bound by the customary rules in that regard, *Kelsen* (supra note 58), 312; see also *de Souza* (supra note 79), 534.

[81]*Kammerhofer* (supra note 12), 78.

having an international community approach in mind, have suggested that a general or common consensus of States, not an individual State consent, would suffice as a requirement for *opinio iuris*.[82]

4.2.3 Traditional Customary International Law: Practical Concerns and Its Slow Development

This overview of different theories analyzed here reveals varying theoretical underpinnings of the two elements of customary international law, State practice and *opinio iuris*. Following the conception of the ICJ that both elements are necessary elements for the formation of customary international law, it is argued that customary international law is best described as a "form of organic law-making".[83] It involves a mixture of both, a material element in the form of State practice, and a subjective element, *opinio iuris*. The second element is construed either as a belief that the practice is required by law, or a legislative will element by States giving either individual consent or establishing common consensus in order to prove the existence of a customary norm.[84]

When one leaves the safe though highly contested waters of the theoretical foundations of traditional customary international law, and tries to test those theoretical concepts in practical cases, one quickly encounters difficulties. Adhering to a two-element approach to customary international law consisting of State practice as a factual element and *opinio iuris* as a belief that the practice is required by law, is easier said than done. The following example shall illustrate: If strictly applied to customary international humanitarian law, one of the components of international criminal law,[85] the traditional approach requires repetitive State action on the battlefield, performed by members of national armies accompanied by *opinio iuris*.[86] However, international humanitarian law in most of its parts prohibits certain acts of warfare, and thus requires the abstention from acting.[87] Various writers agree that abstentions do count as State practice in the process of customary

---

[82]*A. D'Amato*, Consent, Estoppel, and Reasonableness: Three Challenges to Universal International Law, 10 Virginia Journal of International Law (1969), 3 who also interprets the PCIJ's Lotus Case in that way; *A. Pellet*, The Normative Dilemma: Will and Consent in International Law-Making, 12 Australian Yearbook of International Law (1991), 37; *de Souza* (supra note 79), 537; *de Aréchaga* (supra note 17), drawing that conclusion from the case law of the ICJ.

[83]*Kolb* (supra note 11), 144.

[84]*Ibid.*

[85]*M. C. Bassiouni*, Introduction to International Criminal Law (2003), 1.

[86]See the position of a member of the Judge Advocate's Office of the US as cited by *Cassese* in Cassese and Weiler (eds.), Change and Stability in International Law-Making (1988), 24: "State practice on humanitarian law and the laws or warfare is the practice of the battlefield; it is the members of the army who make practice."

[87]*Heinsch* (supra note 65), 298.

law creation,[88] and can be circumscribed as instances of passive practice.[89] However, not every omission can lead to the establishment of customary international law. In certain instances, only if States possessed the means to participate in the State practice (e.g. the technological ability) and knowingly abstained to participate, could that abstention be meaningful for the development of customary international law.[90] Such restrictions decrease the number of subjects that could potentially contribute to the formation of customary international law. Furthermore, in cases of passive practice, *opinio iuris* gains greater significance to show that States have consciously abstained from acting due to a legal duty under international law. As the Permanent Court of International Justice (PCIJ) stated in the *Lotus* Case, "for only if such abstention were based on their being conscious of having a duty to abstain would it be possible to speak of an international custom."[91] One way this passage of the PCIJ has been interpreted is that an abstention can only then be qualified as an instance of State practice if it is underpinned by a corresponding *opinio iuris*.[92] However, such an assertion would abolish the distinctive characteristics of State practice on the one hand and *opinio iuris* on the other. It is not *opinio iuris* that turns omissions into State practice. As stated above, it is a characteristic of State practice in particular that it is value free. The proper approach is to identify instances of omission as State practice, and with just the addition of *opinio iuris* customary international law can be established.[93] The problem is that while State acts consisting of active behavior may be used as relevant evidence for both elements,[94] in the case of abstentions this is not possible.[95] The *opinio iuris* element must be established separately. Therefore, and

---

[88]*M. Akehurst*, Custom as a Source of International Law, 47 British Yearbook of International Law (1977), 10; *Mendelson* (supra note 57), 207; *H. Spieker*, Völkergewohnheitsrechtlicher Schutz der natürlichen Umwelt im internationalen bewaffneten Konflikt (1992), 80ff; *Kammerhofer* (supra note 11), 529 with further references.

[89]*Kammerhofer* (supra note 11), 529; *Danilenko* (supra note 27), 28; *Heinsch* (supra note 65), 298.

[90]*Spieker* (supra note 88), 83ff, in relation to the customary prohibition of warfare that is damaging to the environment, analysis that omissions can only then be coined as State practice if States possess the technological premises to use weapons that are damaging to the environment. See also *M. E. Villiger*, Customary International Law and Treaties (1997), 39; *D'Amato* (supra note 23), 81, 82: "surely one cannot draw any conclusion from the fact that a state did not do what it was not capable of doing."

[91]PCIJ, Lotus Case, 28; A similar approach is taken by the ICRC in its Custom Study (supra note 66), Vol. I: Rules, xxxviii.

[92]*Heinsch* (supra note 65), 299: "Die einzige Methode, um ein Unterlassen auch als relevante Staatenpraxis zu akzeptieren, besteht darin, dass das Unterlassen von einer entsprechenden *opinio iuris* begleitet wird."; ICRC Custom Study (supra note 66), Vol. I: Rules, xlvi *Elias* (surpa note 53), 502 referring to the role of *opinio iuris* in "qualifying State practice". See also *Byers* (supra note 27), 148 who considers that *opinio iuris* can be used to distinguish between legally relevant and legally irrelevant State practice.

[93]*Spieker* (supra note 88), 81.

[94]See supra note 66.

[95]*Spieker* (supra note 88), 82–83 with further references.

somewhat regrettably, it is much easier to demonstrate that States are not willing to adhere to rules of customary humanitarian law, by attacking civilians for example, than proving that the sparing of civilians resulted from deliberate compliance.[96] With that being said, it is safe to conclude that the prohibitive demands of international humanitarian law demonstrate the limits of the traditional approach to customary international law.

Apart from these practical difficulties in establishing proof of the existence of customary international law, another weighty critique of the traditional approach is its necessarily slow development. The requirements of uniformity, generality and duration of State practice prevent it from partaking in legal advances. The tension between the cumbersome process of a traditional customary law creation and the need for a speedy legal adaption to new challenges has been expressed by the ICJ in its Advisory Opinion on the *Legality or Threat or Use of Nuclear Weapons*. Referring to the *Continental Shelf Cases*, the Court adhered to the requirement of actual practice and *opinio iuris* of States,[97] but not without regrets:

> The emergence, as *lex lata*, of a customary rule specifically prohibiting the use of nuclear weapons as such is hampered by the continuing tensions between the nascent *opinio juris* on the one hand, and the still strong adherence to the practice of deterrence on the other.[98]

It was the conviction that a traditional understanding of customary international law could not adequately respond to pressing moral and global challenges that generated other theories to customary law, which have been labeled "modern customary law".

4.3 Modern Customary International Law

4.3.1 Preliminary Remarks

The shortcomings of traditional perception of international customary law have led to a broad variety of more dynamic or modern approaches. These "modern" conceptions have been developed in order to ensure that customary international law can respond adequately and more quickly to global challenges. These modern conceptions can be divided into two groups: Firstly, there are approaches that focus on the procedural alteration of customary international law, that is to say the way customary international law can be identified, either by widening the scope of State

---

[96]One might consider that for these reasons the ICTY, *Tadić* Appeals Chamber Jurisdiction Decision, at para 99 disclaimed "the actual behavior of the troops" as relevant State practice and prefers that "on account of the inherent nature of this subject-matter, reliance must primarily be placed on such elements as official pronouncements of States, military manuals and judicial decisions."

[97]ICJ, Nuclear Weapons Advisory Opinion, para 64.

[98]ICJ, Nuclear Weapons Advisory Opinion, para 73.

practice or elevating *opinio iuris* to the real determining element. Secondly, there are approaches that use the underlying subject matter in order to argue that certain contexts require different forms of determining customary international law.

4.3.2 The Procedural Aspect of Modern Customary International Law

When establishing the existence of customary international law, for some authors the element of State practice had to be broadened, to embrace not only physical acts of States but also their verbal acts such as policy statements and press releases, and their conduct in international organizations including the resolutions for which they vote.[99] In short: "State practice covers any act or statement by a State from which views can be inferred about international law."[100] The International Law Association (ILA) is one of the key proponents arguing that resolutions of international or intergovernmental organizations are also a form of State practice, viewing them as "a series of verbal acts by the individual member States participating in that organ."[101] According to the ICTY *Tadić* Appeals Chamber in the field of international humanitarian law, the utilization of actual State behaviour is not suitable to establish customary international law, making verbal acts and paper practice indispensable:

> In appraising the formation of customary rules or general principles one should [...] be aware that, on account of the inherent nature of this subject-matter, reliance must primarily be placed on such elements as official pronouncements of States, military manuals and judicial decisions.[102]

The International Committee of the Red Cross (ICRC), while accepting the traditional dichotomy between State practice and *opinio iuris*, also included both physical and verbal acts within the element of State practice.[103] The ICRC caveats

---

[99]ILA (supra note 18), Part II: The Objective Element: State Practice, pp. 13–20, the ILA however opens up the possibility that verbal practice, while being able to evince State practice could be attributed less weight than "actual" practice; *M.N. Shaw*, International Law (2008), 82; *I. Brownlie*, Principles of Public International Law (2008), 6; *Simma, Alston* (supra note 1), 89 referring to a "dubious metamorphosis" of State practice.

[100]Cf. *Akehurst* (supra note 88), 10, see also 53.

[101]ILA (supra note 18), Section 11 at p. 19. This view is also shared by *Akehurst* (supra note 88), 53.

[102]ICTY, *Tadić* Appeals Chamber Jurisdiction Decision, para 99.

[103]See ICRC Custom Study (supra note 66), Vol. I: Rules, xxxviii. However, the ICRC has been criticized by the US expressing its concern about the methodology stating that the State practice delivered by the ICRC Custom Study is "insufficiently dense to meet the 'extensive and virtually uniform' standard generally required to demonstrate the existence of a customary rule" and that it "places too much emphasis on written materials, such as military manuals and other guidelines published by States, as opposed to actual operational practice by States during armed conflict". See further *J. B. Bellinger and W. J. Haynes*, A US government response to the International Committee of the Red Cross study Customary International Humanitarian Law, 89 Review of the Red Cross (2007), 444–445.

its classification with the reminder that the separation of practice and *opinio iuris* is "very difficult and largely theoretical".[104] It is evident that expanding the scope of State practice to instances that were traditionally used to establish *opinio iuris* comes at the expense of the *opinio iuris* element.[105] Indeed, the element loses any significance if the State's verbal claim of a right forms State practice and at the same time *opinio iuris*.[106] *Mendelson* tries to solve the problem by means of prohibiting the dual exploitation of one instance as both State practice and *opinio iuris*.[107] This remedy, however, smacks of a frantic adherence to the traditional two-element theory of customary law. A modern understanding of State practice may result in a "purposive (subjective) concept" of State practice as the psychological element is already incorporated within the instance of State practice.[108] However, it would be wrong to assume that a wide understanding of State practice, including verbal statements, necessarily results in a single element approach to customary international law.[109] Technically speaking, one cannot assume on this basis that State practice should be seen as the sole constituent element of customary international law. State practice and *opinio iuris* would both still remain constitutive elements, while

---

[104]ICRC Custom Study (supra note 66), Vol. I: Rules, xlvi.

[105]See for instance *De Witte* in relation to the discussion "The Classical "Sources" of International Law Revisited in Cassese, Weiler (eds.), Change and Stability in International Law-Making (1988), 14; contrary *Wolfke* states that "customs arise from acts of conduct and not from promises of such acts." He would thus distinguish between physical acts and verbal acts. While verbal acts deliver evidence of the *opinio iuris* by their content they can only be used as State practice in a narrow sense as State practice on making verbal statements, but they do not provide for State practice in relation to their content. See *Wolfke* (supra note 75), 42–43; for a strict separation of State practice as physical acts and *opinio iuris* see *D'Amato* (supra note 23), 88: "[A] claim is not an act. [...] But the claims themselves, although they may articulate a legal norm, cannot constitute the material component of custom."

[106]See further: *Kammerhofer* (supra note 11), 525;. R. *Müllerson*, The Interplay of Objective and Subjective Elements in Customary Law, in K. Wellens (ed.), International Law: Theory and Practice: Essays in Honour of Eric Suy (1998), 162; see also *I. Brownlie*, Principles of Public International Law (2008), 8, who does not differentiate between State practice and *opinio iuris* in his list of evidence for customary international law: "diplomatic correspondence, policy statements, press releases, the opinions of official legal advisers, official manuals on legal questions, e.g. manuals of military law, executive decisions and practices, orders to naval forces etc., comments by governments on drafts produced by the International law Commission, state legislation, international and national judicial decisions, recitals in treaties and other international instruments, a pattern of treaties in the same form, the practice of international organs, and resolutions relating to legal questions in the United Nations General Assembly."

[107]*Mendelson* (supra note 57), 206–7, who considers however that *opinio iuris* needs to be established only in cases of doubt, see *ibid*, 292.

[108]*Kammerhofer* (supra note 12), 66–67.

[109]See P. *Haggenmacher*, La doctrine des deux éléments du droit coutumier dans la pratique de la Cour internationale, 90 Revue générale de droit international public (1986), 114: "Les deux prétendus éléments n'ont en réalité aucune individualité propre; ils se trouvent inextricablement mêlés au sein d'une 'pratique' unitaire. Cette pratique forme pour ainsi dire un seul 'élément' complexe, fait d'aspects 'matériels' et 'psychologiques'."

their evidence would be established on the same instances.[110] Although practically one and the same evidence could thus establish both elements, customary international law would nevertheless consist of two distinct constituent elements.

Another modern interpretation of customary international law suggests that *opinio iuris* is the dominating element. *Cheng's* notion of "instant custom" reduces the role of State practice to a purely evidentiary function: no usage is required in the sense of repeated practice as long as the belief or will of States (*opinio iuris*) is clearly established.[111] Through general statements, proclamations, and incantations deduced from the international *fora* by reference to multilateral treaties or resolutions of international organizations—that is by means of a deductive approach— international customary law can be instantly established by voiced *opinio iuris*.[112] That approach sits uneasily with the very notion of customary law, since when supplanting the element of repetitive State practice through *opinio iuris*, very little custom is left within customary international law.[113] It appears revolutionary in the light of the ICJ's mantra-like emphasis on both *opinio iuris* and State practice. However, a closer look at the Court's jurisprudence reveals remarkable concessions, many of them concealed. When the ICJ was concerned with customary international law relating to the prohibition of the use of force in the *Nicaragua Case,* it formally adhered to the two element requirements. While stating that "the Court may not disregard the essential role played by general practice", it added that "the existence of the rule in the *opinio juris* of States is confirmed by practice".[114] Some authors interpret these lines as evidence for the growing predominance of *opinio iuris* while State practice is reduced to an evidentiary function.[115] When analyzing the abstention from using force, the ICJ focused on *opinio iuris* deduced from General Assembly resolutions, the States' attitude toward these resolutions

---

[110]*Wolfke* (supra note 75), 42–45 states that there is a "notorious confusion of that element [referring to *opinio iuris*] with its evidence." *Zemanek* considers that "separating material recording 'State practice' from material recording *opinio juris*, though theoretically perhaps desirable, is practically impossible because the first may, through its language, evidence the second.", K. *Zemanek*, What is State Practice and Who Makes it?, in Beyerlin et al. (eds.), Recht zwischen Umbruch und Bewahrung: Völkerrecht, Europarecht, Staatsrecht: Festschrift für Rudolf Bernhardt (1995), 292; see also *Kammerhofer* (supra note 12), 69–70, who considers that the distinction of element and evidence would only shift the problem and reveal an "epistemological uncertainty".

[111]*Cheng* (supra note 32), 251; see also *Simma, Alston* (supra note 1), 89 and *Guzman* (supra note 11), 149.

[112]*Roberts* (supra note 36), 758ff; *Simma, Alston* (supra note 1), 89.

[113]R. Y. *Jennings*, The Identification of International Law, in Cheng (ed.), International law: Teaching and Practice (1982), 5: "[W]hat we perversely persist in calling customary international law is not only *not* customary law: it does not even faintly resemble a customary law." *Wolfke* (supra note 75), 40–41: "Without practice (*consuetudo*), customary international law would obviously be a misnomer, since practice constitutes precisely the main *differentia specifica* of that kind of international law." (emphasis in original).

[114]ICJ, Nicaragua Case, paras 183–4.

[115]See e.g. T. *Meron*, The Humanization of International Law (2006), 102. See also G. *Werle*, Principles of International Criminal Law (2009), 368.

and other soft law instruments[116]; indeed, the Court entirely neglected traditional State practice despite its "lip service"[117] to the formal requirements of customary law formation. One could therefore conclude that in abstract theory the ICJ adheres to the traditional requirements, State practice and *opinio iuris*, but that in fact it applied a modern customary law approach focusing on *opinio iuris*. However, the Nicaragua judgment does not prejudge the Court's approach, given that its Advisory Opinion on the Legality of the Threat or Use of Nuclear Weapons demonstrates a strong adherence to the State practice of deterrence which trumped the nascent *opinio iuris*.[118] Again in 2013 the ICJ upheld the traditional two elements approach, stating that "the existence of a rule of customary international law requires that there be 'a settled practice' together with *opinio juris*" and that it "is of course axiomatic that the material of customary international law is to be looked for primarily in the actual practice and *opinio juris* of States".[119] Nevertheless, the *Nicaragua Case* can be seen as an acceptance of a modern approach to customary international law by the ICJ.

4.3.3   The Substantive Aspect of Modern Customary International Law

The lack of consistency in the ICJ's approach to customary international law and consideration of the different theoretical approaches indicates that there is no single approach to customary law, but a "multiplicity of custom-creative processes".[120] Indeed, *Verdross* suggested such a possibility in 1968.[121] Different approaches for

---

[116]ICJ, Nicaragua Case, paras 188–195 ("this *opinio juris* may be deduced from, *inter alia*, the attitude of the Parties and States towards certain General Assembly resolutions"); see also *Simma, Alston* (supra note 1), 97.

[117]*Roberts* (supra note 36), 758; *Simma, Alston* (supra note 1), 96; *V. Gowlland-Debbas*, Judicial Insights into the Fundamental Values and Interests of the International Community, in Muller et al (eds.), The International Court of Justice, Its future role after fifty years (1997), 348. The approach of the ICJ has heavily been criticized by *A. D'Amato*, Trashing Customary International Law, 81 American Journal of International Law (1987), 101ff.

[118]ICJ, Nuclear Weapons Advisory Opinion, para 73.

[119]ICJ, Jurisdictional Immunities Case, para 55 referring to the North Sea Continental Shelf Cases, and Continental Shelf Case (Libya v. Malta).

[120]*Kammerhofer* (supra note 12), 204. See with regard to the ICJ's rather flexible approach to customary international law Special Rapporteur *M. Wood*, First Report on Formation and Evidence of Customary International Law, International Law Commission, 65th Session, 6 May-7 June and 8 July-9 August 2013, Official Records of the General Assembly, UN Doc. A/CN.4/663, para 64 footnote 123 with further references.

[121]*Verdross* (supra note 11), 636: "Because it is probable that each of the different theories [on customary law] contain some correct element, the presumption of one mode of creation for all norms of customary international law is probably not correct." See also *Kammerhofer* (supra note 12), 204; recently, *d'Aspremont* in a contemporary formulation has compared "customary international law with a dance floor where (almost) anything goes", see http://www.ejiltalk.org/customary-international-law-as-a-dance-floor-part-i/#more-10650 (last visited 16 June 2017).

the determination of customary international law might be indicated for specific issues such as human rights or humanitarian law,[122] or from a structural hierarchical perspective for norms and rules derived from the constitutional foundations of the international community.[123]

Schachter argued that human rights obligations could not be evaluated in the usual, traditional methods of proof of customary law formations. As States do not comment on the human rights situation in other States if their own nationals were not affected, "one can find scant State practice accompanied by *opinio juris*".[124] In his theory of the "humanization of law", *Meron* focuses on the content of human rights norms as containing community values that are centred on the individual and not the State. He claims that "the burden of proof that must be discharged to demonstrate the establishment of a customary human rights norm should indeed be lighter than in other fields of international law, which are based on reciprocal interests of states."[125] To give an example: an inductive historical assessment of State practice could not have led to a customary prohibition of torture, as it is one of the most common forms of human rights violations, which by definition involves organs of the State. It thus provides ample evidence for a widespread State practice of torture, and not against it.[126] While generally it is argued that contrary State practice could not alter an already established customary norm if it lacks supporting *opinio iuris*, *Meron* is right in concluding that under a traditional view such a view presumes that at some point in time there has already been consistent, lasting and widespread State practice supported by *opinio iuris* to establish such a customary

---

[122]Arguing for a modern approach for customary human rights law: *O. Schachter*, International Law in Theory and Practice, 178 Recueil des Cours (1982), 334; *Baker* (supra note 33), 180; *Roberts* (supra note 36), 759; see also *T. Meron*, Human Rights and Humanitarian Norms as Customary Law (1989).

[123]See the differentiation of "consuetudine-fondamento" (fundamental custom) and "consuetudine-fonte" (custom as a source) in *G. Sperduti*, La fonte suprema dell'ordinamento internazionale (1946), 155ff; *C. Tomuschat*, Obligations Arising for States without or against Their Will, 241 Recueil des Cours (1993), 73; *Kolb* (supra note 11), 123ff.

[124]*Schachter* (supra note 122), 334.

[125]*Meron* (supra note 122), 131.

[126]See *O. Schachter*, New Custom: Power, Opinio Juris and Contrary Practice, in Theory of International Law at the Threshold of the 21st Century: Essays in Honour of Krzysztof Skubiszewski (1996), 538; on the factual "practice" of torture see the Report of the Special Rapporteur on torture and other forms of cruel, inhuman or degrading treatment, Study on the phenomena of torture, cruel, inhuman, or degrading treatment or punishment in the world, including an assessment of conditions of detention, submitted on 5 February 2010 to the United Nations Human Rights Council, UN-Doc. A/HRC/13/39/Add.5: "Despite the fact that torture constitutes one of the most brutal attacks on human dignity and one of the most serious human rights violations, and notwithstanding the absolute nature of the prohibition of torture and ill-treatment even in the most exceptional circumstances, such as war, internal disturbances and terrorism, torture and ill-treatment are widespread practices in the majority of the countries on our planet. Almost no society is immune against torture, but in many societies torture is practiced systematically, both in fighting ordinary crime and in combating terrorism, extremism or similar politically motivated offences."

rule.[127] However, according to human rights reports on the widespread practice of torture, that has to be doubted. It is in such instances that a traditional inductive method for determining customary international law is more myth than reality. Rather, it is true that despite contrary State practice a customary norm is established on basis of prevailing *opinio iuris*. However, it is argued that such an approach that challenges the basic premise of customary law would only be applicable for a restricted number of issues that are human-centered, such as human rights or humanitarian law. Other State-centred fields, such as jurisdiction, immunities, State responsibility, diplomatic privileges, and so forth,[128] would still be governed by a traditional method of customary international law.

Thus, some authors claim that for certain issues the context determines the requirements for the establishment of customary international law. Such an approach reveals a value-oriented ascertainment of customary law: The greater the moral pull, the easier contrary State practice is neglected, and it is assumed that noble humanitarian principles and human rights ideas are positive norms of customary law. It appears that the separation of "morality" and "law" as promulgated by positivism, was abandoned when *Meron* declared that "[t]he 'ought' merges with the 'is', the *lex ferenda* with the *lex lata*" exposing the legislative process of customary law that is determined by noble ideas.[129] Morality is the reason why many academics are willing to apply less strict requirements for the formation of customary international law when the fundamental values of the international community are concerned. Most eloquently *Kirgis* proposed the sliding scale theory:

> The more destabilizing or morally distasteful the activity – for example, the offensive use of force or the deprivation of fundamental human rights – the more readily international decision makers will substitute one element for the other, provided that the asserted restrictive rule seems reasonable.[130]

Faced with these challenges it must be asked how positivistic our moral convictions command us to be. *Koskenniemi* takes a deconstructive position, stating that in the fields of humanitarian and human rights law, legal formalism has revealed its limits, and he simply abandons the idea that these fields are susceptible to a positivistic investigation.[131]

---

[127]*Meron* (supra note 115), 372–373 referring to *R. Higgins*, Problems & Process: International Law and How We Use It (1994), 22.

[128]*Schachter* (supra note 126), 538.

[129]*T. Meron*, The Geneva Conventions as Customary Law, 81 American Journal of International Law (1987), 361.

[130]Compare further *Kirgis* (supra note 11), 149. See also *T. Meron*, International Law in the Age of Human Rights, 301 Recueil des Cours (2003), 388.

[131]Cf. *Koskenniemi* (supra note 2), 1961: "which rights are customary is less a matter of formal tests of legal validity than a deference to their ethico-political importance; indeed, 'elementary considerations of humanity' and 'basic rights of the human person' receive legal protection regardless of whether lawyers come up with any number of precedents to support them; indeed, the more shocking the violation, the more open is the law for allowing responsibility to be triggered. Would any other conclusion have been acceptable, or possible?"

Other writers defend different categories of customary international law on the basis that not all rules share the same normativity.[132] Accordingly, some authors differ between 'ordinary' customary law that requires a traditional two-element formation, and 'exceptional' customary law that is suitable for a single-element formation since the laws and rules that are deduced constitute the very foundation of the international community.[133] Such a constitutional custom is either determined by *opinio iuris* of the international community or must be based on a logical presumption.[134] One example for this higher class of rules, advanced by *Tomuschat*, are rules flowing from common values of mankind, most present in humanitarian law by way of incorporating the Martens Clause into treaties of international humanitarian law.[135] The International Military Tribunal at Nuremberg, for example, treated the Martens Clause without much ado as a legally binding norm on individuals, even though it is difficult to show that the punitive character of these elementary norms of international humanitarian law evolved through State practice supported by *opinio iuris*.[136] What is evidenced by *Tomuschat's* approach is a meshing of "constitutional" principles, general principles of law and the deduction thereof of customary international law.[137] But he is in good company as even the ICJ appears to stray from its traditional path when customary international humanitarian law must be evidenced, given that the Court generally qualifies international humanitarian conventions as a codification of customary norms.[138] It is interesting to see that on several occasions the ICJ refers

---

[132] *O. Schachter*, Entangled Treaty and Custom, Dinstein (ed.), International Law at a Time of Perplexity: Essays in Honour of Shabtai Rosenne (1988), 734, referring to a "higher normativity" of certain norms which he considers as resulting from a fact of contemporary life; *P. Weil*, Towards Relative Normativity in International Law, 77 American Journal of International Law (1983), 413ff is strictly opposed to relative normativity.

[133] See the references in supra note 123f.

[134] *Kolb* (supra note 11), 123; see also *Tomuschat* (supra note 123), 292, who considers that the constitutional foundations of the international community have not evolved in State practice and must necessarily be a core element of the constitutional framework.

[135] Preamble of Hague Conventions of 1899 and 1907 respecting the Laws and Customs of War on Land and included in Common Article 3 of the Geneva Conventions 1949.

[136] *Tomuschat* (supra note 123), 300–2.

[137] *Ibid.* The meshing of different sources of international law finds followers in ICL as *K. Ambos*, Der allgemeine Teil des Völkerstrafrechts (2002), 43f proposed that customary international law in *statu nascendi* shall be verified by general principles.

[138] See for instance the evaluation of Common Article 3 of the Geneva Conventions which the ICJ considers to be the minimum yardstick applicable to international and non-international armed conflicts. See ICJ, Nicaragua Case, paras 218–229; ICJ, Nuclear Weapons Advisory Opinion, para 75 referring to "The Hague Law" and "Geneva Law". ICJ, Wall Case, Advisory Opinion, para 78, referring to the customary international law as reflected in Art. 42 Hague Regulations of 1907. ICJ, Armed Activities Case (Democratic Republic of the Congo v. Uganda), Judgment, 19 December 2005, ICJ Reports (2005), para 219 referring to customary international law as reflected in Art. 25, 27, 28, 43, 46, 47 Hague Regulations of 1907.

to recognized principles that underlie the specific norms of these conventions,[139] such as "fundamental general principles of humanitarian law",[140] "cardinal principles",[141] "elementary considerations of humanity"[142] and to the Martens Clause.[143] These references keep the reader in the dark as to whether the Court is in fact applying customary international law or general principles of international law.[144] Without over-rigorously interpreting the Court's jurisprudence, its position towards international humanitarian law can be summarized as follows: the rules contained in the codifications of humanitarian law reflect not only fundamental humanitarian principles but also, to a large extent, customary law.[145] With no hard and fast walls dividing the two sources, the ICJ is in the comfortable position to combine them as it sees fit. It might even be said that the mere fact that most provisions of humanitarian conventions reflect higher principles or elementary considerations

---

[139]ICJ, Corfu Channel Case (United Kingdom v. Albania), Judgment, 9 April 1949, ICJ Reports (1949), 22 referring to the recognized principle of elementary considerations of humanity; ICJ Nicaragua Judgment, para 215, referring to principles of humanitarian law underlying Hague Convention VIII of 1907; furthermore in para 218 it referred to "elementary considerations of humanity" that are reflected in Common Article 3.

[140]ICJ, Nicaragua Judgment, paras 218–220.

[141]ICJ, Nuclear Weapons Advisory Opinion, para 78, referring to the principle of protection of civilians and the prohibition on causing unnecessary suffering as the fabric of humanitarian law.

[142]First referred to in the ICJ, Corfu Channel Case, 22; ICJ, Advisory Opinion Nuclear Weapons, para 79; ICJ, Wall Case, Advisory Opinion, para 157, the Court stating that these obligations have an *erga omnes* character.

[143]In its modern formulation in Additional Protocol I it states that states are bound by "the principles of international law derived from established custom, from the principles of humanity and from the dictates of public conscience." The Martens Clause was referred to and considered customary law in ICJ, Nuclear Weapons Advisory Opinion, paras 84, 87.

[144]That confusion is also present in academic writing: G. *Zyberi*, The Humanitarian Face of the International Court of Justice. Its Contribution to Interpreting and Developing International Human Rights and Humanitarian Law Rules and Principles (2008), 285, alleges that the ICJ applied in Nicaragua *fundamental principles of customary international humanitarian law*; T. *Meron*, Editorial Comment, Revival of Customary Humanitarian Law, 99 American Journal of International Law (2005), 819: "In that case, the Court held that common Articles 1 and 3 of the Geneva Conventions constitute general principles of humanitarian law that are binding on the United States – *in other words, that they are customary law*" (emphasis added); J. *Wouters*, C. *Ryngaert*, The Impact on the Process of the Formation of customary International Law, in Kamminga, Scheinin (eds.), The Impact of Human Rights Law on General International Law (2009), 123f holding that the ICJ in relation to international humanitarian law was "relying on *general principles*" (emphasis added).

[145]See, ICJ, Nuclear Weapons Advisory Opinion, paras 79–82, referring to "intransgressible principles of international customary law", the "affirmation" of which as customary law is established by the Nuremberg Tribunal and Report of the Secretary-General Pursuant to Paragraph 2 of Security Council Resolution 808 (1993), 3 May 1993, UN Doc S/25704 (SG Report on ICTY); See also the Dissenting Opinion of Judge *Koroma* at p. 580: "By reference to the humanitarian principles of international law, the Court recognized that the Conventions themselves are reflective of customary law and as such universally binding".

of humanity makes these norms customary in character.[146] In the Nicaragua Case the ICJ does not even seek to identify the evidence for the determination of customary humanitarian law, and spares itself the difficulty of establishing State practice and *opinio iuris*.[147] Even though its Advisory Opinion on the Legality of the Threat or Use of Nuclear Weapons is famous for reemphasizing the traditional approach to customary law, the Court refers to "intransgressible principles of international customary law" as reflected in humanitarian treaties, the customary character of which it simply establishes by reference to the Nuremberg Judgments, the establishment of the ICTY, the UN-Secretary General's approval of Hague and Geneva Law, the Genocide Convention and the Nuremberg Charter, thus establishing the acceptance of the customary nature of humanitarian law by other international bodies.[148] There is still no trace of hard State practice when the Court continued: "[t]he extensive codification of humanitarian law and the extent of the accession to the resultant treaties, as well as the fact that the denunciation clauses that existed in the codification instruments have never been used, have provided the international community with a *corpus* of treaty rules the great majority of which had already become customary and which reflected the most universally recognized humanitarian principles."[149]

The doctrinal confusion between the different sources of international law comes as no surprise. Indeed, general principles of international law[150] have been described as "an *opinio iuris* without concordant state practice".[151] If customary international law is also merely based on *opinio iuris* the barriers separating customary international law and general principles of law become not only blurred, but non-existent. That is the reason why due to doctrinal constraints, such as the "irreparable violence to the very concept" of custom, *Simma* and *Alston* argued against a modern application of customary law and saw human rights norms better suited within the context of general principles of law.[152] The difference of classification as either general principle or customary law would only matter in relation to application, as long as treaty and custom take precedent, and general principles are only used to close gaps to prevent a possible *non liquet*. *Simma* and *Alston*,

---

[146]*B. Schlütter*, Developments in Customary International law (2010), 154 (in relation to the ICJ Nicaragua Case); *V. Chetail*, The Contribution of the International Court of Justice to International Humanitarian Law, 85 ICRC Review No. 850 (2003), 245.

[147]*Chetail, id*, 244.

[148]ICJ, Nuclear Weapons Advisory Opinion, paras 79–81.

[149]ICJ, Nuclear Weapons Advisory Opinion, para 82.

[150]The perception of general principles is not restricted to those derived from the *foro domestico* but also include general principles of international law that have been generated by acceptance on the international plane *via, e.g.* declarations of the UN General Assembly.

[151]*B. Simma*, International Human Rights and General International Law, in collected Courses of the Academy of European Law, Volume IV (1995), 225; compare also *M.C. Bassiouni*, A Functional Approach to General Principles of International Law, 11 Michigan Journal of International Law (1990), 768ff.

[152]*Simma, Alston* (supra note 1), 102–6; see also *Schachter* (supra note 126), 539; compare also *A. Verdross, B. Simma*, Universelles Völkerrecht (1984), 386, § 606.

however, circumvent such a *de facto* hierarchical problem by stating that *ius cogens* norms are not created by custom but through the formation of general principles.[153]

The jurisprudence of the ICJ on customary international law reveals that the case law on customary international law is not methodologically pure or clear. It appears to indicate that there are different approaches to custom, depending on the subject matter and the dispute at hand. Others have argued that the ICJ "has a marked tendency to assert the existence of a customary rule more than to prove it."[154] It is, however, wrong to suppose that the ICJ bows to moral considerations imposed by the dispute in question. Indeed, the ICJ appears to be immune, as demonstrated in the 2012 Judicial Immunity judgment when the Court's traditional approach to State immunity under customary law prevented Italian World War II forced laborers from pursuing their claims against Germany before Italian courts. In the light of the moral implications of the case, the Court saw itself forced to stress the inhumanity of forced labor and the "complete disregard for the 'elementary considerations of humanity'" without, however, bending the law or its methodological foundations.[155]

Despite seemingly varying approaches to customary international law in the ICJ's jurisprudence, Judge *Tomka*, president of the ICJ, held that "the Court has never abandoned its view, firmly rooted in the wording of the Statute, that customary international law is 'general practice accepted as law'",[156] advocating the traditional identification of customary international law *via* the two elements of State practice and *opinio iuris*.

4.4 The Identification of Customary International Law: The Challenge Ahead

The different approaches to customary international law outlined above suggest uncertainty with regard to the doctrinal foundations of customary international law and the methods for identifying it. Hoping to shed some light onto this dilemma, the International Law Commission decided to include the topic "Formation and evidence of customary international law" in its "long-term programme of work" in 2011,[157] and in 2012 the topic was placed into its current programme. Sir Michael

---

[153]*Simma, Alston* (supra note 1), 104.

[154]*A. Pellet*, Shaping the Future of International Law: The Role of the World Court in Law-Making, in Arsanjani et al. (eds.), Looking to the Future: Essays on International Law in Honor of W. M. Reisman (2011), 1076.

[155]ICJ, Jurisdictional Immunities Case, paras 52 and 81–91.

[156]*P. Tomka*, Custom and the International Court of Justice, 12 The Law and Practice of International Courts and Tribunals (2013), 197.

[157]Official Records of the General Assembly, UN Doc. A/CN.4/L.796, International Law Commission, 63rd Session, 26 April – 3 June and 4 July – 12 August 2011, Report of the Planning Group; See also Official Records of the General Assembly, Sixty-sixth Session, Supplement No. 10 (A/6610), paras 365ff.

Wood was appointed Special Rapporteur, delivering his first report in 2013,[158] his second the following year[159] and his third and fourth report in 2015 and 2016.[160] That the ILC is an appropriate forum to discuss this topic is evident from Art. 24 of its Statute[161]:

> The Commission shall consider ways and means for making the evidence of customary international law more readily available, such as the collection and publication of documents concerning State practice and of the decisions of national and international courts on questions of international law, and shall make a report to the General Assembly on this matter.

Although the ILC reported to the General Assembly on how to evidence customary international law, and the availability of this evidence, as early as 1950,[162] the UN Secretary General was not enthusiastic about this work. In 1949 the Secretary General submitted a survey to the ILC determining that the definition of sources of international law was adequately covered in Art. 38 ICJ Statute, and that no further investigation was necessary.[163] That cautious position did not change over time. In 1998 it was held that:

> The ILC should not inscribe the topic 'Sources' (with the exception of treaties) on its agenda. It is counterproductive, and may be impossible, to codify the relatively flexible processes by which rules of customary international law are formed.[164]

---

[158]First Report of Special Rapporteur *Wood* (supra note 120).

[159]Special Rapporteur *M. Wood*, Second Report on Identification of Customary International Law, International Law Commission, 66th Session, 5 May-6 June and 7 July-8 August 2014, Official Records of the General Assembly, UN Doc. A/CN.4/672.

[160]Special Rapporteur *M. Wood*, Third Report on Identification of Customary International Law, International Law Commission, 67th Session, 4 May-5 June and 6 July-7 August 2015, Official Records of the General Assembly, UN Doc. A/CN.4/682. Special Rapporteur *M. Wood*, Third Report on Identification of Customary International Law, International Law Commission, 67 Session, 4 May – 5 June and 6 July – 7 August 2015, Official Records of the General Assembly, UN Doc. A/CN.4/682. Special Rapporteur *M. Wood*, Fourth Report on Identification of Customary International Law, International Law Commission, 68th Session, 2 May – 10 June and 4 July – 12 August 2016, Official Records of the General Assembly, UN Doc. A/CN.4/695.

[161]Statute of the International Law Commission, adopted by the General Assembly in Resolution 174 (II), 21 November 1947, and amended by resolutions 485 (V), 12 December 1950, 984 (X), 3 December 1955, 985 (X), 3 December 1955 and 36/39, 18 November 1981, Art. 24.

[162]See Yearbook of the International Law Commission (1950), Volume II, 24ff Working Paper by *M. O. Hudson*, Special Rapporteur and addendum thereto as well as 364ff Report of the International law Commission to the General Assembly, Document A/1316.

[163]Survey of International Law in Relation to the Work of Codification of the International Law Commission, Memorandum submitted by the Secretary General, 10 February 1949, UN Doc. A/CN.4/1/Rev.1, para 33: "It is doubtful whether any useful purposes would be served by the attempts to make it more specific, as, for instance by defining the conditions of the creation and of the continued validity of international custom"; see also First Report of Special Rapporteur *Wood* (supra note 120), 4–5.

[164]See First Report of Special Rapporteur *Wood* (supra note 120), 5, referring to the 1998 unofficial survey as quoted in Report of the Study Group on the Future Work of the International Law Commission, in Anderson et al. (eds.), The International Law Commission and the Future of International Law (1998), 42.

Despite this resistance, the ILC decided to take the topic of customary international law onto its agenda. As the first report of SR *Wood* reveals, the Special Rapporteur changed the topic from the 'formation and evidence' to the 'identification' of customary international law, fearing that the question was too broad and too theoretical.[165] Although the title of the topic was accordingly revised by the Commission in 2013 at its sixty-fifth session, the ILC stated that "the proposed work of the Commission would nevertheless include an examination of the requirements for the formation of rules of customary international law, as well as the material evidence of such rules, both being necessary to the determination of whether a rule of customary international law existed."[166] However, in practice it appears that the ILC will focus on means and ways for the "identification" of customary international law, setting aside the nature of customary international law.[167] Furthermore, the result of the ILC will not produce a list of norms forming part of customary international law, but will focus on theoretical principles for the identification of customary rules.[168] SR *Wood* indicated that there might be different approaches to customary international law depending on the context. At the same time SR *Wood* apparently contradicted himself: with reference to Judge *Greenwood*, he noted that subsystems in international law are not to be viewed in clinical isolation to one other but are part of a "single, unified system of law". This in turn would conflict with different approaches to customary international law depending on the content (human rights, humanitarian, international criminal law etc.).[169] Consequently, several members of the commission held that rather than varying approaches to customary international law, the ILC should elaborate on a "common, unified approach to the identification of rules of customary international law".[170] The discussions of the ILC implied a broad support for a two-element approach to customary international law that includes State practice and *opinio iuris* as necessary elements for the identification of customary international law. The ILC adopted a set of 16 draft conclusions, together with commentaries thereto, on the identification of customary international law. Furthermore, the ILC decided to

---

[165]First Report of Special Rapporteur *Wood* (supra note 120), 6.

[166]ILC Report on the Work of its 65th Session to the General Assembly, 6 May – 7 June and 8 July – 9 August 2013, Supplement No. 10 (A/68/10), paras 69 and 76. SR *Wood* was criticized that his approach would not take into account the distinction between formal and material sources of law, see *id*, para 87.

[167]Thus the ILC will not shed light on the first layer of sources of law, see Sect. 4.1, Preliminary Remarks.

[168]ILC Report on the Work of its 65th Session (supra note 166), para 83: "General support was also expressed for the proposed focus on the practical process of identifying rules of customary international law, rather than the content of such rules."

[169]First Report of Special Rapporteur *Wood* (supra note 120), 7–8, referring to ICJ, Ahmadou Sadio Diallo Case (Republic of Guinea v. Democratic Republic of the Congo), Judgment – Compensation owed by the Democratic Republic of the Congo to the Republic of Guinea, 19 June 1012, ICJ Reports (2012), 391ff, Declaration of Judge Greenwood, para 8.

[170]ILC Report on the Work of its 65th Session (supra note 166), paras 84 and 86. In his Second Report Special Rapporteur *Wood* (supra note 159), para 28 adheres to the commission's proposal.

transmit these draft conclusions to governments for comments with the request that such comments are submitted to the Secretary-General by 1 January 2013.[171]

4.5 Concluding Remarks

This chapter has shown that customary international law is indeed "situated in a theoretical minefield."[172] Various conceptions of customary international law exist that stand in direct competition to one other, and none of them can claim to have universal validity. One could agree with *Verdross* that "[b]ecause it is probable that each of the different theories [of customary international law] contain some correct element, the presumption of one mode of creation for all norms of customary international law is probably not correct."[173] The ILC, however, seems to be certain that there is a "common, unified approach to the identification of rules of customary international law"[174] and that the requirements of both, State practice and *opinio iuris* are generally accepted as necessary elements for the formation and determination of customary international law.[175] Even with the ILC adopten of a set of 16 draft conclusions, it is safe to say that at the moment there is no generally accepted unified theory of customary international law. Nor is there agreement on the necessary constituent elements for the formation of customary international law, or on the possible instances of evidence for the identification of these elements. However, it seems that one-element approaches to customary international law are rather to be treated as the exception than the rule for the establishment of customary international law.[176] It needs to be remembered that innovative, modern approaches to customary international law in the inter-State context might be welcomed, as they progressively develop the law in order to adequately respond to pressing social, moral and global challenges. However, it is uncertain how such theories could be adequately applied within the context of international criminal law. In contrast to inter-State disputes in international criminal proceedings, the lives of individuals are at stake. The human rights of the accused individual may place

---

[171] ILC Report on the Work of its 68th Session to the General Assembly, 2 May – 10 June and 4 July – 12 August 2016, Supplement No. 10 (A/71/10), Chapter V.

[172] *Koskenniemi* (supra note 2), 1947.

[173] *Verdross* (supra note 11), 636.

[174] ILC Report on the Work of its 65th Session (supra note 166), para 102. Second Report of Special Rapporteur *Wood* (supra note 159), para 28.

[175] ILC Report on the Work of its 65th Session (supra note 166), para 102, para 101. Second Report of Special Rapporteur *Wood* (supra note 159), Draft Conclusion 2.

[176] Second Report of Special Rapporteur *Wood* (supra note 159), para 27, determining that "[w]hile such writings [i.e. on one-element approaches] are always interesting and provocative, and have been (and should be) duly taken into account, it remains the case that they do not seem to have greatly influenced the approach of States or courts. The two-element approach remains dominant." The Special Rapporteur lists numerous examples in the legal literature (para 26), State practice (para 24) and international courts (para 25) to substantiate this finding.

greater restrictions on judges in international criminal tribunals than judges "convicting" States as abstract entities. While these different contextual settings need to be taken duly into account, one must first understand what role is given to judges when determining customary international law.

Chapter 5
The Role of Judges When Determining Customary International Law

5.1 The Initial Position: Being a Judge in the 1990s

As has been suggested by *Shahabuddeen*, "[t]he state of international criminal law was meager at the time of the establishment of the ICTY".[1] This comes to no surprise as the ICTY has been the only international criminal tribunal established since the IMT at Nuremberg and the IMTFE at Tokyo. Despite some considerable work in the field by the ILC, there has been no enforcement of international criminal law on the international plane, with only occasional cases held on the domestic level.[2] The rather "poor" state of international criminal law in the 1990s was highlighted by the International Committee of the Red Cross, which concluded in 1993 that "the notion of war crimes is limited to situations of international armed conflict."[3] The newly established international criminal tribunals were therefore faced with seemingly insurmountable difficulties when tasked with delivering criminal judgments on the horrendous atrocities that occurred in the 1990s in Rwanda and the former Yugoslavia. Due to the scarcity of available legal material it is understandable that judges must have felt that they were "thrown in at the deep end", lacking the tools necessary to fulfill their task of applying norms that are "beyond doubt part of customary international law".[4] Moreover, international criminal tribunals deal with large-scale atrocities that are exposed to public

---

[1]*M. Shahabuddeen*, Judicial Creativity and Joint Criminal Enterprise, in Darcy, Powderly (eds.), Judicial Creativity at the International Criminal Tribunals (2010), 187.

[2]See e.g. Israeli Supreme Court, *Eichmann* Case, 277; French Court de Cassation, *Barbie Case*, 125. See in that regard also ECtHR, *Kononov v. Latvia*, Application No. 36376/04, Judgment, 17 May 2010, para 208.

[3]Preliminary Remarks of the ICRC, 25 March 1993 as cited by *C. Greenwood*, The Development of International Humanitarian Law by the International Criminal Tribunal for the Former Yugoslavia, 2 Max Planck Yearbook of United Nations Law (1998), 131.

[4]See Report of the Secretary-General Pursuant to Paragraph 2 of Security Council Resolution 808 (1993), 3 May 1993, UN Doc S/25704), para 34 (SG Report on ICTY).

© Springer International Publishing AG 2017
T. Rauter, *Judicial Practice, Customary International Criminal Law and* Nullum
Crimen Sine Lege, DOI 10.1007/978-3-319-64477-6_5

expectations and pressure. From this perspective, it is perfectly understandable that international criminal judges are tempted not only to adjudicate upon the existing law—thereby acting in conformity with fundamental principles of criminal law—but also to adjudicate upon the law as it should be, mixing *de lege ferenda* with *de lege lata*.[5] In these difficult surroundings the question arises of the role given to judges: the application of law as it is, or the creation of law.[6]

5.2   The Role of Judges: Determining, Developing or Creating Customary International Criminal Law?

According to *Montesquieu*, the judge is "the mouth that reproduces the words of the law".[7] This view suggests that the role of the judges is reduced to the application of law and not the creation of law. However, the application of law includes declaring, formulating, clarifying, interpreting and developing the law and as such the difference between a mere determination of existing law and rule-creation is one of degree.[8] Where to draw the line between application and creation of law is thus rather difficult. However, as noted by *Jennings*, generally judges, national and international, are not given the authority to create law; their "ultimate source of authority" rests upon a permissible interpretation of the existing law.[9] It is thus clear that the source of authority of judges rests upon the application of existing legal principles. Once judges take the path to adjudicate beyond the realms of existing law, they are losing their source of authority. Although it might be tempting for

---

[5]In its Custom Study the ICRC also concluded that "[i]t appears that international courts and tribunals on occasion conclude that a rule of customary international law exists when that rule is a desirable one for international peace and security or for the protection of the human person, provided that there is no important contrary *opinio juris*." See *J.-M. Henckaerts*, Customary International Humanitarian Law (2005) (ICRC Custom Study), Vol. I: Rules, xlii.

[6]A position contrary to a legislative role of judges has been taken by Judge *Li* in his separate opinion to ICTY, *Tadić* Appeals Chamber Jurisdiction Decision, para 13, determining that the ICTY Appeals Chamber in that decision acted under "an unwarranted assumption of legislative power which has never been given to this Tribunal by any authority."

[7]*C. de Secondat, Baron de Montesquieu*, De l'Esprit des lois. Livre XI, Chapitre 6 (1748), Chapitre 6.

[8]*R. Y. Jennings*, General Course on Principles of International Law, 121 Recueil des Cours (1967), 341.

[9]*R. Y. Jennings*, The Judiciary, National and International and the Development of International Law, 45 International Comparative Law Quarterly (1996), 3: "Judges, whether national or international, are not empowered to make new laws. Of course we all know that interpretation does, and indeed should, have a creative element in adapting rules to new situations and needs, and therefore also in developing it even to an extent that might be regarded as changing it. Nevertheless, the principle that judges are not empowered to make new law is a basic principle of the process of adjudication. Any modification and development must be seen to be within the parameters of permissible interpretation. For otherwise judges lose their ultimate source of authority."

judges to neglect the distinction of *de lege ferenda* and *de lege lata* due to pressing social or moral needs, it must be kept in mind as stated by the ICJ that being "a court of law" it "can take account of moral principles only in so far as these are given a sufficient expression in legal form. Law exists, it is said, to serve a social need; but precisely for that reason, it can do so only through and within the limits of its own discipline. Otherwise, it is not a legal service that would be rendered. Humanitarian considerations may constitute the inspirational basis for rules of law, just as, for instance, the preambular parts of the United Nations Charter constitute the moral and political basis for the specific legal provisions thereafter set out. Such considerations do not, however, themselves amount to rules of law."[10]

Moreover, international criminal law, being at the interception of human rights, humanitarian law and criminal law, appears to be torn by moral aspirations that determine the way the law needs to be interpreted and applied. The human factor in yielding to the moral pull is quite understandable. Critics such as *Robinson* consider that international criminal tribunals apply a "victim-focused teleological reasoning aggravated by utopian aspirations".[11] However, the source of authority for judges of international criminal tribunals rests upon the application of existing customary international criminal law. Thus the UN Secretary General's demand that international criminal tribunals apply norms "which are beyond any doubt part of customary international law",[12] is its legitimizing source of authority. Consequently, judges adjudicating on the strength of law must keep a clear distinction between *de lege lata* and *de lege ferenda*. Humanitarian and moral considerations can only be taken into account by judges when they have found adequate expression in legal form.

This obligation to maintain a clear distinction between *de lege lata* and *de lege ferenda* owes in particular to the dual nature of international criminal law. While it is embedded in public international law it must simultaneously adhere to fundamental principles of criminal law. For this reason *Meron* considers that progressive approaches to customary international law by international criminal tribunals could not be reconciled with criminal law principles such as *nullum crimen sine iure*.[13]

Nevertheless, according to the ICTY Appeals Chambers, the NCSI principle "does not prevent a court from *interpreting and clarifying* the elements of a

---

[10]ICJ, South West Africa Cases (Ethiopia and Libera v. South Africa), Judgment, 18 July 1966, ICJ Reports (1966), paras 49–50.

[11]C.f. *D. Robinson*, The Identity Crisis of International Criminal Law, 21 Leiden Journal of International Law (2008), 944f; see also *A. Nollkaemper*, The Legitimacy of International Law in the Case Law of the International Criminal Tribunal for the Former Yugoslavia, in Vandamme/ Reestman (eds.), Ambiguity in the Rule of Law (2001), 18, characterizing the approach of the ICTY to the determination of law as "quintessentially teleological".

[12]As demanded by the SG Report on ICTY (supra note 4), para 34 and affirmed by the jurisprudence of the ICTY: see for instance, *Tadić* Appeals Chamber Judgment, para 662, *Blaškić* Appeals Judgment, para. 114; ICTY, *Delalić* Trial Judgment, paras. 415–18.

[13]*T. Meron*, Editorial Comment, Revival of Customary Humanitarian Law, 99 American Journal of International Law (2005), 825.

particular crime,"[14] even going so far as to claim that *nullum crimen sine iure* does not "preclude *the progressive development* of the law".[15] *Shahabuddeen* is the major proponent of the possibility of a progressive development of international criminal law by judges that is supposedly in accordance with the NCSI principle. Referring to the case law of the ECtHR, he considers that existing international core crimes can be clarified or adapted to new circumstances as long as they "can reasonably be brought under the original concept of the offence" and that "the resultant development is consistent with the essence of the offence and could reasonably be foreseen".[16] The most important authority he cites is the ECtHR Case in *CR v. the United Kingdom*, Application No 20190/92. In this case the ECtHR held that the judicial removal of the common law marital immunity for rape committed by a husband against his estranged wife had become a "reasonably foreseeable development of the law" that was "consistent with the very essence of the offence"; thus the husband could be convicted for the crime of rape. This development—so the ECtHR implies—would not as such run counter the *nullum crimen sine lege* principle as enshrined in Art. 7 of the Convention.[17] Prominent proponents considered using the same approach for a progressive development of international criminal law.[18] It seems, however, questionable whether the same reasoning of that particular case before the ECtHR can be applied generally in international criminal proceedings.[19] Indeed, in the cited ECtHR case the criminal-

---

[14]ICTY, *Delalić* Appeals Judgment, para 173 (emphasis added); see also *Aleksovski* Appeals Judgment, para 126.

[15]ICTY, *Ojdanić* Appeals Chamber Decision, para 38 (emphasis added).

[16]*M. Shahabuddeen*, International Criminal Justice at the Yugoslav Tribunal, A Judge's Recollection (2012), 72–73, referring to the ECtHR, *X Ltd and Y v. the United Kingdom*, Application No 8710/79, Judgment, 7 May 1982, para 9 and ECtHR, *CR v. the United Kingdom*, para 34; see also *M. Shahabuddeen*, Does the Principle of Legality Stand in the Way of Progressive Development of Law?, 2 Journal of International Criminal Justice (2004), 1007ff. A similar position is taken by *A. Cassese* International Criminal Law (2008), 45f, who considers that an "evolutive adaptation" of international criminal law is permissible if it is in line with "the essence of the offence", it confirms to fundamental principles of ICL, and is reasonably foreseeable.

[17]See ECtHR, *CR v. the United Kingdom*, para 41, note, however, that the ECtHR seemingly also referred to the *malum in se* argument referring to the "manifest debasing character of rape" (para 42); see also ECtHR, *SW v. the United Kingdom*, Application No. 20166/92, Judgment, 22 November 1995, para 43; These two cases before the ECtHR, both dealing with the question of marital immunity for rape, were considered on the same day by a single chamber. *K. S. Gallant*, The Principle of Legality in International and Comparative Criminal Law (2009), 222–3, is critical of these cases of the ECtHR as it overly broadens the concept of foreseeability.

[18]See the references in supra note above.

[19]*Meron* (supra note 13), 826, rightly criticized such a generous interpretation of progressive development of ICL demonstrating that there is a "difference between removing personal immunity for liability for an obviously criminal act and extrapolating from it a theory of evolution and ex post facto application of criminal liability for acts that were not unlawful at the time of their commission."

ity of the underlying conduct was not in doubt.[20] The only question was whether the common law immunity as a procedural immunity would still be applicable, preventing the English courts from convicting the husband, who clearly had committed the crime of rape. In that regard the ECtHR considered that the immunity defence has been increasingly limited by the English case law over a considerable period of time, and that in this case the domestic English courts merely "continue[d] a perceptible line of case-law development dismantling the immunity of a husband from prosecution for rape upon his wife."[21] Thus, this ECtHR case exhibits distinctive particularities and as such it seems questionable whether the specific facts of this case before the ECtHR could be used to substantiate a general theory of evolution, progressive development or evolutive adaptation of international criminal law. It is evident that in a first step judges in international criminal proceedings must establish the criminality of the underlying conduct on the basis of its existence as a customary international criminal norm. Only then questions concerning the scope of application arise, such as whether factual developments are pertinent to the "essence of the offence", or whether expanding the scope of application for established elements of crimes or forms of liability to new facts goes beyond the permissible.[22] The ECtHR case in *CR v. the United Kingdom* "merely" considered the applicability of immunity to undoubtedly criminal conduct, and as such a wider application to a general theory of progressive development of international criminal law seems exaggerated. Admittedly, as stated above a clear demarcation between a mere application—interpretation or clarification—of existing international criminal law and a possible *ex post facto* law creation can never be exactly defined. Thus *Jennings* is right to claim that "the difference between making and determining law is one of degree."[23] Unfortunately, the ECtHR case of *CR v. the United Kingdom* cannot shed further light on this difficult task.

It should, however, be stressed that fundamental criminal principles do apply to the determining of customary international criminal law, its application and its interpretation. The requirements of *nullum crimen sine iure praevia* and *nullum crimen sine iure certa* prevent, according to the ICTY Appeals Chamber, "a court from creating new law or from interpreting existing law beyond the reasonable limits of acceptable clarification."[24]

While the *nullum crimen sine iure* guarantees with regard to customary international criminal law have already been analyzed above,[25] it is not the only

---

[20]ECtHR, *CR v. the United Kingdom*, paras 39–40. Even the husband admitted that if not for the marital immunity his acts constituted the crime of rape, of which he could be convicted.

[21]ECtHR, *CR v. the United Kingdom*, para 41.

[22]See further A. *Cassese*, International Criminal Law (2013), 32.

[23]*Jennings* (supra note 8), 341.

[24]ICTY, *Ojdanić* Appeals Chamber Decision, para 38.

[25]See Sect. 3.10, The Guarantees of the *Nullum Crimen Sine Lege* Principle in International Criminal Law: The Principle of *Nullum Crimen Sine Iure*.

fundamental criminal principle relevant when considering the existence and interpretation of law. The principle *in dubio pro reo* is of utmost importance. This
principle is foremost concerned with the presumption of innocence, meaning that an
individual could only be convicted of a crime if on the basis of the facts he could be
proven guilty beyond reasonable doubt.[26] Admittedly, there have been views put
forward in ICTY jurisprudence that restrict the application of the principle *in dubio
pro reo* solely to findings of facts[27]—in other words whether on the basis of the
facts the alleged perpetrator has committed the crime or not. Other judgments,
however, consider that the principle *in dubio pro reo* covers both findings of facts
and of law,[28] which has far reaching consequences for the determination and
interpretation of law. Even in the case of a restricted application of the principle
to findings of facts, such a conception may include "legal facts". As has been put
forward by Judge *Schomburg*: "Such legal facts, e.g. the existence of a domestic
statute, *state practice, customary law* or foreign law in general, are subject to the
normal fact-finding process of the court, as the power to interpret these norms is not
vested to the International Tribunal. *In case of doubt on such legal facts, the
International Tribunal must also decide in favour of the accused.*"[29]

If the principle *in dubio pro reo* covers findings of law or legal facts, when
applied to customary law as the underlying legal basis for individual criminal
responsibility, doubts in relation to the existence of a customary law might have
to be resolved in favor of the defendant. Such doubts may originate in varying
methodological approaches to the existence of customary international law or
different approaches to the interpretation and application of customary international
criminal law.[30] At the ECCC, the Pre-Trial chamber decided that if there is
ambiguity of customary international law by the absence of clear State practice

---

[26]ICTY, *Delalić* Trial Judgment, para 601: "the Prosecution is bound in law to prove the case
alleged against the accused beyond a reasonable doubt. At the conclusion of the case the accused is
entitled to the benefit of the doubt as to whether the offence has been proved."

[27]ICTY, *Stakić* Trial Judgment, para 416: "The Trial Chamber explicitly distances itself from the
Defence submission that the principle *in dubio pro reo* should apply as a principle for the
interpretation of the substantive criminal law of the Statute. As this principle is applicable to
findings of fact and not of law, the Trial Chamber has not taken it into account in its interpretation
of the law." See also the partially dissenting and separate opinion and declaration of Judge
Schomburg to *Prosecutor v. Limaj et al*, IT-03-66-A, Appeals Chamber, Judgment, 27 September
2007, paras 15ff.

[28]ICTY, *Delalić* Trial Judgment, para 413; Declaration of Judge Shahabuddeen to *Limaj* Appeals
Judgment, paras 2ff; see also *G. Mettraux*, International Crimes and the *ad hoc* Tribunals (2005),
226, proposing "the application of the general principle of criminal law that where there is a doubt
in the interpretation of the law, that doubt should always be interpreted in favour of the accused (*in
dubio pro reo*)". Due to conflicting jurisprudence in that regard *Robinson* (supra note 11),
934 (footnote 37), considers that it is yet undecided in ICL whether the principle can be used
for both questions of fact and of law.

[29]Partially dissenting and separate opinion and declaration of Judge Schomburg to *Limaj* Appeals
Judgment, para 20 (emphasis added).

[30]*Meron* (supra note 13), 823 calling such a solution 'outcome conservatism'.

and *opinio iuris*, such ambiguity has to be resolved in favor of the accused according to the principle of *in dubio pro reo*.[31]

Thus, judges at international criminal tribunals are advised to adhere to the role ascribed to them, to deliver convictions on the basis of existing legal principles. In determining the existence and scope of international criminal norms, fundamental criminal principles such as *nullum crimen sine iure* and *in dubio pro reo* have to be taken into account.

---

[31] ECCC, Pre-Trial Chamber, Public Decision on Appeals by *Nuon Chea* and *Ieng Thirith* against the Closing Order, para 144, holding it necessary to include an armed conflict nexus requirement to crimes against humanity therewith an individual before the ECCC could be convicted for crimes against humanity. However, in subsequent decisions both the Trial Chambers and the Appeals Chamber have denied that such ambiguity existed and did not require an armed nexus requirement to crimes against humanity under customary international law; see ECCC, Decision on Co-Prosecutors' Request to Exclude Armed Conflict Nexus Requirement from the Definition of Crimes Against Humanity, Trial Chamber, Case No. 002/10-09-2007/ECCC/TC, 26 October 2011 (ECCC Trial Chamber Decision Armed Conflict Nexus Requirement); see also *Duch* Trial Judgment, para 291; *Duch* Appeals Judgment, paras 106ff.

Chapter 6
Methodological Approaches to Customary International Law by International Criminal Tribunals

6.1 The Disclosure of the Method

In the previous chapter I argued that the role of the judge is to apply the law, with restricted possibilities to develop the law in relation to new factual circumstance. Judges are, however, not allowed to create law when merely "determining" customary international criminal law. When the applicable law consists of unwritten norms, the question is whether judges should have an obligation to disclose the method used to determine a customary international criminal norm. When the ICRC published its customary international humanitarian law study[1] it chose to disclose the method used to identify customary law, listing what it considers to be relevant State practice and *opinio iuris*.[2] The ICRC itself simultaneously claimed that the separation of State practice and *opinio iuris* is "very difficult and largely theoretical."[3] Although the ICRC Custom Study has been subject to critique,[4] the disclosure of method is to be welcomed in that it allows the ascertainment of customary international law to be comprehensible. However, one could argue that the role of international criminal tribunals is to deliver judgments and that—to draw on *Pellet's* comments on the ICJ—they are only judicial bodies and not teachers or

---

[1]*J.-M. Henckaerts*, Customary International Humanitarian Law (2005) (ICRC Custom Study).

[2]ICRC Custom Study, *id*, xxxvii ff (Assessment of customary international law).

[3]ICRC Custom Study, *id*, Vol. I: Rules, xlvi.

[4]See the critique of *Bellinger* and *Haynes* on the non-traditional methodology used by the ICRC, *J. B. Bellinger and W. J. Haynes*, A US government response to the International Committee of the Red Cross study Customary International Humanitarian Law, 89 Review of the Red Cross (2007). See also the critique on the ICRC Custom Study by *R. Cryer*, Of Custom, Treaties, Scholars and the Gavel: The Influence of the International Criminal Tribunals on the ICRC Customary Law Study, 11 Journal of Conflict & Security Law (2006), 239ff, and *H. Krieger*, A Conflict of Norms: The Relationship between Humanitarian Law and Human Rights Law in the ICRC Customary Law Study, 11 Journal of Conflict & Security Law (2006), 265ff.

© Springer International Publishing AG 2017
T. Rauter, *Judicial Practice, Customary International Criminal Law and* Nullum Crimen Sine Lege, DOI 10.1007/978-3-319-64477-6_6

scholars in relation to the underlying methodology.[5] Nevertheless, it is maintained here that the issue is different with regard to criminal proceedings. An accused is entitled to know the exact underlying jurisdictional legal basis of the charges against him, whether they form part of conventional or customary international criminal law,[6] and similarly a convicted criminal is entitled to comprehend the legal basis of his conviction. A part of the fair trial guarantee is that the rationale of a trial judgment shall be explained, accompanied by a reasoned opinion.[7] This obligation on the part of the trial chambers safeguards the accused's right of appeal, and that the Appeals Chamber can evaluate the Trial Chambers findings. In practice Appeal Chambers have rebuked Trial Chambers for their evaluation of factual evidence.[8] While overturning certain customary law findings of the Trial Chambers, such as the result, the Appeal Chambers have rarely criticized the applied methodology of the Trial Chambers.[9] Since the rationale or legal reasoning of a judgment must clearly be explained,[10] the underlying legal basis of the criminal conviction must have already been clearly set out as a prerequisite. In relation to "ordinary" domestic statutory criminal norms this problem does not generally arise. As established above in the domestic context, the *nullum crimen sine lege certa* requirement as an "imperative for improvement"[11] is addressed to the legislator to define *ex ante* the underlying criminal norms with adequate precision. Ideally, everyone who can read should be able to comprehend the underlying legal basis as long as the criminal norms are drafted in a clear and comprehensible manner. For customary international criminal law the matter is far more complex.[12] Here the disclosure of how the respective chamber arrived at a customary international criminal norm is a necessary element therewith an individual can comprehend the legal reason and normative basis of his conviction, and as such be able to challenge

---

[5]*A. Pellet*, Article 38, in Zimmerman et al (eds.), The Statute of the International Court of Justice – A Commentary (2012), 761, MN 236.

[6]See e.g. ICTY, *Strugar* Appeals Chamber Decision, para 13.

[7]See Art. 23 (2) ICTY Statute; see in this regard ICTY, *Prosecutor v. Furundžija*, IT-95-17/1, Appeals Chamber, Judgment, 21 July 2000, para 69; *Prosecutor v. Kunarac* et al, IT-96-23 & IT-96-23/1, Appeals Chamber, Judgment, 12 June 2002, para 42; see also Art. 23 (2) ICTR Statute, Art; 74 (5) Rome Statute; Art. 18 SCSL Statute; Rule 101 Extraordinary Chambers in the Court of Cambodia, Internal Rules (Rev. 8) (2011).

[8]See in that regard, *M. D. Öberg*, Processing Evidence and Drafting Judgments in International Criminal Trial Chamber, 24 Criminal Law Forum (2013), 120ff with further references to case law.

[9]See e.g. the critique of the ICTY, *Stakić* Appeals Judgment, para 62, stating that the liability of co-perpetration as established by the *Stakić* Trial Chamber "does not have support in customary international law".

[10]See ICTY, *Kunarac* Appeals Judgment, para 42.

[11]*P. Hauck*, The Challenge of Customary International Crimes to the Principle of Nullum Crimen Sine Lege, 21 Humanitäres Völkerrecht – Informationsschriften (Journal of International Law of Peace and Armed Conflict) (2008), 61.

[12]See Sect. 3.10.6.2, The *certa* Requirement as an Imperative for Improvement.

possible methodological shortcomings on part of the judges.[13] However, judges are often reluctant to disclose the applied method(s). Like magicians, the judges are not willing to reveal how they pull the rabbit—customary international criminal law—out of the hat. The opportunity to quantify the way customary law is determined by international criminal tribunals begins with a duty to disclose the method used. On the basis of the disclosed method one would be in a position to verify or challenge a judgment or decision, that is to say, if it had been delivered on sound methodological grounds. Regrettably, this proposed duty of a methodological disclosure is far from being a political and legal reality.

6.2   A Word of Caution

Since international criminal tribunals generally avoid disclosing the way they find customary international law, a word of caution is required. Any methodological analysis can only ever be as good as the case law is susceptible to examination and classification. The non-disclosure of international criminal tribunals with regards to the applied method(s) is thus problematic, as researchers must seek to interpret which method(s) the tribunals were in fact applying. Such interpretation is necessarily contestable. Nevertheless, any methodological analysis of the jurisprudence of international criminal tribunals contributes to the general debate of how customary international criminal norms can be found.

It has to be noted that not all the case law of international criminal tribunals can be methodologically analyzed. This is particularly true with regards to the jurisprudence of the ICTR. While the present author has no intention to contribute to bench bashing, one has to endorse the view expressed by *van den Herik* that the ICTR appears to claim the existence of customary international criminal law rather than proving it through an examination of adequate evidences of State practice and *opinion iuris*.[14] Thus, the case law of the ICTR has only been taken into consideration where it was susceptible to a methodological analysis.

Nevertheless, the author has examined and classified the existing jurisprudence of international criminal tribunals by analyzing the adequacy of instruments and elements they used when determining customary international law.

---

[13]Similar *G. Mettraux*, International Crimes and the *ad hoc* Tribunals (2005), 14–5, argues that a "court must carefully reason and explain its conclusion as to the customary or non-customary status of a norm [as it is] an element of the fair trial guarantee and the rationale of a judgment must therefore be 'clearly explained'."

[14]*L. van den Herik*, The Contribution of the Rwanda Tribunal to the Development of International Law (2005), 275.

6.3   Detectable Approaches to Customary International Criminal Law

6.3.1   The Traditional Two Elements Approach

6.3.1.1   Preliminary Remarks

The jurisprudence of international criminal tribunals reveals that when they elaborate on customary international law in the abstract, the various chambers share the prevailing view that customary international law consists of two constituent elements, State practice and *opinio iuris*.[15] However, when determining the concrete underlying customary international criminal norm or mode of liability, they generally spare themselves the cumbersome task of establishing lasting, uniform and widespread State practice accompanied by *opinio iuris*, or they do not assign the listed evidence to the two elements. Thus, in relation to the methodological underpinnings of their decisions and judgments, international criminal tribunals are merely paying lip service to the traditional "two-element" requirement for customary law formation, and they generally do not explicitly or implicitly specify which elements they consider adequate to establish State practice and which elements are proof of *opinio iuris*.

In the 40 ICTY Trial Chamber judgments[16] that have been analyzed, only 11 make explicit reference to State practice and/or *opinio iuris*.[17] In those

---

[15]See for the ICTY: *Prosecutor v. Hadžihasanović*, IT-01-47-T, Trial Chamber, Judgment, 15 March 2006, para 254: "To prove the existence of a customary rule, the two constituent elements of the custom must be established, namely, the existence of sufficiently consistent practices (material element), and the conviction of States that they are bound by this uncodified practice, as they are by a rule of positive law (mental element)"; *Hadžihasanović* Appeals Chamber Decision, para 12: "to hold that a principle was part of customary international law, it has to be satisfied that State practice recognized the principle on basis of supporting *opinio juris*"; *Furundžija* Appeals Judgment), Declaration of Judge Patrick Robinson, para 281: "in seeking to ascertain international custom [...] what one is looking for is a sufficiently widespread practice of states accompanied by *opinio juris*." See for the SCSL: *Norman* Appeals Chamber Decision, para 17: "The formation of custom requires both state practice and a sense of pre-existing obligation (opinio juris)." For the ECCC see Trial Chamber Decision on Armed Conflict Nexus Requirement, para 12 (footnote 40): "The content of customary international law derives from the actual practice of states and opinio juris"; see also Pre-Trial Chamber JCE Appeals Decision, para 53: "The Pre-Trial Chamber recalls that, when determining the state of customary international law in relation to the existence of a crime or a form of individual responsibility, a court shall assess existence of common, consistent and concordant state practice, or *opinio juris*, meaning that what States do and say represents the law. A wealth of state practice does not usually carry with it a presumption that *opinio juris* exists".

[16]The ICTY Trial Chamber Judgment *Prosecutor v. Prlić*, IT-04-74-T, 28 Mai 2013, has been omitted from the analysis as it is only available in French on the ICTY homepage.

[17]The 11 ICTY Trial Chamber judgments are the following: *Delalić* Trial Judgment; *Furundžija* Trial Judgment; *Prosecutor v. Jelisić*, IT-95-10-T, Trial Chamber, Judgment, 14 December 1999; *Kupreškić* Trial Judgment; *Kunarac* Trial Judgment; *Krstić* Trial Judgment; *Vasiljević* Trial Judgment; *Prosecutor v. Simić*, IT-95-9-T, Trial Chamber, Judgment, 17 October 2003; *Galić* Trial Judgment; *Hadžihasanović* Trial Judgment; *Boškoski* Trial Judgment.

11 judgments the ICTY trial chambers explicitly referred to State practice 22 times and to *opinio iuris* 16 times.[18] Only in rare instances has State practice been allocated to specific evidence.[19] *Opinio iuris* has been allocated to specific evidence in 12 instances.[20]

An analysis of the ICTY Appeals Chamber judgments does not improve this situation. In the 37 ICTY Appeals Chamber judgments that have been analyzed, only 7 Appeals Chambers make explicit reference to State practice and/or *opinio iuris*.[21] Those 7 judgments explicitly referred to State practice 22 times and to

---

[18]The search terms included "State practice", "national practice", "practice", "opinio juris" and "opinio iuris". Instances when trial chambers merely used quotations of previous judgments that contained these phrases have not been counted.

[19]When elaborating on the crime of genocide the ICTY *Jelisić* Trial Chamber has identified State practice in the form of national case law, see *Prosecutor v. Jelisić*, IT-95-10-T, Trial Chamber, Judgment, 14 December 1999, paras 51ff; see in that regard also ICTY, *Krstić* Trial Judgment, para 541, treating national legislation and judicial practice as State practice and referring in the subsequent paragraphs to French legislation (para 571) and German case law (para 579); when elaborating on a possible obligation to prosecute international crimes under customary law, the *Hadžihasanović* Trial Chamber treated national case law as an instance of State practice, *Hadžihasanović* Trial Judgment, paras 254, 257; *Boškoski* Trial Judgment, para 191 treating statements by States as possible evidence for State practice and *opinio iuris* when distinguishing NIACs from "merely" terroristic acts not rising to the level of armed conflict. See also the references in infra note 39.

[20]In that regard the Rome Statute of the International Criminal Court has been used 7 times to evince *opinio iuris*: ICTY, *Furundžija* Trial Judgment, para 227, in relation to the mode of liability of aiding and abetting; ICTY, *Kupreškić* Trial Judgment, para 580, stated that the Rome Statute may be indicative of the *opinio iuris* of many States but with regard to the crime of persecution (Art. 7 (1) (h) Rome Statute) it is not consonant with customary international law, as it requires a nexus between persecution and "any act referred to in this paragraph or any crime within the jurisdiction of the Court"; *Kunarac* Trial Judgment, para 495 when elaborating on the crime of torture, footnote 1225 elaborating on the crime of outrages upon personal dignity, footnote 1333 when elaborating on the crime of enslavement; ICTY, *Krstić* Trial Judgment, para 541 when elaborating on the crime of genocide; *Prosecutor v. Simić*, IT-95-9-T, Trial Chamber, Judgment, 17 October 2003, footnote 212 elaborating on the law on deportation; furthermore UN General Assembly Resolution where used as indicative for *opinio iuris*, when dealing with reprisals (ICTY, *Kupreškić* Trial Judgment, para 532) and the protection of the civilian population from the dangers arising from hostilities (*Galić* Trial Judgment, footnote 78); the number of ratification of the Geneva Conventions or the AP I have been used to evince *opinio iuris*, see *Simić* Trial Judgment, para 1153 and ICTY, *Kupreškić* Trial Judgment, para 532. And as stated before the *Boškoski* Trial Judgment treated statements by States as possible evidence for State practice and *opinio iuris* when distinguishing NIACs from "merely" terroristic acts not rising to the level of armed conflict.

[21]Those 7 ICTY Appeal Chamber judgments are the following: *Tadić* Appeals Judgment; *Delalić* Appeals Judgment; *Aleksovski* Appeals Judgment; *Blaškić* Appeals Judgment; *Krnojelac* Appeals Judgment; *Kordić* Appeals Judgment; *Prosecutor v. Đorđević*, IT-05-87/1-A, Appeals Chamber, Judgment, 27 January 2014.

opinio iuris 7 times.[22] In only 5 instances has the Appeals Chambers allocated the element of State practice with specific evidence,[23] and they have allocated specific evidence to *opinio iuris* 4 times.[24]

It is astonishing to see that the ICTR chambers neither did allocate specific evidence to State practice and/or *opinio iuris* in their judgments, nor explicitly even refer to State practice and/or *opinio iuris* as elements for the establishment of customary international law.

At the SCSL, two Trial Chambers and two Appeals Chambers explicitly mention State practice and/or *opinio iuris* in their judgments,[25] while only in 4 instances has

---

[22]The analysis only counted the references in the judgments themselves, whereas references to State practice and/or *opinio iuris* in separate or dissenting opinions were not included in the analysis.

[23]ICTY, *Tadić* Appeals Chamber Judgment, paras 124ff, stated that the "effective control" test of the ICJ Nicaragua Case was "at variance with international judicial and State practice". After elaborating on international judicial practice, the Appeals Chamber referred to State practice in the form of national judicial practice (at footnotes 155–6 referring to the German Jorgić Case and footnote 167) and statements of States in SC Res debates (at footnotes 157 and 167) and by "judging from international case law and State practice" the *Tadić* Appeals Judgment came to the conclusion that the appropriate test to attribute acts of military or paramilitary groups to a State is "overall control". Furthermore, the *Tadić* Appeals Judgment determined that crimes against humanity under customary international law do not require the proof of a discriminatory intent (apart of the crime of persecution) referring to State practice in the form of national legislation and national jurisprudence, ICTY, *Tadić* Appeals Chamber Judgment, para 190. Furthermore the ICTY, *Kordić* Appeals Judgment, para 66, elaborated on State practice in the form of national legislation and case law and determined that State practice was not settled on the question of a result requirement for unlawful attacks on civilians. It is not clear when referring to the "controversial negotiations" of the Rome Statute how the Appeals Chamber treated it as "evidence of the unsettled nature of State *opinio juris* and practice". *Krnojelac* Appeals Judgment, para 221 referred to the Rome Statute as an evidence of State practice in order to evince that forcible displacement can constitute the crime of persecution under customary international law. ICTY, *Galić* Appeal Judgment, para 92ff, referred to State practice in the form of statements, national legislation and domestic court decisions when elaborating on the crime of terror under customary international law.

[24]The ICTY, *Tadić* Appeals Chamber Judgment, paras 222–223, referred to the Rome Statute as *opinio iuris* when elaborating on Joint Criminal Enterprise; in that regard the *Đorđević* Appeals Chamber, para 35 defended the ICTY *Tadić* Appeals Chamber's reference to the Rome Statute; ICTY, *Delalić* Appeals Judgment, footnote 255 relied on the Rome Statute as *opinio iuris* when establishing the necessary element of "effective control" for command responsibility under customary international law; *Blaškić* Appeals Judgment, para 158 referred to UN GA Resolutions when elaborating on the prohibition of attacking the civilian population under customary international law.

[25]These SCSL judgments are: *Fofana* Trial Judgment; *Sesay* Trial Judgment; *Fofana* Appeals Judgment; SCSL, *Taylor* Appeals Judgment.

the element of State practice been allocated with specific evidence,[26] and in 3 instances has *opinio iuris* been allocated with specific evidence.[27]

At the ECCC in the three judgments available at the time of writing, the two trial chambers have explicitly referred to State practice 4 times and to *opinio iuris* 2 times, whereas State practice has been allocated two times to specific evidence.[28] The ECCC Supreme Court Chamber in its *Duch* Judgment has referred to State practice 8 times and to *opinio iuris* 7 times. Both elements have been allocated to specific evidence only once.[29]

6.3.1.2 ICTY *Tadić* Appeals Chamber Jurisdiction Decision

Interestingly, the famously progressive ICTY *Tadić* Appeals Chamber Jurisdiction Decision is one of the rare occasions a chamber of international criminal tribunals tried to establish customary international law on basis of State practice accompanied with *opinio iuris*. This occurred in its most revolutionary sub-section: when determining the existence of individual criminal responsibility for war crimes committed in non-international armed conflicts under customary international law.[30]

In a prelude, before analyzing individual criminal responsibility for war crimes committed in non-international armed conflicts (NIACs), the ICTY *Tadić* Appeals Chamber stated that "a word of caution on the law-making process in the law of armed conflict is necessary. When attempting to ascertain State practice with a view

---

[26]With regard to the crime of intentionally directing attacks against personnel involved in a peacekeeping mission, SCSL, *Sesay* Trial Judgment, paras 213ff referred to official pronouncements of States before the UN Security Council as State practice and the Rome Statute has been treated as evidence of State practice and *opinio iuris*; SCSL, *Fofana* Appeals Judgment, paras 391ff with regard to the distinction of the prohibition against pillage and the prohibition against destruction not justified by military necessity treated military manuals as evidence of State practice. SCSL, *Taylor* Appeals Judgment when establishing the *mens rea* standard of knowledge for aiding and abetting under customary international law, referred to national legislation as State practice (para 430) and the Rome Statute as not evincing contrary State practice (para 436); furthermore a standard of specific direction was considered to be contrary to State practice (para 474) as evinced by domestic legislation, the Arms Trade Treaty and the creation of international criminal tribunals as established by States.

[27]The Rome Statue and the Arms Trade Treaty have been used to evidence *opinio iuris*, see for the Rome Statute SCSL, *Sesay* Trial Judgment, para 218 and SCSL, *Fofana* Appeals Judgment, para 403 and for the Arms Trade Treaty, SCSL, *Taylor* Appeals Judgment, para 461.

[28]ECCC, *Duch* Trial Judgment, para 589 referring to "Cambodian practice" as contained in the penal code; *Prosecutor v. Nuon*, Case File No. 002/19-09-2007/ECCC/TC, Trial Chamber, Judgment, 7 August 2014, para 719 (in conjunction with footnote 2241) referring to US case law as an instance of State practice.

[29]ECCC, *Duch* Appeals Judgment, para 225 referring to State practice with regard to post World War II convictions by "hybrid military NMTs [Nuremberg Military Tribunals]" and national courts and para 109 referring to General Assembly Resolution 95 (I) as evincing *opinio iuris*.

[30]ICTY, *Tadić* Appeals Chamber Jurisdiction Decision, paras 128–134.

to establishing the existence of a customary rule or a general principle, it is difficult, if not impossible, to pinpoint the actual behaviour of the troops in the field for the purpose of establishing whether they in fact comply with, or disregard, certain standards of behavior. This examination is rendered extremely difficult by the fact that not only is access to the theater of military operations normally refused to independent observers (often even to the ICRC) but information on the actual conduct of hostilities is withheld by the parties to the conflict; what is worse, often recourse is had to misinformation with a view to misleading the enemy as well as public opinion and foreign Governments. In appraising the formation of customary rules or general principles, one should therefore be aware that, on account of the inherent nature of this subject-matter, reliance must primarily be placed on such elements of official pronouncements of States, military manuals and judicial decisions."[31]

This statement prompted diverging opinions in the legal literature concerning its methodological approach. Some authors argued that it is not clear whether the Appeals Chamber treated "official pronouncements of States, military manuals and judicial decisions" as State practice or *opinio iuris*, or merely as subsidiary means for the determination of a rule of law.[32] On the other hand *Meron* suggested that the ICTY *Tadić* Appeals Chamber "in effect weighed statements both as evidence of practice and as articulation of *opinio juris*".[33] *Meron's* comment may be of particular importance, as the above quoted paragraph of the ICTY *Tadić* Appeals Chamber appears to be a paraphrase of an article he published in 1987.[34]

However, regarding the decision in its totality, the *Tadić* Appeals Chamber adhered to the classical distinction of State practice and *opinio iuris* when determining individual criminal responsibility for war crimes committed in NIAC under customary international law. In the present author's opinion the Appeals Chamber treated "official pronouncements of States, military manuals and judicial decisions" as instances of State practice. Such a conclusion is clear: the Appeals Chamber referred explicitly to "State practice" when addressing its "word of caution"[35] as quoted above. Furthermore, it also explicitly referred to State practice in the

---

[31] ICTY, *Tadić* Appeals Chamber Jurisdiction Decision, para 99.

[32] See W. *Heintschel von Heinegg*, Criminal International Law and Customary International Law, in Zimmermann (ed.), International Criminal Law and the Current Development of Public International Law (2003), 35; see also R. *Heinsch*, Die Weiterentwicklung des humanitären Völkerrechts durch die Strafgerichtshöfe für das ehemalige Jugoslawien und Ruanda (2007), 299.

[33] T. *Meron*, The Continuing Role of Custom in the Formation of International Humanitarian Law, 90 American Journal of International Law (1996), 239.

[34] T. *Meron*, The Geneva Conventions as Customary Law, 81 American Journal of International Law (1987), 361; "because of the difficulty of ascertaining significant state practice in periods of hostilities, manuals of military law and legislation of states providing for the implementation of humanitarian law norms as internal law should be considered as among the best types of evidence of such practice and, sometimes perhaps, as a statement of *opinio juris* as well."

[35] ICTY, *Tadić* Appeals Chamber Jurisdiction Decision, para 99.

subsequent paragraphs when elaborating on "official pronouncements of States"[36] and "judicial decisions."[37] When the ICTY *Tadić* Appeals Chamber analyzed individual criminal responsibility for war crimes committed in NIAC, although not expressly referring to the term State practice, it quoted a case before the Supreme Court of Nigeria during the Nigerian Civil War, four military manuals, and Yugoslavian and Belgium national legislation, designed to implement the Geneva Conventions. After listing the material evidence, it explicitly referred to two unanimous Security Council resolutions (SC Res 793 (1992) and SC Res 814 (1993) as being of "great relevance to the formation of *opinio juris*".[38] Thus, it is evident that the ICTY *Tadić* Appeals Chamber intended to uphold the traditional requirements of establishing State practice and *opinio iuris* when determining individual criminal responsibility for war crimes committed in NIAC under customary international law. Subsequent ICTY jurisprudence, when referring to the *Tadić* case's listing of "official pronouncements of States, military manuals and judicial decisions", expressly treated them as instances of State practice.[39]

The doctrinal confusion with regard to the classification of "official pronouncements of States, military manuals and judicial decisions" as either instances of State practice or *opinio iuris* or both is quite understandable, since the Appeals Chamber by denouncing the quality of actual State conduct by troops as untrustworthy, dismisses their value for determining customary international law. It thus focuses on "verbal" or "paper" practice.[40] This "modern positivistic"[41] conception of State practice has been adequately described by *Kress* as on the border-line between actual State practice and *opinio iuris*.[42] As we have seen, widening the scope of the element of 'State practice' to include verbal and paper practice renders the exact contours and delimitation of the two elements rather unclear.[43] However, for the reasons stated above, it would be

---

[36]ICTY, *Tadić* Appeals Chamber Jurisdiction Decision, para 100 with regard to the Spanish Civil War and para 102 with regard to the instructions of Mao Tse-Tung to the Peoples' Liberation Army, para 105 with regard to a public statement of the Prime Minister of Congo.

[37]ICTY, *Tadić* Appeals Chamber Jurisdiction Decision, para 125 with regard to a case before the Supreme Court of Nigeria.

[38]ICTY, *Tadić* Appeals Chamber Jurisdiction Decision, 133.

[39]See ICTY, *Galić* Appeal Judgment, para 92; *Prosecutor v. Strugar*, IT-01-42-T, Trial Chamber, Judgment, 31 January 2005, footnote 754; *Prosecutor v. Boškoski*, IT-04-82-T, Trial Chamber, Judgment, 10 July 2008, footnote 1273; *Prosecutor v. Đorđević*, IT-05-87/1-T, Trial Chamber, Judgment, 23 February 2011, footnote 5779. *Prosecutor v. Stanišić and Župljanin*, IT-08-91-T, Trial Chamber, Judgment, 27 March 2013, footnote 86.

[40]ICTY, *Tadić* Appeals Chamber Jurisdiction Decision, para 99. See also *J. Wouters, C. Ryngaert*, The Impact on the Process of the Formation of customary International Law, in Kamminga, Scheinin (eds.), The Impact of Human Rights Law on General International Law (2009), 116.

[41]A term coined by *B. Simma* and *A.L. Paulus*, The Responsibility of Individuals for Human Rights Abuses in Internal Conflicts: A Positivist View, in 93 American Journal of International Law (1999), 306ff.

[42]*C. Kress*, War Crimes Committed in Non-international Armed Conflict and the Emerging System of International Criminal Justice, 30 Israel Yearbook on Human Rights (2001), 108.

[43]See Sect. 4.3.2, The Procedural Aspect of Modern Customary International Law.

wrong to assume that the *Tadić* Appeals Chamber tried to turn the classical two-elements approach into a one-element approach, or used the listed paper or verbal practice as instances of both State practice and *opinio iuris*.

6.3.1.3 High Frequency and High Consistency of State Practice

The approach chosen by the ICTY *Tadić* Appeals Chamber in relation to the determination of criminal responsibility for war crimes committed in NIAC under customary international law is problematic. Whereas one could also question the qualitative value of these instances of State practice, that is, whether they could actually qualify as proof for the criminalization of war crimes committed in NIAC,[44] at this point we will focus on the quantity of the quoted State practice: one domestic case, four military manuals and two national legislations.[45] These instances of State practice leave much to be desired when applying the high frequency and high consistency test as established by the ICJ in the North Sea Continental Shelf Cases, which requires that State practice should be both "extensive and virtually uniform."[46] The Appeals Chamber has rightly been criticized by scholars as to whether it could not have made greater effort in its search for instances of State practice.[47]

Despite this criticism, the findings of the *Tadić* Appeals Chamber with regard to criminal responsibility for war crimes committed in NIAC are settled jurisprudence.[48] Subsequent jurisprudence has placed a favorable gloss on the sheer quantity of the quoted State practice of the *Tadić* Appeals Chamber.[49] Whereas the ICTY *Tadić* Appeals Chamber itself did not explicitly elaborate on the ICJ's

---

[44]The ICTY *Tadić* Appeals Chamber appeared not to be overconfident in its proof: the military manuals of the US and Great Britain only "lend themselves to the interpretation" that war crimes included NIAC situations and also the norms of the Criminal Code of the FRY only "seem[ed] to imply that they also apply to internal armed conflicts." See, ICTY, *Tadić* Appeals Chamber Jurisdiction Decision, para 131–132; see also the critique by *Heintschel von Heinegg* (supra note 32), 35ff.

[45]ICTY, *Tadić* Appeals Chamber Jurisdiction Decision, paras 128–132.

[46]See ICJ, North Sea Continental Shelf Cases, para 74.

[47]*Heintschel von Heinegg* (supra note 32), 35ff; Kress (supra note 42), 107; *Meron* (supra note 33), 240. *Cassese* himself in that regard admitted that "we came up with a lot of evidence . . . *well some evidence* [laughter]." See Editorial, Nino – In His Own Words, 22 European Journal of International Law (2011), 942.

[48]See e.g. for the ICTY: *Tadić* Trial Judgment, para 614; ICTY, *Delalić* Appeals Judgment, paras 153ff; see for the ICTR: *Akayesu* Trial Judgment, para 613; *Prosecutor v. Rutaganda*, ICTR-96-3-T, Trial Chamber, Judgment, 6 December 1999, para 87; see for the SCSL: *Prosecutor v. Fofana*, SCSL-2004-14-AR72(E), Appeals Chamber, Decision on Preliminary Motion on Lack of Jurisdiction Materiae: Nature of Armed Conflict, 25 May 2004, para 24: "Any argument that these norms [CA 3 and Art. 4 (2) AP II] do not entail individual criminal responsibility has been put to rest in ICTY and ICTR jurisprudence."

[49]In the *Delalić* Case it has been stated that the *Tadić* Appeals Chamber "illustrate[d] that there are many instances of penal provisions for violations of the laws applicable in internal armed conflicts", see ICTY, *Delalić* Trial Judgment, para 307; ICTY, *Delalić* Appeals Judgment, paras 175ff.

high frequency and high consistency test of State practice, it is safe to conclude that it tacitly ignored it. The Appeals Chambers of other international criminal tribunals were more expressive concerning the non-applicability of the high frequency and high consistency test of State practice.

The Appeals Chamber of the SCSL, when concerned with a preliminary motion alleging that it lacks jurisdiction in relation to child recruitment—a war crime according to Art. 4 SCSL Statute—affirmed that the "formation of custom requires both state practice and a sense of pre-existing obligation (*opinio iuris*)."[50] It considered that the prohibition on child recruitment had been established as customary law prior to November 1996, the date when its temporal jurisdiction began, referring to the State practice as contained in national legislation,[51] and the widespread acceptance of conventional norms that prohibit child recruitment contained in, for example, the convention on the Rights of the Child and Additional Protocol II.[52] However, the central issue was whether that prohibition also entailed individual criminal responsibility as a war crime for the acts of conscripting or enlisting children under the age of 15 into armed forces, or using them to participate actively in hostilities, already existed as of 1996.[53] The Appeals Chamber referred to the inclusion of the crime in the Rome Statute (adopted in 1998, entry into force 2002) as well as its elements of crime (adopted in 2000). In response to the defense's objection that these instruments created new law, it stated that the preparation of the Rome Statute was a codification of existing customary norms rather than the formation of new rules. It treated the US position in the negotiating proceedings of the Rome Conference, stating that child recruitment "did not reflect international customary law, and was more a human rights provision than a criminal law provision", more or less as the sole persistent objection,[54] a position that can be doubted.[55]

---

[50]SCSL, *Norman* Appeals Chamber Decision, para 17.

[51]As annexed to the *Amicus Curiae* Brief of the United Nations Children's fund (UNICEF).

[52]See Art. 4 (3e) Additional Protocol II and Art. 38 (3) Convention on the Rights of the Child, 20 November 1989, 1577 UNTS 3.

[53]See SCSL, *Norman* Appeals Chamber Decision, paras 30ff. The issue of individual criminal responsibility has already been raised by the Secretary General in his report on the SCSL, at para 17, where he stated "while the prohibition on child recruitment has by now acquired a customary international law status, it is far less clear whether it is customarily recognized as a war crime entailing the individual criminal responsibility of the accused." Indeed the Secretary General in a previous draft of the SCSL Statute prepared by him "only" criminalized "abduction and forced recruitment" while voluntary enlistment was not included.

[54]SCSL, *Norman* Appeals Chamber Decision, para 33.

[55]It seems that more States than just the US shared this position – c.f. *H. von Hebel and D. Robinson*, Crimes within the Jurisdiction of the Court, in Lee, The International Criminal Court: The Making of the Rome Statute: Issues, Negotiations, Results (1999), 117. See also *M. Happold*, International Humanitarian Law, War Criminality and Child Recruitment: The Special Court for Sierra Leone's Decision in Prosecutor v. Samuel Hinga Norman, 18 Leiden Journal of International Law (2005), 290.

Furthermore, it looked into other conventions[56] that however post-dated the SCSL's temporal jurisdiction. Finally, the Appeals Chamber looked into State practice demonstrating "few examples of national legislation criminalizing child recruitment prior to 1996".[57] It also made references to national legislation that prohibits child recruitment in military law, to administrative legislation, and to legislation that simply makes it impossible for an individual to recruit children. These instances of State practice would hardly pass the high frequency and high consistency test. However, the SCSL Appeals Chamber circumvents this issue by reference to *Akehurst*, stating that "a practice followed by a very small number of states can create a rule of customary law if there is no practice which conflicts the rule".[58] While not determined to set a specific date, it considered that criminalization of child recruitment had been established before being explicitly included in international conventions, and certainly by November 1996.[59] Judge *Robertson* filed a dissenting opinion criticizing the Appeals Chamber for not differentiating between forced recruitment, which he considered to be a war crime, and voluntary enlisting. He considered that under customary international law as it stood by the end of 1996, voluntary enlisting of children or involving them in hostilities was prohibited by humanitarian law, triggering State responsibility, but that this prohibition did not entail individual criminal responsibility.[60] Despite this cutting critique by Judge *Robertson*, the findings of the Appeals Chamber have been followed in the subsequent judgments of the SCSL,[61]

---

[56] 1999 ILO Convention 182 Concerning the Prohibition and Immediate Action for the Elimination of the Worst Forms of Child Labour, the Optional Protocol II to the Convention on the Rights of the Child on the Involvement of Children in Armed Conflict (signed in 2000, entry into force 2002). These instruments are questionable since they strictly speaking do not criminalize the conduct themselves, but merely oblige State parties to take immediate and effective measures (in the case of the ILO convention) or to adopt legal measures necessary to prohibit and criminalize such practices (in the case of the CRC Optional Protocol) or in the case of the CRC, referred to in para 41 to take all feasible measures.

[57] SCSL, *Norman* Appeals Chamber Decision, para, 45. The Appeals Chamber refers to the UNICEF Amicus Brief that lists 5 national legislations that explicitly criminalized the recruitment of children (Colombia's national law, the Code of Military Justice of Argentina, Spain's Penal Code, Ireland's Geneva Conventions Act and Norway's Military Penal Code).

[58] SCSL, *Norman* Appeals Chamber Decision, para 49, referring to M. *Akehurst*, Custom as a Source of International Law, 47 British Yearbook of International Law (1977).

[59] SCSL, *Norman* Appeals Chamber Decision, para 53.

[60] SCSL, *Norman* Appeals Chamber Decision, Dissenting opinion of Justice *Robertson*, para 60: "what had emerged, in customary international law, by the end of 1996 was a humanitarian rule that obliged states, and armed factions within states, to avoid enlisting under fifteens or involving them in hostilities, whether arising from international or internal armed conflict. What had not, however, evolved was an offence cognisable by international criminal law which permitted the trial and punishment of individuals accused of enlisting (i.e. accepting for military service) volunteers under the age of fifteen. It may be that in some states this would have constituted an offence against national law, but this cannot be determinative of the existence of an international law crime." Judge *Robertson* refers to the difference of forcible recruitment and enlistment in paras 8–10.

[61] SCSL, *Fofana* Trial Judgment, para 184; *Brima* Trial Judgment, para 728; *Sesay* Trial Judgment, para 184.

and the ICC has used the SCSL case law as a source for interpretation of the Rome Statute.[62] It is indeed stunning to see the SCSL Appeals Chamber circumventing the high frequency and high consistency test with reference to one single legal scholar, thereby conveniently avoiding the task of searching for an adequate number of instances of State practice.

Also the Supreme Court Chamber of the ECCC elaborated on the frequency and consistency of State practice for the determination of customary international criminal law. It plainly stated that in this particular field of law "the traditional requirement of 'extensive and virtually uniform' state practice may actually be less stringent than in other areas of international law".[63]

These examples of the Appeals Chambers of three different international criminal tribunals suggest a reluctance to adhere to the high frequency and high consistency test with regards to State practice. Moreover, it appears that its non-applicability has met common agreement before international criminal tribunals. The ICTY *Tadić* Appeals Chamber in its Jurisdiction Decision opened the possibility of establishing customary international law merely on "trace elements" of State practice, but remained silent with regard to its doctrinal problems. However, the highest chambers of other international criminal tribunals, the SCSL Appeals Chamber and the ECCC Supreme Court Chamber, did not shy away from proclaiming that the traditional method of establishing customary international law on basis of "extensive and virtually uniform" State practice is not applicable to determining customary international criminal law. This is in line with a modern understanding of customary international law: that in certain fields of law the context is relevant for ascertaining different requirements for its establishment.[64] It reveals a value-oriented ascertainment of customary international law. As the existence of a norm of customary international criminal law is desirable, requirements for the ascertainment of customary international law are less stringent, resulting in the omission of the high frequency/consistency test of State practice when establishing customary international criminal norms.

6.3.1.4 Denying the Existence of Customary International Criminal Law on the Basis of the Traditional Two Elements Approach

It seems that the findings of the Appeals Chamber in the *Tadić* Jurisdiction Decision is one of the rare instances of ICTY case law that sought to establish instances of concrete State practice and *opinio iuris* when proving the existence of a customary

---

[62]ICC, Trial Chamber I, ICC-01/04-01/06, Situation in the Democratic Republic of the Congo in the Case of the *Prosecutor v. Thomas Lubanga Dyilo*, Judgment, 14 March 2012, para 603: "The SCSL's case law therefore potentially assist in the interpretation of the relevant provisions of the Rome Statute."

[63]ECCC, *Duch* Appeals Judgment, para 93.

[64]See Sect. 4.3.3, The Substantive Aspect of Modern Customary International Law.

norm. Generally, however, the traditional method, the explicit reference to State practice and *opinio iuris*, has often been used to negate the existence of custom, claiming that the alleged norm in question lacks sufficient support of State practice and/or *opinio iuris*.

Generally, when adhering to the traditional method, denials of the existence of a customary norm are given without further indication. There is rarely a deeper discussion on the possible evidences of State practice and *opinio iuris*, and the customary character of a norm is sweepingly denied. This occurred in the Trial Chamber Judgment in the *Čelebici* Case, which analyzed the applicability of Art. 2 ICTY Statute and the question as to whether the alleged victims were to be considered "protected persons" within the meaning of the Geneva Conventions.[65] The customary law duty of a successor State to grant nationality to all of the nationals of the predecessor State residing in its territory, and the right the individual to accept or decline that nationality, was negated by the *Čelebici* Trial Chamber. It determined that it "cannot be said to yet reflect binding customary international law, on the basis of State practice and *opinio juris*."[66] This conclusion was based entirely on a publication by a legal scholar, who argued that "from the widespread but not universal treaty practice and from other instances of State practice" a customary norm could not be established. However, the Trial Chamber itself did not conduct an independent analysis of customary international law.[67] Furthermore, the *Čelebici* Appeals Chamber determined that "effective control" is a necessary element in order to establish superior responsibility and denied the prosecution's submission of "substantial influence" as it "lacks sufficient support in State practice and judicial decisions".[68] In the *Kupreškić* Case, the Trial Chamber affirmed the irrelevance of the principle of reciprocity for obligations deriving from international humanitarian law and consequently denied the application of the *tu quoque* principle, as it had no support in State practice.[69] In the *Vasiljević* Case, the Trial Chamber could not find conclusive evidence of State practice that would define the crime of "violence to life and person", a crime charged pursuant to Art. 3 ICTY Statute, and rebuked the Trail Chamber in *Blaškić* for not citing relevant State

---

[65]ICTY, *Delalić* Trial Judgment, paras 245, analyzing the requirement "in the hands of a party to the conflict or occupying power of which they are not nationals" as stipulated in Art. 4 Geneva Convention IV.

[66]ICTY, *Delalić* Trial Judgment, paras 255–6, analyzed on basis of the ILC Draft Articles on Nationality in Relation to the Succession of States and the Declaration on the Consequences of State Succession for the Nationality of Natural Person of the European Commission for Democracy through Law (Venice Commission).

[67]ICTY, *Delalić* Trial Judgment, at footnote 283 referring to *P. Weis*, Nationality and Statelessness in International Law (1979).

[68]ICTY, *Delalić* Appeals Judgment, para 266.

[69]ICTY, *Kupreškić* Trial Judgment, para 516, listing for its conclusion only one post World War II case. Furthermore the Trial Chamber stated that the *tu quoque* is a "flawed in principle" as IHL is not based on reciprocity.

practice when it previously defined that crime.[70] Furthermore the ICTY *Vasiljević* Trial Chamber did not follow ICTR case law in relation to the crime of extermination charged under Art. 5 ICTY Statute. Whereas the ICTR *Kayishema and Ruzinanda* Trial Chamber held that a single killing could be qualified as extermination, as long as it forms "part of a mass killing event",[71] the ICTY *Vasiljević* Trial Chamber rebuked its sister trial chamber for not citing one single instance of State practice. It determined that extermination under customary international law requires that the individual is responsible for a large number of deaths.[72] In the *Krstić* Case, the Trial Chamber referred to the State practice of the Federal Constitutional Court of Germany, which stated that genocide "extends beyond physical and biological extermination".[73] The German Constitutional Court opened the possibility that attacks on the cultural, religious or sociological characteristics of a group could fall under the definition of the crime of genocide. However, the *Krstić* Trial Chamber, by referring to the restraints set by the NCSI principle, held that "despite recent developments, customary international law limits the definition of genocide to those acts seeking the physical or biological destruction of all or part of the group."[74] The Appeals Chamber in *Aleksovski* stated that war crimes charged under Art. 3 ICTY Statute do not require a proof of discriminatory intent since "[t]here is no evidence of State practice which would indicate the development of customary international law".[75] Furthermore, the Trial Chamber in the *Ojdanić* Decision decided that the mode of liability of co-perpetration, introduced previously by the *Stakić* Trial Chamber, had no support under customary law due to the lack of State practice and *opinio iuris*.[76]

---

[70]ICTY, *Vasiljević* Trial Judgment, para 194, furthermore stating that the "residual character of a criminal prohibition such as Article 3 of the Statute does not by itself provide for the criminalisation by analogy to any act which is even vaguely or potentially criminal." In para 199 the Trial Chamber refers to the possibilities of determining that a given act is criminal under customary international law stating that "a vast number of national jurisdictions have criminalized it, or a treaty provision which provides for its criminal punishment has come to represent customary international law." A critical position to this judgment was taken by A. Cassese, Black Letter Lawyering v. Constructive Interpretation, 2 Journal of International Criminal Justice (2004), 271ff.

[71]ICTR, *Kayishema* Trial Judgment, para 147.

[72]ICTY, *Vasiljević* Trial Judgment, para 227. In a footnote the Trial Chamber determines that due to the lack of an adequate analysis of the elements of customary international law the ICTR, *Kayishema* Trial Judgment cannot be considered to have precedential value. In the same vein it denounces the Rome Statute as it blindly followed the ICTR precedent.

[73]Federal Constitutional Court of Germany, 2 BvR 1290/99, 12 December 2000, para (III) (4) (a) (aa).

[74]ICTY, *Krstić* Trial Judgment, para 580. The Trial Chamber treats national judicial decisions as instances of State practice, see para 541.

[75]ICTY, *Aleksovski* Appeals Judgment, para 23.

[76]ICTY, *Prosecutor v. Milutinović* et al, IT-05-87-PT, Trial Chamber, Decision on Ojdanić's Motion Challenging Jurisdiction: Indirect Co-perpetration, 22 March 2006, para 39; Compare also ICTY, *Stakić* Appeals Judgment, para 62, stating that it "does not have support in customary international law or in the settled jurisprudence of this Tribunal which is binding on the Trial Chambers" and sees that in contrast Joint Criminal Enterprise (JCE) is "firmly established in customary international law", which it considered to be settled jurisprudence.

The majority in the Appeal Chamber Judgment in the *Erdemović* Case considered that "duress does not afford a complete defence to a soldier charged with a crime against humanity and/or a war crime involving the killing of innocent human being."[77] The Appeals Chamber referred to the Joint Separate Opinion of Judge McDonald and Judge Vohrah, who after an analysis of war crimes cases, criminal codes and legislation, could not find consistent and uniform State practice underpinned by *opinio iuris* to confirm the existence of duress as a defence under customary international law. This case is troubling from one particular angle: it is evident that the majority here explicitly referred to and applied the high frequency and high consistency test of the ICJ for State practice for the determination of customary international criminal law to the detriment of the accused.[78] In contrast, Judge *Cassese*, in his dissenting opinion in the *Erdemović* Case, held that the prosecution has failed to establish a special customary rule that would exclude the applicability of duress in international criminal proceedings, as the prosecution could only rely on one case and two military manuals, and that in that regard the State practice was manifestly inconsistent.[79] At the SCSL, the *Fofana* Appeals Chamber determined that acts of burning could not be included under the customary crime of pillage, stating that the prosecution's reference to three military manuals could not be considered thorough enough to satisfy the extensive and virtually uniform test for State practice.[80] However the defence was also rebuked by the SCSL Appeals Chamber in the *Taylor* Case when it sought to modify the *mens rea* standard of "knowing participation" as an element of aiding and abetting. While the Appeals Chamber acknowledged that existing customary international law "can be modified if the combination of *opinio juris* and state practice show a continuing and consistent adherence to the new custom by the international community," it stated that "the Defence has failed to identify any examples of such *opinio juris* and state practice, much less a continuing and consistent adherence."[81]

That is not to suggest that these chambers were wrong concerning the result, the non-existence of customary international law in relation to the content in these respective cases. However, these examples illustrate an ambivalent application of the traditional method to determine customary international criminal law. When the judges are faced with a claim of the existence of a customary international law that contradicts their legal conviction, they require proof of the existence of customary international criminal law according to a traditional approach, namely strict evidence of State practice –in some cases explicitly referring to the high frequency and high consistency test—and *opinio iuris*. By applying such a strict standard the

---

[77]ICTY, *Erdemović* Appeals Judgment, para 19.

[78]ICTY, *Erdemović* Appeals Judgment, Joint Separate Opinion of Judge McDonald and Judge Vohrah, paras 46–55, explicitly referring to the authoritative statement of the ICJ in the North Sea Continental Shelf Cases.

[79]ICTY, *Erdemović* Appeals Judgment, Separate and Dissenting Opinion of Judge Cassese, para 40.

[80]SCSL, *Fofana* Appeals Judgment, paras 389ff, 405.

[81]SCSL, *Taylor* Appeals Judgment, para 484. The Appeals Chamber was not willing to accept an alternate purpose or specific direction under customary international law.

judges conveniently allow themselves to sweep away claims of the existence of customary international law contrary to their personal beliefs.

Despite this critique, there are examples when the chambers applied a more sophisticated elaboration on the non-existence of customary international criminal law. The ICTY *Kordić* Appeals Chamber sought to determine whether the war crime of "unlawful attacks on civilians" required the showing of serious injury, death, or damage. After a careful analysis it stated that in relation to unlawful attacks on civilians, "State practice was not settled as some required the showing of serious injury, death or damage as a result under their national penal legislation, while others did not."[82] As a result it held that criminal responsibility for unlawful attacks on civilians requires the proof of a result element, causing death, serious injury to body or health.[83]

Interestingly, chambers also responded favourably to the methodological approach of determining customary international law of previous judgments. For example, the ICTY Appeals Chamber in the *Ojdanić* JCE Decision stated that it "does not propose to revisit its finding in *Tadić* concerning the customary status of this form of liability [*i.e.* JCE]. It is satisfied that the *state practice and opinio juris reviewed in that decision* was sufficient to permit the conclusion that such a norm existed under customary international law".[84] In that regard it is evident that the ICTY *Ojdanić* Appeals Chamber misconstrued the methodological approach of the ICTY *Tadić* Appeals Chamber. While the ICTY *Tadić* Appeals Chamber considered international conventions in its analysis[85] as well as national legislation,[86] it nevertheless based its customary law finding of Joint Criminal Enterprise entirely on post World War II case law. According to the ICTY *Tadić* Appeals Chamber, the other evidences merely "warrant the conclusion that case law [referred to by the Chamber in its analysis of the different forms of JCE] reflects customary rules of international criminal law."[87] The

---

[82]ICTY, *Kordić* Appeals Judgment, paras 62–66. The Appeals Chamber highlighted the fact that even under the grave breaches regime of AP I in relation to unlawful attacks against civilians, it would be required that these cause "death or serious injury to body or health", see Art. 85 (3) AP I.

[83]ICTY, *Kordić* Appeals Judgment, para 67.

[84]ICTY, *Ojdanić* Appeals Decision on JCE, para 29 (emphasis added).

[85]International Convention for the Suppression of Terrorist Bombing (adopted by consensus by the General Assembly Resolution 52/164 (15 December 1997), Art. 2 (3) (c)); Art. 25 of the ICC Rome Statute (viewing it as an expression of *opinio iuris*).

[86]Although the Appeals Chamber demonstrated that common purpose is "rooted" in the domestic legal system of many States, it seems as if it did not factor those laws and decisions in its assessment of applicable law. They did not constitue general principles of law due to the small number of examples. Furthermore the domestic laws did not incorporate customary international humanitarian law and thus could not be considered for the formation of customary international law. See ICTY, *Tadić* Appeals Chamber Judgment, para 225.

[87]ICTY, *Tadić* Appeals Chamber Judgment, para 226. Also the *Đorđević* Appeals Chamber misconstrues the methodological approach of the *Tadić* Appeals Chamber. It quotes para 226 of the *Tadić* Appeals Judgment referring to the "consistency and cogency of case law and the treaties referred to [. . .] as well as their consonance with the general principles on criminal responsibility laid down both in the Statute and general international criminal law and in national legislation" but omits the essential conclusion of para 226 that the "case law reflects customary rules of international criminal law". *Đorđević* Appeals Judgment, paras 41 and 35.

Tadić Appeals Chamber was effusively willing to declare that these cases themselves are indicative of the existence of customary international law, although without conducting an adequate inquiry into State practice or *opinio iuris*. The existence of JCE as a mode of liability under customary international law is thus a question of what "authoritative value" shall be attributed to those post World War II cases, and the extent to which they could be used as subsidiary means for determining customary international law as a methodological shortcut, as will be considered in a later chapter.[88]

6.3.2   Non-allocation to Elements Method

The identification of concrete evidence for (lasting, consistent, widespread) State practice and *opinio iuris* is a cumbersome task, which international criminal tribunals willingly choose to avoid were possible.[89] Rather than applying a meticulous analysis of customary international criminal law by establishing concrete evidences for State practice and *opinio iuris*, international criminal tribunals generally prefer not to allocate the listed evidence to the elements of State practice or *opinio iuris*.[90] It allows the chambers the comfortable position of simply enumerating all instances of evidence for the determination of customary international criminal law, without being required to address the quantity of the evidence, which in terms of State practice would correspond to the consistency/uniformity test as established by the ICJ Continental Shelf Case. Nor do they need to ascertain the legal relevance attached to these instances. The conception of sources is wide, comprising international conventions, resolutions of international organizations, the work of the ILC and the ICRC, international and domestic case law, official pronouncements of States or other international actors, national legislation and the writings of legal scholars. Mere enumeration of these sources allow the chambers of international criminal tribunals to avoid the task of classifying the listed elements as instances of State practice, *opinio iuris*, or both, or as mere subsidiary means for the determination of a rule of law.[91] Since there is no allocation of these evidences to the elements of State practice and *opinio iuris*, the reader of these judgments is left uninformed as to the value of these evidences for the determination of customary international criminal law. Such a "non-allocation" approach is by far the most commonly applied "method" for the determination of customary international

---

[88] See further Sect. 6.3.4, Methodological Shortcuts; see also Sect. 7.7, Jurisprudence.

[89] See the scarce use of the terminology of State practice and *opinio iuris* by international criminal tribunals under Sect. 6.3.1.1, Preliminary Remarks.

[90] See also *B. Schlütter*, Developments in Customary International law (2010), 187, naming such an approach to customary international law the "sources based approach".

[91] In order to make the identification of customary international criminal law a tangible venture this thesis will try to identify the legal value of these different instances under Chap. 7, Relevant Material for Proving the Existence of Customary International Criminal Law.

criminal law and has been applied by all international criminal tribunals. While it would go beyond the scope of the thesis to elaborate on each and every instance of the "non-allocation" approach, some representative examples will serve to illustrate.

At the ICTY, the *Tadić* Trial Chamber elaborated on the customary status of crimes against humanity and various conditions of its applicability. This included the nexus requirement to armed conflicts as demanded by the ICTY Statute but which according to the Trial Chamber departs from customary law; and the civilian population requirement, the need to demonstrate the widespread or systematic occurrence of the acts in question. Moreover, the Trial Chamber determined that a State policy is not a necessary requirement for crimes against humanity under customary international law, and it determined that knowledge can be implied from the circumstances with regard to *mens rea*.[92] These analyses share a key feature: in each example the *Tadić* Trial Chamber does not seek to establish concrete evidence for State practice or *opinio iuris*, but instead refers to various international and national instruments without indicating their authoritative value for the determination of customary international law. These references include statutes of other international criminal tribunals such as the Nuremberg and Tokyo Charter and the ICTR Statute, resolutions of the General Assembly, statements of States before the UN Security Council, the ILC Nuremberg principles and ILC Draft Codes, national legislation such as Control Council Law No. 10, international conventions such as the 1968 Convention on the Non-Applicability of Statutory Limitations to War Crimes and Crimes Against Humanity, the 1948 Genocide Convention, the 1973 Convention on Apartheid, the writing of legal scholars and national and international case law (mainly referring to the ICTY's own decisions). Again, this is not to say that the ICTY *Tadić* Trial Chamber was wrong in its result with regard to the existence of the requirements of crimes against humanity under customary international law. However, by the non-allocation of the evidences to which it refers, the Trial Chamber avoids a sound methodological review of its customary law determination, because in the judgment there is no trace of specific allocated evidence for the elements of State practice and *opinio iuris*.

The non-allocation of evidence to the concrete elements of State practice and *opinio iuris* is a recurring theme through the entire jurisprudence of the ICTY. It has been applied in relation to specific crimes, including the crime of genocide[93],

---

[92]ICTY, *Tadić* Trial Judgment, paras 618–659.

[93]ICTY, *Jelisić* Trial Judgment, paras 59ff, that excepting national case law does not allocate evidence to specific instances of State practice or *opinio iuris*; see also ICTY, *Krstić* Trial Judgment, paras 541ff referring to several sources in its analysis of customary international law, *inter alia* the 1948 Genocide Convention, ILC Draft Codes, the reports of the sub-commission on prevention of discrimination and protection of minorities of the UN but which allocated only the Rome Statute and national legislation and jurisprudence as specific evidence for State practice or *opinio iuris*. *Prosecutor v. Popović*, IT-05-88-T, Trial Chamber, Judgment, 10 June 2010, paras 807ff.

imprisonment[94], extermination[95], persecution[96], other inhumane acts[97], enslavement[98] and deportation[99] as crimes against humanity, its chapeau requirements[100], as well as modes of liability such as command responsibility.[101]

As stated above, at the ICTR customary international law is asserted rather than proven.[102] Since the ICTR chambers do not even explicitly refer to State practice and/or *opinio iuris* as elements for the establishment of customary international law in their judgments, the evidence listed cannot be allocated to the element of State practice or *opinio iuris*.

The SCSL also applied the non-allocation to elements approach in its case law. It was used in relation to specific crimes, such as the crime of acts of terrorism[103] and pillage,[104] both being charged as war crimes under Art. 3 SCSL Statute, enlisting

---

[94]ICTY, *Kordić* Trial Judgment, paras 295ff

[95]ICTY, *Vasiljević* Trial Judgment, paras 216ff; *Prosecutor v. Blagojević & Jokić*, IT-02-60-T, Trial Chamber, Judgment, 17 January 2005, paras 570ff; *Krstić* Trial Judgment, paras 490ff.

[96]ICTY, *Tadić* Trial Judgment, paras 694ff; *Prosecutor v. Blaškić*, IT-95-14-T, Trial Chamber, Judgment, 3 March 2000, paras 219ff; *Prosecutor v. Krajišnik*, IT-00-39-T, Trial Chamber, Judgment, 27 September 2006, paras 733ff.

[97]ICTY, *Blaškić* Trial Judgment, paras 237ff.

[98]ICTY, *Kunarac* Trial Judgment, paras 518ff.

[99]ICTY, *Stakić* Appeals Judgment, paras 274ff establishing that deportation requires that individuals are transferred across a State border or *de facto* border, referring to post World War II jurisprudence, international conventions, the ILC Draft code, the ICRC Custom Study and ICTY jurisprudence, but not explicitly referring to State practice or *opinio iuris*.

[100]E.g. the ICTY *Kupreškić* Trial Chamber in its Judgment at para 577 determined that under customary international law the nexus requirement between crimes against humanity and war crimes vanished, referring to Control Council Law No. 10, national legislation and case law, international conventions and prior ICTY jurisprudence without indicating their value for the establishment of State practice and/or *opinio iuris*. The *Martić* Appeals Chamber determined that the chapeau of crimes against humanity does not require that the individual victim has civilian status but determined that persons *hors de combat* can also be victims of crimes against humanity. It came to this conclusion by a consideration of various international instruments without allocating them to instances of State practice or *opinio iuris*; see Appeals Chamber, *Prosecutor v. Martić*, IT-95-11-A, Appeals Chamber, Judgment, 8 October 2008, paras 303ff. See also ICTY, *Kunarac* Appeals Judgment, para 98 (footnote 114), that the existence of a State plan or policy is not a requirement for crimes against humanity under customary international law.

[101]ICTY, *Prosecutor v. Aleksovski*, IT-95-14/1, Trial Chamber, Judgment, 25 June 1999, paras 66ff; ICTY, *Delalić* Trial Judgment, paras 333ff; ICTY, *Delalić* Appeals Judgment, paras 228ff; *Prosecutor v. Halilović*, IT-01-48-T, Trial Chamber, Judgment, 16 November 2005, paras 38ff.

[102]See Sect. 6.2, A Word of Caution.

[103]SCSL, *Brima* Trial Judgment, paras 660ff *inter alia* referring to AP II, ICTY case law, the report of the United nations War Crimes Commission, domestic military manuals.

[104]SCSL, *Brima* Trial Judgment, paras 750ff; *Sesay* Trial Judgment, paras 204ff.

children[105] charged under Art. 4 SCSL Statute, and to other inhumane acts[106] and enslavement[107] as crimes against humanity.

Thus the chambers of international criminal tribunals, when applying the non-allocation approach to the determination of customary international criminal law, fail to indicate the value of the listed evidence as either proving State practice and/or *opinio iuris* or as subsidiary means for the determination of a rule of law. In order to make the identification of customary international criminal law a tangible venture this study will seek to identify the legal value of these different instruments for the determination of customary international law in a later chapter.[108]

6.3.3   Deductive Approach

6.3.3.1   Preliminary Remarks

In addition to the traditional two elements approach and the "non-allocation" method, the deductive method is another approach applied by international criminal tribunals to identify customary international criminal norms. The deductive method can be described as going from the general to the specific, finding specific customary rules that are derived from general and universally accepted principles.[109] Thus the jurisprudence takes recourse to general principles of international humanitarian law, most importantly as contained in the Martens Clause, the principles of humanity and the dictates of public conscience, the principle of distinction, the principle of responsible command, the principle of human dignity, or the elementary considerations of humanity.

6.3.3.2   Value-Based Deductive Approach and Deduction from Technical Humanitarian Principles

When the ICTY began it was faced with the problem that there was a contrast between the vast number of rules applicable to international armed conflicts, and the few rules for NIACs. To bridge this gap the ICTY chambers referred to a

---

[105] SCSL, *Fofana* Trial Judgment, paras 182ff *inter alia* referring to AP I and AP II. the 1989 Convention on the Rights of the Child, the Rome Statute.

[106] SCSL, *Brima* Trial Judgment, paras 697ff referring to ICTY case law, the IMT Nuremberg Charter, Control Council Law No. 10, the Rome Statute and national case law.

[107] SCSL, *Brima* Trial Judgment, paras 739ff.

[108] See Chap. 7, Relevant Material for Proving the Existence of Customary International Criminal Law.

[109] On the inductive and deductive method in relation to the determination of customary international law, see generally, W. T. *Worster*, The Inductive and Deductive Methods in Customary International Law Analysis: Traditional and Modern Approaches, Georgetown Journal of International Law (2014), 445ff. *Worster* suggests that in relation to customary international law induction and deduction are not opposing but intertwined methods.

concept established by ICJ jurisprudence: "the elementary considerations of humanity".[110] The ICTY considered that Common Article 3 of the 1949 Geneva Conventions was applicable to both international and non-international armed conflicts, stipulating a "minimum yardstick" reflecting customary international law simply because it was based on "elementary considerations of humanity."[111] Again, the famous ICTY *Tadić* Appeals Chamber Jurisdiction Decision is of particular importance here. That decision has already been used to demonstrate that international criminal tribunals adhere to the traditional requirements of State practice and *opinio iuris* when establishing criminal responsibility for war crimes committed in NIACs under customary international law.[112] However, the Appeals Chamber simultaneously applied different methods to identify customary international law. It also adhered to a deductive reasoning when establishing customary rules of international humanitarian law that govern IACs.[113] According to the *Tadić* Appeals Chamber, the traditional distinction between rules applicable in IACs and in NIACs had been blurred, since a "State-sovereignty-oriented approach has been gradually supplanted by a human-being-oriented approach".[114] It proclaimed that "*elementary considerations of humanity* and common sense make it preposterous that the use by States of weapons prohibited in armed conflicts between themselves be allowed when States try to put down rebellion by their own nationals on their own territory. *What is inhumane, and consequently proscribed, in international wars, cannot but be inhumane and inadmissible in civil strife.*"[115]

It is doctrinally questionable whether the *Tadić* Appeals Chamber drew that conclusion by analogy, arguing that certain rules of IACs also covered situations of NIACs, or whether it relied on a deductive approach on basis of vague humanitarian principles. The mere fact that rules of humanitarian law are based on "elementary considerations of humanity" was apparently considered valid enough to argue that these rules also reflect customary international law applicable in NIAC. But the *Tadić* Appeals Chamber did not stop there. Although admitting that Common

---

[110]ICJ Corfu Channel Case, 22, claiming that a notification obligation of the existence of a minefield in Albanian territorial waters in order to warn approaching ships stems from "elementary considerations of humanity". The ICJ in the Nicaragua Case, para 218, applied these "elementary considerations of humanity" with regard to Common Article 3. The ICJ in Legality of the Threat of Nuclear, para 29, held that rules being based on "elementary considerations of humanity" constitute "intransgressible principles of international customary law".

[111]ICTY, *Prosecutor v. Mrkšić*, IT-95-13/1, Appeals Chamber, Judgment, 5 May 2009, para 70; *Krajišnik* Trial Judgment, para 706; *Prosecutor v. Naletilić*, IT-98-34-T, Trial Chamber, Judgment, 31 March 2003, para 228; *Delalić* Trial Judgment, para 303; *Delalić* Appeals Judgment, para 140; *Prosecutor v. Aleksovski*, IT-95-14/1, Trial Chamber, Judgment, 25 June 1999, para 50; ICTY, *Tadić* Appeals Chamber Jurisdiction Decision, para 102; *Tadić* Trial Judgment, para 609.

[112]See Sect. 6.3.1.2, ICTY *Tadić* Appeals Chamber Jurisdiction Decision.

[113]ICTY, *Tadić* Appeals Chamber Jurisdiction Decision, paras 96ff. See also *Schlütter* (supra note 90), 225 determining that the Appeals Chamber "combines the traditional two-element approach with deductive reasoning".

[114]ICTY, *Tadić* Appeals Chamber Jurisdiction Decision, para 97.

[115]ICTY, *Tadić* Appeals Chamber Jurisdiction Decision, para 119 (emphasis added).

Article 3 of the 1949 Geneva Conventions does not contain "explicit reference to criminal liability for violation of its provisions", it had no doubt that these violations, whether committed in IACs or NIACs, entail individual criminal responsibility:

> Principles and rules of humanitarian law reflect *"elementary considerations of humanity"* widely recognized as the mandatory minimum for conduct in armed conflicts of any kind. *No one can doubt the gravity of the acts at issue, nor the interest of the international community in their prohibition.*[116]

It is only after the result—the existence of individual responsibility for violations of rules of international humanitarian law applicable in NIAC under customary law—has already been determined that the Appeals Chamber turns to the task of whether State practice and *opinio iuris* substantiates such a customary law determination.[117] After elaborating on State practice and *opinio iuris*, the ICTY *Tadić* Appeals Chamber concluded that "customary international law imposes criminal liability for serious violations of common Article 3, *as supplemented by other general principles and rules* on the protection of victims of internal armed conflict, and for breaching certain fundamental principles and rules regarding means and methods of combat in civil strife."[118] The ICTY *Tadić* Appeals Chamber's deductive reasoning was based on "elementary considerations of humanity" and the acknowledgment that customary international criminal law with regard to war crimes committed in NIACs can be "supplemented by other general principles", and thus it opened the door for the "humanization of law"[119] reasoning by international criminal tribunals. A general approach for the determination of customary international criminal law adheres to the following deductive steps: Firstly, principles are identified that underlie the components that constitute international criminal law, most of which refer to principles of international humanitarian law. Secondly, it is stated that the customary nature of a law is given as it enshrines these principles or even that criminality is directly derived from these principles. Thirdly, on that basis the chambers develop the concrete elements of the crimes that have been charged.

Elaborating on Art. 3 ICTY Statute and the responsibility for war crimes committed in non-international armed conflicts, the ICTY *Delalić* Appeals

---

[116]ICTY, *Tadić* Appeals Chamber Jurisdiction Decision, paras 128–129 (emphasis added).

[117]ICTY, *Tadić* Appeals Chamber Jurisdiction Decision, 133.

[118]ICTY, *Tadić* Appeals Chamber Jurisdiction Decision, para 134 (emphasis added).

[119]See generally *T. Meron*, The Humanization of International Law (2006); on the role of Judge *Cassese* in this development, see *T. Hoffmann*, The Gentle Civilizer of Humanitarian Law, in Stahn/van den Herik (eds.), Future Perspectives on International Criminal Justice (2010), 58ff. Other writers see that "the proclamation of a new substantive universal (and common good) signifies a 'turn to ethics', a potential moralization of law, which leads actors unconsciously down the path of a deformalization of international law itself. Common juridical values, such as democracy or human rights, become fundamental, and guaranteeing them is sometimes understood as necessary due, in effect, to their own intrinsic value, and not due to the fact that they are inscribed in the texts of positive law", see *E. Jouannet*, Universalism and Imperialism (2007), 389.

Chamber determined that Common Article 3 reflects fundamental humanitarian principles that underlie international humanitarian law as a whole, which promote respect for *human dignity* and is therefore applicable to all armed conflicts.[120] The Chamber claimed that the protection of human dignity was the very purpose of the Geneva Conventions and as such the discrepancies in the legal regimes applicable to IACs and NIACs had to be resolved.[121] Based upon the fundamental principle of respect for human dignity, the *Delalić* Appeals Chamber not only established the customary law basis for Common Article 3, but added individual criminal responsibility. By stating that the NCSI principle "does not prevent a court form interpreting and clarifying the elements of a particular crime"[122] the ICTY *Delalić* Appeals Chamber defended the way its Trial Chamber has defined the elements of crimes for charges made under Art. 3 ICTY Statute, *inter alia* murder, torture and cruel treatment. It conveniently circumvents the requirement to establish State practice and *opinio iuris* for the international crimes charged. After all, murder, torture and cruel treatment all violate the dignity of the human person.

In some way or the other, in the early phase of the ICTY all chambers took recourse to a purposive elaboration on customary international criminal law in the general spirit of international humanitarian law, which is said to safeguard *human dignity* or *human treatment/protection*,[123] while other chambers apply the Martens

---

[120]ICTY, *Delalić* Appeals Judgment, para 143.

[121]ICTY, *Delalić* Appeals Judgment, para 172 (emphasis added).

[122]ICTY, *Delalić* Appeals Judgment, para 173.

[123]See e.g. ICTY, *Furundžija* Trial Judgment, para 162, when elaborating and defining torture under Art. 3 ICTY Statute; ICTY, *Aleksovski* Trial Judgment, elaborating and defining "outrages upon personal dignity" under Art. 3 ICTY Statute, paras 49ff; *Delalić* Trial Judgment, para 263 eliminating a strict nationality requirement in order to determine a broad category of protected persons under the grave breaches regime based on ethnicity; ICTY, *Jelisić* Trial Judgment, para 83 determining that "international custom admits the characterization of genocide even when the exterminatory intent only extends to a limited geographic zone" based on the object and purpose of the Genocide Convention; *Blaškić* Trial Judgment, para 167ff stating that Common Article 3 expresses the fundamental principle underlying the Geneva Conventions, humane treatment, and that it covers acts of AP I relating to unlawful attacks upon civilian targets. The *Aleksovski* Appeals Judgment, para 146 defended the "overall control" test against the "effective control" test of the ICJ as the former "provides for greater protection of civilian victims of armed conflicts, this different and less rigorous standard is wholly consistent with the fundamental purpose of Geneva Convention IV, which is to ensure protection of civilians to the maximum extent possible." At the ICTR the *Akayesu* Appeals Chamber determined that the "purpose of common Article 3 [is] to ensure respect for the few essential rules of humanity which all civilized nations consider as valid everywhere and under all circumstances" and determined that protection of victims is at the core of Common Article 3. The *Akayesu* Appeals Chamber on basis of this purpose determined that individual responsibility on that basis could not be restricted to specific perpetrators merely belonging to the members of armed forces but chose a wide application; see ICTR, *Prosecutor v. Akayesu*, ICTR-96-4-A, Appeals Chamber, Judgment, 1 June 2001, paras 439ff.

Clause,[124] which refers to the *principles of humanity* and the *dictates of public conscience*.[125] It may be argued that, methodologically speaking, the chambers were applying an object and purpose interpretation of the conventional norms of international humanitarian law that underlie the statutes of international criminal tribunals on basis of these fundamental humanitarian principles.[126] However, in that regard the lines between treaty interpretation and customary international law are not only being blurred, as maintained by some authors,[127] but are non-existent. This conclusion can be drawn as the chambers did not differ between the conventional norm and its customary mirror. For example, the ICTY *Kupreškić* Trial Chamber used the Martens Clause as an interpretative guideline to construe the humanitarian rule of precaution in attacks and their effects as narrowly as possible, so as to maximise the protection of civilians. By referring to the prescriptions of "Articles 57 and 58 [AP I] (*and of the corresponding customary rules*)" its reasoning applies to both conventional norms and customary norms.[128] As a result the margin of discretion allowed to belligerents is narrowed. The Trial Chamber has conveniently used the Martens Clause to reach that conclusion by a narrow interpretation of the humanitarian treaty norms and their customary mirror.

Such an object and purpose approach on the basis of the underlying humanitarian values has met with only little resistance in the jurisprudence. The ICTY *Krnojelac* Trial Chamber notably sought to curb such a deductive approach when criticizing previous trial chambers that expanded the crime of torture with a *mens*

---

[124] ICTY, *Tadić* Trial Judgment, para 618 referring to the Martens Clause to determine that crimes against humanity was not a "novel concept" of the IMT Charter; ICTY, *Furundžija* Trial Judgment *inter alia* referring to the Martens Clause to determine that "a general prohibition against torture has evolved in customary international law" (para 137) and that "the prohibition of rape and serious sexual assault has also evolved in customary international law" (para 168); *Kupreškić* Trial Judgment, para525ff elaborating on the customary rules of precaution in attacks on military objectives causing damage to civilians; *Hadžihasanović* Trial Chamber Decision, para 64 referring to the Martens Clause as containing fundamental principles of international humanitarian law and, in the very next paragraph on the principle of criminal responsibility, establishing the principle of responsible command and the principle of command responsibility. The Appeals Chamber did not refer to the Martens Clause in its decision on interlocutory appeal, but adhered to another deductive reasoning, see supra note 154 and accompanying text.

[125] The original Martens Clause was contained in the preamble to the 1899 Hague Convention concerning the laws or customs of war on land: "Until a more complete code of the laws of war is issued, the High Contracting Parties think it right to declare that in cases not included in the Regulations adopted by them, populations and belligerents remain under the protection and empire of the principles of international law as they result from the usages established between civilized nations, from the laws of humanity, and the requirements of the public conscience." A modern version of the Martens Clause is found in Art. 1 (2) AP I and the preamble of AP II referring to "the principles of humanity" and "the dictates of public conscience".

[126] With regard to the Martens Clause it has been argued that it could be used as an interpretative guideline to international humanitarian rules, see e.g. *A. Cassese*, The Martens Clause: Half a Loaf or Simply Pie in the Sky?, 11 European Journal of International Law (2000), 212–3.

[127] E.g. *Schlütter* (supra note 90), 254ff.

[128] ICTY, *Kupreškić* Trial Judgment, para 525.

rea requirement of "humiliation" of the torture victim. It stated that "[i]n light of the principle of legality, the proposition that 'the primary purpose of humanitarian law is to safeguard human dignity' is not sufficient to permit the court to introduce, as part of the *mens rea*, a new and additional prohibited purpose, which would in effect enlarge the scope of criminal prohibition against torture beyond what it was at the time relevant to the indictment under consideration."[129] Such critical appraisals are, however, the exception and not the rule.

Interestingly, fundamental humanitarian principles have also been used to challenge the traditional requirements for the formation of customary international law. The ICTY *Kupreškić* Trial Chamber did not "merely" use the Martens Clause as an interpretative guideline of rules of customary norms of IHL. Although it stated that the Martens Clause is not an autonomous source of law,[130] when analyzing the customary rules of reprisals against civilians it utilized the clause as a justification for a differentiated methodology when determining customary international humanitarian rules. The Trial Chamber was faced with the problem that the treaty provisions that prohibit reprisals, as contained in Arts. 51 (6) and 52 (1) AP I, had not been ratified by powerful States, such as the US, France, India, Indonesia, Israel, Japan, Pakistan and Turkey. Therefore it could not be argued that the treaty norms were a codification of existing customary norms or crystallizing new customary norms.[131] It also admitted that it could not detect adequate recent State practice to establish customary international law by a traditional method. Despite this apparent deadlock, the ICTY *Kupreškić* Trial Chamber pushed for a methodological *coup d'état* when determining customary international humanitarian law:

> This is however an area where *opinio iuris sive necessitatis* may play a much greater role than *usus*, as a result of the aforementioned Martens Clause. In the light of the way States and courts have implemented it, this Clause clearly shows that principles of international humanitarian law may emerge through a customary process under the pressure of the demands of humanity or the dictates of public conscience, even where State practice is scant or inconsistent. The other element, in the form of *opinio necessitatis*, crystallizing as a

---

[129]ICTY, *Prosecutor v. Krnojelac*, IT-97-25-T, Trial Chamber, Judgment, 15 March 2002, para 186.

[130]ICTY, *Kupreškić* Trial Judgment, para 525. See also the positions of the UK with regard to the ICJ's Nuclear Weapons Advisory Opinion, as quoted in T. *Meron*, The Martens Clause, Principles of Humanity, and the Dictates of Public Conscience, 94 American Journal of International Law (2000), 85: "While the Martens Clause makes clear that the absence of a specific treaty provision on the use of nuclear weapons is not, in itself, sufficient to establish that such weapons are capable of lawful use, the Clause does not, on its own, establish their illegality." This conclusion is drawn despite the clause's loose wording that seems that seems to elevate "the principles of humanity" and "the dictates of public conscience" to the same level as "usages established between civilized nations"; see in that regard T. *Rensmann*, die Humanisierung des Völkerrechts durch das *ius in bello* – Von der Martens'schen Klausel zu "Responsibility to Protect", 68 Zeitschrift für ausländisches öffentliches Recht und Völkerrecht (2008), 114; *Cassese* (supra note 126), 188, 193ff.

[131]On the role of treaties for the determination of customary international law see Sect. 7.5, International Conventions.

result of the imperatives of humanity or public conscience, may turn out to be the decisive element heralding the emergence of a general rule or principle of humanitarian law.[132]

The following conclusions can be drawn from the ICTY *Kupreškić* Trial Chamber's approach to customary international humanitarian law: Firstly, it is indifferent to State practice as a necessary element for the formation of customary international law. The Trial Chamber even quotes State practice in the form of military manuals that allow reprisals against civilians but does not take them into account for its determination of customary international law.[133] Secondly, while some writers argue that the utilization of the Martens Clause "reinforces a trend, which is already strong in international institutions and tribunals, toward basing the existence of customary law primarily on *opinio juris*",[134] corresponding to a modern approach to customary international law,[135] the *Kupreškić* Trial Chamber went even further. It made a deliberate distinction between *opinio iuris* and *opinio necessitatis*.[136] It did not require that customary law is based on a "legal conviction", but contented itself with the existence of extra-legal convictions based on social, moral, or political necessity in order to establish the prevailing psychological element for the determination of customary international law.[137] The ICTY *Kupreškić* Trial Chamber explicitly based its customary law finding on the prohibition of reprisals entirely on the existence of *opinio necessitatis*. This was, it claimed, manifested in UN General Assembly Resolution 2675 (1970), the number of States that have ratified AP I, and the fact that States generally refrained from claiming to have a right to use reprisals against civilians.[138] While these manifestations might very well be used to prove a legal conviction, *i.e. opinio iuris*,[139] the wording used by the ICTY *Kupreškić* Trial Chamber suggests that customary law can be based on *opinio necessitatis* alone, that is to say, out of social, moral, or political necessity. This methodological artifice is, according to the ICTY *Kupreškić* Trial Chamber, made possible by the Martens Clause, the demands of humanity and the dictates of public conscience.

---

[132]ICTY, *Kupreškić* Trial Judgment, para 527.

[133]ICTY, *Kupreškić* Trial Judgment, para 532

[134]*Meron* (supra note 130), 88; in a similar vein *Rensmann* (supra note 130), 114.

[135]See Sect. 4.3.2, The Procedural Aspect of Modern Customary International Law.

[136]ICTY, *Kupreškić* Trial Judgment, para 531.

[137]On *opinio iuris sive necessitatis* see Sect. 4.2.2, Opinio Iuris Under a Traditional Interpretation. See also *Cassese*, presiding judge in the *Kupreškić* Trial Chamber, in his scholarly writing *Cassese* (supra note 126), at 214: "Put differently, the requirement of *opinio iuris* or *opinio necessitatis* may take on a special prominence. As a result, the expression of legal views by a number of states and other international subjects concerning the binding value of a principle or a rule, *or the social and moral need for its observance by states*, may be held to be conductive to the formation of a principle or a customary rule, even when those legal views are *not backed up by widespread and consistent state practice, or even by no practice at all.*" (emphasis added).

[138]ICTY, *Kupreškić* Trial Judgment, paras 532–533.

[139]See further Sect. 7.6.2, UN General Assembly Resolutions.

In his legal writing *Cassese* considered the Martens Clause to be "an ingenious blend of natural law and positivism".[140] The Martens Clause, being itself enshrined in positive law, in international humanitarian law conventions, could be viewed as providing a bridge between the polarizing positions of positivism and naturalism. However, it is more appropriate to say that such a use of the Martens Clause for the determination of customary international law conceals the re-invocation of naturalism in positivistic clothing.[141] It is evident that the way the Martens Clause has been applied by the ICTY *Kupreškić* Trial Chamber is nothing less than the equation of morial, social or political necessity with customary international law.[142] It has to be noted that the ICTY *Kupreškić* Trial Chamber's finding—that reprisals against civilians are absolutely prohibited under customary international law—has been criticized in the legal literature.[143] It has not been followed by subsequent ICTY jurisprudence and national State practice.[144] Despite this renunciation of the absolute prohibition of reprisals under customary international humanitarian law, the ICTY *Kupreškić* Trial Chamber's methodological approach to the determination of customary international law has left its mark in the case law of another international criminal tribunal. At the ECCC the Supreme Court Chamber has held that when "evaluating the emergence of a principle or general rule concerning conduct that offends the laws of humanity or the dictates of public conscience (. . .) the requirement of *opinio juris* may take pre-eminence over the

---

[140]*Cassese* (supra note 126), 189.

[141]See also *R. Cryer*, The Philosophy of International Criminal Law, in Orakhelashvili (ed.), Research Handbook on the Theory and History of International Law (2011), 250, stating in regard to the ICTY *Kupreškić* Trial Chamber reasoning that "the argumentation is notionally, or presentationally, positivist. The argument of the Chamber was that custom accepted the position, and, again some State practice was (mis)quoted. It is clear, though, that the underlying ideal of the opinion is naturalist."

[142]See also *T. Hoffmann*, The Gentle Civilizer of Humanitarian Law, in Stahn/van den Herik (eds.), Future Perspectives on International Criminal Justice (2010), 76.

[143]See e.g. *F. Kalshoven*, Reprisals and the Protection of Civilians, in Vohrah *et al* (eds.), Man's Inhumanity to Man: Essays in Honour of Antonio Cassese (2003), 481ff.

[144]See ICTY, *Prosecutor v. Martić*, IT-95-11-T, Trial Chamber, Judgment, 12 June 2007, paras 465ff arguing that reprisals can be considered lawful under international humanitarian law subject to strict conditions. That finding has been accepted by the Appeals Chamber, *Prosecutor v. Martić*, IT-95-11-A, Appeals Chamber, Judgment, 8 October 2008, paras 263ff. Concerning State practice see for example the explanatory note regarding the German draft law for the German Code of Crimes against International Law, Bundesratsdrucksache 29/02 of 15 January 2002, 33, considering that reprisals subject to strict conditions may constitute a justification for the commission of international crimes. The UK Joint Service Manual of the Law of Armed Conflict (2004), JSP 383, 423 explicitly criticizes the ICTY *Kupreškić* Trial Chamber stating that "the court's reasoning is unconvincing and the assertion that there is a prohibition in customary law flies in the face of most of the state practice that exists. The UK does not accept the position as stated in this judgment." Available at: https://www.gov.uk/government/publications/jsp-383-the-joint-service-manual-of-the-law-of-armed-conflict-2004-edition (last visited: 16 June 2017).

usus element of custom."[145] While the ECCC Supreme Court Chamber was not following the ICTY *Kupreškić* Trial Chamber's conception that *opinio necessitatis* can be considered as forming an adequate basis of customary international law, it was willing to declare that the *opinio iuris* element may trump State practice as the prevailing element for its determination.

In conclusion it can be said that the impact of value-based humanitarian principles on the determination of customary international law follows two different lines of legal reasoning: On the one hand, we encounter a deductive method that determines that customary international criminal law exists as it is derived from and interpreted according to general principles underlying international humanitarian law, such as elementary considerations of humanity, human dignity, or the Martens Clause containing the principles of humanity and the dictates of public conscience. Concerning the Martens Clause, on the other hand, it has also been argued that the clause enables international criminal tribunals to deviate from the traditional method to determine customary international law on basis of State practice and *opinio iuris*, by allowing them to base the existence of customary law primarily on *opinio iuris* or *opinio necessitatis*. However, in order to establish these "legal convictions" or "extra-legal convictions" recourse is again taken to a deductive approach, as *opinio iuris* or *opinio necessitatis* derive from declarations on the international forum, especially General Assembly resolutions.[146]

Within customary international law deductive reasoning in the jurisprudence of international criminal tribunals is not restricted to specific crimes or violations of international humanitarian law. It is also detectable in relation to modes of liability. In the *Hadžihasanović* Case the chambers had to determine whether command responsibility was applicable in non-international armed conflicts. Although the Chamber elaborated on a number of instruments, such as conventions, case law and military manuals that include command responsibility, all of these instruments applied in the context of international armed conflicts.[147] Indeed, with regard to the humanitarian law treaties applicable to non-international armed conflicts, there is a suspicious silence concerning command responsibility. The ICTY *Hadžihasanović* Trial Chamber determined that fundamental principles underlying international humanitarian law are the principles of responsible command and command responsibility,[148] and stated that it could "apply all principles of international criminal law to achieve the purposes of international humanitarian law".[149]

---

[145]ECCC, *Duch* Appeals Judgment, para 93. Note, however, that in that regard the ECCC Supreme Court Chambers referred to *Cassese's* legal writing and not to the ICTY *Kupreškić* Trial Chamber over which he presided.

[146]See also A. E. *Roberts*, Traditional and Modern Approaches to Customary International Law: A Reconciliation, 95 American Journal of International Law (2001), 758.

[147]ICTY, *Hadžihasanović* Trial Chamber Decision, paras 68ff, 151, 165.

[148]ICTY *Hadžihasanović* Trial Chamber Decision, para 65.

[149]ICTY *Hadžihasanović* Trial Chamber Decision, para 165.

It claimed that command responsibility has its roots in responsible command,[150] a principle also enshrined in the law applicable in NIACs, referring to the preamble of AP II;[151] and thus deduced command responsibility from the principle of responsible command. When the defence appealed the decision, the *Hadžihasanović* Appeals Chamber[152] determined that "to hold a principle was part of customary international law it has to be satisfied that State practice recognized the principle on the basis of supporting *opinio juris*",[153] thus affirming the traditional requirements for the determination of customary international law. However, this formal affirmation of the traditional requirements can be considered once more as a chamber paying lip-service to State practice and *opinio iuris* as necessary elements for the determination of customary international law. The Appeals Chamber did not conduct an inductive analysis of instances of State practice and *opinio iuris* to determine whether command responsibility in NIACs has a customary basis by a traditional method, but—just like its Trial Chamber—deduced command responsibility from the principle of responsible command. In the wording of the Appeals Chamber, "military organization implies responsible command and that responsible command in turn implies command responsibility."[154] The ICTY *Halilović* Trial Chamber affirms and adheres to the deductive approach of the *Hadžihasanović* Case, adding an alternative deductive reasoning by stipulating that the "principle of command responsibility may be seen in part to arise from one of the basic principles of international humanitarian law aiming at ensuring protection for protected categories of persons and objects during armed conflicts. This protection is at the very heart of international humanitarian law."[155] Despite this deductive reasoning, the ICTY Appeals Chamber in the *Hadžihasanović* Case switched to a traditional approach when determining whether a commander can be held responsible for crimes that have been committed by his subordinates before he took command. The Appeals Chamber stated that in "this particular case, no practice can be found, nor is there any evidence of *opinio juris* that would sustain the proposition that a commander can be held responsible for crimes committed by a subordinate prior to the commander's assumption of command over that subordinate."[156] Although a different result could have been achieved by a deductive reasoning being based on "responsible command", the Appeals Chamber has used a traditional approach to

---

[150]ICTY *Hadžihasanović* Trial Chamber Decision, paras 163ff.

[151]ICTY *Hadžihasanović* Trial Chamber Decision, para 87.

[152]ICTY, *Hadžihasanović* Appeals Chamber Decision.

[153]ICTY, *Hadžihasanović* Appeals Chamber Decision, para 12.

[154]ICTY, *Hadžihasanović* Appeals Chamber Decision, para 17. See also at para 22: "the elements of command responsibility are derived from the elements of responsible command." Compare also Partially Dissenting Opinion and Declaration of Judge *Liu* to *Prosecutor v. Orić*, IT-03-68-A, Appeals Chamber, Judgment, 3 July 2008, para 31.

[155]ICTY, *Halilović* Trial Judgment, para 39f.

[156]ICTY, *Hadžihasanović* Appeals Chamber Decision, para 45.

customary international law in order to deny the existence of customary international law in that specific instance.[157]

6.3.3.3   Concluding Remarks

As stated above, the deductive method can be described as going from the general to the specific, finding specific customary rules that are derived from general and universally accepted principles.[158] In terms of the question of a reflection of conventional humanitarian law as customary international law, *Baxter* argued that every new codification of humanitarian law is nothing more than a specification of a more general standard already laid down in earlier conventions. He argued, therefore, that humanitarian treaties should be viewed as reflecting customary international law without requiring much proof of a basis in the traditional elements of State practice and *opinion iuris*.[159] Indeed, it is a tempting simplification of the task of establishing customary international humanitarian law; however, it would result in a complete overlap of conventional humanitarian law and customary humanitarian law, as every norm of international humanitarian law can be derived from a core principle of humanitarian law, such as principle of distinction, proportionality, humanity and so forth.[160] Within the context of defining crimes and modes of liability under international criminal law such an approach is misplaced. One has to agree with Judge *Schomburg's* critique that simply deducing crimes from principles of humanitarian law "appears to be incorrect since it could be made in any context in relation to any and every violation of international humanitarian law."[161] Accordingly, such a deductive approach would equate every violation of a principle of international humanitarian law with a crime under international criminal law. However, without proof of the *criminalization* of norms of international humanitarian law, the present author advocates a clear distinction between State responsibility under international humanitarian law and individual criminal responsibility under international criminal law.[162] Since international criminal law is a separate and distinct legal discipline it is necessary to ensure that violations of international humanitarian law have been criminalized separately under customary international law in order to qualify as an international customary crime.

---

[157]For the issue of command responsibility before the commander's assumption of command see ICTY, *Hadžihasanović* Appeals Chamber Decision, para 45 and the dissenting opinions thereto.

[158]*Worster* (supra note 109), 445ff.

[159]R. *Baxter*, Multilateral Treaties as Evidence of Customary International Law, 41 British Yearbook of International Law (1965–66), 286 (emphasis added).

[160]*Spieker* (supra note 88), 59

[161]Separate and Partially Dissenting Opinion of Judge Schomburg to the ICTY, *Galić* Appeal Judgment, para 17.

[162]See already Sect. 3.10.5, The *praevia* Requirement and the Sources of International Law.

6.3.4   *Methodological Shortcuts: The Case Law Approach*

6.3.4.1   Preliminary Remarks

On various occasions international criminal tribunals would not attempt an analysis, to use *Schwarzenberger's* words, of the "law-creating process" ingredients that lead to the formation of customary international law generally indicating the existence of State practice and *opinio iuris*[163] or the other approaches established above. Instead, as has been evinced in the jurisprudence of international criminal tribunals, the existence of law is proven in particular with reference to case law. The predominant role of case law has been explained by the ICTY *Kupreškić* Trial Chamber: "The Tribunal's need to draw upon judicial decisions is only to be expected, due to the fact that both substantive and procedural criminal law is still at a rudimentary state in international law."[164]

The personal backgrounds of the judges that compose the bench in international criminal proceedings are relevant here. It is quite clear that judges that have a common law origin are generally used to cite cases as authority to support a legal position.[165] While the relevance of the decisions of different courts, inter-State courts, international and internationalized criminal tribunals, and national courts for the determination and formation of customary international law will be discussed in more detail in a latter chapter,[166] at this point one must consider why tribunals follow previous decisions. As we are dealing with methodological shortcuts for the determining of rules of law, the question as to whether international criminal tribunals might follow the *authority* of adjudicating bodies, in order to adhere to a binding *stare decisis* doctrine applicable at the international level that views previous decisions as binding precedents, will generally not be addressed.[167] International criminal tribunals have established a system of binding precedents within the same institutional setting. Here Trial Chambers are bound by the precedents of their Appeals Chambers, who themselves should only depart from

---

[163]See *G. Schwarzenberger*, The Inductive Approach to International Law (1965), 5; *G. Schwarzenberger*, International Law as Applied by International Courts and Tribunals (1957), Vol. 1, 28ff.

[164]ICTY, *Kupreškić* Trial Judgment, para 537; See also ICTY, *Furundžija* Trial Judgment, para 193: "Little light is shed on the definition of aiding and abetting by the international instruments providing for major war trials: the London Agreement, the Charter of the International Military Tribunal for the Far East, establishing the Tokyo Tribunal, and Control Council Law No. 10. It therefore becomes necessary to examine the case law."

[165]See also *I. Bantekas*, Reflections on Some Sources and Methods of International Criminal and Humanitarian Law, 6 International Criminal Law Review (2006), 131–2; *A. Cassese*, The Influence of the European Court on Human Rights on International Criminal Tribunals – Some Methodological Remarks, in Bergsmo (ed.), Human Rights and Criminal Justice For the Downtrodden: Essays in Honour of Asbjorn Eide (2003), 21; *A. Z. Borda*, The Use of Precedent as Subsidiary Means and Sources of International Criminal Law, 18 Tilburg Law Review (2013), 73.

[166]See Sect. 7.7, Jurisprudence.

[167]On that issue see *X. Tracol*, The Precedent of Appeals Chambers Decisions in the International Criminal Tribunals, 17 Leiden Journal of International Law (2004), 67ff.

precedents of previous Appeals Chambers for "cogent reasons in the interests of justice".[168] In this chapter the use of case law will be analyzed in light of Art. 38 (1) (d) ICJ Statute as "subsidiary means for the determination of rules of law". Accordingly, international criminal tribunals might use case law as a "genuine" subsidiary source whenever international conventions, customary international law, or general principles of law do not provide for an answer, to avoid a *non liquet* situation. Furthermore, international criminal tribunals could take pre-existing case law into consideration as subsidiary means to determine an existing rule of international law, *i.e.* a conventional or customary norm or a general principle of law. It is in this sense that *Schwarzenberger* speaks of courts as "law-determining agencies."[169]

6.3.4.2 Case Law as a Genuine "Subsidiary" Source of Law

Apart from binding precedents within the same institutional setting,[170] international criminal tribunals generally do not consider themselves bound by previous decisions of other international (criminal) courts.[171] However, as has been suggested by *Shahabuddeen*, this does not mean that they lack of any precedential value.[172] This is what Art. 38 (1) (d) ICJ Statute terms as "subsidiary means for the determination of rules of law".

One way to interpret the reference to case law in Art. (1) (d) ICJ Statute is to see case law as a genuine subsidiary source of law: If neither a treaty norm, nor customary law, nor a general principle of law is available, previous case law can be consulted to suggest a solution and avoid a *non liquet* situation. It is, however, in such instances that the case law itself would in turn have to be considered as a source of law, albeit subsidiary.[173] Although such an understanding of judicial

---

[168]See the leading case at the ICTY for the role of precedent within the ICTY, *Aleksovski* Appeals Judgment, paras 89–115.

[169]G. *Schwarzenberger*, The Inductive Approach to International Law (1965), 5.

[170]See e.g. ICTY, *Aleksovski* Appeals Judgment, paras 89–115.

[171]E.g. the ICTY *Delalić* Appeals Chamber stated that "there is no hierarchical relationship" between the ICTY and the ICJ and that it is not bound by ICJ precedents, see ICTY, *Delalić* Appeals Judgment, paras 21, 24. In relation to international criminal case law both the SCSL chambers and ECCC chambers rejected any form of binding precedents of ICTY and ICTR case law. See for the SCSL *W.A. Schabas*, The UN International Criminal Tribunals (2006), 108 referring to the SCSL case law in *Prosecutor v. Sesay*, SCSL-03-05-PT, Trial Chamber, Decision, 23 May 2003, para 11; *Prosecutor v. Gbao*, SCSL-03-09-PT), Decision, 10 October 2003. para 31; *Prosecutor v. Norman et al.*, SCSL-04-14-AR73, Decision on Amendment of the Consolidated Indictment, 17 May 2005, para 46; see also *Prosecutor v. Kamara*, SCSL-04-16-PT, Decision and Order on Defence Preliminary Motion on Defects in the Form of the Indictment, 1 April 2004, paras 22–25. See for the ECCC: *Duch* Appeals Judgment, para 97.

[172]M. *Shahabuddeen*, Precedent in the World Court (1996), 237.

[173]On this understanding of judicial decisions as a subsidiary source of law, see K. *Doehring*, Die Rechtsprechung als Rechtsquelle des Völkerrechts. Zur Auslegung des Art. 38 Abs. 1 Ziff. d des Statuts des Internationalen Gerichtshofs, in Reinhart (ed.), Richterliche Rechtsfortbildung – Erscheinungsformen, Auftrag und Grenzen, FS Heidelberg (1986), 546.

decisions as a genuine subsidiary source of law is widely rejected in the legal literature, and does not find support in the *travaux préparatoires* to Art. 38 ICJ Statute,[174] there are some isolated instances in the jurisprudence of international criminal tribunals that support such an approach.

When the ICTY Appeals Chamber had to consider whether duress was an applicable defence in the *Erdemović* Case,[175] Judge *Li* in his separate and dissenting opinion stated that on this question neither conventional nor customary international law, nor a general principle of law, was available. Nevertheless, in such instances according to Judge *Li* "recourse is to be had to the decisions of Military Tribunals, both international and national, which apply international law."[176] On the basis of case law he deduced both a general rule of applicability of duress as a complete defence under certain requirements and an exception to that rule when heinous acts are concerned, such as the killing of prisoners of war or innocent civilians. In such circumstances duress can only be used as a mitigating factor for sentencing but not as a complete defence.[177] In the *Erdemović* case, Judge *Li* apparently did not use case law as subsidiary means for the determination of a rule of customary law, but referred to the case law as a genuine subsidiary source of law.[178]

When the ECCC Supreme Court Chambers in the *Duch* Case had to determine whether cumulative convictions were possible under international law, it had to decide whether its Trial Chamber erred in law when adhering to a test established by the ICTY *Čelebići* Appeals Chamber for resolving the same issue.[179] The Supreme Court Chambers stated that "[t]he question still arises whether the Trial Chamber was correct in resorting to rules established in *ad hoc* jurisprudence *as opposed to primary sources of international law*. In this regard, the Supreme Court Chamber finds that there is no treaty or customary international law specifically addressing *concursus delictorum* for international crimes" and could also not find a general principle of law.[180] Despite the silence in the primary source of

---

[174]*Heinsch* (supra note 32), 346–352 with further references.

[175]ICTY, *Erdemović* Appeals Judgment.

[176]Separate and dissenting opinion Judge *Li* to the ICTY, *Erdemović* Appeals Judgment, para 2–4.

[177]*Ibid*, para 5.

[178]See also *Borda* (supra note 165), 75–76 referring to *B.B. Jing*, Judicial Decisions as a Source of International Law and the Defence of Duress in Murder or Other Cases Arising from Armed Conflict, in Yee and Wand (eds.), International Law in the Post-Cold War World (2001), 77ff. See also *A. Nollkaemper*, Decisions of National Courts as Sources of International Law: An Analysis of the Practice of the ICTY, in Boas/Schabas (eds.), International Criminal law Developments in the Case Law of the ICTY (2003), 290

[179]ECCC, *Duch* Appeals Judgment, paras 285ff. The Trial Chamber in its Judgment, paras 559ff applied the *Čelebići* test as established in ICTY, *Delalić* Appeals Judgment, paras 412ff, but did not indicate its authoritative value. According to the *Čelebići* test "multiple criminal convictions entered under different statutory provisions but based on the same conduct are permissible only if each statutory provision involved has a materially distinct element not contained in the other" which also includes *chapeau* requirements.

[180]ECCC, *Duch* Appeals Judgment, para 290 (emphasis added).

international law, in treaty law, customary law or general principle of law, the ECCC Supreme Court Chambers in the *Duch* Case considered the ICTY *Čelebići* test to be appropriate as it serves the interest of justice and that cumulative convictions accurately reflected the individual's criminal culpability.[181] The Supreme Court Chamber justified this conclusion by stating that the ICTY *Čelebići* test had been uniformly applied by the ICTY, ICTR, SCSL and ICC.[182] Although the ECCC Supreme Court Chambers did not expressly elaborate on the methodological underpinning, and although within the same judgment it rebuked the Trial Chamber for its heavy reliance on ICTY and ICTR jurisprudence,[183] concerning the applicability of cumulative convictions it was willing to use the ICTY *Čelebići* Appeals Judgment as a genuine subsidiary source of law.[184]

6.3.4.3   International Case Law as Subsidiary Means for the Determination of Customary International Law

Another reading of "subsidiary means for the determination of law" as enshrined in Art. 38 (1) (d) ICJ Statute concerns the use of case law as subsidiary means to establish an existing rule of international law, most notably customary international law or general principles of law.[185] Courts function, in *Schwarzenberger's* words, as "law-determining agencies."[186] It is important to note that in this sense judicial decisions as subsidiary means for determining a rule of law are in themselves not a source of law. As *Pellet* remarks, they are mere "documentary sources" that give indications on the existence of the three sources of law as established in Art. 38 ICJ Statute.[187] Indeed, according to the jurisprudence of international criminal tribunals, pre-existing case law has been referred to as it reflects or is indicative of customary international criminal law.[188] Despite some chambers paying lip service

---

[181] ECCC, *Duch* Appeals Judgment, paras 291–295.

[182] ECCC, *Duch* Appeals Judgment, para 300.

[183] ECCC, *Duch* Appeals Judgment, para 97.

[184] See also *Borda* (supra note 165), 74.

[185] See e.g. ICTY *Kupreškić* Trial Judgment, para 540.

[186] See G. *Schwarzenberger*, The Inductive Approach to International Law (1965), 5.

[187] *Pellet* (supra note 5), 854, MN 305.

[188] See for the ICTY *Kupreškić* Trial Judgment, para 605 when elaborating on the customary law status of the crime of persecution as a crime against humanity; see also ICTY *Tadić* Trial Judgment, para 674 determining that "[t]he most relevant sources for such a determination [participation as a basis of liability] are the Nürnberg war crimes trials"; ICTY, *Tadić* Appeals Chamber Judgment, para 255ff referring to case-law as the sole evidence of customary international law to determine that purely personal motives are irrelevant for establishing crimes against humanity; for the customary law status of the mode of liability of Joint Criminal Enterprise being based on case law see for example ICTY, *Tadić* Appeals Chamber Judgment, para 226, and ICTY, *Prosecutor v. Brđanin*, IT-99-36-A, Appeals Chamber, Judgment, 3 April 2007, para 41C. See for the ECCC, Case No 002 Pre-Trial Chamber Public Decision on the JCE Appeals, para 53 in conjunction with para 60.

to the traditional approach to identify customary international law—the establishment of the two elements[189]—the jurisprudence of international criminal tribunals reveals that in certain instances the chambers were willing to declare that the case law is indicative of the existence of customary international law without an inquiry into the traditional elements of State practice or *opinio iuris*. The reference to case law alone spared the tribunals the cumbersome task of establishing adequate proof of State practice and *opinio iuris* for the determination of a customary international norm. One could thus describe recourse to judicial decisions as a "methodological shortcut" for the determination of customary international law.

But under what circumstances can case law be used as subsidiary means for the determination of customary international law, or, in other words, what "authoritative value" shall be attributed to case law? It has been argued in the legal literature that the value attributed to previous cases when determining customary international law is dependent on the persuasive legal quality of the decision, that is, its underlying analysis of the constitutive elements of customary international law.[190] Indeed, international criminal tribunals have critiqued the use of courts as a "law-determining agencies" for customary international criminal law, when those courts fail to cite adequate State practice and *opinio iuris* to substantiating their customary law findings.[191] However, when case law has been used as an affirmation for the existence of customary international law, it has generally been done without an inquiry into the legal explanation of the courts. Since international criminal tribunals are not bound by the decisions of other international courts, the authority of external judicial decisions as subsidiary means for the determination of customary international law can only rest upon the content of the underlying customary law analysis; that is to say, on the legal quality of the decision, never on the authority of the respective judicial body itself that rendered the decision.[192]

Nevertheless, in contrast to such a restrictive approach, international criminal tribunals have been somewhat flexible when using case law of other courts as "law-determining agencies". In place of an analysis of the constitutive elements that underlie previous case law, particular importance is given to distinguishing between different categories of decisions: whether the decision has been rendered by "international" or "national" judicial authorities. International criminal tribunals

[189]See e.g. ICTR, *Prosecutor v. Rwamakuba*, ICTR-98-44-AR72.4, Appeals Chamber, Decision on Interlocutory Appeal Regarding Application of Joint Criminal Enterprise to the Crime of Genocide, 22 October 2004, para 14.

[190]See for example *Mettraux* (supra note 13), 15, with regard to a possible precedential value of judicial pronouncements: "A statement that a norm is customary is therefore only ever as good as the explanation referred to by the court in support of its finding to that effect."

[191]See for instance the ICTY *Vasiljević* Trial Chamber in its Judgment rebuking the trial chambers of both the ICTY and ICTR for not conducting an adequate analysis of State practice and *opinio iuris* to substantiate their customary law findings, see further supra note 70 and 72.

[192]*Cryer* (supra note 4), 246–7, with references to *H. Lauterpacht*, The Development of International Law by the International Court (1958), 18, and *Schwarzenberger* (supra note 163), 30; *Mettraux* (supra note 13), 15.

have highlighted that the case law of international courts plays a more important role as "law-determining agencies", as these operate in the same forum and apply international law, whereas national case law must be used cautiously in determining customary international law.[193] However, the jurisprudence of international criminal tribunals does not generally indicate which criteria must be fulfilled for case law to be considered "international" in character.[194] Indeed, in the legal literature it is debated whether domestic judicial decisions could be regarded as subsidiary means for the determination of a rule of customary international law within the meaning of Art. 38 (1) (d) ICJ Statute.[195] A restrictive approach for using domestic decisions as "law-determining agencies" appears in the jurisprudence of international criminal tribunals: In the words of the ECCC Pre-Trial Chamber, "cases, in which domestic courts applied domestic law, do not amount to international case law and the Pre-Trial Chamber does not consider them as proper precedents for the purpose of determining the status of customary law in this area."[196] The ICTY *Kupreškić* Trial Chamber also noted that tribunals "should apply a stricter level of scrutiny to national decisions than to international judgments, as the latter are at least based on *the same corpus of law as that applied by international courts*, whereas the former tend to apply national law, or primarily that law, *or else interpret international rules through the prism of national legislation*."[197] However, it is not necessarily the case that only "true" international courts render "international judgments". Indeed in the *Eichmann* Case the Israeli Supreme Court declared it would adjudicate on the case "in the capacity of a guardian of

---

[193]See in that regard the two leading cases on the "authoritative value" of external case law at the ICTY: the *Kupreškić* Trial Judgment, paras 541–2, and the *Furundžija* Trial Judgment, para 194.

[194]The ICTY considered itself to be an "international court" for the following reasons: It corresponds to the Security Council's intent when establishing the ICTY, the tribunal's structure and function, and the applicable law being international law; see ICTY *Kupreškić* Trial Judgment, para, 539. There is, however, no discussion in relation other "international" courts detectable in the jurisprudence.

[195]Most prominently *Pellet* (supra note 5), MN 321, in his commentary on Art. 38 ICJ Statute argued that domestic decisions "should better be treated as elements of State practice in the customary process, or, maybe, as being at the crossroads between evidence of practice and *opinio juris*." Other authors argue, however, that domestic judicial decisions can be used as subsidiary means for the determination of a rule of law, see e.g. A. Nollkaemper, National Courts and the International rule of Law (2011), 270. *Nollkaemper* sees such a possibility under the conditions that the court is independent, based the decision on what the court believed is international law, and reasoned to a high standard.

[196]ECCC, Case No 002 Pre-Trial Chamber Public Decision on the JCE Appeals, para 82 Similar ICTY *Kupreškić* Trial Judgment, para 541: "depending upon the circumstances of each case, generally speaking decisions of national courts on war crimes or crimes against humanity delivered on basis of national legislation would carry relatively less weight." See also ICTY, *Furundžija* Trial Judgment, para 194: "one should constantly be mindful of the need for great caution in using national case law for the purpose of determining whether customary rules of international criminal law have evolved in a particular matter."

[197]ICTY, *Kupreškić* Trial Judgment, para 542 (emphasis added).

international law and an agent for its enforcement".[198] It could very well be argued
that the Israeli Supreme Court in that regard rendered an "international judgment".
Basing the use of case law not on the *quality* of the decision itself but solely upon
the question of applicable law—as the ICTY *Kupreškić* Trial Chamber considered
whether they apply "the same corpus of law as that applied by international
courts"—but at the same time excluding national courts applying international
law as "law-determining agencies", appears rather arbitrary for the determination
of international. That might be particularly true in light of the fact that in certain
domestic legal systems international law is directly applicable before domestic
courts. Furthermore, it can also be argued that the mere domestic transformation
or implementation of international law "does not deprive the original source of its
true character."[199] However, the ICTY *Kupreškić* Trial determined that even under
such circumstances domestic courts might see international law through the "prism
of national legislation". Domestic courts might then apply a national interpretation
of international law. Such an undesirable result would be detrimental to the purpose
of using that case law as a subsidiary means for the determination of customary
international law.[200] There is some value to this finding of the ICTY *Kupreškić*
Trial Chamber. In such instances, methodologically speaking, it would be better to
argue that domestic decisions applying international law, what they think is international law, or a domestic transformation of international law, provide evidence
for the "law-creating process" ingredients. In that regard domestic decisions can be
used to evidence both the elements of State practice and *opinio iuris*.[201] In these
instances the domestic courts as State organs do not only contribute to the formation
of State practice through their decisions, but also indicate *opinio iuris*, since they
apply law that domestic judges believe is part of, or conforms to, international law.
Such an evincing function for the constitutive elements of customary international
law, however, needs to be distinguished from a role of judicial decisions as
subsidiary means for the its determination. Regrettably, it seems that such a clear
and strict distinction is not made in the jurisprudence of international criminal
tribunals. The ICTY *Kupreškić* Trial Chamber Judgment also fails to adhere to its
own caveats of using domestic decisions cautiously. Despite the warning that
domestic courts apply international law through the "prism of national legislation",

---

[198]Israeli Supreme Court, Eichmann Case, 304.

[199]See *H. Lauterpacht*, Decisions of Municipal Courts as a Source of International Law, 10 British
Yearbook of International Law (1929), 77.

[200]See also *P. M. Moremen*, National Court Decisions as State Practice: A Transnational Judicial
Dialogue?, in 32 North Carolina Journal of international Law & Commercial Regulation (2006),
291, pointing to the problem that domestic "courts considering customary international law issues
may be restricted to considering domestic law transpositions of international law, such as
implementing statutes or prior judicial decisions. National court decisions, therefore, may reflect
not international law but a national interpretation of international law. The result could be a court
decision significantly out of step with current international law, which would limit its relevance."

[201]*Nollkaemper* (supra note 178), 281–283. *Pellet* (supra note 5), MN 321; see further Sect. 7.7.4,
Domestic Case Law.

it elevated post World War II domestic military decisions operating under Control Council Law No. 10 as law-determining agencies to the same level as the decisions of the IMTs of Nuremberg and Tokyo.[202] It further stated that "[i]n many instances no less value may be given to decisions on international crimes delivered by national courts operating pursuant to the 1948 Genocide Convention, or the 1949 Geneva Conventions or the 1977 Protocols or similar international treaties. In these instance the international framework on the basis of which the national court operates and the fact that *in essence the court applies international substantive law*, may lend great weight to rulings of such courts."[203]

By subjecting the utility of case law as customary law-determining agencies to caveats of "applicable law", it appears that international criminal tribunals are rather flexible when determining the "international character" of judicial decisions. Without an analysis of the legal reasoning, one could argue that previous "judicial precedents" applying international substantive law have themselves acted as catalysts bringing about customary international criminal law. Such a perception blurs the borders between the "law-creating processes" and the "law-determining agencies". It has been argued that judicial decisions within the domestic English common law system have "the merit of making the custom and therefore the law certain".[204] According to *Blackstone* "judicial decisions are the principal and most authoritative evidence, that can be given, of the existence of such a custom as shall form a part of the common law."[205] One might be tempted to transpose such an evincing function of the judiciary as an authoritative, declaratory source of customary law from the English common law system to the international legal order.[206] Such an approach, however, needs to be rejected for the following reasons: Firstly, within the English common law context these judicial decisions demonstrate custom that is based on "long and immemorial usage."[207] It would be hardly justifiable to adopt the same approach to international judges applying innovative

---

[202]ICTY, *Kupreškić* Trial Judgment, para 541.

[203]ICTY, *Kupreškić* Trial Judgment, para 542 (emphasis added).

[204]*J.C. Gardner*, Judicial Precedent in the Making of International Public Law, 17 Journal of Comparative Legislation and International Law (1935), 256.

[205]See *W. Blackstone*, Commentaries on the Laws of England, Vol. 1 (1756), 69.

[206]There are, however, critical voices in the legal literature concerning the transposition of domestic concepts to the international legal order. See for instance *J.S. Watson*, Legal Theory, Efficacy and Validity in the Development of Human Rights Norms in International Law, 3 University of Illinois Law Forum (1979), 621, stating that the "transference of the domestic law philosophy is seen in its most elementary form in the unrelenting use of decisions of the International Court as though they were legally binding precedents. These opinions are analyzed by some writers in much the same fashion as one would analyze the opinions of a national supreme court in a common law jurisdiction, inducing from what is said in relation to various sets of facts the existence of rules or principles sufficiently broad in scope to state the law in other unrelated cases. This use of the decisions of the International Court ignores the unique socio-political context of that organ and the fact that each decision is presented in a blend of highly political factors which makes any such analysis of the opinions entirely speculative."

[207]*Blackstone* (supra note 205), 68.

and modern theories to customary international law. Furthermore, within the English legal system the legislator still can function as an "available corrective" to the customary law determination of the judiciary. By adopting new laws the legislator can either adapt to new circumstances or modify outdated customary norms.[208] Yet this is not possible, or at least is seriously hampered, within the international legal sphere. Without a genuine centralized legislator it appears misguided to think that States could fulfill such a corrective function. As was held by Judge *Robertson* at the SCSL "[e]very law student can point to cases where judges have been tempted to circumvent the *nullum crimen* principle to criminalise conduct which they regard as seriously antisocial or immoral, but which had not been outlawed by legislation or by categories of common-law crimes. This temptation must be firmly resisted by international law judges, with no legislature to correct or improve upon them".[209] International judicial decisions are thus best viewed as mere "documentary sources". Whether previous decisions of courts can function as "law-determining agencies" is thus dependent on the underlying *quality* of the decision.

Bearing such caution in mind, the actual importance of the case law of post World War II tribunals for the determination of customary international law is striking. It has been argued that international criminal tribunals have elevated the case law of international and domestic courts into essentially primary sources of international law.[210] Taking recourse to these cases, according to the ICTY *Kupreškić* Trial Chamber, is necessary "due to the fact that both substantive and procedural criminal law is still at a rudimentary state in international law."[211] International criminal tribunals have relied extensively on the jurisprudence of post World War II trials for the determination of customary international criminal law:[212] The chambers have referred to post World War II case law in relation to the contextual elements of crimes against humanity, eliminating any nexus requirement between crimes against humanity and war crimes under customary international

---

[208]*Gardner* (supra note 204), 256.

[209]See Dissenting Opinion Judge Robertson to the SCSL, *Norman* Appeals Chamber Decision, para 13.

[210]*Bantekas* (supra note 165), 129f.

[211]ICTY, *Kupreškić* Trial Judgment, para 537; See also ICTY, *Furundžija* Trial Judgment, para 193: "Little light is shed on the definition of aiding and abetting by the international instruments providing for major war trials: the London Agreement, the Charter of the International Military Tribunal for the Far East, establishing the Tokyo Tribunal, and Control Council Law No. 10. It therefore becomes necessary to examine the case law."

[212]It needs to be highlighted that there are fundamental differences between different categories of post World War II trials, such as the IMT Nuremberg and IMTFE Tokyo, the "zone trials" operating under the "authority" of Control Council Law No. 10, or other domestic courts operating outside the occupied zones, including The Australian Military Court, the Canadian Military Court, the Chinese War Crimes Court, USSR Military Courts, the Netherlands Special Courts, Norwegian Courts, the Supreme National Tribunal of Poland or Danish Military Courts. These differences need to be taken into account for establishing their authoritative value for the determination of customary international criminal law. See further Sect. 7.7, Jurisprudence.

law,[213] although the ICTY Statute expressly required such a nexus in its Art. 5. Moreover, the requirement that crimes against humanity were conducted in order to pursue a State plan or policy was abolished.[214] On basis of case law the chambers determined that the status of a possible victim of a crime against humanity is not restricted to "civilians" and that the presence of individual combatants in the midst of civilians does not alter the status of an attack on a "civilian population" as required for the application of crimes against humanity.[215] The chambers determined that the personal motive (for "purely personal reasons") is irrelevant for the application of crimes against humanity.[216] Furthermore, reference to the jurisprudence of post World War II tribunals was made when elaborating on individual crimes, such as the war crime of plunder,[217] the crimes against humanity

---

[213]ICTY, *Kupreškić* Trial Judgment, para 577, referring to US Military Tribunal, *Altstötter and Others Case*, 974; US Military Tribunal, *Ohlendorf and Others* Case ("Einsatzgruppen Case"), in Trials of War Criminals Before the Nuremberg Military Tribunals under Control Council Law No. 10, Vol. IV, 49; see also ECCC, *Duch* Trial Judgment, para 291; however, the analysis is flawed since not all related cases have been evaluated by the chambers. *Heller* rightly points out the fact that the tribunals forget to mention (the Pohl and Ministries Case) or rightly evaluate (Flick Case) other Control Council Law No. 10 Cases before the US Military Tribunals that uphold the necessity to demonstrate a nexus requirement, such as the *Flick Case*; *Pohl and Others Case*, in Trials of War Criminals Before the Nuremberg Military Tribunals under Control Council Law No. 10, Vol. V, 193ff; *Von Weizsaecker and Others* ("Ministries Case"), in Trials of War Criminals Before the Nuremberg Military Tribunals under Control Council Law No. 10, Vol. XII, 1ff; see K. J. Heller, The Nuremberg Military Tribunals and the Origins of International Criminal Law (2011), 383. *Schabas* considers that "*Eichmann* stands as the first conviction for crimes against humanity committed without a formal link to armed conflict." See W. Schabas, The Contribution of the Eichmann Trial to International Law, 26 Leiden Journal of International Law (2013), 679.

[214]For the ICTY see *Kunarac* Appeals Judgment, para 98 (see footnote 114); followed by *Blaškić* Appeals Judgment, para 120; this result is astonishing since the *Kunarac* Trial Judgment, para 432, previously claimed that the case law is divergent on the question of whether a policy element is a necessary contextual element to crimes against humanity under customary international law; see also the critique of W. A. Schabas, State Policy as an Element of International Crimes, 98 Journal of Criminal Law & Criminology (2008), 959ff: "the result reached – that a State plan or policy is not a required element – appears to be a results-oriented political decision rather than a profound analysis."

[215]ICTY, *Martić* Appeals Judgment, para 309 referring to US Military Tribunal, *Leeb and Others Case* ("High Command Case"), Law Reports of the Trials of War Criminals, Vol. XII, 1; *Von Weizsaecker and Others*; as well as 3 cases before the Supreme Court in the British Occupied Zone, OGHSt 1, 217–229, OGHSt 2, 231–246, OGHSt 1, 45–49; see also *Blaškić* Trial Judgment, para 210 (footnote 405).

[216]ICTY, *Tadić* Appeals Chamber Judgment, para 255, referring *i.a.* to the denunciation cases before the Supreme Court for the British Zone and German national courts.

[217]ICTY, *Naletilić* Trial Judgment, paras 612ff referring to US Military Tribunal, *Flick Case*, 1; US Military Tribunal, *Krupp Case*, *Krauch Case*; French Military Tribunal, in re *Roechling and others*, 15 Annual Digest and Reports of Public International Law Cases (1948), 408; Austrian Supreme Court, *Austrian Treasury v. Auer*, 14 Annual Digest and Reports of Public International Law Cases (1947), 276; Italian Court of Appeals of Bologna, *Maltoni v. Companini*, 71 Foro Italiano (1948), Vol. I, 1090, Norway Court of Appeal, *Johansen v. Gross*, 16 Annual Digest and Reports of Public International Law Cases (1949), 481; French Court of Cassation, *Soubrouillard contre Kilbourg*, Gazette du Palais (1948), Vol. II, 163; see also ICTY, *Kordić* Trial Judgment, para 351 also referring to the US Military Tribunal, *Krauch* Case.

of extermination,[218] other inhuman acts[219] and persecution and persecutory acts.[220] In this context the ICTY *Kupreškić* Trial Chamber stated that "the case-law referred to above reflects, and is indicative of, the notion of persecution as laid down in customary international criminal law".[221]

The case law of post World War II military tribunals also left its mark on possible defences, as on its basis the application of *tu quoque*,[222]

---

[218]ICTY, the *Krstić* Trial Judgment, para 492, determined that extermination is widely recognized despite that the case law did not provide for a specific definition of the crime, referring to the US Military Tribunal, *Altstötter and Others Case*, Supreme National Tribunal of Poland, *Trial of Hauptsturmführer Amon Leopold Goeth*, Law Reports of the Trials of War Criminals, Vol. VII, 1ff, US Military Tribunal, *Krauch* Case, US Military Tribunal, *Krupp Case*, US Military Tribunal, *Leeb* Case; US Military Tribunal, *Greifelt and Others* Case ("the RuSHA Case"), Trials of War Criminals Before the Nuremberg Military Tribunals under Control Council Law No. 10, Vol. IV, 597ff, Supreme National Tribunal of Poland, *Trial of Gauleiter Greiser*, Law Reports of the Trials of War Criminals, Vol. XIII, 70f; ICTY, *Vasiljević* Trial Judgment, para 222, referring to US Military Tribunal, *Altstötter and Others Case*, US Military Tribunal, *Ohlendorf* Case, 49; and US Military Tribunal, *Brandt and Others Case* ("Medical Case"), in Trials of War Criminals Before the Nuremberg Military Tribunals under Control Council Law No. 10, Vol. I, 1ff;

[219]ICTY, *Blagojević* Trial Judgment, para 624 referring to US Military Tribunal, *Brandt and Others Case*; US Military Tribunal, *Leeb* Case; US Military Tribunal, *Von Weizsaecker and Others* and US Military Tribunal, *Altstötter and Others Case*; see also ICTY, *Stakić* Appeals Judgment, para 315.

[220]ICTY, *Kupreškić* Trial Judgment, para 598ff, referring to US Military Tribunal, *Leeb* Case, US Military Tribunal, *Von Weizsaecker and Others*, US Military Tribunal, *Greifelt and Others* Case; Supreme National Tribunal of Poland, *Greiser Case*; Netherlands Special Court in Amsterdam and Netherlands Special Court of Cassation, *Trial of Willy Zuehlke*, Law Reports of the Trials of War Criminals, Vol. XIV, 139ff, and also referring to Israeli Supreme Court, Eichmann Case, 277ff, French Court de Cassation, *Barbie* Case, 125; see also *Krajišnik* Trial Judgment, paras 736ff further referring to Netherlands Special Court of Cassation, *Trial of Hans Albin Rauter*, Law Reports of the Trials of War Criminals, Vol. XIV, 89ff, and Supreme National Tribunal of Poland, *Trial of Dr. Joseph Buhler*, Law Reports of the Trials of War Criminals, Vol. XIV, 23ff; ICTY, *Stakić* Trial Judgment, para 773 also referring to the US Military Tribunal, *Altstötter and Others Case*; ICTY, *Blaškić* Appeals Judgment, para 149 with reference to the US Military Tribunal, *Flick Case*, that stated that compulsory taking of industrial property would not constitute a crime against humanity. However, the Appeals Chamber determining that plunder depending on its extent and nature may constitute a crime of persecution; furthermore in para 150 with reference to the *Blaškić* Trial Judgment, para 223–4 referring to cases before the Supreme National Tribunal of Poland, the Netherlands Special Court in Amsterdam and the *Eichmann* Case.

[221]ICTY, *Kupreškić* Trial Judgment, para 605.

[222]ICTY, *Kupreškić* Trial Judgment, para 516, referring to US Military Tribunal, *Leeb* Case; see however S. Yee, The Tu Quoque Argument as a Defence to International Crimes, Prosecution or Punishment, 3 Chinese Journal of International Law (2004), 87ff, who argues that the IMT Nuremberg allowed the *tu quoque* defence in relation to Admirals Dönitz and Raeder for "unrestricted submarine warfare" as a defence against punishment since the British and US Navies had behaved similarly, *id.*, 103.

duress,[223] and military necessity in relation to the intentional attack on civilians[224] was rejected.

Furthermore, the chambers have used the post World War II jurisprudence to establish customary law in relation to modes of liability, including aiding and abetting,[225] command responsibility,[226] and the joint criminal enterprise (JCE) doctrine. Concerning the latter, ICTY Appeals Chambers have stated that the case law "reflects" customary international criminal law[227] or was "persuasive as to the contours of joint criminal enterprise liability in customary international law".[228]

In most of these instances, one does not encounter a methodological discussion as to why these cases establish customary international law and under which conditions case law can be used as "law-determining agencies" for the determination

---

[223]Whereas in ICTY, *Erdemović* Sentencing Judgment, para 17ff, the Trial Chamber accepted that duress can constitute a complete defence on basis of post World War II case law, the *Erdemović* Appeals Judgment, para 19, rejected duress as a valid defence. The Appeals Judgment makes reference to the Joint Separate Opinion of Judge *McDonald* and Judge *Vohrah*, paras 43–5, who consider that the "only express affirmation of the availability of duress as a defence" is given in the US Military Tribunal *Ohlendorf* Case. Furthermore, the judges question the authoritative value of these cases before the military tribunals and concluding in para 55: "We do not think that the decisions of these tribunals or those of other national courts and military tribunals constitute consistent and uniform state practice underpinned by *opinio juris sive necessitates*." For a contrary view, see Separate and Dissenting Opinion of Judge Cassese, para 27; compare also *V. Epps*, The Soldier's Obligation to Die When Ordered to Shoot Civilians or Face Death Himself, 37 New England Law Review (2003), 987ff.

[224]ICTY, *Galić* Trial Judgment, para 44 referring to US Military Tribunal, *List Case*, 757ff: "Military necessity permits (…) the destruction of life of armed enemies and other persons whose destruction is incidentally unavoidable (…) There must be some reasonable connection between the destruction of property and the overcoming of the enemy forces."; see also ICTY, *Prosecutor v. Orić*, IT-03-68, Trial Chamber, Judgment, 30 June 2006, para 588, also referring to the British Military Court, *Trial of Kapitänleutnant Eck and Others* ("Peleus Trial"), Law Reports of the Trials of War Criminals, Vol. I, 1ff.

[225]ICTY, *Furundžija* Trial Judgment, paras 193ff, referring to British Military Court, *Trial of Franz Schonfeld and Others*, Law Reports of the Trials of War Criminals, Vol. XI, 64ff, British Military Court, *Trial of Werner Rohde and Others*, Law Reports of the Trials of War Criminals, Vol. V, 54ff, British Military Court, *Trial of Otto Sandrock and Others* ("Almelo Trial"), Law Reports of the Trials of War Criminals, Vol. I, 35ff; British Military Court, *Trial of Max Wielen and Others* ("Stalag Luft III Case"), Law Reports of the Trials of War Criminals, Vol. XI, 33ff; German Supreme Court in the British Occupied Zone, K. und A., StS 18/48, Entscheidungen des Obersten Gerichtshofs für die Britische Zone. Entscheidungen in Strafsachen, Vol. I (1949).

[226]ICTY, *Delalić* Trial Judgment, paras 338 referring to US Supreme Court, *Yamashita* Case, US Military Tribunal, *Brandt* Case, US Military Tribunal, *List Case*, US Military Tribunal, *Leeb* Case; for the responsibility of non-military superiors see *id.*, para 359–362 with reference to US Military Tribunal, *Flick Case* and French Military Tribunal, in re *Roechling and others*; ICTY, *Delalić* Appeals Chamber in its Judgment, para 228ff also referring to US Military Tribunal, *Pohl* Case; ICTY, *Strugar* Trial Judgment, paras 363–364; ICTY, *Prosecutor v. Delić*, IT-04-83-T, Trial Chamber, Judgment, para 59; ICTY, *Blaškić* Trial Judgment, paras 317f; ICTY, Appeals Chamber *Hadžihasanović* Decision, para 50.

[227]ICTY, *Tadić* Appeals Chamber Judgment, para 226.

[228]ICTY, *Brđanin* Appeals Judgment, para 410.

of customary international criminal law. The ICTY *Erdemović* Appeals Judgment,[229] however, reveals slight disagreement of the bench on the question of the authoritative value of post World War II cases adjudicating upon the "strength" of Control Council Law No. 10. Judge *Cassese* appointed more weight to those judgments in comparison with "ordinary" domestic courts, because "Control Council Law No. 10 can be regarded as an international agreement among the four Occupying Powers (subsequently transformed, to a large extent, into customary law), the action of the courts established or acting under that Law acquires an international relevance that cannot be attributed to national courts pronouncing solely on the strength of national law."[230] In contrast, judges *McDonald* and *Vohrah*, while acknowledging that the "constitution, character and competence" of these tribunals might rest on international law, nevertheless clarified that in substance "[t]here was no statement to the effect that the tribunals applied purely international law" and that "they invariably drew on the jurisprudence of their own national jurisdictions."[231] Thus, judges *McDonald* and *Vohrah* treated the case law of the US Military Courts operating under Control Council Law No. 10, at least with regard to the question of applicability of duress as a defence, as "ordinary" domestic judgments applying domestic law that could not be used as subsidiary means for the determination of customary international criminal law. The ICTY Appeals *Erdemović* Judgment is thus worth considering to show that with regards to post World War II judicial decisions as subsidiary means for the determination of customary international law, the case law of international criminal tribunals lacks methodological uniformity and clarity.

In addition to the post World War II cases, the emergence of a vast number of decisions and judgments of modern international criminal tribunals has left a mark on the way chambers of the same or other international criminal tribunals determine customary international law. Looking at the jurisprudence of the ICTY, ICTR, SCSL and ECCC, one encounters chains of international judicial cross references. When determining the applicable law tribunals at times refer exclusively to their own jurisprudence.[232] International criminal tribunals also make use of the rich

---

[229] ICTY, *Erdemović* Appeals Judgment.

[230] ICTY, *Erdemović* Appeals Judgment, Separate and Dissenting Opinion of Judge Cassese, para 27.

[231] ICTY, *Erdemović* Appeals Judgment, Joint Separate Opinion of Judge McDonald and Judge Vohrah, para 54.

[232] See. for the ICTY references to previous ICTY case law when establishing the chapeau requirements of Art. 3 ICTY Statute under customary international law *Blagojević* Trial Judgment, paras 535ff; *Galić* Appeal Judgment, paras 111ff; *Prosecutor v. Kvočka*, IT-98-30/1-T, Trial Chamber, Judgment, 2 November 2001, paras 123ff; *Prosecutor v. Brđanin*, IT-99-36-T, Trial Chamber, Judgment, 1 September 2004, paras 126ff; references to previous ICTY case law when establishing the chapeau requirements of crimes against humanity under customary international law *Galić* Trial Judgment, paras 139ff; *Simić* Trial Judgment, paras 34ff; *Prosecutor v. Limaj et al*, IT-03-66-T, Trial Chamber, Judgment, 30 November 2005, paras 180ff; references to previous ICTY case law when establishing command responsibility under customary international law *Krnojelac* Trial Judgment, paras 91ff; *Galić* Trial Judgment, paras 173ff; *Naletilić* Trial Judgment, paras 64ff; *Prosecutor v. Mrkšić*, IT-95-13/1-T, Trial Chamber, Judgment, 27 September 2007, paras 557ff.

jurisprudence of their international criminal "sister" tribunals[233] when determining the applicable law. Since there is no inter-institutional *stare decisis* doctrine[234] applicable between the different international criminal tribunals, the chambers follow these decisions for their "persuasive value."[235] Rather than analyzing the constitutive elements for the formation of customary international law, reference is generally made to the case law of modern international criminal tribunals that previously dealt with the same or similar legal issues. For example, with regard to the application of Art. 7 (1) ICTY Statute and the modes of liability under customary international law, the ICTY *Aleksovski* Trial Chamber held:

> This question was already the subject of in-depth debate in several cases heard before the International Criminal Tribunal for the Former Yugoslavia and the International Criminal Tribunal for Rwanda *inter alia* in the Tadić, Čelebici, Furundžija and Akayesu cases [...] The Trial Chamber therefore sees no point in making the same analysis and will rely on the two essential elements which entail responsibility within the meaning of Article 7 (1) as unanimously established in all the other cases.[236]

Thus it appears that it is a judicial practice not to repeat a customary law analysis if the chamber concurs with the earlier analysis. Once an issue has been determined to be settled jurisprudence, the underlying legal basis is rarely called into question. However, some delicate divergences in the determination of customary international criminal law are discernable among the various tribunals.[237]

---

[233] See for example the references to the jurisprudence of different international criminal tribunals for establishing the chapeau requirements of crimes against humanity under customary international law, the ICTY, *Krnojelac* Trial Judgment, paras 53ff; *Naletilić* Trial Judgment, paras 232ff; SCSL, *Fofana* Trial Judgment, paras 110ff; *Sesay* Trial Judgment, paras 75ff; ECCC, *Duch* Trial Judgment, paras 297ff.

[234] See Sect. 6.3.4.2, Case Law as a Genuine "Subsidiary" Source of Law.

[235] See Art. 20 (3) SCSL Statute providing that "[t]he judges of the Appeals Chamber of the Special Court shall be guided by the decisions of the Appeals Chamber of the International Tribunals for the former Yugoslavia and for Rwanda." The SCSL chambers refer to the jurisprudence of the other UN *ad hoc* tribunals "solely" for their "persuasive value", see SCSL, *Sesay* Trial Judgment, para 48; *Fofana* Trial Judgment, para 88; *Brima* Trial Judgment, para 639.

[236] ICTY, *Aleksovski* Trial Judgment, para 60.

[237] There are different views on the existence or non-existence of customary international law detectable among international criminal tribunals: for example the ICTY, *Prosecutor v. Perišić*, Appeals Chamber, Judgment, 28 February 2013, paras 25ff, determined that specific direction was a component of the *actus reus* of aiding and abetting liability under customary international law, while the *Prosecutor v. Taylor*, Case No. SCSL-03-01-A, Appeals Chamber, Judgment, 26 September 2013 at para 486 stated " that 'specific direction' is not an element of the *actus reus* of aiding and abetting liability [...] under customary international law." The ICTY Appeals Chamber, *Prosecutor v. Šainović*, IT-05-87-A, Appeals Chamber, Judgment, 23 January 2014, paras 1617ff followed the conception of the SCSL Appeals Chamber. The ECCC Trial Chamber also adhered to that conception, see *Prosecutor v. Nuon*, Case File No. 002/19-09-2007/ECCC/TC, Trial Chamber, Judgment, 7 August 2014, paras 707ff. Another example concerns the JCE doctrine, where the ECCC Pre-Trial Chamber openly challenged the customary law finding of the ICTY Appeals Chamber in its *Tadić* Judgment concerning the third form or "extended form" of joint criminal enterprise, as it did not deliver consistent and widespread State practice and *opinio iuris* at the time relevant to the temporal jurisdiction of the ECCC. See ECCC, Case No 002 Pre-Trial Chamber Public Decision on the JCE Appeals, para 77. Consequently, the third form of JCE has found no application in ECCC jurisprudence.

Within the same institutional setting a doctrine of binding precedent has gradually been installed.[238] At the ICTY, before the 2001 *Aleksovski* Appeals Judgment, the chambers had referred to previous ICTY decisions mainly "to set out the rules of existing customary international law on the subject".[239] Such an approach would refer to previous decisions as subsidiary means to determine customary international law. However, the ICTY *Aleksovski* Appeals Chamber changed the rules of the game. Relying on "a proper construction" of the ICTY Statute, it determined that within the ICTY a system of binding precedents applied.[240] The Appeals Chamber affirmed the existence of binding precedents of ICTY Appeals Chamber jurisprudence on ICTY Trial Chambers, which is to say, strict *stare decisis*.[241] According to ICTY case law, Trial Chambers cannot simply disregard the legal principles applied by their Appeals Chambers.[242] When the *Blaškić* Trial Chamber departed from the standard of "had reason to know"—as elaborated by the *Čelebici* Appeals Chamber when establishing command responsibility—the *Blaškić* Appeals Chamber stated that the *Čelebici* Appeals Chamber "has settled the interpretation of the standard of 'had reason to know'", and found that the Trial Chamber's approach "is not consistent with the jurisprudence of the Appeals Chamber in this regard and must be corrected accordingly."[243] When the *Stakić* Trial Chamber introduced the mode of liability of "co-perpetration" as an alternative to the critiqued JCE

---

[238] *Tracol* (supra note 167), 67ff; *P. M. Wald*, Tribunal Discourse and Intercourse: How the International Courts Speak to One Another, 30 Boston College International and Comparative Law Review (2007), 15ff; *Schabas* (supra note 171), 107ff.

[239] See, ICTY, *Aleksovski* Trial Judgment, para 60.

[240] See ICTY, *Aleksovski* Appeals Judgment, paras 89–115. The Appeals Chamber found reasons for binding precedents in the hierarchical structure of the ICTY Statute, the assurance of certainty and predictability and the right of the accused to have like cases treated alike. The *Aleksovski* jurisprudence was expressly endorsed by other chambers of the ICTY, see *Galić* Appeal Judgment, para 117; *Kordić* Appeals Judgment, para 1040; *Blaškić* Appeals Judgment, para 62; and by the ICTR, see e.g. *Prosecutor v. Semanza*, ICTR-97-20-A, Appeals Chamber, Decision, 31 May 2000, para 92.

[241] Concerning the situation for Appeals Chambers the ICTY *Aleksovski* Appeals Chamber stated that "in the interests of certainty and predictability, the Appeals Chamber should follow its previous decisions, but should be free to depart from them for cogent reasons in the interests of justice." ICTY, *Aleksovski* Appeals Judgment, para 107.

[242] Trial Chambers are bound by the *ratio decidendi* of their Appeals Chambers, which can be understood as a "the statement of legal principle (express or implied)", see ICTY, Separate Opinion Judge *Hunt*, Appeals Chamber Decision in *Ojdanić's* Motion Challenging Jurisdiction, para 43, positioning himself contrary to the rather "fluid concept" of *ratio decidendi* adopted by Judge *Shahabuddeen* in his Separate Opinion to the same decision. As such these binding precedents cover only "issues of law, but not issues of fact" *Schabas* (supra note 171), 107, referring to the ICTY case law, *Prosecutor v. Krnojelac*, IT-97-25-PT, Decision on the Defence preliminary Motion on the Form of the Indictment, para 43, *Prosecutor v. Simić et al*, IT-95-9-PT, Decision on the Pre-Trial Motion by the Prosecution Requesting the Trial Chamber to take Judicial Notice of the International Character of the Conflict in Bosnia-Herzegovina.

[243] ICTY, *Blaškić* Appeals Judgment, para 62 holding a commander responsible "only if information was available to him which would have put him on notice" of crimes committed by the subordinates..

doctrine,[244] the Appeals Chamber determined that it "must intervene to whether the mode of liability applied by the Trial chamber is consistent w jurisprudence of this Tribunal." It came to the conclusion that JCE is "s jurisprudence of this Tribunal, which is binding on the Trial Chambers."[245] examples show the existence of the *stare decisis* doctrine within the same institutional setting, creating a hierarchy from the Appeals Chamber decisions down to the Trial Chambers. However, when Trial Chambers "dared" to leave the Appeals Chamber's track, they have not only been rebuked by their Appeals Chambers for not adhering to the binding precedent doctrine. The duty of compliance with the Appeals Chamber's case law is two-lane as the Appeals Chamber simultaneously considers its jurisprudence as an authoritative statement of customary international law. Returning to the example of the ICTY *Stakić* Trial Chamber that introduced the mode of liability of "co-perpetration" the Appeals Chamber simultaneously held that the mode of liability of "co-perpetration" has no support in customary international law and runs contrary to the JCE doctrine that is "firmly established in customary international law".[246] Such a determination, however, did not prevent the Trial Chambers from openly challenging the customary law findings of the Appeals Chambers in their judgments; judgments which they nevertheless found binding on themselves due to the *stare decisis* doctrine. Consequently Trial Chambers were forced to apply "law" that according to their belief was not reflective of customary international law.[247]

---

[244]ICTY, *Stakić* Trial Judgment, para 438 stating that JCE was only one of various possibilities to interpret the term of "commission" under Art. 7 (1) ICTY Statute arguing that "a more direct reference to 'commission' in its traditional sense should be given priority before considering responsibility under the judicial term 'joint criminal enterprise'." The Trial Chamber was presided by Judge *Schomburg* who was the most prominent advocate for an alternative to the JCE doctrine at the ICTY: see also his partially dissenting and separate opinion and declaration to the *Limaj* Appeals Judgment.

[245]ICTY, *Stakić* Appeals Judgment, paras 58–63.

[246]See e.g. ICTY, *Stakić* Appeals Judgment, para 62.

[247]The *Orić* Trial Chamber expressed its wish to establish a superior's responsibility for their failure to punish crimes that occurred before taking effective control of the relevant subordinates, but considered itself bound by Appeals Chamber precedents contrary to that effect. ICTY, *Orić* Trial Judgment, para 335, stating that "a superior's duty to punish is not derived from a failure to prevent the crime, but rather is a subsidiary duty of its own." However, the Appeals Chamber in the *Hadžihasanović* Decision, para 45 prevented this possibility: "In this particular case, no practice can be found, nor is there any evidence of *opinio juris* that would sustain the proposition that a commander can be held responsible for crimes committed by a subordinate prior to the commander's assumption of command over that subordinate." The *Orić* Appeals Chamber declined to overrule the *ratio decidendi* of the *Hadžihasanović* Appeals Chamber Decision on Jurisdiction: ICTY, *Orić* Appeals Judgment, para 167. In contrast at the SCSL, the *Sesay* Trial Chamber considered that the principle of command responsibility would be broad enough under customary international law to cover situations in which a superior has taken command only after the crime has been committed and knew or had reason to know that his subordinates had committed such a crime, but failed to punish the subordinates from the time he assumes effective control, SCSL, *Sesay* Trial Judgment, paras 295ff.

6.3.5 Concluding Remarks

This chapter has illustrated that there are different methodologies detectable in the tribunals' jurisprudence, from the traditional two elements approach to customary international law, the non-allocation to the elements method, the deductive approach and methodological shortcuts on the basis of pre-existing international case law. One could thus assert that the case law of international criminal tribunals in terms of the determination of customary international criminal law, does not adhere to a "common, unified approach to the identification of rules of customary international law"[248]—as has been proclaimed by the ILC. This finding might surprise, since in the abstract international criminal tribunals do consider that customary international law must be established on basis of the traditional method of State practice and *opinio iuris*. However, international criminal tribunals generally fail to establish proof of these elements *in concreto* when elaborating on specific crimes and modes of liability. Indeed there are only a handful of cases in the jurisprudence of international criminal tribunals that seek to adhere to the traditional requirements of State practice and *opinio iuris* for the determination of customary international criminal law. The reluctance of international criminal tribunals to refer to State practice and *opinio iuris* explicitly, or to allocate specific evidence to these elements in their judgments as elaborated above, is eye-catching. That is not to say that the end result, the existence or non-existence of customary international law, is necessarily mistaken. However, it is difficult to assess the customary law findings of international criminal tribunals doctrinally. The present author considers that the international criminal tribunals could have been more careful in their analysis of the material and evidence they listed when establishing customary international criminal law. It is not clear what authoritative value for proving the existence of customary international criminal law is to be given to *inter alia* statements of States, resolutions of international organizations, statutes of international criminal tribunals, international conventions, national and international case law. Can these instances be used to give evidence to the element of State practice, *opinion iuris*, or both; or are they to be considered as subsidiary means for the determining of a rule of customary law? The next chapter will seek to address into these questions.

---

[248]ILC Report on the Work of its 65th Session to the General Assembly, 6 May – 7 June and 8 July – 9 August 2013, Supplement No. 10 (A/68/10), para 102. Special Rapporteur *M. Wood*, Second Report on Identification of Customary International Law, International Law Commission, 66th Session, 5 May-6 June and 7 July-8 August 2014, Official Records of the General Assembly, UN Doc. A/CN.4/672., para 28.

Chapter 7
Relevant Material for Proving the Existence of Customary International Criminal Law

7.1 Preliminary Remarks

This chapter will assess the evidence that has been referred to by international criminal tribunals when establishing the existence of customary international criminal law. It will determine what function the listed material can fulfill when proving the existence of customary international criminal law. For this task I consider it useful to maintain the distinction made by *Schwarzenberger* between the "law-creating processes" of public international law and the "law-determining agencies" as subsidiary means for the determination of a rule of law.[1]

The "law-creating processes" concern the question as to which entities possess law-making capacities on the international plane. Despite some authors attributing a law-making role to non-State actors,[2] the prevailing opinion still considers that law-making in the international legal sphere is primarily reserved to States.[3] That position does not exclude the practice of international organizations, or more

---

[1] *G. Schwarzenberger*, The Inductive Approach to International Law (1965), 5, 19ff.

[2] See. *A. Boyle, C. Chinkin*, The Making of International Law (2007); *R. McCorquodale*, An Inclusive International Legal System, 17 Leiden Journal of International Law (2004), 492ff. See also *K. S. Gallant*, International Criminal Court and the Making of Public International Law: New Roles for International Organizations and Individuals, 43 John Marshall Law Review (2010), 603ff, proposing a law-making capacity of international criminal courts.

[3] See e.g. Special Rapporteur *M. Wood*, Second Report on Identification of Customary International Law, International Law Commission, 66th Session, 5 May-6 June and 7 July-8 August 2014, Official Records of the General Assembly, UN Doc. A/CN.4/672, Draft Conclusion 5: "The requirement, as an element of customary international law, of a general practice means that it is primarily the practice of States that contributes to the creation, or expression, of rules of customary international law." See also *id.*, para 33; cf. *G. M. Danilenko*; Law-Making in the International Community (1993), 193ff; *A. Pellet*, The Normative Dilemma: Will and Consent in International Law-Making, 12 Australian Yearbook of International Law (1991), 22; *A. Roberts, S. Sivakumaran* admitting that "the notion of international lawmaking embodied in the doctrine of sources has remained remarkably statist in character", see *A. Roberts, S. Sivakumaran*,

© Springer International Publishing AG 2017
T. Rauter, *Judicial Practice, Customary International Criminal Law and* Nullum Crimen Sine Lege, DOI 10.1007/978-3-319-64477-6_7

precisely the practice of intergovernmental organizations, as being useful for the determination of the "law-creating processes". Generally, organs of intergovernmental organizations are composed of State representatives and as such their practice can be traced back to the participating States.[4] While it would go beyond the scope of this thesis to elaborate on the question of the requirements to qualify as a State entity,[5] we must consider the scope of State practice and *opinio iuris*, and the nature of the acts and organs of state that can be used to support these constitutive elements of customary international law.

There is no general agreement on the scope of State practice in the legal literature. Some authors argue for a narrow concept of State practice, suggesting that only physical practice[6] counts, or that only "concrete and/or specific acts of States [...] are relevant as *usus*", whereas the position of States *in abstracto* could not be considered adequate to establish State practice.[7] The ILA proposed that State practice concerns only the practice of States "in their international legal relations."[8] A wider concept of State practice includes physical acts of States, verbal acts such as policy statements and press releases, and their conduct in international organizations including the resolutions they support. Taken together these could reveal the State's view on international law.[9] *Akehurst* famously stated that "State practice covers any act or statement by a State from which views can be inferred about international law."[10] Within this chapter I adhere to a wide concept of State practice in order to infer the State's position with regard to international law. As *Bos* has remarked:

Lawmaking by Nonstate Actors: Engaging Armed Groups in the Creation of International Humanitarian Law, 37 The Yale Journal of International Law (2012), 111–115.

[4]*International Law Association*, London Conference (2000), Committee on Formation of Customary (General) International Law, Final Report of the Committee, Statement of Principles Applicable to the Formation of General Customary International Law, Section 11 at p. 19 views resolutions of intergovernmental organizations as "a series of verbal acts by the individual member States participating in that organ." See also Second Report of Special Rapporteur *Wood* (supra note 3), paras 43, 41 (i); he claims, however, in para 44 that the case is different for the European Union in areas where the member States have transferred exclusive competences to the EU. In such a case the practice of the supranational organization shall count as State practice, otherwise "its Member States would be deprived or reduced of their ability to contribute to State practice in cases where the Member States have conferred some of their public powers to the organization."

[5]See *Jellinek's* doctrine of three elements: territory, population, and government, *G. Jellinek*, Allgemeine Staatslehre (1914), 396ff.

[6]*A. D'Amato*, The Concept of Custom in International Law (1971), 88ff. See also the dissenting opinion of Judge Read in the ICJ Fisheries Case (United Kingdom v. Norway), Judgment, 18 December 1951, ICJ Reports (1951), 191.

[7]*G. J. H. van Hoof*, Rethinking the Sources of International Law (1983), 108.

[8]ILA (supra note 4), Part I: Definitions, 9.

[9]See Sect. 4.3.2, The Procedural Aspect of Modern Customary International Law.

[10]Cf. *M. Akehurst*, Custom as a Source of International Law, 47 British Yearbook of International Law (1977), 10, see also 53.

If custom is 'what one is in the habit of doing', practice can be anything within the scope of a State's jurisdiction. All actions or, more generally, forms of behavior so qualified are eligible to become the basis of a customary rule of international law. It is quite useless, therefore, to try to limit the material element in custom to one or more categories of such behaviour.[11]

Since States are the principal law-making entities it is evident that the practice must be attributable to the State.[12] Consequently, a wide concept of State practice also corresponds to the currently predominant view that accepts that all organs[13] of a State, the executive, legislative and judicial, can contribute to the formation of customary international law. Earlier writers, in contrast, would only take acts of organs that could bind States in their external relations into consideration.[14] Furthermore, these State acts have to be accessible, which means they need to be made public, or at least be made public to one other State.[15]

Within this study the view is rejected that *opinio iuris* can simply be deduced from State practice,[16] or that the function of *opinio iuris* is restricted to determine which instances of State practice count for the formation of customary international law.[17] State practice is a generalization of a pattern of behavior (factual behavior, paper or verbal practice), which is in itself value-free. Without some further element the practice alone can be descriptive but not prescriptive.[18] The addition of *opinio iuris* serves as a means to distinguish acts based on legal obligations from exceeding acts of good will, habit or courtesy.[19] However, by widening the scope of State practice to include verbal or paper practice, one could indeed argue that this is a "purposive" development of State practice.[20] Nevertheless, it is proposed that despite the widening of the scope of State practice, customary international law still consists of two distinct constitutive elements, State practice and *opinio iuris*. It is "merely" the evidence for both elements that could be found within the same evidential source.[21] Consequently certain examples of paper/verbal practice not

---

[11]*M. Bos*, A Methodology of International Law (1984), 229.

[12]Second Report of Special Rapporteur *Wood* (supra note 3), Draft Conclusion 6.

[13]Comprising *de jure* as well as *de facto* organs, see Second Report of Special Rapporteur *Wood* (supra note 3), para 34.

[14]ILA (supra note 4), Section 9, pp. 17–18, referring to the early view as stipulated by *inter alia D. Anzilotti*, Cours de droit international (1929), 74ff.

[15]ILA (supra note 4), Section 5.

[16]See Sect. 4.2.2, Opinio Iuris Under a Traditional Interpretation; see also Second Report of Special Rapporteur *Wood* (supra note 3), paras 72–74, who determines that *opinio iuris* is not merely proven by a large number of State practice.

[17]ILA (supra note 4), Part I: Definitions, p. 10: "in the context of the formation of general customary law (. . .) the main function of the subjective element is to indicate what practice counts (or, more precisely, does not count) towards the formation of a customary rule."

[18]*J. Kammerhofer*, Uncertainty in International Law – A Kelsenian Perspective (2011), 61.

[19]ICJ, Right of Passage over Indian Territory, 42–43; Asylum Case, 276–277; Jurisdictional Immunities Case, para 55.

[20]See Sect. 4.3, Modern Customary International Law.

[21]See the references to the legal literature in Sect. 4.3.2, The Procedural Aspect of Modern Customary International Law.

may also contain indications for the
the same instance, evidence for State
lement of customary international law
e such a double function will be elabo-
the concrete evidences for customary
nal criminal tribunals. However it must
t give evidence for State practice *ipso*
ion the *opinio iuris* element has a broad
to the formation of customary inter-
at a certain act is already required by
onsent element would enable custom-
king tool for States, which can initiate
customary international law, inviting
g rule. Customary international law is
generality, consistency and duration of
State practice, the subjective element would evolve from a law-creating, constitutive will/consent element into an element of belief or conviction that certain acts
are required by an existing customary norm.[25] Due to this evolving, continuing
process, State acts conforming to an existing customary international norm are both
constitutive to as well as declaratory evidence of the existence of a customary
international rule.[26] This conclusion derives from the "law-creating processes" of
customary international law, in which State practice and *opinio iuris* remain
constitutive elements of custom, even if the customary international rule is already
well established. Therefore, it is not necessary that practice needs to be distinguished as "constitutive" or "declarative" evidence for the formation or determination of customary international law. *Opinio iuris* can be established on basis of

---

[22]See Sect. 4.3.2, The Procedural Aspect of Modern Customary International Law. See also
Second Report of Special Rapporteur *Wood* (supra note 3), para 70.

[23]See also *Danilenko* (supra note 3), 121–123, stating that "[n]ot all acts which are usually
included into the broad category of state practice may express the required *opinio juris*".

[24]The ILA apparently also proposes that the subjective element could include a will/consent and a
belief element, see ILA (supra note 4), Part III, The Subjective Element, 29ff. As it seems with
regard to the "World Court" the PCIJ, Lotus Case seems to be the only case were the will element
was predominant. The ICJ holds on to a conception of *opinio iuris* as belief, see further *A. Pellet*,
Article 38, in Zimmerman et al (eds.), The Statute of the International Court of Justice – A
Commentary (2012), 819, MN 225.

[25]It is in that regard that the ICJ, North Sea Continental Shelf Cases, para 78, stated: "Some States
have at first probably accepted the rules in question, as States usually do, because they found them
convenient and useful, the best possible solution for the problems involved. Others may also have
been convinced that the instrument elaborated [. . .] was to become and would in due course
become general law. [. . .] Many States have followed suit under the conviction that it was law.
[. . .]." The ILA (supra note 4), Part I: Definition, 9–12, considers that the process is a continuing
one and that State practice can be constitutive of a new rule but could also evince an existing rule.
See also *Danilenko* (supra note 3), 100ff.

[26]See also ILA (supra note 4), Part I: Definition, 9 footnote 21.

individual State acts. Furthermore, *opinio iuris* can also be established by revealing a general or common consensus of the existence of a customary international norm by the generality of States.[27]

Beyond these "law-creating processes" of customary international law, other evidence referred to in order to prove the existence of customary international law can "merely" be used as subsidiary means for its determination. In this sense *Schwarzenberger* speaks of "law-determining agencies".[28] Art. 38 (1) (d) ICJ Statute highlights the roles of "judicial decisions" and the legal doctrine described as "the teachings of the most highly qualified publicists of the various nations". It is important to note once more the fact that these subsidiary means for the determination of a rule of law are not in themselves a primary source of law. *Pellet* terms them "documentary sources" that give indications of the existence of the three sources of law as established in Art. 38 ICJ Statute: international conventions, customary international law and general principles of law.[29] In terms of judicial decisions as stated above, it would be preferable to consider them as suitable subsidiary means for the determination of a rule of customary law only if the decision itself attains a qualitative standard by adequately demonstrating State practice and *opinio iuris*.[30]

The next chapters will analyze the value of the listed material referred to by international criminal tribunals for the determining of customary international law on the basis of the distinction between the "law-creating processes" and the "law-determining agencies". The following chapters are not divided into the methodological categories of 'State practice', '*opinio iuris*', or 'subsidiary means for the determination of customary law'. Since one and the same evidential source may indicate more than just one of these methodological categories, it is more fruitful to subdivide the chapters according to the materials to which international criminal tribunals refer.

7.2 Official Pronouncements by States

In what has turned out to be one of the most influential decisions in the case law of the ICTY, the Appeals Chamber in the *Tadić* Appeals Chamber Jurisdiction Decision[31] laid the foundations of the treatment of State practice by international criminal tribunals. By conveniently labeling actual military conduct in the field as

---

[27]See ILA (supra note 4), Part I: Definition, 8; *Pellet* (supra note 24), 819, MN 225. Second Report of Special Rapporteur *Wood* (supra note 3), para 64.

[28]G. *Schwarzenberger*, The Inductive Approach to International Law (1965), 5, 19ff.

[29]*Pellet* (supra note 24), 854, MN 305.

[30]See further Sect. 6.3.4.3, International Case Law as Subsidiary Means for the Determination of Customary International Law.

[31]ICTY, *Tadić* Appeals Chamber Jurisdiction Decision.

untrustworthy, the *Tadić* Appeals Chamber circumvented the necessity of analyzing actual battlefield behavior.[32] It adhered to a wide conception of State practice, stating that "on account of the inherent nature of this subject-matter" *inter alia* "official pronouncements of States" are of particular importance for determining customary international criminal law.[33] For the reasons stated above, it appears that the *Tadić* Appeals Chamber treated official pronouncements of States as an instance of State practice,[34] a position that has been confirmed by subsequent ICTY jurisprudence.[35] To the present author's knowledge, only on rare occasions have international criminal tribunals explicitly referred to official pronouncements of States as also indicating *opinio iuris*.[36]

The jurisprudence of international criminal tribunals demonstrates that official pronouncements of States occur in various forms: They include public statements by States commenting on international law applicable within their own internal legal order,[37] general comments on international law and comments on the situations in foreign States,[38] the attitude of States towards resolutions of international organizations,[39] statements of States or group of States in the

---

[32]ICTY, *Tadić* Appeals Chamber Jurisdiction Decision, para 99.

[33]ICTY, *Tadić* Appeals Chamber Jurisdiction Decision, para 99 also referring to military manuals and judicial decisions; see above Sect. 6.3.1.2, ICTY *Tadić* Appeals Chamber Jurisdiction Decision.

[34]See Sect. 6.3.1.2, ICTY *Tadić* Appeals Chamber Jurisdiction Decision.

[35]See Sect. 6.3.1.2, ICTY *Tadić* Appeals Chamber Jurisdiction Decision.

[36]ICTY, *Boškoski* Trial Judgment, para 191, distinguishing NIACs from "merely" terroristic acts not rising to the level of armed conflict. See also ICTY, *Tadić* Appeals Chamber Jurisdiction Decision, para 83, viewing the US *Amicus Curiae* Brief proposing to expand the scope of the grave breaches regime also to cover NIACs as "the first indication of a possible change in *opinio juris* of States".

[37]See e.g. ICTY, *Tadić* Appeals Chamber Jurisdiction Decision, para 105, referring to a public statement of the prime minister of the Congo and para 113 statement of the Ministry of Defence and Security of El Salvador.

[38]See e.g. ICTY, *Tadić* Appeals Chamber Jurisdiction Decision, para 100, citing a speech concerning the Spanish Civil War of the British Prime Minister Chamberlain before the House of Commons, para 117, referring to a statement of the Deputy Legal Adviser of the United States State Department at a conference, paras 121f referring to British, German and US practice condemning the Iraqi use of chemical weapons; *Kupreškić* Trial Judgment, paras 521 and 524 also referring to the statement of Chamberlain and para 532 referring to the report of the US deputy legal adviser and head of the US delegation to the Geneva Diplomatic Conference of 1974–77 to the US Secretary of State; ICTY, *Galić* Appeal Judgment, para 89, referring to the position of the US deputy legal adviser at a conference and a letter from the department of the army to the legal adviser of the US army forces deployed in the gulf region.

[39]ICTY, *Tadić* Appeals Chamber Jurisdiction Decision, paras 110 und 111, referring to the US position regarding UN GA Resolution 2444 (1968) as "declaratory of existing customary international law" or the positions of Norway and Cuba towards UN GA Resolution 2675 (1970); ICTY, *Delalić* Appeals Judgment, para 356, referring to the explanation of vote by the US to Security Council Resolution 827 (1993).

framework of multilateral diplomacy,[40] and official pronouncements of a group of States.[41]

In the present author's opinion and in accordance with the jurisprudence of international criminal tribunals, these instances of "official pronouncements" can provide evidence of State practice. Moreover, under certain conditions they could also be used to establish a possible *opinio iuris*.[42] *Opinio iuris* cannot simply be deduced from official pronouncement as an instance of State practice.[43] The language of the official pronouncements is particularly important for also providing evidence of *opinio iuris*. When a State explicitly refers to customary international law when making a specific pronouncement, it is safe to assume that this statement also reflects the belief of the particular state in the existence and content of customary international law.[44] Without such an explicit reference to customary international law, these pronouncements can still provide proof for the element of State practice, but it remains questionable as to whether they can serve as an indication of the subjective element of customary international law. A State may very well make a specific pronouncement out of political opportunity. Without an adequate indication that the State was expressing its views on the content of customary international law, one could thus only speculate as to the reason for the pronouncement. Without further indication it is untenable to claim that official pronouncements by States *ipso facto* also provide evidence for an *opinio iuris*. However, as stated above, generally the case law of international criminal tribunals has used official pronouncements of States as evidence only for establishing the element of State practice.

---

[40]ICTY, *Tadić* Appeals Chamber Jurisdiction Decision, para 120 referring to the position of Greece on behalf of the European Community in sessions of the First Committee of the UN General Assembly, para 121 referring to the German position on the Iraqi use of chemical weapons before the First Committee of the UN General Assembly; see also *Tadić* Appeals Chamber Judgment, paras 130 and 136 referring to statements of States in debates of the UN Security Council; see also *Hadžihasanović*, Trial Chamber Decision, paras 116ff. See also SCSL, *Sesay* Trial Judgment, para 288 referring to statements of States before the UN General Assembly and the UN Security Council.

[41]ICTY, *Tadić* Appeals Chamber Jurisdiction Decision, referring to the declarations of the Member States of the European Community in paras 113 (on Liberia), 115 (on Chechnya) and 120 (on Iraq); *Boškoski* Trial Judgment, para 192 referring *inter alia* to the Council Common Position 2005/847/CFSP (29 November 2005) of the European Union; SCSL, *Taylor* Appeals Judgment referring to the Council Common Position 2008/944/CFSP (2 December 2008) of the European Union.

[42]See also Second Report of Special Rapporteur *Wood* (supra note 3), paras 41ff and 76ff.

[43]See Sect. 4.3.2, The Procedural Aspect of Modern Customary International Law with reference to the jurisprudence of the ICJ and legal literature. Also Special Rapporteur *Wood* in his Second Report of Special Rapporteur *Wood* (supra note 3), paras 72–74, determines that *opinio iuris* is not merely proven by a large number of State practice.

[44]*H. Spieker*, Völkergewohnheitsrechtlicher Schutz der natürlichen Umwelt im internationalen bewaffneten Konflikt (1992), 104 and 144 coming to the same conclusion with regard to military manuals.

7.3 Passive Practice

On rare occasions international criminal tribunals have also referred to instances of passive practice: an abstention from claiming to be entitled to a certain practice has been used to establish the existence of customary international law.[45] These rare references were made without a clear indication by international criminal tribunals whether these instances give evidence for State practice, *opinio iuris*, or both. A stated above, while instances of omission may qualify as State practice, the existence of *opinio iuris* must be proven separately.[46]

7.4 National Legislation

7.4.1 Preliminary Remarks

As held by various authorities, domestic legislation can play an important role in determining customary international law.[47] Generally, international criminal tribunals have treated national legislation as an instance of State practice.[48] However, such a determination requires concretion. Not all legislation of a State is relevant for the formation or determination of customary international law, but it requires some nexus to the international legal order. As early as 1950 the ILC tasked with collecting evidence of customary international law held that national legislation shall have "bearing on matters of international concern" or shall be "relating to particular topics of international interest".[49] In his report on the ICTY the UN Secretary General stated that "[s]uggestions have been made that the international tribunal should apply *domestic law in so far as it incorporates customary international humanitarian law*."[50] The ICTY *Tadić* Appeals Chamber, considering

---

[45]See ICTY, *Kupreškić* Trial Judgment, para 533 referring to the abstention from claiming a right of reprisals upon enemy civilians and ICTY, *Furundžija* Trial Judgment, para 138 stating that "no State has ever claimed that it was authorized to practice torture in time of armed conflict".

[46]See Sect. 4.2.3, Traditional Customary International Law: Practical Concerns and Its Slow Development.

[47]Dissenting Opinion of Judge *Gaja* to ICJ, Jurisdictional Immunities Case, para 3: "Legislation is an important aspect of State practice." See also Second Report of Special Rapporteur *Wood* (supra note 3), para 41 (d); ILA (supra note 4), Part II The Objective Element: State Practice, 13ff; *I. Brownlie*, Principles of Public International Law (2008), 6.

[48]ICTY, *Krstić* Trial Judgment, paras 541, 571; *Galić* Appeal Judgment, paras 92ff; *Kordić* Appeals Judgment, para 66; SCSL, *Fofana* Appeals Judgment, paras 391, 405ff; SCSL, *Taylor* Appeals Judgment, para 430,

[49]Report of the ILC to the General Assembly, Yearbook of the International Law Commission (1950), Volume II, 371.

[50]Report of the Secretary-General Pursuant to Paragraph 2 of Security Council Resolution 808 (1993), 3 May 1993, UN Doc S/25704), para 36 (SG Report on ICTY) (emphasis added).

whether the JCE doctrine has an underpinning in domestic legislations, concluded that "domestic law does not originate from the implementation of international law but, rather, to a large extent runs parallel to, and precedes, international regulation."[51] It could therefore not use the cited domestic legislations as relevant material for the customary law foundation of JCE. As has been stated before, the *Tadić* Appeals Chamber instead relied on post World War II jurisprudence as subsidiary means for the determination of a rule of customary law.[52] Consequently, domestic legislation that develops irrespective of a connecting factor to public international law is not relevant for the determination of State practice or *opinio iuris*, even though in that regard domestic legislation may be relevant material for proving a general principle of law according to Art. 38 (1) (c) ICJ Statute.

7.4.2 International Crimes Laws and National Criminal Codes

The first category of national legislation that is of particular importance for the determination of customary international criminal law is domestic legislation that incorporates international crimes and modes of liability into the domestic legal order. The national legislators may choose to incorporate international criminal law by merely amending domestic penal codes,[53] or it may establish a specific code or statute dealing with international crimes.[54] The mere incorporation of international law is a sufficient connecting factor to consider these laws as relevant material for the determination of customary international law, and the jurisprudence of international criminal tribunals has relied heavily upon them.[55] As stated above, when

---

[51]ICTY, *Tadić* Appeals Judgment, para 225; see also SCSL, *Taylor* Appeals Judgment, para 429: "Domestic law, even if consistent and continuous in all State, is not necessarily indicative of customary international law. This is particularly true in defining legal elements and determining forms of criminal participation in domestic jurisdictions, which may base their concepts of criminality on differing values and principles."

[52]See Sect. 6.3.4.3, International Case Law as Subsidiary Means for the Determination of Customary International Law.

[53]See for example Arts. 211 and 212 of the French Penal Code incorporating the crime of genocide and crimes against humanity, or §§ 321ff of the Austrian Criminal Code as amended by 29 December 2014 incorporating the crime of genocide, crimes against humanity and war crimes.

[54]See for example German Code of Crimes against International Law, Parliamentary Documents (Bundestagsdrucksache) 14/8524 and 14/8892, Federal Gazette I (2002) 2254.

[55]See for example. ICTY, *Galić* Trial Judgment, para 31 and *Galić* Appeal Judgment, para 95 when elaborating on the crime of terror; *Krstić* Trial Judgment, para 571 and *Prosecutor v. Krstić*, IT-98-33A, Appeals Chamber, Judgment, 19 April 2004, para 141 elaborating on the crime of genocide; *Kupreškić* Trial Judgment, para 577 when eliminating the nexus requirement between crimes against humanity and war crimes; *Blaškić* Trial Judgment, para 212 when elaborating on crimes against humanity; *Kordić* Appeals Judgment, para 66 showing that national legislation was not settled on the question of showing a result requirement under the crime of

explicitly allocating these materials to the constitutive elements of customary international law, international criminal tribunals have used domestic criminal laws as instances of State practice.[56] But they did not inquire under which conditions domestic legislation could be used to evidence *opinio iuris*. For this one would require proof that the State considered the domestic legislation or certain norms thereof as reflecting customary international law. Indeed, the explanatory notes to domestic laws might prove to be of particular importance in certain instances when giving evidence of the legal convictions of States towards customary international law, such as the explanatory note regarding the draft law to the German Code of Crimes against International Law.[57] Without such additional evidence one could very well argue that a State merely corresponded to an obligation to implement based on an international convention, or that a State enacted national legislation out of political opportunity or moral pressure. Nevertheless, States might use national legislation to initiate the first State practice with a will to *create* customary international law. Such a will/consent element could very well be used to establish *opinio iuris*. However, in such a case the explanatory notes should provide evidence that the State intended to use national legislation as a tool to develop customary international law. While a particular national legislation might not reflect the current state of customary international law, States could use their law making powers, the explanatory notes thereto, as means to develop or create it. Such a conscious approach on part of the States of using customary international law as a law-making tool has been advocated above.[58] If States are not clear in their views on the implementation of international law through domestic legislation, other actors might read an *opinio iuris* element into a domestic legislation that was never intended by the implementing State. Consequently, one has to agree with *Schmitt* and *Watts* that States are ceding influence on shaping international law to non-State actors by neglecting to give adequate proof of their legal views.[59]

---

unlawful attacks against civilians and civilian objects. See also SCSL, *Brima* Trial Judgment, para 663 elaborating on the crime of terror; *Sesay* Trial Judgment, para 217 when elaborating on the crime of intentionally directing attacks against personnel involved in a peacekeeping mission.

[56] See supra note 48.

[57] See in that regard the explanatory note regarding the draft law to the German Code of Crimes against International Law, Bundesratsdrucksache 29/02 of 15 January 2002, reprinted in Lüder/Vormbaum (eds.) Materialien zum Völkerstrafgesetzbuch (2002). For instance at p. 47 the explanatory note explicitly states that its inclusion of sexual coercion as a crime against humanity (§ 7 (1) (7) corresponds with customary international law. At p. 56 it applies the definition of non-international armed conflict contained in AP II as reflecting customary international law: At p. 62f the explanatory note explicitly determines that § 8 (1) (8) (b) (taking body tissue or organs) and § 8 (1) (8) (c) (using treatment methods that are not medically recognised) are war crimes under customary international law.

[58] See Sect. 3.10.6.2, The *certa* Requirement as an Imperative for Improvement.

[59] M. N. Schmitt, S. Watts, State *Opinio Juris* and International Humanitarian Law Pluralism, 91 International Law Studies (2015), 171ff.

7.4.3 Military Manuals and Military Penal Codes

Another category of national legislation that may be of particular importance is military manuals.[60] Drafting military manuals is one method of States use to disseminate international humanitarian law.[61] Through such manuals States can ensure respect for IHL in armed conflicts, although strictly speaking international humanitarian law treaties do not oblige State parties to draft and issue military manuals.[62] The famous ICTY *Tadić* Appeals Chamber Jurisdiction Decision[63] considered that military manuals are of particular importance for determining customary international criminal law.[64] For the reasons stated above, the *Tadić* Appeals Chamber treated military manuals of States as an instance of State practice,[65] a position that has been confirmed by subsequent ICTY jurisprudence.[66] The jurisprudence of international criminal tribunals has relied heavily on military manuals and military penal codes.[67] The "dubious metamorphosis"[68] of State practice to include verbal and paper practice has been most fiercely debated in relation to military manuals as possible evidence for customary international humanitarian law, with several writers criticizing the failure to analyse actual military State practice, especially battlefield behavior, post

---

[60]The present analysis is restricted to national military manuals; international manuals such as the 1994 San Remo Manual on International Law Applicable to Armed Conflicts at Sea fall outside the scope of the present survey.

[61]Additional Protocol I, Art. 83.

[62]See further *H.P. Gasser*, Military Manuals, Legal Advisers and the First Additional Protocol of 1977, in Hayashi (ed.), National Military Manuals on the Law of Armed Conflict (2008), 56ff.

[63]ICTY, *Tadić* Appeals Chamber Jurisdiction Decision.

[64]ICTY, *Tadić* Appeals Chamber Jurisdiction Decision, para 99 also referring to official pronouncements and judicial decisions; see above Sect. 6.3.1.2, ICTY *Tadić* Appeals Chamber Jurisdiction Decision.

[65]See Sect. 6.3.1.2, ICTY *Tadić* Appeals Chamber Jurisdiction Decision.

[66]See ICTY, *Galić* Appeal Judgment, para 92; *Prosecutor v. Strugar*, IT-01-42-T, Trial Chamber, Judgment, 31 January 2005, footnote 754; *Prosecutor v. Boškoski*, IT-04-82-T, Trial Chamber, Judgment, 10 July 2008, footnote 1273; *Prosecutor v. Đorđević*, IT-05-87/1-T, Trial Chamber, Judgment, 23 February 2011, footnote 5779. *Prosecutor v. Stanišić and Župljanin*, IT-08-91-T, Trial Chamber, Judgment, 27 March 2013, footnote 86.

[67]See for example ICTY Hadžihasanović Trial Judgment, para 44 when stating that also a "partial destruction" falls under the crime of wanton destruction of towns and villages not justified by military necessity and para 51 when stating that war booty is exempted from plunder; ICTY, *Galić* Trial Judgment, para 31 and *Galić* Appeal Judgment, para 95 when elaborating on the crime of terror; *Kordić* Appeals Judgment, para 66 showing that national legislation was not settled on the matter of evidence for the crime of unlawful attacks against civilians and civilian targets; *Delalić* Appeals Chamber Judgment, para 230 when elaborating on command responsibility; see also SCSL, *Brima* Trial Judgment, para 663 elaborating on the crime of terror; *Sesay* Trial Judgment, para 217 when elaborating on the crime of intentionally directing attacks against personnel involved in a peacekeeping mission.

[68]*B. Simma* and *P. Alston*, The Sources of Human Rights Law: Custom, Jus Cogens, and General Principles, 12 Australian Yearbook of International Law (1988–1989), 89.

battlefield practice, and disciplinary measures in cases of troop misconduct.[69] However, a wide concept of State practice comprises both actual State behavior and military manuals as relevant evidence for the determination of customary international law. Nevertheless, although an instance may qualify as evidence for State practice, it must still fulfill certain requirements, *inter alia* the practice needs to be attributable to the State and it has to be accessible, meaning it needs to be made public, at least to one other State.[70] The ICRC Custom Study has been prominently criticized for relying on a manual attributed to Israel that *Dinstein* considered did not represent the official views of the State of Israel.[71] Consequently, it is important to note that the military manual in question is attributable to the State, usually published by the government or the military. The need that the document has to be made public disqualifies internal manuals as instances of State practice.[72] If these criteria are fulfilled military manuals can indeed be referred to in order to establish State practice.

Various authors consider that military manuals may simultaneously indicate *opinio iuris*.[73] Indeed, within the UK Military Manual one finds the following statement: "The publication of this Manual should be seen as another step in stating publicly the UK's interpretation of what the Law of Armed Conflict requires."[74] However, according to some authors that does not in turn mean that the military manual gives evidence for the UK view of the customary law of armed conflict, as it may very well simply restate provisions that have been agreed on a mere

---

[69]See in this regard the critique of *J. B. Bellinger and W. J. Haynes*, A US government response to the International Committee of the Red Cross study Customary International Humanitarian Law, 89 Review of the Red Cross (2007), on the non-traditional methodology used by the ICRC Custom Study, 445: "Although manuals may provide important indications of State behavior and *opinio juris*, they cannot be a replacement for meaningful assessment of operational State practice in connection with actual military operations." See also *W. H. Parks*, The ICRC Customary Law Study: A Preliminary Assessment, 99 Proceedings of the Annual Meeting (American Society of International Law) (2005), 210: "Government-authorized actions in war speak louder than peace-time government statements".

[70]See Sect. 7.1, Preliminary Remarks.

[71]See *D. Turns*, Military Manuals and the Customary Law of Armed Conflict, in Hayashi (ed.), National Military Manuals on the Law of Armed Conflict (2008), 68 referring to *Y. Dinstein*, The ICRC Customary Humanitarian Law Study, 36 Israel Yearbook on Human Rights (2006), 6f.

[72]*Turns* (supra note 71), 68.

[73]*C. Garraway*, Military Manuals, Operational Law and the Regulatory Framework of the Armed Forces, in Hayashi (ed.), National Military Manuals on the Law of Armed Conflict (2008), 51: "national manuals provide evidence of state practice and *opinio juris*". See also *T. Meron*, The Geneva Conventions as Customary Law, 81 American Journal of International Law (1987), 361: "manuals of military law and legislation of states providing for the implementation of humanitarian law norms as internal law should be considered as among the best types of evidence of such practice and, sometimes perhaps, as a statement of *opinio juris* as well."

[74]UK Military Manual JSP 383 The Joint Service Manual of the Law of Armed Conflict (2004), available at https://www.gov.uk/government/uploads/system/uploads/attachment_data/file/27874/JSP3832004Edition.pdf (last visited 16 June 2017).

conventional basis.[75] Furthermore, some authors consider that States might include norms within military manuals because of policy considerations rather than adhering to a customary international norm.[76] However, similar to what has been stated above in relation to international crimes laws, the more clear States are on their view on international law when issuing military manuals the more adequate proof of *opinio iuris* can be established by military manuals. Therefore, it is appropriate that military manuals are generally a useful indication of the *opinio iuris* element when establishing customary international law.[77]

7.5 International Conventions

7.5.1 Preliminary Remarks

The relationship between international conventions and customary international law is a complex one. Although the two are distinct sources of public international law according to Art. 38 (1) (a) and (b) ICJ Statute, their relationship with one another has been aptly described as "entangled".[78] To ensure that treaty norms influence the formation of customary international law, the ICJ presupposes that treaty rule should be of a *fundamentally norm-creating character* in order to form the basis of a general rule of law.[79] As such the ICJ appears to assume that a conventional norm has to be drafted in a general and abstract manner to be able to influence the development of customary international norms.

There are various ways treaties and customary international law interact: A convention might be drafted to codify pre-existing customary international law, which has been described by the ICJ as a convention's "recording" function.[80] Furthermore, a treaty might be the point of the "crystallization" of an emergent

---

[75]*Turns* (supra note 71), 69 listing the example that the UK has prohibited the use of chemical weapons in armed conflicts because it is State party to the Convention on the Prohibition of the Development, Production, Stockpiling and Use of Chemical Weapons and on their Destruction, 3 September 1992, 1974 UNTS 45.

[76]*Spieker* (supra note 44), 144; *Turns* (supra note 71), 69.

[77]See also Second Report of Special Rapporteur *Wood* (supra note 3), para 76 (d).

[78]*O. Schachter*, Entangled Treaty and Custom, Dinstein (ed.), International Law at a Time of Perplexity: Essays in Honour of Shabtai Rosenne (1988), 717ff; see on this issue also *M. E. Villiger*, Customary International Law and Treaties (1997), and *B.B. Jia*, The Relations between Treaties and Custom, 9 Chinese Journal of International Law (2010), 81ff. Also the ECCC Supreme Court Chambers stated that it "must be recognised that treaty law and customary international law often mutually support and supplement each other." See ECCC, *Duch* Appeals Judgment, para 94.

[79]ICJ, North Sea Continental Shelf Cases, para 72.

[80]ICJ, Continental Shelf Case (Libya v. Malta), para 27: ""multilateral conventions may have an important role to play in recording and defining rules deriving from custom".

customary international law. In both instances the convention or norms thereof would be declaratory of customary international law. Furthermore, a conventional norm may be subsequently mirrored by a customary norm if it is accepted as such.[81] In this way a treaty could be regarded as "historical or material source",[82] triggering the subsequent development of customary international law. The question is how we can perceive these interactions in the proposed structure of the "law-creating processes" and the "law-determining agencies".

A wide concept of State practice warrants the conclusion that all State acts in relation to international conventions—negotiating, signing, ratifying or implementing—are relevant material for the formation of customary international law as a form of State practice.[83] Thus, even "declaratory" treaties, or more precisely the different State acts in relation to these treaties, can simultaneously be conceived as constitutive for the formation of customary international law. But treaties that do not have a "codifying" or "crystallizing" effect, may also in themselves be the starting point of a developing process of customary law.[84] Consequently also in that regard conventions should not be reduced to the role of a mere "historical or material source" triggering subsequent State practice, but the practice in relation to international conventions itself can be used to prove the element of State practice. It is in that regard that the so-called *Baxter* paradox, which has also been referred to by the ICTY *Čelebići* Trial Chamber, is overstated. Describing this paradox the Trial Chamber stated that the "evidence of the existence of such customary law – State practice and *opinio iuris* – may, in some situations, be extremely difficult to ascertain, particularly where there exists a prior

---

[81]On these three different interactions between treaties and customary law see ICJ, North Sea Continental Shelf Cases, paras 60–82.

[82]For a discussion of the terms historical or material source of law see Sect. 4.1, Preliminary Remarks.

[83]*Akehurst* (supra note 10), 43, who "has no difficulty in regarding treaties as State practice." See also Second Report of Special Rapporteur *Wood* (supra note 3), para 41 (h) also referring to A. D'Amato, Custom and Treaty: A Response to Professor Weisburd, 21 Vanderbilt Journal of Transnational Law (1988), 462: "What makes the content of a treaty count as an element of custom is the fact that the parties to the treaty have entered into a binding commitment to act in accordance with its terms. Whether or not they subsequently act in conformity with the treaty, the fact remains that they have so committed to act. The commitment itself, then, is the 'state practice' component of custom". See, however, A. M. *Weisburd*, Customary International Law: The Problem of Treaties, 21 Vanderbilt Journal of Transnational Law (1988), 24, arguing that if "a treaty demonstrates that the parties believe they would have no legal obligation to behave as the treaty requires but for the treaty, it follows that practice under the treaty cannot supply the usage element necessary to establish a rule of customary international law." For the reasons established under Sect. 4.2.3, Traditional Customary International Law: Practical Concerns and Its Slow Development the present author concurs with the opinion of *D'Amato* as State practice is an independent element that does not need to be "qualified" by *opinio iuris*.

[84]ILA (supra note 4), Section 24; see also ICTY, *Tadić* Appeals Judgment, para 290 stating that "treaty provisions which are at the very origin of the customary process".

multilateral treaty which has been adopted by the vast majority of States".[35] Since according to the Ĉelebici Trial Chamber only practice outside of a convention would be significant for the element of State practice, widely ratified conventions would hinder the development of customary international law. This strict separation between treaties and customary international law is artificial when accepting a wide concept of State practice. All State acts in relation to international conventions are a form of State practice and as such relevant for the material element of customary international law.

Whether a treaty or State practice in relation to a convention can also be used as evincing *opinio iuris*, depends on whether one can establish a belief of the existence of a legal duty beyond the contractual obligation. It is thus necessary to differentiate between the *opinio iuris* element for the establishment of customary international law and a pure *opinio iuris conventionis*.[86] The mere conclusion of a treaty does not imply the existence of the *opinio iuris* element for the determination of customary international law.[87] If a treaty aims at being declaratory of customary international law, such an acknowledgment must be given directly or indirectly within the treaty or the negotiations leading to its conclusion. As such the preamble, the treaty text and the *travaux préparatoires* are of particular importance.[88] However, it must be stated that only the acts of State delegates could be used to establish an *opinio iuris*, and not acts of members of the ILC, irrespective of any direct or indirect State acknowledgment.[89] Furthermore, it appears that in practice international conventions would sometimes contain elements of progressive development of the law and simultaneously contain certain norms that are drafted with the intention of restating customary international law. Which norms of a treaty are intended to reflect customary international law and whether adequate *opinio iuris* exists generally has to be established on basis of available material in relation to individual treaty norms.[90] Assuming that these materials are available, it must be added that

---

[85]ICTY *Delalić* Trial Judgment, para 302. See further *R. Baxter*, Treaties and Custom, 129 Recueil des Cours (1970), 64; see also ICJ, North Sea Continental Shelf Cases, para 76: "From their action [State Parties to the 1958 Geneva Convention] no interference could legitimately be drawn as to the existence of a rule of customary international law in favour of the equidistance principle." It seems, however, that the ICJ did not adhere to its own restrictive ruling and took the practice of State parties to the UN Charter into account when elaborating on the customary prohibition of use of force in the *Nicaragua* Case, see also *Spieker* (supra note 44), 69 and *Schachter* (supra note 78), 726f.

[86]*Villiger* (supra note 78), 28. See also *Meron*, who in relation to the 1948 Geneva Conventions determined: "*Opinio juris* is thus critical for the transformation of treaties into general law. To be sure, it is difficult to demonstrate such *opinio juris*, but this poses a question of proof rather than of principle." See *Meron* (supra note 73), 367.

[87]*Weisburd* (supra note 83), 24; *Spieker* (supra note 44), 149.

[88]Second Report of Special Rapporteur *Wood* (supra note 3), para 76 (f) with further references to the legal literature and jurisprudence. See also *Villiger* (supra note 78), 231ff.

[89]See also *R. Pisillo-Mazzeschi*, Treaty and Custom: Reflections on the Codification of International Law, 23 Commonwealth Law Bulletin (1997), 553. See on the role of the ILC for the determination of customary international law Sect. 7.8, International Law Commission.

[90]See further *Villiger* (supra note 78), 230ff.

even if the States party to the convention were mistaken in thinking certain norms of the treaty were declaratory of customary international law, it nevertheless still "amounts to an explicit acknowledgment by the parties to the treaty that they would be legally bound to the treaty's rules even if the treaty did not exist,"[91] thus providing evidence of *opinio iuris* for a customary norm. In contrast, however, reservations towards conventional norms are generally detrimental to any evincing function of *opinio iuris* since it can be assumed that the States consider that they are not bound by an equivalent customary norm. Otherwise what would be the sense in making the reservation?[92]

Furthermore, practice subsequent to a treaty can also manifest an *opinio iuris*. This is probably most relevant in situations where a convention triggers the subsequent development of customary international law. States parties may subsequently refer to treaty norms, viewing them as a manifestation of existing or developing customary international law in their relations with States parties as well as non-States parties, while and also non-States parties may indicate that they accept that the treaty or certain norms thereof either reflected customary international law at the time of its conclusion or subsequently developed into customary international law.[93] Thus, whether *opinio iuris* can be established in relation to the conclusion or performance of a treaty is "a question of fact. One has to look at statements, claims, and State conduct to determine whether the treaty rule has embodied prior customary law rules, enshrined a developing rule as custom or has passed into customary law after its adoption."[94] One might fear that such an "entangled" approach between treaties and customary international law would blur the lines between the two distinct sources of law. Nevertheless, while customary international law and international conventions are intertwined, it must be noted that the evidence for the existence of State practice and *opinio iuris* on the basis of treaties and practice in connection with treaties, is but one step for determining customary international law. All other relevant material must be consulted to verify or deny the existence of customary international law.[95] Other instances of State

---

[91]*Weisburd* (supra note 83), 23.

[92]*Villiger* (supra note 78), 261: "A reservation (but not a reservation clause!) may hence be a sign of disapproval of the underlying customary law." See also Second Report of Special Rapporteur *Wood* (supra note 3), para 76 (f) with further references to the jurisprudence.

[93]*Spieker* (supra note 44), 149; *Villiger* (supra note 78), 28; see also *Meron* (supra note 73), 370: "As with other widely ratified treaties, if states parties comply with the Geneva conventions in actual practice, verbally affirm their vital normative value, and accept them in *opinio juris*, states and tribunals will be reluctant to make and to accept the argument that the law of Geneva is solely, or even primarily, conventional."

[94]*Schachter* (supra note 78), 734.

[95]*Baxter* (supra note 85), 43f: "the evidence of the practice of the parties consolidated in the treaty must be weighed in the balance with all other evidence of customary international law according to the normal procedure employed in the proof of customary international law". Second Report of Special Rapporteur *Wood* (supra note 3), para 76 (f) and Third Report on Identification of Customary International Law, International Law Commission, 67th Session, 4 May-5 June and 6 July-7 August 2015, Official Records of the General Assembly, UN Doc. A/CN.4/682.

practice beyond the treaty practice, such as official pronouncements or actual State behavior, may be used to deny the uniformity or generality of State practice despite the existence of a widely ratified convention.

Furthermore, such an "entangled" relationship does not violate the *pacta tertiis* principle as contained in Art. 34 VCLT, which makes the treaty binding on non-State parties by using the "backdoor" of customary international law. Rather the necessity for States to make use of the persistent objector doctrine in relation to the treaty practice of other States is a natural consequence of a wide range of the element of State practice. Customary international law as an opt-out system requires that States use the persistent objector doctrine in order to avoid that it is binding on them.[96] Under a wide concept of State practice that also holds true with regard to State practice in relation to international conventions.

The previous paragraphs have dealt with State acts in relation to conventions for the purposes of establishing the "law-creating processes". However, in the words of the ICJ, "conventions may have an important role to play in *recording* (. . .) rules deriving from custom."[97] Such a position presupposes that apart from playing a role in the determination of constitutive elements, international treaties may very well be used as documentary evidence of customary international law. This corresponds to *Schwarzenberger's* "law-determining agencies" as subsidiary means for the determination of a rule of law.[98] Indeed, rather than consulting all possible instances of State acts that could indicate State practice and *opinio iuris*, several authors have restricted themselves to the "internal view" of a treaty in order to confirm the existence of a customary mirror norm.[99] For example *Baxter*, discussing a treaty that is supposed to be declaratory of customary international law, considers that it is to "be regarded as an expression of the concordant State practice of the parties" and that it would be "self-defeating" to compare State practice beyond the treaty with the treaty rule itself.[100] According to his view the value of a declaratory treaty for proving customary international law increases with the number of contracting States.[101] Such a position corresponds with that of *D'Amato*, who in contrast to *Baxter* would not consider whether the treaty in question was intended to be declaratory of customary international law, but expands his discussion to all treaties, whether declaratory of or progressive for customary international law. He focuses on a widely adopted multilateral convention to verify

---

[96]See *N. Petersen*, The Role of Consent and Uncertainty in the Formation of Customary International Law, in Lepard (ed.), Reexamining Customary International Law, available at: www.coll. mpg.de/pdf_dat/2011_04online.pdf (last visited 16 June 2017), 2.

[97]ICJ, Continental Shelf Case (Libya v. Malta), para 27.

[98]See also *Villiger* (supra note 78), 132 stating that treaties that reflect or declare customary rules are evidence of a customary rule although not evincing the constitutive elements.

[99]See *Pisillo-Mazzeschi* (supra note 89), 556ff with further references.

[100]*Baxter* (supra note 85), 52–56.

[101]*Pisillo-Mazzeschi* (supra note 89), 557.

the existence of the "consensus of States" as a basis for customary international law.[102] *D'Amato* would take quasi-universally ratified treaties as catalysts for customary international law without analysing the elements of State practice and *opinio iuris*.[103] However, such a suggestion does appear to be going too far. As established above, the existence of a treaty norm is but one step for the determination of customary international law. As 'documentary sources" to customary international law, their legal value can only ever be as good as the explanation leading to its result, namely proof of the underlying elements in relation to customary international law. As treaties generally do not lay down the constitutive elements of pre-established customary international law as a "documentary source,"[104] their use as genuine subsidiary source appears limited. It is thus safer to consider treaties for identifying customary international law under the law-creating processes, rather than as law-determining agencies.

However, it is evident that in practice there is a noticeable tendency to take a shortcut for determining customary international law by relying on conventional norms. For example, when the Secretary General in his report on the ICTY determined rules of international humanitarian law that had "beyond doubt become part of international customary law", he immediately referred to the 1949 Geneva Conventions, the 1907 Hague Convention IV, the 1948 Genocide Convention and the IMT Nuremberg Charter,[105] without providing a clear legal reasoning why these conventional instruments are reflective of customary international law. The Secretary General is, however, in good company, as the ICJ was quick to declare that international humanitarian law treaties reflect customary international law, without giving lengthy legal explanations.[106] Indeed, it appears that there are certain conventional norms considered as being undoubtedly part of customary international law, and for which separate proof of the constituent elements of customary international law is not required. Reference is just made to the black letter law conventions that reflect customary international law. The following section will analyse the ways in which international criminal tribunals have referred to international conventional law in order to determine customary international law. It will also ask whether they have been referred to as instances of State practice and *opinio iuris*, and what other legal material has been considered as relevant when determining whether a conventional norm reflects customary international law. The discussion will focus on the most relevant conventions in the case law: *i.e.* humanitarian law conventions and the statutes of other international criminal tribunals.

---

[102]A. A. *D'Amato*, The Concept of Custom in International Law (1971), 165.

[103]See this conclusion also drawn by *Pisillo-Mazzeschi* (supra note 89), 558.

[104]*Pellet* (supra note 24), 854, MN 305.

[105]SG Report on ICTY (supra note 50), para 35.

[106]See the reference to the ICJ jurisprudence in Sect. 4.3.3, The Substantive Aspect of Modern Customary International Law.

7.5.2   *Humanitarian Law Conventions*

Humanitarian law conventions, in particular the 1907 Hague Convention IV and the Regulations annexed thereto,[107] and the 1949 Geneva Conventions[108] and its additional protocols of 1977,[109] are among the most cited sources by international criminal tribunals when establishing customary international humanitarian law. Generally it appears that international criminal tribunals do not consider it necessary to devote much attention to the task, as it could be argued that these humanitarian law conventions simply codified "old" core principles of customary international humanitarian law.[110] ICTY chambers have placed particular emphasis on the fact that the UN Secretary General explicitly listed the 1907 Hague Convention IV, and the Regulation annexed thereto, and the 1949 Geneva Conventions as examples of rules that have "beyond doubt become part of international customary law".[111] As already stated, the report of the Secretary General on the ICTY Statute has been equated with the *travaux préparatoires* for the interpretation of the ICTY Statute.[112]

Consequently, international criminal tribunals when referring to international humanitarian law conventions have only occasionally addressed the complex relationship between treaties and customary international law. As seen in the

---

[107] 1907 Hague Convention (IV) respecting the Laws and Customs of War on Land and regulations annexed thereto, 36 Stat. 2277, 3 Martens Nouveau Recueil (ser. 3) 461; see for example with regard to plunder the reference made to the 1907 Hague Convention by the ICTY in *Delalić* Trial Judgment, para 315 and *Blaškić* Appeals Judgment, para 147; see also ICTY Strugar Trial Judgment, para 227 for the destruction and devastation of property, including cultural property.

[108] The four Geneva Conventions of 1949: Geneva Convention for the Amelioration of the Condition of the Wounded and Sick in Armed Forces in the Field, 75 U.N.T.S. 31; Geneva Convention for the Amelioration of the Condition of Wounded, Sick and Shipwrecked Members of Armed Forces at Sea, 75 U.N.T.S. 85; Geneva Convention relative to the Treatment of Prisoners of War, 75 U.N.T.S. 135; Geneva Convention relative to the Protection of Civilian Persons in Time of War, 75 U.N.T.S. 287; reference to the Geneva Conventions are frequent, see *inter alia* with regard to the prohibition of attacks on civilians, ICTY, *Galić* Trial Judgment, paras 44ff, ICTY and *Galić* Appeal Judgment, para 88. The Geneva Conventions have been labelled without much ado as an "an expression of customary international law", see *Blaškić* Appeals Judgment, para 145 and *Krnojelac* Appeals Judgment, para 220.

[109] Protocol Additional to the Geneva Conventions of 12 August 1949, and Relating to the Protection of Victims of International Armed Conflicts (Protocol I), 1125 U.N.T.S. 3; Protocol Additional to the Geneva Conventions of 12 August 1949, and Relating to the Protection of Victims of Non-International Armed Conflicts (Protocol II), 1125 U.N.T.S. 609; for reference to the additional protocols see *inter alia* with regard to the prohibition of attacks on civilians and the prohibition of terror, ICTY, *Galić* Trial Judgment, paras 44ff; ICTY, *Galić* Appeal Judgment, paras 86ff; *Martić* Trial Judgment, paras 66ff.

[110] See ECCC, *Duch* Trial Judgment, para 405. See also Sect. 6.3.3, Deductive Approach

[111] See for example ICTY; *Kordić* Appeals Judgment, para 76; *Delalić* Appeals Judgment, para 113.

[112] See e.g. *V.D. Degan*, On the Sources of International Criminal Law, 4 Chinese Journal of International Law (2005), 63.

Čelebići Case, the ICTY Trial Chamber referred to the so called *Baxter* paradox: It assumes that the number of States that could contribute to the formation of State practice necessary for developing customary international law will decrease in proportion to the number of State parties to a multilateral convention, as only the State practice outside the treaty is relevant for proving the separate existence of a customary norm.[113] In order to circumvent such an unsatisfactory solution, it appears that international criminal tribunals, when considering whether conventional humanitarian law norms reflect or turned into customary international, paid particular attention to the number of States parties to the conventions.[114] The chambers did, however, not specify how the number of States parties to a convention is relevant for the determination of customary international law. As such there is a detectable tendency in the jurisprudence that would turn conventions that fall within the "category of universal multilateral treaties" into norms of customary international law.[115] When conventions have not been universally ratified, which is the case for the additional protocols to the Geneva Conventions, on some occasions the *travaux préparatoires* have been consulted to verify whether the drafters of the conventional norms intended to codify pre-existing customary international law.[116] Generally, however, it should be noted that international criminal tribunals did not devote much effort considering the traditional concepts of State practice and *opinio iuris* as constitutive elements when determining that international humanitarian law conventions were considered to reflect customary international law.[117]

It needs to be reemphasized that humanitarian law conventions are generally drafted to stipulate inter-State obligations, but not criminal norms.[118] While there are examples in the jurisprudence that would equate inter-State prohibitions with

---

[113]ICTY, *Delalić* Trial Judgment, para 302.

[114]ICTY, *Galić* Appeal Judgment, para 89, which also indicated a specific role to non-State parties of the conventions for the determination of customary international law. It seems, however, that this is an isolated case where the acts of non-State parties were taken into consideration in the jurisprudence of international criminal tribunals.

[115]ICTY, *Delalić* Appeals Judgment, para 112 referring to the Geneva Conventions falling within the "category of universal multilateral treaties which reflect rules accepted and recognised by the international community as a whole." ICTY, *Furundžija* Trial Judgment, para 138 stating that the Geneva Conventions reflect customary international law as they "have been ratified by practically all States of the world".

[116]See with regard to Additional Protocol I: ICTY, *Delalić* Trial Judgment, para 340 with regard to command responsibility as enshrined in Art. 87 of Additional Protocol I; *Galić* Trial Judgment, para 45 (footnote 78) referring to the customary law prohibition of attacking civilians as enshrined in Additional Protocol I; see in that regard also ICTY, *Blaškić* Appeals Judgment, para 158.

[117]Only two judgements of the ICTY referred to the traditional elements with regard to international humanitarian law conventions: *Kupreškić* Trial Judgment, para 532 which uses the high number of States that ratified Additional Protocol I for establishing *opinio iuris*. See also *Simić* Trial Judgment, para 1153 treating the ratification of the 1948 Geneva Conventions by 188 States as *opinio iuris*.

[118]Cf. the discussion on this issue in Sect. 3.10.5.2, The *praevia* Requirement and International Conventions.

(individual) criminality,[119] in general international criminal tribunals have referred to various other instances in order to establish a separate customary international norm that entails individual criminal responsibility.[120]

7.5.3 Other Statutes of International Criminal Tribunals

7.5.3.1 Statutes of the IMT, IMTFE and Control Council Law No. 10

International criminal tribunals refer regularly to the statutes of their predecessors, namely, the statutes of the IMT Nuremberg, the IMTFE Tokyo and Control Council Law No. 10.[121] References to these instruments stand to reason as on the basis of these statutes individuals have been held criminally accountable for crimes existing under international law in the past. The question is how to assess these statutes for the purpose of determining customary international criminal law.

When praising the importance of these international instruments, the ICTY *Tadić* Appeals Chamber held that they are "treaty provisions [...] at the very origin of the customary process".[122] Strictly speaking, however, only the IMT Nuremberg Charter is to be considered an international convention. It was annexed to the London Agreement, an international convention between the United States of America, the French Republic, the United Kingdom and the Soviet Union, and has subsequently been ratified by 19 other States.[123] In contrast, the IMTFE Tokyo Charter was annexed to the Special Proclamation by the Supreme Commander for

---

[119]See for example ICTY, *Galić* Trial Judgment, para 127ff determining that individual criminal responsibility for the crime of terror is given under conventional law as "is evident from the content and context of Additional Protocol I". See also *Kordić* Appeals Judgment, para 75 equating grave breaches with crimes *qua* custom.

[120]See for example ICTY, *Galić* Appeal Judgment, paras 91ff which in contrast to its Trial Chamber referred to various instances of State practice in the form of national legislation and jurisprudence in order to establish the criminalisation of terror against the civilian population under customary international law. See however, Separate and Partially Dissenting Opinion of Judge Schomburg to the *Galić* Appeal Judgment, who on basis of the listed materials merely saw a "trend" of criminalization of the prohibition of terror.

[121]See *inter alia* the references to all three statutes by the ICTY, *Tadić* Appeals Chamber Judgment, para 287ff in order to establish that generally crimes against humanity do not require the proof of a discriminatory intent, *Tadić* Trial Judgment, paras 618ff in order to establish the general customary law basis of crimes against humanity, whereas the *Stakić* Appeals Judgment in para 315 established that other inhumane acts were a crime against humanity under customary international law. The ECCC also referred to all three statutes in the *Duch* Case in order to establish the customary law basis of crimes against humanity, see ECCC, *Duch* Trial Judgment, para 293; for persecution, *Duch* Appeals Judgment, para 219; or to determine that the doctrine of joint criminal enterprise (the first and second form) have a basis in customary international law, see ECCC, Case No 002 Pre-Trial Chamber Public Decision on the JCE Appeals, para 57.

[122]ICTY, *Tadić* Appeals Chamber Judgment, para 290.

[123]IMT Nuremberg Charter.

the Allied Powers, which is to be viewed as occupation law.[124] Similarly, Control Council Law No. 10 can be regarded as a legislative act jointly promulgated by the occupying powers. *Bassiouni* argues that Control Council Law No. 10 "was not intended to be an international instrument but national legislation" enacted by the Allies in their role as "the supreme legislative authority" over Germany.[125] In contrast, in his dissenting opinion to the *Erdemović* Appeals Judgment Judge *Cassese* argued that "Control Council Law No. 10 can be regarded as an international agreement among the four Occupying Powers (subsequently transformed, to a large extent, into customary law)".[126] Similarly other chambers also held that Control Council Law No. 10 was an expression of customary international law at that time.[127] Whatever legal basis is given to Control Council Law No. 10, whether it is conceived as national occupation legislation or an international agreement, it seems that its status as reflecting customary international law is not questioned by international criminal tribunals. However, international criminal tribunals do not generally give an explanation as to why Control Council Law No. 10 should be viewed as an expression of customary international law. One could argue that the relevance of Control Council Law No. 10 for the development of customary international criminal law could not be on the same footing as the IMT Nuremberg Charter: Unlike the IMT Nuremberg Charter the report of the UN Secretary General did not list Control Council Law No. 10 as an example for a codification of customary international law.[128] Furthermore, the international community, via a General Assembly resolution, unanimously affirmed the jurisprudence of the IMT Nuremberg as well as the underlying IMT Charter.[129] There was no such act, however, for Control Council Law No. 10. One could take an overly formalistic

---

[124]Tokyo Charter, as annexed to the Special Proclamation by the Supreme Commander for the Allied Powers, 19 January 1946, Treaties and Other International Agreements of the United States of America 1589.

[125]*M C. Bassiouni*, Crimes Against Humanity in International Law (1999), 33. See also *W. Schabas*, The Contribution of the Eichmann Trial to International Law, 26 Leiden Journal of International Law (2013), 677, arguing that the Allied Powers "understood the Charter of the International Military Tribunal to be international law and therefore applicable to them as well as to the Nazis, whereas they viewed Control Council Law No. 10 as domestic legislation in force only with respect to Germany."

[126]ICTY, *Erdemović* Appeals Judgment, Separate and Dissenting Opinion of Judge Cassese, para 27.

[127]See for the ICTY: *Tadić* Appeals Chamber Judgment, paras 288ff; *Kupreškić* Trial Judgment, para 577; *Stakić* Appeals Judgment, para 315.

[128]SG Report on ICTY (supra note 50), para 35 referring to the IMT Nuremberg Charter. That fact has also been highlighted in the jurisprudence of international criminal tribunals, such as ICTY, *Tadić* Trial Judgment, para 622.

[129]UN GA Res. 95 (I), A/RES/95 (I). *M. P. Scharf*, Seizing the "Grotian Moment": Accelerated Formation of Customary International Law in Times of Fundamental Change, 43 Cornell International Law Journal (2012), 454–5 determined that UN GA Res. 95 (I) "had all the attributes of a resolution entitled to great weight as a declaration of customary international law: it was labeled an 'affirmation' of legal principles; it dealt with inherently legal questions; it was passed by a unanimous vote; and none of the members expressed the position that it was merely a political

stand by suggesting that on such a basis Control Council Law No. 10 could not play as an important role for the development of customary international criminal law as does the IMT Nuremberg Charter.[130] However, Control Council Law No. 10 had been adopted by the Occupying Powers in order to incorporate the London Agreement and the IMT Nuremberg Charter. Art. 1 Control Council Law No. 10 determines that the 1945 London Agreement, to which the IMT Nuremberg Charter is annexed, is an integral part of that law. According to its wording Control Council Law No. 10 should "establish a uniform legal basis in Germany for the prosecution of war criminals and other similar offenders, other than those dealt with by the International Military Tribunal".[131] In so far as the provisions of Control Council Law No. 10 incorporate provisions of substantive international criminal law as already contained in the IMT Nuremberg Statute, its legal authority can be deduced from the London agreement,[132] as well as the subsequent affirmation by the General Assembly. In the present author's opinion the subsequent "affirmation" of the Nuremberg Charter by a General Assembly resolution is of particular relevance for its determination of customary international law, an issue to which we will return in a later chapter.[133]

It is thus clear that with regard to the legal principles of the "Nuremberg Era", a strict separation of various possible sources for the determining of customary international criminal law is not possible. The relevance of Control Council Law No. 10 is necessarily intertwined with the Nuremberg Charter. Evidentially, the IMT Charter and, following *Cassese*, Control Council Law No. 10 are to be perceived as international conventions. For a correct appraisal of these conventional instruments as also reflecting customary international criminal law, however, we must take into account the jurisprudence of the IMT Nuremberg and other post World War II tribunals adjudicating on the strength of Control Council Law No. 10,[134] as well as the affirmation of the legal principles as enshrined in the Nuremberg Charter and applied to the IMT Nuremberg by the General Assembly.[135] Thus, the evidence for customary international criminal law is not restricted to the question of whether the convention was drafted in order to conform to or subsequently developed into customary international law. It is a multi-layered

---

statement". On the role of GA Resolutions for the determination of customary international law see further Sect. 7.6, UN Resolutions.

[130]*R. K Woetzel*, The Nuremberg Trials in International Law with a Postlude on the Eichmann Case (1962), 243 (footnote 49); *K. J. Heller*, The Nuremberg Military Tribunals and the Origins of International Criminal Law (2011), 112.

[131]Control Council Law No. 10, Punishment of Persons Guilty of War Crimes, Crimes Against Peace and Against Humanity, 20 December 1945, 3 Official Gazette Control Council for Germany 50–55 (1946).

[132]Similar SCSL, *Taylor* Appeals Judgment, para 419 (footnote 1298).

[133]See Sect. 7.6, UN Resolutions.

[134]See further Sect. 7.7.3, IMT Nuremberg and Post World War II Tribunals Operating Under the Strength of Control Council Law No. 10.

[135]See further Sect. 7.6.2, UN General Assembly Resolutions.

issue, which must be addressed, in order to assess the relevance of these statutes for the determination of customary international criminal law adequately.

7.5.3.2 Statutes of the ICTY, ICTR, SCSL and ECCC

International criminal tribunals have also referred to the statutes of their sister tribunals when analyzing customary international law, although generally without indicating the specific role these international instruments might play.[136] The legal basis of their underlying statutes differ: the statutes of the ICTY and ICTR were established on the basis of a binding Chapter VII resolution of the UN Security Council whose authority is based on the UN Charter, the SCSL Statute is based on a bilateral treaty between the UN and the government of Sierra Leone, and the ECCC Statute is domestic legislation.[137] Nevertheless, what they have in common is that their subject matter jurisdiction is based on the provisions of other, earlier international conventions, such as international humanitarian law conventions, the genocide convention and the IMT Nuremberg Statute.[138] Consequently, the value of the statutes of international criminal tribunals for the determining customary international law is dependent on the value of the original underlying conventions.

Since the legal basis of the convictions of international criminal tribunals is dependent on the existence of crimes under customary international law, their underlying statutes have also been interpreted in conformity with it.[139] It has occasionally been argued that the statutes of international criminal tribunals can give insight into the views of those who drafted them. For example, referring to command responsibility as enshrined in the ICTY Statute, the *Hadžihasanović* Trial Chamber held that the "inclusion of Article 7, paragraph 3, should be read as a reflection of the well-supported views of the Security Council [...] that this norm formed part of customary international law at the time covered by the mandate of the International Tribunal."[140] Indeed, the view taken in this study is that resolutions of inter-governmental organizations, being composed of State representatives, can be traced back to the participating States and as such can be considered as

---

[136]For example determining that crimes against humanity do not require a nexus to an armed conflict, see ICTY, *Đorđević* Trial Judgment, para 1587; *Mrkšić* Trial Judgment, para 531; ECCC, Trial Chamber Decision Armed Conflict Nexus Requirement, para 10; see also SCSL, *Taylor* Appeals Judgment, para 383 analyzing individual criminal responsibility under Art. 6 (1) SCSL Statute.

[137]See Sect. 3.10.2, The Quest for Applicable Law.

[138]See Sect. 3.10.3, The *scripta* Requirement and the Sources of International Law: International Conventions as the Sole Legal Basis for Individual Criminal Responsibility?

[139]ICTY, *Tadić* Appeals Chamber Judgment, para 287; see also W. *Schabas*, Customary Law or "Judge-Made" Law: Judicial Creativity at the UN Criminal Tribunals, in Doria (ed.), The Legal Regime of the International Criminal Court (2009), 82.

[140]ICTY, *Hadžihasanović* Trial Chamber Decision, para 171 with reference to the verbatim records of the 3217th Security Council meeting.

constitutive elements for the determination of customary international law.[141] However, when the ICTY chambers perceived that the ICTY statute were departing from customary international law, it was suggested that the Security Council had defined crimes under the Statute "more narrowly than necessary under customary international law."[142] In that instance the "view" of the Security Council was not considered relevant for the determination of a new development of customary international law, but as a deviation from customary international law. Consequently, the armed conflict nexus requirement for crimes against humanity as contained in Art. 5 ICTY Statute has been considered to be a specific feature of the ICTY Statute that is not found in customary international law.[143]

7.5.3.3 Rome Statute

It appears that international criminal tribunals use the traditional terminology of State practice and *opinio iuris* when determining customary international law with regard to international conventions only in relation to the Rome Statute. Generally, its ratification has been treated in the jurisprudence as an indication of the *opinio iuris* of the contracting States.[144] The Rome Statute has been referred to by international criminal tribunals on various occasions, despite the fact that it generally post-dates the temporal jurisdiction of the ECCC, ICTY, ICTR and SCSL. Be that as it may, it has been argued in the legal literature that there was a "general agreement that the definitions of crimes in the ICC Statute were to reflect existing customary international law, and not to create new law".[145] Nevertheless, the ICTY *Furundžija* Trial Chamber correctly held that in "many areas the [Rome] Statute may be regarded as indicative of the legal views, *i.e. opinio juris* of a great number of States [. . .] resort may be had *cum grano salis* to these provisions to help

---

[141] See supra note 4. UN Security Council resolutions are the practice of the participating States. See further Sect. 7.6, UN Resolutions.

[142] See for example ICTY, *Mrkšić* Trial Judgment, para 431 with regard to the nexus requirement to an armed conflict under Art. 5 ICTY Statute.

[143] See *inter alia* ICTY, *Tadić* Appeals Chamber Jurisdiction Decision, paras 140ff; *Tadić* Appeals Chamber Judgment, para 251. The ECCC in Trial Chamber Decision Armed Conflict Nexus Requirement determined that the nexus requirement was already not part of customary international law as of 1975.

[144] See the references to the jurisprudence of the ICTY and SCSL in Sect. 6.3.1.1, Preliminary Remarks. Only the *Krnojelac* Appeals Judgment treated the Rome Statute as an instance of State practice.

[145] P. *Kirsch*, in Dörmann (ed.), Elements of War Crimes under the Rome Statute of the International Criminal Court: Sources and Commentary (2003), Foreword, xiii; see also *J.-M. Henckaerts*, Customary International Humanitarian Law (2005) (ICRC Custom Study), Introduction, xlv. Critical *R. Cryer*, Of Custom, Treaties, Scholars and the Gavel: The Influence of the International Criminal Tribunals on the ICRC Customary Law Study, 11 Journal of Conflict & Security Law (2006), 251, on such a "broad-brush approach", in particular referring to Art. 10 Rome Statute.

elucidate customary international law. Depending on the matter at issue, the Rome Statute may be taken to restate, reflect or clarify customary rules or crystallize them, *whereas in some areas it creates new law or modifies existing law.*"[146]

The ICTY *Furundžija* Trial Chamber thus proposes a differentiated role for the Rome Statute when determining customary international law, as in certain instances it may serve as an adequate codification of customary international law, whereas in other instances it might modify it or even create new law. Nevertheless, the chambers of international criminal tribunals generally did not consult, for example, the *travaux préparatoires* when determining whether the Rome Statute or more precisely a specific norm thereof codified customary international law. In contrast, in subsequent judgments such a differentiated treatment of the Rome Statute has not been upheld, and it has been considered to reflect the *opinio iuris* of its contracting States.[147] Such an approach is not only methodologically problematic, since the chambers did not distinguish between an *opinio iuris* and *opinio iuris conventionis*, but also has practical implications: It does not stand to reason to accept on the one hand that the Rome Statute can sweepingly be used to provide evidence for the *opinio iuris* of its State parties, and on the other simply to state that certain provisions thereof are "not consonant with customary international law"[148] when the chambers have doubts about the customary basis of certain norms contained therein. For example, the Rome Statute's provision on persecution, which requires a nexus to another crime within the ICC's jurisdiction, has been dismissed as not reflecting customary international law.[149] The legal reasoning for such a conclusion was, however, found outside the convention. Yet, if the Rome Statute were an undifferentiated document useful for demonstrating the *opinio iuris* of its contracting States, one could have argued that a modern variation of persecution requiring a nexus to another crime had been established under customary international law by the State parties to the Rome Statute.

A more appropriate handling of the relationship between customary international law and the Rome Statute can be found in the ICTY *Kordić* Appeals Chamber's judgment with regard to the question whether the crimes of unlawful attack against civilians and civilian objects would require a result requirement

---

[146]ICTY, *Furundžija* Trial Judgment, para 227 (emphasis added). This assessment of the importance of the Rome Statute for the determination of customary international law has been approved by the *Tadić* Appeals Chamber Judgment, para 223. Also the *Kunarac* Trial Judgment, para 495 indicated that "the ICC Statute does not necessarily represent the present status of international customary law".

[147]See for the ICTY, *Delalić* Appeals Judgment, para 196 (footnote 255); see for the SCSL, *Fofana* Appeals Judgment, para 403.

[148]ICTY, *Kupreškić* Trial Judgment, para 580 when determining that persecution as enshrined in the Rome Statute under Art. 7 (2) (h) requiring a nexus to another crime within the ICC's jurisdiction does not reflect customary international law. That position was upheld by the *Kordić* Trial Judgment, para 197, claiming that the Rome Statute in that regard is "more restrictive than is necessary under customary international law".

[149]*Ibid.*

under customary international law, such as showing serious injury, death or damage. The Appeals Chamber referred to the "controversial negotiations" at the Rome Conference that led to Art. 8 (2) (b) (i) and (ii) Rome Statute, which do not require a result element. Nevertheless, the Appeals Chamber considered that these provisions may merely "be indicative of a progressive development of international law on this issue."[150] As held above, the treaty practice must be weighed with other available evidence of customary international law.[151] The ICTY *Kordić* Appeals Chamber, by analyzing national legislation and case law, came to the conclusion that "State practice was not settled as some required the showing of serious injury, death or damage as a result under their national penal legislation, while others did not."[152] As a result—to the benefit of the individual accused—the ICTY *Kordić* Appeals Chamber held that criminal responsibility for unlawful attacks on civilians requires the proof of a result element that emanates from such an attack.[153] This analysis by the ICTY *Kordić* Appeals Chamber, viewing the Rome Statute as one of many possible instances of evidence for the constitutive elements of customary international law, is a valuable approach.

Another problem with the Rome Statute lies in the fact that when the international criminal tribunals cite it, they are restricted to a plain reading of the text, and cannot yet refer to a rich ICC jurisprudence that interprets the Rome Statute. For example, when the SCSL *Taylor* Appeals Chamber had to interpret "purpose" for aiding and abetting under its Statute, it did not consider Art. 25 (3) (c) Rome Statute as relevant material for the determination of customary international law, since "purpose" under the liability scheme of the Rome Statute might be interpreted in various directions by the ICC Appeals Chamber. Consequently it stated that until the ICC Appeals Chamber "has made its views known, speculative exercises do not assist in the identification of the law, and established customary international law, as consistently articulated and applied in the jurisprudence of international criminal tribunals from the Second World War to today, must bear more weight than suppositions as to what Article 25 (3) (c) [Rome Statute] does or does not mean."[154]

7.5.4 Other International Conventions

On various other occasions the chambers of international criminal tribunals referred to a multitude of other international conventions, *inter alia* the 1973 Convention on

---

[150]ICTY, *Kordić* Appeals Judgment, para 66 (footnote 73).

[151]See supra note 95 and accompanying text.

[152]ICTY, *Kordić* Appeals Judgment, paras 62–66. The Appeals Chamber highlighted the fact that even under the grave breaches regime of AP I in relation to unlawful attacks against civilians it would be required that these cause "death or serious injury to body or health", see Art. 85 (3) AP I.

[153]ICTY, *Kordić* Appeals Judgment, para 67.

[154]SCSL, *Taylor* Appeals Judgment, para 451.

Apartheid,[155] the 1984 Torture Convention,[156] human rights conventions,[157] and so forth. The reference to international conventions was used as one of many sources to bolster an argument under customary international law. However, in such references the chambers of international criminal tribunals generally did not elaborate specifically on the relation between conventional norms and customary international law, nor did they refer to State practice or *opinio iuris* in that regard. Consequently, in these instances the jurisprudence does not give clear indications for the relevance of these conventions for the determination of customary international law. For the sake of completeness, the 1948 Genocide Convention must also be mentioned.[158] Genocide is one of the core crimes under the jurisdiction of international criminal tribunals and international criminal tribunals regularly referred to the convention when elaborating on the crime of genocide. However, they have generally not considered it necessary to conduct a detailed analysis of the customary international law status of the Genocide Convention.[159] Indeed, the Genocide Convention is one of the most widely ratified conventions,[160] and international criminal tribunals have generally referred to the report of the Secretary General on the ICTY Statute and the jurisprudence of the ICJ to determine that it is an uncontested part of customary international law and even part of *ius cogens*.[161]

---

[155]International Convention on the Suppression and Punishment of the Crime of Apartheid, 30 November 1973, 1015 UNTS 243; for reference to the convention see for example ICTY, *Kupreškić* Trial Judgment, para 577 or ECCC, Trial Chamber Decision Armed Conflict Nexus Requirement, para 30 when determining that crimes against humanity do not require a nexus to another crime under international law.

[156]Convention against Torture and Other Cruel, Inhuman or Degrading Treatment or Punishment, 10 December 1984, 1465 UNTS 85; for reference to the convention see ICTY, *Furundžija* Trial Judgment, para 159; ICTY, *Delalić* Trial Judgment, para 453 elevating it by reference to Special Rapporteur for Torture to the level of a *ius cogens* norm.

[157]For example, International Covenant on Civil and Political Rights, 16 December 1966, 999 UNTS 171; for reference to the convention see ICTY, *Delalić* Trial Judgment, para 452 for the definition of torture under customary international law; ICTY, *Kupreškić* Trial Judgment, para 566 when elaborating on "other inhumane acts".

[158]Convention on the Prevention and Punishment of the Crime of Genocide, 9 December 1948, 78 UNTS 277.

[159]For example, ICTY, *Jelisić* Trial Judgment, para 60: "There can be absolutely no doubt that its provisions fall under customary international law".

[160]*Ibid.*

[161]For the ICTR compare further *Akayesu* Trial Judgment, para 495; *Rutaganda* Trial Judgment, para 46; *Prosecutor v. Bagilishema*, ICTR-95-1A-T, Trial Chamber, Judgment, 7 June 2001, para 54; *Musema* Trial Judgment, para 151; for the ICTY compare: *Stakić* Trial Judgment, para 500; *Krstić* Trial Judgment, paras 541ff; ICTY, *Jelisić* Trial Judgment, para 60; see also *Popović* Trial Judgment, para 807.

7.5.5 Concluding Remarks

The complex relationship between conventional norms, customary international law and its methodological problems, has been treated only occasionally in the jurisprudence of international criminal tribunals. Generally, however, it should be noted that international criminal tribunals did not devote much effort to the determining of traditional concepts of State practice and *opinio iuris* as constitutive elements, when determining that international law conventions were considered to reflect customary international law.

7.6 UN Resolutions

7.6.1 Preliminary Remarks

There seems to be agreement in the legal literature that in general UN resolutions, and resolutions of the General Assembly in particular, play a significant role in the formation and determination of customary international law.[162] Adhering to the proposed structure of the law-creating processes and law-determining agencies,[163] there is, however, wide disagreement in the legal literature at what stage of the customary process—concerning its formation and/or determination—UN resolutions and State acts connected thereto shall play a part: it has been suggested that they may give evidence for the constitutive elements for the formation of customary international law, State practice[164]

---

[162]See *M. D. Öberg*, The Legal Effects of Resolutions of the UN Security Council and General Assembly in the Jurisprudence of the ICJ, 15 European Journal of International Law (2006), 879ff; *S. M. Schwebel*, The Effect of Resolutions of the U.N. General Assembly on Customary International Law, 73 Proceedings of the Annual meeting (American Society of International Law) (1979), 301ff; *J. Castañeda*, Legal Effects of United nations Resolutions (1969); *B. Cheng*, United Nations Resolutions on Outer Space: "Instant" International Customary Law, in Cheng (ed.), International law: Teaching and Practice (1982). Other writers have even considered that General Assembly Resolutions are to be considered as a new source of law, see *Danilenko* (supra note 3), 204 (footnote 55) with further references.

[163]See Sect. 7.1, Preliminary Remarks.

[164]ILA (supra note 4), Part II: The Objective Element: State Practice, Section 11, p. 19, which views resolutions of international organizations as a series of verbal State acts; Second Report of Special Rapporteur *Wood* (supra note 3), para 41 (i) referring to the State acts connected to the adoption of the resolution, *i.e.* voting or attaching explanations; *Schwebel* (supra note 162), 302, proposes that the General Assembly offers a forum for States to express their views and that the "expressed views of states undeniably may be elements of that state practice which can give rise to customary international law", however, he caveats this conclusion with a reminder that "what states do is more important than what they say." However, critical voices have also been raised stating that "[o]ne should thus be mindful not to equate the practice of international organizations with state practice." See *J Wouters, P. De Man*, International Organizations as

and/or *opinio iuris*,[165] whereas others have claimed that UN resolutions do not concern the law-creating process but could be used as law-determining agencies, as they may be declaratory of international law.[166] In the following chapters, the distinction between the law-creating processes and the law-determining agencies with regard to UN General Assembly and UN Security Council Resolutions will be upheld. The ways in which international criminal tribunals have used these resolutions when determining customary international law will be analyzed.

7.6.2   UN General Assembly Resolutions

7.6.2.1   UN General Assembly Resolutions as a Law-Creating Process

It certainly does appear somewhat curious that the UN General Assembly should play a part in the process of creating (customary) international law. After all, the San Francisco Conference establishing the UN Charter did not provide the General Assembly with legislative powers.[167] According to the UN Charter, excepting internal administrative or financial issues, the General Assembly can only make recommendations that are non-binding on the UN Member States.[168] This cautious approach in relation to any legislative authority of the UN General Assembly is reflected in the case law of the ICJ in the 1960s and 1970s that determine that

---

Law-Makers, Klabbers, Wallendahl (eds.), Research Handbook on the Law of International Organizations (2011), 208.

[165] Second Report of Special Rapporteur *Wood* (supra note 3), para 76 (g); *Cheng* (supra note 162), 251, who considers that customary international law only consists of one true constitutive element *i.e. opinio iuris*, which can be deduced from General Assembly resolutions, whereas State practice would be reduced to an evidentiary function; the ICJ in its jurisprudence has thus far established *opinio iuris* on basis of UN General Assembly resolutions and did not inquire whether these resolutions could also evince State practice, see ICJ, Nicaragua Case and ICJ, Nuclear Weapons Advisory Opinion, see also on that issue *Öberg* (supra note 162), 898, and *Danilenko* (supra note 3), 208.

[166] *J. Higashi*, The Role of Resolutions of United Nations General Assembly in the Formative Process of International Customary Law, 25 Japanese Annual of International Law (1982), 23: "Resolutions never create rules of law by themselves. They merely acknowledge and declare what the law is, sometimes with the effect of making the contents of the existing law clear and definite." See also *Castañeda* (supra note 162), 168: "The essential trait of the resolutions under study here, no matter how they are designated, is that they do not *create* law, but that they *recognize* and *declare* it" (emphasis in original). Such a declaratory function may according to *Castañeda* express "legally irrefutable proof", see *id*, 193 referring to UN GA Resolutions 95 (I) and 96 (I).

[167] *Higashi* (supra note 166), 15, referring to the Philippine proposal to give the General Assembly legislative authority, which was rejected by a vote of 26 to 1, see UNCIO Doc., Vol. 9 (1945), 316. See also *M. P. Scharf*, Customary International Law in Times of Fundamental Change (2013), 51.

[168] Arts. 10f UN Charter; *Higashi* (supra note 166), 14.

General Assembly resolutions are recommendatory in nature.[169] However, with the *Nicaragua* Case the ICJ began to shift its perception, viewing UN General Assembly resolutions as relevant material when establishing the constitutive elements of customary international law. According to the ICJ "*opinio juris* may, though with all due caution, be deduced from, inter alia, the attitude of the Parties and the attitude of States towards certain General Assembly resolutions",[170] adding that "the adoption by States of this text [of Resolution 2625 (XXV)] affords an indication of their *opinio juris* as to customary international law on the question."[171] In the Advisory Opinion on the Legality of Nuclear Weapons the ICJ also clearly stated that "General Assembly resolutions, even if they are not binding, may sometimes have normative value. They can, in certain circumstances, provide evidence important for [. . .] the emergence of an *opinio juris*."[172] The inclusion of the UN General Assembly resolution as relevant material for the formation of customary international law has the benefit that the UN is an international organization with universal membership and thus provides the opportunity for expressing the collective will of States.[173] Moreover, this inclusion of General Assembly resolutions is not in contradiction with the idea that law-making on the international plane is a role primarily reserved to States.[174] Since the General Assembly is composed of State representatives its resolutions can be traced back as relevant practice of the participating States since they adopt the resolutions (voting against, contrary or abstaining from vote or by consensus). Other writers have taken a rather critical stance: most notably *Arangio-Ruiz* held that these resolutions should not play a role in legislating international law, simply because States do not "mean it" when adopting unbinding General Assembly resolutions.[175] This position is based on the idea that since the General Assembly merely adopts recommendatory resolutions, States do not adopt them from a legal perspective but out of political opportunity. Such an argument does not stand. Since the ICJ took UN General Assembly resolutions into account as relevant material in order to establish *opinio iuris* and legal writers have referred to these resolutions as evidence for the

---

[169]ICJ, South West Africa Cases, para 98; Legal Consequences for States of the Continued Presence of South Africa in Namibia (South West Africa) Notwithstanding Security Council Resolution 276 (1970), Advisory Opinion, ICJ Reports (1971), para 105.

[170]ICJ, Nicaragua Case, para 188.

[171]*Ibid*, para 191. Whereas the ICJ in the *Nicaragua* Case was not specific about what conditions have to be fulfilled in order that General Assembly resolutions can be used to give evidence to *opinio iuris*, the later Advisory Opinion on the Legality of the Threat of Nuclear Weapons provided further guidelines on this issue.

[172]ICJ, Nuclear Weapons Advisory Opinion, para 70.

[173]*Higashi* (supra note 166), 13. Some writers have highlighted that the United Nations elevates international law to an "organized international community", see *Danilenko* (supra note 3), 203 with further references.

[174]See Sect. 7.1, Preliminary Remarks.

[175]*G. Arangio-Ruiz*, The Normative Role of the General Assembly of the United Nations and the Declaration of Principles of Friendly Relations, 3 Recueil des Courts (1972), 457.

constitutive elements of customary international law, States are put on notice that their practice in relation to General Assembly resolutions matters for the formation of law. The question is whether these resolutions can be used to demonstrate State practice or *opinio iuris*, or both, and under what circumstances they can do so.

UN General Assembly resolutions do fall into the wide conception of State practice that is applied within this study. Nevertheless, there are strong arguments as to why UN General Assembly resolutions should not be used as evincing both State practice and *opinio iuris*, but that they "merely" are relevant material for establishing *opinio iuris*. Firstly, adhering to the case law of the ICJ, it is evident that when referring to UN General Assembly resolutions the World Court used the resolutions to establish *opinio iuris* and not State practice.[176] Secondly, unlike other material under a wide concept of State practice, any double-evincing function of General Assembly resolutions would lead to an "instant quasi-legislative effect."[177] Indeed, due to the universal membership of the United Nations, if General Assembly resolutions could be used to give evidence to both State practice and *opinio iuris*, their adoption (unanimous, by overwhelming majority or *consensus*) would effectively equate to the establishment of "instant customary international law".[178] Such a development of "instant customary international law", however, is hardly reconcilable with the UN Charter, as the General Assembly was established with only recommendatory powers.[179] Others, most prominently *Simma*, have argued that General Assembly resolutions grow "like a flower in a hot-house and that it is anything but sure that such creatures will survive in the much rougher climate of actual state practice."[180] However, this last argument could be raised with regard to any verbal or paper practice under a wide conception of State practice.[181] Nevertheless, even following a wide concept of State practice, the law-creating processes General Assembly resolutions do appear to be better suited "merely" to establish *opinio iuris*.

A further question concerns which conditions have to be fulfilled therewith a resolution can potentially evidence *opinio iuris*. In that regard the ICJ has stated

---

[176]See the reference to the ICJ case law in supra note 165; see further *Öberg* (supra note 162), 898ff with further references to the legal literature, who, however, determines that strictly speaking the ICJ case law did, however, not rule out that General Assembly resolutions may be used to evidence State practice.

[177]*Öberg* (supra note 162), 899.

[178]The notion of "instant customary international law" dates to *Cheng* (supra note 162), who, however, determines that *opinio iuris* is the sole constitutive element of customary international law.

[179]See also *Scharf* (supra note 167), 51; *Öberg* (supra note 162), 899.

[180]*B. Simma*, International Human Rights and General International Law, in collected Courses of the Academy of European Law, Volume IV (1995), 217, as quoted in *Scharf* (supra note 167), 52.

[181]*Schwebel* (supra note 162), 302, also argues that "what states do is more important than what they say."

that "it is necessary to look at its *content* and the *conditions of its adoption*; it is also necessary to see whether an *opinio juris exists as to its normative character*."[182]

The content concerns the normative language used in the resolutions, "whether it is couched in legally binding terms".[183] The conditions of its adoption concern the voting process of the resolution and thus resolutions with a significant number of negative votes and abstentions[184] cannot be used to establish a general *opinio iuris*.[185] Resolutions that are put to a vote thus give a clear indication to the normative weight due to the voting outcome. However, the situation is less clear in *consensus* resolutions that are adopted without an actual vote. In those instances one cannot clearly establish whether the States genuinely consented to the resolutions only by failing to raise a formal objection. As such it seems *consensus* resolutions can hardly provide as clear a picture for an *opinio iuris* compared to resolutions that are adopted unanimously or by overwhelming majority.[186] Distinguishing "whether an *opinio juris* exists as to its normative character" from "content", and thus the legal implications of the vote, depends on the question as to why States voted in favor of a resolution. *Schwebel* determined that members of the General Assembly often do not consider that their votes "are evidence of a practice accepted as law", but vote a certain way "because it is politically unpopular to vote otherwise".[187] It is by drawing on the discussions leading to the resolution, and the position taken by various States, that one can reveal whether a resolution was adopted in the belief that it expresses a legally binding rule.[188]

International criminal tribunals generally have not referred to UN General Assembly Resolutions as evidence for establishing the constitutive elements of State practice or *opinio iuris*. They appear to list these resolutions as relevant material for the determination of customary international law without doctrinally determining their authoritative value.[189] Some chambers have suggested that the

---

[182]ICJ, Nuclear Weapons Advisory Opinion, para 70 (emphasis added). While the ICJ also referred to "a *series of resolutions* [that] may show the gradual evolution of the *opinio juris* required for the establishment of a new rule", it is more appropriate to determine that this is not strictly speaking a requirement for the establishment of *opinio iuris* on basis of UN General Assembly resolutions, and "it seems more reasonable to interpret the *Nuclear Weapons* reference to repetition as a simple statement that *opinio juris* may evolve", *Öberg* (supra note 162), 903.

[183]*Öberg* (supra note 162), 901; Second Report of Special Rapporteur *Wood* (supra note 3), para 76 (g).

[184]ICJ, Nuclear Weapons Advisory Opinion, para 71.

[185]Second Report of Special Rapporteur *Wood* (supra note 3), para 76 (g); *Öberg* (supra note 162), 900; *Scharf* (supra note 167), 55.

[186]*Öberg* (supra note 162), 901 with further references. *Scharf* (supra note 167), 55, considers that States may be "pressured to remain silent (even if they have objections) so as not to break consensus."

[187]*Schwebel* (supra note 162), 302.

[188]*Schachter* (supra note 78), 730; Second Report of Special Rapporteur *Wood* (supra note 3), para 76 (g); *Öberg* (supra note 162), 902.

[189]Consequently the "No Allocation to Elements Method" is of particular relevance when dealing with UN General Assembly resolutions, see Sect. 6.3.2, Non-allocation to Elements Method.

voting conduct is relevant for taking General Assembly resolutions into consideration,[190] while others avoided asking how these resolutions came into existence.[191] It seems astonishing that international criminal tribunals have not made greater effort to allocate the listed General Assembly resolutions as "international instruments" for the constitutive elements for the formation of customary international law, as in certain instances the references thereto were of particular importance. For example, ICTY chambers had to decide whether the crime of genocide could be committed when the intent to destroy a group was restricted to a limited geographic zone. Two ICTY Trial Chambers stressed that in 1982 the General Assembly had declared the massacre of 800 Palestinians an act of genocide.[192] Whereas, the previous *Jelisić* Trial Chamber reminded that "it is appropriate to look upon this evaluation with caution due to its undoubtedly being more of a political assessment than a legal one",[193] no such words of warning are to be found in the later *Krstić* Trial Chamber Judgment.[194]

Therefore international criminal tribunals could have placed greater emphasis on elaborating the relationship between these resolutions and the evolution of customary international law. In the rare cases in which they have noted the importance of UN General Assembly resolutions as explicitly giving evidence to *opinio iuris* when establishing customary international law,[195] the remarks on their relevance are rather sparse. The ICTY *Blaškić* Appeals Chamber simply stated that evidence for *opinio iuris* can be demonstrated by UN General Assembly resolutions,[196] and the ICTY *Kupreškić* Trial Judgment highlighted the fact that UN General Assembly resolution 2675 (1970) was adopted by "a vast majority".[197] The present author considers a more thorough analysis is necessary: by adhering to the conditions laid

---

[190]For example, with regard to the crime of torture under Art. 3 ICTY Statute the *Furundžija* Trial Chamber held that the General Assembly "Torture Declaration" was adopted by consensus showing that "no member State of the United Nations had any objection to such definition". See ICTY, *Furundžija* Trial Judgment, para 160; see also ICTY, *Delalić* Trial Judgment, para 453.

[191]See for the SCSL case law, *Sesay* Trial Judgment, para 260 when elaborating on attacks on peacekeepers or *Brima* Trial Judgment, para 673 when elaborating on collective punishments.

[192]ICTY, *Krstić* Trial Judgment, para 589, and *Jelisić* Trial Judgment, para 83, referring to UN GA Res. 123D (1982), A/RES/37/123D, 16 December 1982. The resolution was adopted by 123 affirmative votes and 22 abstentions, which was not, however, taken into considerations by the chambers.

[193]ICTY, *Jelisić* Trial Judgment, para 83.

[194]ICTY, *Krstić* Trial Judgment, para 589.

[195]To the present author's knowledge only in 2 judgments have General Assembly resolutions been allocated with the element of *opinio iuris*: ICTY, *Blaškić* Appeals Judgment, para 158 when elaborating on the prohibition to launch attacks against the civilian population: "Evidence of the existence of *opinio juris* is demonstrated in the General Assembly Resolution 2444 (1968) [. . .] and in Resolution 2675 (1970)". ICTY, *Kupreškić* Trial Judgment, para 531 using General Assembly Resolution 2675 (1970) to establish *opinio necessitatis*.

[196]ICTY, *Blaškić* Appeals Judgment, para 158.

[197]ICTY, *Kupreškić* Trial Judgment, para 531. UN General Assembly Resolution 2675 (1970) was adopted by 109 affirmative votes and 8 abstentions.

down by the ICJ in its Advisory Opinion concerning the Legality of the Threat of Nuclear Weapons, General Assembly resolutions could be shown to establish *opinio iuris*.[198]

However it should be noted that international criminal tribunals have not only referred to the law-creation processes of General Assembly resolutions in order to establish *opinio iuris* as one of the two necessary elements for the formation of customary international law. The ICTY *Kupreškić* Trial Judgment and its relevance for the deductive approach has been elaborated above.[199] The Trial Chamber determined that reprisals against civilians are absolutely prohibited under customary international law on the basis of *opinio necessitatis* as deduced from General Assembly Resolution 2675 (1970), even where State practice is "scant or inconsistent".[200] This finding has been endorsed by the ECCC Supreme Court Chamber, stating that "the requirement of *opinio juris* may take pre-eminence over the *usus* element of custom."[201] While these two references seem to be isolated events in the case law of international criminal tribunals, the underlying methodological approach has isolated advocates in the legal literature: *Cheng* determined that "instant customary international law" can be created on basis of the sole constituent element of *opinio iuris*,[202] and the ILA proposed that General Assembly resolutions "are capable, very exceptionally, of creating general customary law by the mere fact of their adoption".[203]

7.6.2.2   UN General Assembly Resolutions as Law-Determining Agencies

In addition to a role in the law-creating process, the ICJ has highlighted that UN General Assembly resolutions may "reflect" customary international law.[204] Indeed, some authors argue that these resolutions shall not be used as relevant material for the creation of customary international law as a "law-creating process",

---

[198]ICJ, Nuclear Weapons Advisory Opinion, para 70.

[199]See further on the *Kupreškić* Trial Judgment's methodological approach Sect. 6.3.3.2, Value-Based Deductive Approach and Deduction from Technical Humanitarian Principles.

[200]ICTY, *Kupreškić* Trial Judgment, para 527.

[201]ECCC, *Duch* Appeals Judgment, para 93. Note, however, that in that regard the ECCC Supreme Court Chambers referred to *Cassese's* legal writing and not to the ICTY *Kupreškić* Trial Chamber over which he presided.

[202]*Cheng* (supra note 162).

[203]ILA (supra note 4), Section 32, 61ff.

[204]ICJ, Nicaragua Case, para 195 referring to the definition of aggression as annexed to GA Resolution 3314 (1974); in its Nuclear Weapons Advisory Opinion, at para 70 the ICJ also highlighted that General Assembly resolutions "may have normative value" distinguishing between the law-creating process ("the emergence of an *opinio juris*") and the law-determining agency ("provide evidence important for establishing the existence of a rule"); see *Öberg* (supra note 162), 896 with further references to the legal literature.

but are restricted to "authoritatively evidencing the emergent rules as *outcomes of the process*".[205] As such, it is proposed that there are certain resolutions of the General Assembly that in themselves are declaratory of existing customary international law and thus fit into the category of "law-determining agencies", despite the fact that Art. 38 (1) (d) ICJ Statute only lists judicial decisions and the legal doctrine as subsidiary means for the determination of rules of law. Even though writers argue that declaratory General Assembly resolutions do not create law *per se*, nevertheless the legal authority ascribed to them hardly corresponds to the category of a mere *subsidiary* source of law. For instance, *Castañeda* argued that "[t]he recognition and formal expression of a customary rule or a general principle of law by the General Assembly constitutes a *juris et de jure* presumption that such a rule or principle is a part of positive international law, that is to say, a legal assumption or fiction that does not allow proof to the contrary, and in the face of which an opposing individual position therefore lacks legal efficacy."[206] Consequently, according to *Castañeda* in certain instances General Assembly resolutions although not creating law may create "legally irrefutable proof" of the existence of customary international law.[207] He suggest that due to the lack of a genuine legislator on the international plane, the General Assembly as a "broadly representative organ" should fill this void in order "to serve as a valuable and sometimes irreplaceable means of determining in case of doubt, and of authoritatively verifying whether a legal norm exists."[208] Under such conditions General Assembly resolutions may indeed carry much greater weight in the determination of customary international law than by mere subsidiary means. In this view they are—in *Pellet's* words—more than "documentary sources"[209] that simply record pre-existing widespread or uniform State practice accompanied by *opinio iuris*. At the same time, however, *Castañeda* admits that there is no clear uniform approach to General Assembly resolutions, as resolutions may simultaneously contain *de lege lata* and *de lege ferenda* considerations. Consequently "the legal value of declaratory resolutions allows for a wide range of shading. There are no tangible, clear, juridical criteria that demarcate with precision the zones of binding force."[210] Others did not shy away from laying down legal criteria in order to determine whether General Assembly resolutions could have declaratory force for the existence of customary international law. For instance, the sole arbitrator *Dupuy* in the Award on the merits in the Dispute between Texaco Overseas Petroleum Company and the Government

---

[205]*Higashi* (supra note 166), 23 (emphasis added); *Castañeda* (supra note 162), 168: "The essential trait of the resolutions under study here, no matter how they are designated, is that they do not *create* law, but that they *recognize* and *declare* it" (emphasis in original).

[206]*Castañeda* (supra note 162), 172.

[207]*Castañeda* (supra note 162), 193, referring to General Assembly resolution 95 (I) (1946) affirming the Nuremberg principles.

[208]*Castañeda* (supra note 162), 169–171.

[209]*Pellet* (supra note 24), 854, MN 305.

[210]*Castañeda* (supra note 162), 176.

of the Libyan Arab Republic, stated that the legal validity of declaratory UN General Assembly resolutions is dependent on "the examination of voting conditions and the analysis of the provisions concerned".[211] Concerning the latter aspect, *Dupuy* considered the discussions leading to the resolutions in order to distinguish *de lege lata* from *de lege ferenda*. He suggested that political rather than legal declarations are detrimental to the task to establish the legal bindingness of General Assembly resolutions.[212] Various writers have referred to the Texaco Case when elaborating the criteria for determining the legal validity of declaratory UN General Assembly resolutions.[213] Admittedly, these considerations are closely connected to the above-established criteria concerning whether General Assembly resolutions could evidence *opinio iuris* as one of the two constitutive elements.[214] The reason for this overlap of the criteria lies within the ICJ case law itself. In its Advisory Opinion on the Legality of the Threat of Nuclear Weapons the ICJ stated that General Assembly resolutions "can, in certain circumstances, provide evidence important for establishing *the existence of a rule* or *the emergence of an opinio juris*. To establish whether this is true of a given General Assembly resolution, it is necessary to look at its content and the conditions of its adoption, it is also necessary to see whether an *opinio juris* exists as to its normative character."[215]

While the first sentence distinguishes between the "law-creating process" ("the emergence of an *opinio juris*") and the "law-determining agencies" ("the existence of a rule"), the reader is left in the dark whether the second sentence refers to former, the latter, or to both. Depending on the stage at which one believes General Assembly resolutions should play a role, it seems that the ICJ case law, and the criteria established in the Advisory Opinion, can be used to substantiate both the "law-creating process" as well as the "law-determining agencies". Accordingly, the "conditions of its adoption", such as the voting outcome, the text, content and normative character, must be taken into account when using General Assembly resolutions as declaratory of customary international law, that is to say, as law-determining agencies.

However, the case law of international criminal tribunals reveals that generally only the voting outcome has been explicitly considered as relevant.[216] In contrast

---

[211]Texaco Overseas Petroleum Company and the Government of the Libyan Arab Republic, 17 International Legal Materials (1978), 28.

[212]*Ibid*, 30.

[213]See e.g. *K. Skubiszewski*, Resolutions of the U.N. General Assembly and Evidence of Custom, International Law at the Time of its Codification – Essays in Honour of Roberto Ago (1987), 510; *Scharf* (supra note 167), 56, who also attributes importance to the type of resolution, whether it is a mere "recommendation", a "declaration", or an "affirmation", see *id*, 54.

[214]See Sect. 7.6.2.1, UN General Assembly Resolutions as a Law-Creating Process.

[215]ICJ, Nuclear Weapons Advisory Opinion, para 70 (emphasis added).

[216]See for example ICTY; *Kordić* Appeals Judgment, para 59 referring to Resolution 2444 (1968) that was adopted unanimously; *Prosecutor v. Martić*, IT-95-11-R61, Trial Chamber, Decision, 8 March 1996, para 12 referring to Resolution 2444 (1968) and 2675 (1970) both being adopted unanimously; see for the ECCC, *Duch* Trial Judgment, para 353 referring to Resolution 3452

the ICTY *Tadić* Appeals Chamber in its Jurisdiction Decision,[217] when elaborating that the General Assembly Resolutions 2444 (1968) and 2675 (1970) were declaratory of customary international law, highlighted various factors: they were adopted "unanimously", were adopted as "affirmations", contained clear wording by using normative language, and referred to declarations of States during and after the drafting process of the resolutions. These factors determined that the resolutions were declaratory of customary international law. Such a greater awareness as exemplified by the *Tadić* Appeals Chamber when using General Assembly resolutions is to be welcomed. Such an approach, however, is a rare exception in the case law of international criminal tribunals.

One General Assembly resolution that is of particular importance for the development of customary international criminal law must be singled out: UN General Assembly Resolution 95 (I) (1946). It was adopted on 11 December 1946, a little over 2 months after the IMT Nuremberg Judgment had been delivered. Within this resolution the General Assembly "[a]ffirms the principles of international law recognized by the Charter of the Nürnberg Tribunal and the judgment of the Tribunal."[218] When the ECCC Supreme Court Chamber determined that although the IMT Nuremberg Judgment in itself would not constitute binding precedent for the ECCC, it simultaneously determined that "coupled with" UN General Assembly Resolution 95 (I) (1946) "it provides strong evidence of existent and newly emerging principles of international criminal law."[219] The ECCC Supreme Court Chamber is in good company, as in 1962 the Israeli Supreme Court in the *Eichmann* Case held that "if fifty-eight nations [corresponding to all Member States of the UN at that time] unanimously agree on a statement of existing law, it would seem that such a declaration would be all but conclusive evidence of such a rule, and agreement by a large majority would have great value in determining what is existing law."[220] Thus it is clear that the affirmation of the legal principles as enshrined in the IMT Nuremberg Charter and as applied by the IMT Nuremberg *via* the UN General Assembly Resolution, had an effect on the consideration of both the Nuremberg Statute and the jurisprudence being based upon it as customary international law. This view is also widely accepted in the legal literature.[221]

(1975) being adopted by consensus; the *Duch* Trial Chamber has been criticized by the Supreme Court Chambers in the *Duch* Appeals Judgment, para 194: "The 1975 Declaration on Torture is a non-binding General Assembly resolution and thus more evidence is required to find that the definition of torture found therein reflected customary international law at the relevant time." At the same time, however, the Supreme Court Chamber also merely referred to the fact that UN General Assembly Resolution 95 (I) was adopted unanimously to determine that it "reflects" principles of international law, see *id*, para 225.

[217]ICTY, *Tadić* Appeals Chamber Jurisdiction Decision, paras 110 and 111.

[218]UN General Assembly Resolution 95 (I) (1946).

[219]ECCC, *Duch* Appeals Judgment, para 110.

[220]Israeli Supreme Court, Eichmann Case, para 11.

[221]*Cassese* (supra note 51); *Scharf* (supra note 167), 65–66; *Castañeda* (supra note 162), 191–3.

Indeed, when applying the criteria established by the ICJ Advisory Opinion on the Legality of the Threat of Nuclear Weapons of *content* and the *conditions of its adoption* to General Assembly Resolution 95 (I), as aptly held by *Scharf*, the resolution "had all the attributes of a resolution entitled to great weight as a declaration of customary international law: it was labeled an 'affirmation' of legal principles; it dealt with inherently legal questions; it was passed by a unanimous vote; and none of the members expressed the position that it was merely a political statement".[222] With regard to UN General Assembly Resolution 95 (I) (1946), writers have argued that the affirmation gives "irrefutable proof"[223] of the existence of customary international law, or that it is to be considered a "Grotian Moment" that rapidly ripened the IMT Nuremberg Statute and the jurisprudence of the IMT Nuremberg into customary international law.[224] Indeed, the case law of national and international courts alike treats the "General Assembly resolution affirming the principles of the Nuremberg Charter and judgments as an authoritative declaration of customary international law."[225] This "affirmation" of the legal principles by the UN General Assembly does not "merely" benefit the IMT Nuremberg Statute and the IMT Nuremberg Judgment. Since the affirmation concerned the "principles of international law recognized by the Charter and judgment of the Tribunal",[226] this affirmation is best regarded as a process-oriented approach to the underlying legal principles. Since Control Council Law No. 10 was created in order to incorporate the provisions of substantive international criminal law as already contained in the IMT Nuremberg Statute, that instrument, as well as the subsequent case law of the military tribunals operating under the authority and strength of Control Council Law No. 10, can also be regarded as being "affirmed" by the UN General Assembly resolution. It is in this sense that one should read *Cassese's* argument that "Control Council Law No. 10 can be regarded as an international agreement among the four Occupying Powers (*subsequently transformed, to a large extent, into customary law*), the action of the courts established or acting under that Law acquires an international relevance that cannot be attributed to national courts pronouncing solely on the strength of national law."[227] The ICTY *Kupreškić* Trial Chamber also held that the military tribunals acting under Control Council Law No. 10 "operated under international instruments laying down provisions that were either declaratory of existing law or which had been gradually transformed into customary international law."[228]

---

[222]*Scharf* (supra note 129), 254f.

[223]*Castañeda* (supra note 162), 193.

[224]*Scharf* (supra note 167), 63–106.

[225]*Scharf* (supra note 167), 66–67 with further references.

[226]UN General Assembly Resolution 95 (I) (1946).

[227]ICTY, *Erdemović* Appeals Judgment, Separate and Dissenting Opinion of Judge Cassese, para 27 (emphasis added).

[228]ICTY the *Kupreškić* Trial Judgment, paras 541 (emphasis added).

The affirmation by the General Assembly of the underlying international criminal law principles enshrined in the Nuremberg Charter, and as applied by the IMT Nuremberg and the military courts operating under Control Council Law No. 10, is of particular relevance for considering these instances as an authoritative source of declaratory customary international criminal law.[229]

7.6.3   UN Security Council Resolutions

The role of UN Security Council resolutions for the formation and determination of customary international law, in contrast to those of the General Assembly, has attracted little attention in either the legal literature or in the case law of the ICJ. The "decisions" of the UN Security Council, within the meaning of Art. 25 UN Charter, have binding force. Due to the precedence of UN Charter obligations over other obligations under other international agreements,[230] it seems that the legal debate of SC resolutions in relation to customary international concerned the question of whether "SC decisions have an overriding normative power capable of pre-empting obligations following from traditional sources of international law", including customary international law.[231]

However, since according to the focus of this study acts of intergovernmental organizations are considered as relevant material for giving evidence to customary international law,[232] the value of Security Council resolutions should be addressed. It has been argued that the Security Council has entered into its "legislative phase".[233] As such, the legal discourse on "legislative acts" of international organizations shifted from the General Assembly to the Security Council.[234] However, these "legislative acts" of the Security Council are conceived outside the realm of customary international law. Rather, it has been argued that Security Council legislation may be classified under Art. 38 (1) (a) ICJ Statute as "secondary treaty law" of the UN Charter,[235] or that beyond the scope of the traditional sources of

---

[229]On the value of this jurisprudence for the determination of customary international law, see Sect. 7.7.3, IMT Nuremberg and Post World War II Tribunals Operating Under the Strength of Control Council Law No. 10.

[230]Art. 103 UN Charter.

[231]*Öberg* (supra note 162), 884f with further references to ICJ case law.

[232]See Sect. 7.1, Preliminary Remarks.

[233]See *J.E. Alvarez*, Editorial Comment: Hegemonic International Law Revisited, 97 American Journal of International (2003), 874. Note, however, that the power of the Security Council to legislate is a controversial issue, see *E. Rosand*, The Security Council as "Global Legislator": Ultra Vires or Ultra Innovative?, 28 Fordham International Law Journal (2005), 542ff.

[234]M. Payandeh, Internationales Gemeinschaftsrecht (2010), 313 with further references to the legal literature.

[235]See *S. Talmon*, The Security Council as World Legislature, 99 American Journal of International Law (2005), 179.

international law Security Council resolutions could constitute a "new source" of law.[236] However, this study suggests that since organs of intergovernmenta_ organizations are composed of State representatives, the practice of the organization can be traced back to the participating States. There seems to be no logical reason for Security Council resolutions to be excluded from the law-creating process of customary international law. A wide conception of State practice includes the conduct of States in international organizations, including the resolutions for which they vote.[237] Above it was suggested that General Assembly resolutions could not be used to give evidence to both elements, State practice and *opinion iuris*. However the danger of such an "instant quasi-legislative effect"[238] does not apply to the Security Council[239] as it is composed of only 15 members Consequently, assuming that the respective SC resolution was adopted unanimously one could potentially establish the view of only the five permanent members and the 10 non-permanent members. Moreover, one must also consider the content of the normative character of the Security Council resolutions by analyzing the formulation of the respective paragraphs to determine if *opinio iuris* to a certain legal issue can be established.

International criminal tribunals have not regularly referred to Security Council resolutions as relevant material for the formation or determination of customary international law. On the rare occasions where they have been referred to, no clear picture of their relevance is detectable: in some cases they have not been allocated to the constitutive elements of customary international law,[240] while in others they have explicitly been referred to as an instance of State practice,[241] *opinio iuris*,[242] or both.[243] Considering individual criminal responsibility for war crimes committed in a non-international armed conflict, the ICTY *Tadić* Appeals Chamber adhered to the traditional approach of determining customary international law on the basis of

---

[236]*Ibid* footnote 45 referring to *K. Skubiszewski*, International Legislation, Bernhardt (ed.), Encyclopedia of Public International Law, Vol. II (1995), 1261.

[237]See Sect. 4.3.2, The Procedural Aspect of Modern Customary International Law.

[238]*Öberg* (supra note 162), 899.

[239]In his Second Report Special Rapporteur *Wood* (supra note 3), also considered that resolutions of intergovernmental organizations may evince State practice and *opinio iuris*. He claimed that the adoption of resolutions (voting in favour, against or abstaining) is a form of State practice at para 41 (i), from which *opinio iuris* can be deduced (as well as from statements in relation to resolutions), at para 76 (g).

[240]ICTY, *Tadić* Appeals Chamber Jurisdiction Decision, para 114 referring to six Security Council resolutions when elaborating on the customary rules of international humanitarian law governing internal armed conflict; see also SCSL, *Sesay* Trial Judgment, para 216 referring to the condemnation of attacks against peacekeeping personal and material by the Security Council.

[241]SCSL, *Taylor* Appeals Judgment, para 474 in connection with para 462 when determining that "specific direction" is not an element of the *actus reus* of aiding and abetting.

[242]ICTY, *Tadić* Appeals Chamber Jurisdiction Decision, para 133.

[243]ICTY, *Boškoski* Trial Judgment, para 191–2.

State practice and *opinio iuris*.[244] However, it should be noted that the only evidence of *opinio iuris* in this case was given by the reference to two Security Council resolutions adopted unanimously in relation to Somalia. While the formulation of the respective paragraphs in the resolutions are a strong indication that the members of the Security Council considered that individual criminal responsibility exists in such cases, the evidence for an *opinio iuris* given by the ICTY *Tadić* Appeals Chamber only reflects the legal conviction of the 15 States sitting in the Security Council. Accordingly, further evidence that could prove an *opinio iuris generalis*[245] when establishing a universal customary norm would be necessary for the determination of customary international law.

7.7   Jurisprudence

7.7.1   Preliminary Remarks

Some of the crucial issues that will be analyzed in the present chapter have already been addressed above when elaborating on the methodological approaches to customary international law. International criminal tribunals have used "international" case law as a methodological shortcut for the determination of customary international law.[246] In such cases it would be necessary to analyze the *quality* of the international decisions—the underlying analysis of the constitutive elements of customary international law—to determine whether the case law can be used as subsidiary means. However, in place of such an analysis, international criminal tribunals have focused their attention on the question of whether the decision has been rendered by "international" or "national" judicial authorities. They have given the former more authoritative value as subsidiary means for the determination of a rule of customary law. In this chapter the authoritative value of specific courts, international and national alike, will be elaborated in more detail, adhering to the proposed structure of the "law-creating processes" and the "law-determining agencies".

7.7.2   International Court of Justice

This study considers that law-making in the international legal sphere is a task that is primarily reserved to States. Thus it is clear that even the case law of the

---

[244]See Sect. 6.3.1.2, ICTY *Tadić* Appeals Chamber Jurisdiction Decision.

[245]See the references in supra note 27.

[246]See Sect. 6.3.4.3 International Case Law as Subsidiary Means for the Determination of Customary International Law.

International Court of Justice cannot be considered as relevant material for the formation of customary international law, that is, proving the constitutive elements of State practice and/or *opinio iuris*. Consequently, the case law of the International Court of Justice cannot be a source of law in itself, but is merely a "subsidiary means for the determination of a rule of law" according to Art. 38 (1) (d) ICJ Statute.[247] As argued above, such possibility is dependent on the quality of the decision: thus in relation to customary international law its analysis of the constituent elements.[248] Nevertheless, it appears that the case law of the International Court of Justice as "the principal judicial organ of the UN"[249] is given an authoritative value that stands at odds with this conception. *Buergenthal*, for example, stated that "a decision by the ICJ will today, in general, be treated by the international community as the most authoritative statement on the subject and *accepted as the law*."[250] Thus *Lauterpacht* considered that the difference between law-determining agencies and law-creating processes consists in form only, and that the effect of the two may be the same. He suggested that international courts "state what the law is. Their decisions are evidence of the existing rule of law. That does not mean that they do not *in fact* constitute a source of international law. For the distinction between the evidence and the source of many a rule of law is more speculative and less rigid than is commonly supposed."[251]

In terms of the treatment of ICJ case law in the jurisprudence of international criminal tribunals, it must be stated that they operate in a different fields from one another, the ICJ attributing State responsibility and the international criminal tribunals attributing individual criminal responsibility. Nevertheless, international criminal law is not to be considered in clinical isolation from public international law. At the ICTR, Judge *Shahabuddeen* put forward the view that "so far as international law is concerned, the operation of the *desiderata* of consistency, stability and predictability does not stop at the frontiers of the Tribunal. [...] The Appeals Chamber cannot behave as if the general state of the law in the international community whose interest it serves is none of its concern; to act on that blinkered view is to wield power divorced from responsibility."[252]

---

[247] *K. Doehring*, Die Rechtsprechung als Rechtsquelle des Völkerrechts. Zur Auslegung des Art. 38 Abs. 1 Ziff. d des Statuts des Internationalen Gerichtshofs, in Reinhart (ed.), Richterliche Rechtsfortbildung – Erscheinungsformen, Auftrag und Grenzen, FS Heidelberg (1986), 552. See also *H. Lauterpacht*, The Development of International Law by the International Court (1958), 20ff.

[248] See Sect. 6.3.4.3 International Case Law as Subsidiary Means for the Determination of Customary International Law.

[249] Art. 92 UN Charter.

[250] *T. Buergenthal*, Lawmaking by the ICJ and Other International Courts, 103 American Society of International Law Proceedings (2009), 404 (emphasis added); see also *M. Shahabuddeen*, Precedent in the World Court (1996), 239.

[251] *Lauterpacht* (supra note 247), 21 (emphasis added).

[252] ICTR, Separate Opinion of Judge Shahabuddeen to *Semanza* Appeals Chamber Decision, para 24.

This is especially true when the different components that constitute international criminal law do not provide for an answer.[253] For example the ICTY *Tadić* Appeals Chamber stated that IHL does not contain rules of imputability and that therefore it is necessary to rely on the general rules on State responsibility.[254] Taking recourse to concepts of general public international law clearly reveals that the case law of the ICJ is of significant importance to international criminal tribunals. Throughout their case law, international criminal law chambers have referred to the "authoritative" statements of the ICJ for the determination of customary international law. At the same time the chambers have refused to grant precedential value to the case law of the ICJ.[255] However, as a law-determining agency the ICJ stands as perhaps *the* "international" judicial authority, and its decisions have been attributed enormous value as subsidiary means for the determination of customary international law.

International criminal chambers referred to the ICJ judgments in order to determine that certain international treaty norms are part of international customary law, most prominently when determining the customary law status of Common Article 3 of the 1949 Geneva Convention. The customary law status of this treaty norm has mainly been argued with reference to the following passage of the ICJ in the Nicaragua Case[256]: "Article 3 which is common to all four Geneva Conventions of 12 August 1949 defines certain rules to be applied in the armed conflicts of a non-international character. There is no doubt that, in the event of international armed conflicts, these rules also constitute a minimum yardstick, in addition to the more elaborate rules which are also to apply to international conflicts; and they are rules which, in the Court's opinion, reflect what the Court in 1949 called 'elementary considerations of humanity'."[257] The ICTY chambers did not consider it necessary to delve into the reasoning of the ICJ, but were ready to accept the customary law status of Common Article 3 without any further inquiry.

When elaborating on the inclusion of genocide within their statutes, the ICTR and ICTY usually affirmed that their statutes reproduce Arts. II and III of the Genocide Convention, which is widely accepted and the provisions of which are uncontested part of customary law and *ius cogens* as stipulated by the ICJ in its

---

[253]See on the components of ICL Sect. 2.2, International Criminal Law: A Collision of Legal Systems.

[254]ICTY, *Tadić* Appeals Chamber Judgment, para 105.

[255]See for example ICTY, *Delalić* Appeals Judgment, paras 21, 24. *Rosenne* considers that while there is no formal hierarchy between international tribunals the pre-eminence of the case law of the ICJ is generally accepted. See *S. Rosenne*, The Law and Practice of International Courts and Tribunals: Volume III, Procedure (2006), 1553.

[256]For the ICTY compare: *Tadić* Appeals Chamber Jurisdiction Decision, para 98, compare also paras 93, 102 and 117. *Furundžija* Trial Judgment, para 138; *Aleksovski* Trial Judgment, para 50; *Halilović* Trial Judgment, para 25; *Mrkšić* Appeals Judgment, para 70; *Delalić* Trial Judgment, para 303.

[257]ICJ, Nicaragua Case, para 218.

advisory opinion of 1951.[258] Just as with Common Article 3, the chambers did not conduct an inquiry as to how the ICJ has determined the status of those conventional norms, but considered its "authoritative" statement *de facto* as the source of law. It is evident that in this regard the jurisprudence of the ICJ has been granted much greater authority than a mere "subsidiary" source for the determination of one of the primary sources of law contained in Art. 38 (1a–c) ICJ Statute.

While these two examples illustrate the willing adherence of international criminal tribunals to the jurisprudence of the ICJ, such acceptance appears to be restricted to areas where those judgments overlap with the legal conviction of the judges at the international criminal tribunals. Prior to the ICTY *Tadić* Appeals Chamber Judgment there was a dispute at the ICTY while considering the classification of an armed conflict as either international or internal, which is relevant for the application of Art. 2 ICTY Statute. The *Tadić* Trial Chamber analyzed this question through the lens of the ICJ by referring to the "effective control"[259] test as established in the Nicaragua Case, in order to attribute the conduct of military or paramilitary groups to a State. It denied that acts of the army of the Republika Srpska, the Bosnian Serb Army, were attributable to the Federal Republic of Yugoslavia (FRY, Serbia and Montenegro).[260] In contrast, the *Delalić* Trial Chamber stated that "the creation of the VRS and VJ [the successors of the Yugoslav People's Army], constituted a deliberate attempt to mask the continued involvement of the FRY".[261] The *Delalić* Trial Chamber argued that the ICJ's jurisprudence is not relevant in that case due to the difference in nature between inter-State and international criminal tribunals. The Appeals Chamber in its *Tadić* judgment, however, held that the issue was not the distinction between State responsibility and individual responsibility. Rather, as a preliminary matter it stressed the need to clarify which conditions according to international law are necessary to attribute acts of individuals to the State, be it either to determine State responsibility or to

---

[258]For the ICTR compare further *Akayesu* Trial Judgment, para 495 (also referring to the UN SG Report on the ICTY); *Rutaganda* Trial Judgment para 46 (also, to the UN SG Report on the ICTY); *Bagilishema* Trial Judgment, para 54; *Musema* Trial Judgment, para 151 (also referring to the UN SG Report on the ICTY); for the ICTY compare: *Stakić* Trial Judgment, para 500; *Krstić* Trial Judgment, paras 541ff; ICTY, *Jelisić* Trial Judgment, para 60; see also *Popović* Trial Judgment, para 807 referring to the ICJ Bosnia Judgment and other prior opinions of the ICJ.

[259]This test requires that in order that acts of a secessionist movement (in case of the ICJ the contras) can be attributed to an outside, intervening State it needs to be shown that that State "directed or enforced the perpetration of the acts contrary to human rights and humanitarian law". Proof of financing, organizing, training, supplying and equipping and even general control would be insufficient. See ICJ, Nicaragua Case, para 115.

[260]ICTY, *Tadić* Trial Judgment, para 584ff and 607ff.

[261]ICTY, *Delalić* Trial Judgment, para 230, referring to the Dissenting Opinion of Judge McDonald to the *Tadić* Case. See also ICTY, *Delalić* Appeals Judgment, paras 21, 24 stating that "there is no hierarchical relationship" between the ICTY and the ICJ and that it is not bound by ICJ precedents.

render a conflict international as a precondition for the application of the grave breaches regime for the determination of individual criminal liability.[262] While it thus rejected the distinction made by the *Delalić* Trial Chamber, the *Tadić* Appeals Chamber nevertheless came to the conclusion that the ICJ's "effective control" test was not persuasive. According to the Appeals Chamber, firstly, it does not correspond to the logic of the law of State responsibility. And secondly the ICJ case law was not consonant with customary international law, as it is "*at variance with judicial and state practice*".[263] The Appeals Chamber thus doubted the legal reasoning of the ICJ and did not adhere to the "authoritative" ICJ case law. It considered that when it comes to the degree of control required for actions by "organized and hierarchically structured armed groups" the applicable test is "overall control".[264] *Schabas* has argued that the ICTY Appeals Chamber varied the requirements for customary law formation, replacing the *opinio iuris* element with an element of judicial practice.[265] In fact, the Appeals Chamber did not include much State practice in its analysis referring only to one domestic case, the German *Jorgić* case. Rather, the *Tadić* Appeals Judgment based the analysis on case law before other international courts, with reference being made to the case law of the Mexico-US General Claims Commission, the Iran-US Claims Tribunal and the European Court of Human Rights.[266] It should be stressed that the Appeals Chamber did not conduct an inquiry of the constitutive elements of customary international law to establish the "overall control" test. Furthermore it did not consider how those other international courts arrived at their findings by analyzing the underlying evidence in the decisions of those respective courts. It merely substituted the test elaborated by the ICJ with a test it deduced from the jurisprudence of other international tribunals. One could argue that the *Tadić* Appeals Chamber was result-oriented in order to circumvent the strict requirements of the "effective control" test by forming a less stringent test of the attribution of responsibility of "overall control". Other international criminal chambers and courts followed suit and it can be stated that the "overall control" test is now generally considered settled jurisprudence by international criminal tribunals.[267]

This dispute between the "overall control" test and the "effective control" test suggests that international criminal tribunals do not consider the ICJ's findings as authoritative statements concerning the existence of a rule of customary

---

[262]ICTY, *Tadić* Appeals Chamber Judgment, para 104.

[263]ICTY, *Tadić* Appeals Chamber Judgment, paras 124ff (emphasis added).

[264]This test is less strict than the one established by the ICJ, since besides "mere financing and equipping" it only needs to be shown that the outside State was involved in the organizing, co-ordination, planning or supervision, but it is not required to show that it had issued specific instructions. See ICTY, *Tadić* Appeals Chamber Judgment, para 145.

[265]See also *Schabas* (supra note 139), 80.

[266]ICTY, *Tadić* Appeals Chamber Judgment, paras 124ff.

[267]It has been followed by the ICTY, *Naletilić* Trial Judgment, para 183; *Aleksovski* Appeals Judgment, para 134; *Blaškić* Trial Judgment, para 95ff; *Kordić* Appeals Judgment, para 306ff; the ICC also adhered to this test, see *Lubanga* Trial Judgment, para 541.

international law. Regrettably, the ICTY *Tadić* Appeals Chamber failed to elaborate on the underlying legal quality of the decisions of other international tribunals when forming its "overall control" test. Consequently, the "overall contro." test is not underpinned by a more thorough methodological analysis of customary international law. Without an adequate legal analysis of the underlying *quality* of the decisions of these other international tribunals, it seems dubious how these decisions could carry greater authoritative weight than the ICJ jurisprudence.[268] Instead, one could accuse international criminal tribunals of "cherry picking", adhering to the jurisprudence of the ICJ when it fits, but circumventing it when the judges have opposing opinions. The "overall control" test is a good example to show that international criminal tribunals do not attribute the case law of the ICJ a higher authoritative value compared to other international tribunals. They merely treat the ICJ as just one of various "law-determining agencies". Nevertheless, it needs to be reemphasized that in order to use international judicial decisions as "law-determining agencies" the *quality* of the decisions must to be taken into account.[269]

7.7.3 IMT Nuremberg and Post World War II Tribunals Operating Under the Strength of Control Council Law No. 10

The frequent reference to post World War II jurisprudence by international criminal tribunals for the purpose of establishing customary international criminal norms has already been highlighted in a previous chapter.[270] Post World War II "international" decisions have been used by all international criminal tribunals as subsidiary means for the determination of a rule of law according to

---

[268]The ICJ held on to its "effective control" test in the *Bosnian Genocide* Case openly criticising the ICTY at para 403: "The Court has given careful consideration to the Appeals Chamber's reasoning [in the *Tadić* Case] in support of the foregoing conclusion, but finds itself unable to subscribe to the Chamber's view. First, the Court observes that the ICTY was not called upon in the *Tadić* case, nor is it in general called upon, to rule on questions of State responsibility, since its jurisdiction is criminal and extends over persons only. Thus in that Judgment the Tribunal addressed an issue which was not indispensable for the exercise of its jurisdiction."

[269]For example when the ECtHR determined that the ICJ's Jurisdictional Immunities Case was "authoritative as regards the content of customary international law" to establish that no *ius cogens* exception to State immunity has yet crystallized under international law, the ECtHR examined the legal reasoning and customary international law analysis of the ICJ, see European Court of Human Rights, Case of *Jones and Others v. The United Kingdom*, Applications Nos 34356/06 and 40528/06, Judgment, 14 January 2014, paras 198 in conjunction with paras 88–94.

[270]See Sect. 6.3.4.3 International Case Law as Subsidiary Means for the Determination of Customary International Law.

Art. 38 (1) (d) ICJ Statute[271]: International criminal tribunals determined that the post World War II cases "reflect"[272] customary international law, are "persuasive as to the contours"[273] of a crime or mode of liability in customary international law, are "indicative of customary international law"[274] or provide "conclusive evidence for the state of customary international law."[275] In this chapter it will be demonstrated why the case law of the IMT Nuremberg and the US military court cases held under Control Council Law No. 10 as contained in the "green series" can be used as subsidiary means for the determination of a rule of customary international law.

Generally, in the legal literature the discussion of the "authoritative value" of these cases centres on the question of whether the tribunals were "international" in nature and applied "international law".[276] *Schwarzenberger* argued that the IMT Nuremberg is "a *municipal* tribunal of extraordinary jurisdiction which the four Contracting Powers share in common."[277] In contrast, *Kelsen*, although arguing that the Nuremberg Judgment could not constitute a precedent in international law due to a lack of neutral judges, stated that the IMT Nuremberg was "expressly designated an 'International' Military Tribunal, and its members were not appointed by the Control Council for Germany but by the governments of the United States, Great Britain, France and the Soviet Union, with the consent, subsequently given, of the States which adhered to the Agreement."[278] Concerning the applicable law, the IMT Nuremberg endeavored to show that the Nuremberg Charter was "not an arbitrary exercise of power on the part of the victorious Nations, but [...] the expression of international law existing at the time of its creation".[279] Nevertheless,

---

[271]The ECCC Pre-Trial Chamber explicitly acknowledged the use of judicial decisions as subsidiary means for the determination of a rule of law, see ECCC, Case No 002 Pre-Trial Chamber Public Decision on the JCE Appeals, para 53. Note however at para 60 the Pre-Trial Chamber considers that the jurisprudence of post World War II military tribunals may "offer an authoritative interpretation of their constitutive instruments and can be relied upon to determine the state of customary international law", thus also advocating to use the case law as relevant material for the interpretation of the underlying treaty provisions.

[272]ICTY, *Tadić* Appeals Chamber Judgment, para 226.

[273]ICTY, *Brđanin* Appeals Judgment, para 410.

[274]SCSL, *Taylor* Appeals Judgment, para 417. See also ICTR, *Rwamakuba* Appeals Chamber, Decision, para 14.

[275]ECCC, *Duch* Appeals Judgment, para 146.

[276]See on these issues in relation to the US Nuremberg Military Tribunals, *Heller* (supra note 130), 110ff; see in relation to the IMT Nuremberg, *R. K Woetzel*, The Nuremberg Trials in International Law with a Postlude on the Eichmann Case (1962), 40ff.

[277]*G. Schwarzenberger*, The Judgment of Nuremberg, Mettraux (ed.), Perspectives on the Nuremberg Trial (2008), 171 as quoted in *Heller* (supra note 130), 110.

[278]*H. Kelsen*, Will the Judgment in the Nuremberg Trial Constitute a Precedent in International Law?, 1 International Law Quarterly (1947), 168.

[279]IMT Nuremberg Judgment, Vol. 1, 218.

there has been persistent critique that the IMT Nuremberg applied *ex post facto* law thereby violating the *nullum crimen sine lege* principle.[280]

From a present day standpoint it is not necessary to delve into the question of whether the IMT Nuremberg is to be considered an "international" court adjudicating on what it considered to be part of international law at the time of rendering its judgment. As shown above,[281] UN General Assembly Resolution 95 (I) (1946) cast away any doubt on the customary law nature of the IMT Nuremberg's jurisprudence. Within this resolution the General Assembly "[a]ffirms the principles of international law recognized by the Charter of the Nürnberg Tribunal and the judgment of the Tribunal."[282] Even if one was to assume that the IMT did not apply existing international law[283] as enshrined in Art. 38 ICJ Statute at the time of the Nuremberg Judgment, the subsequent General Assembly affirmation would safeguard that the applied legal principles are valid principles of international law, at least since the point in time of this "affirmation". At the IMTFE judge *Pal* in his dissentient judgment stated that "[u]nder international law, as it now stands, a victor nation or a union of victor nations, would have the authority to establish a tribunal for the trial of war criminals, but no authority to legislate and promulgate a new law of war crimes."[284] However, Judge *Pal* was not blind to the power of world politics and the dynamic process of international legislation, and declared that even though there was no justification for *ex post facto* law creation on the international level, "law can also be created illegally otherwise than by the recognized procedures – *ex injuria jus oritur*: Any law now created in this manner and applied will perhaps be the law henceforth."[285] This raises the possibility that the "illegality" of the judgment at the time of its rendering, applying law that supposedly was not covered by the general sources of law in Art. 38 ICJ Statute, would not hinder that the judgment is subsequently given significant meaning for the determination of a rule of law. With such reasoning any possible *ex post facto* law critique of the original judgment would not hold valid for future perpetrators, as long as the judgment had been subsequently affirmed by the international community as containing

---

[280]*C. Burchard*, The Nuremberg Trial and its Impact on Germany, 4 Journal of International Criminal Justice (2004), 800ff with further references.

[281]See Sect. 7.6.2.2, UN General Assembly Resolutions as Law-Determining Agencies.

[282]UN General Assembly Resolution 95 (I) (1946). *Woetzel* (supra note 276), 49–57, has attributed this affirmation by the UN General Assembly enormous value, stating that "[t]he United Nations affirmed the principles applied at Nuremberg and thereby expressed its endorsement of the principles applied by the court. This approval is of special importance, since the IMT did not directly apply general international law as the Permanent International Court at The Hague is authorised to do, according to Article 38 of its Statute, but was bound by the London Agreement and the Charter which constituted the law to be applied. This additional endorsement by the United Nations represents further tangible evidence for assuming that the principles of the Charter as well as those in the Judgment of the IMT were valid principles of international law, and that their application was justified."

[283]*Woetzel* (supra note 276), 55–57.

[284]Judge *R. Pal*, Dissentient Judgement (1953), 26.

[285]*Pal, id*, 26.

binding legal principles. This certainly has been the case with the legal principles contained in the Nuremberg Statute and as applied by the IMT Nuremberg.

While the Nuremberg Judgment concerned the trial of the major war criminals before the IMT Nuremberg, the Nuremberg Charter itself did not rule out the possibility that subsequent trials against other "minor" war criminals may also be held before the international tribunal. Art. 22 IMT Charter stated that "[t]he first trial shall be held at Nuremberg, and any subsequent trials shall be held at such places as the Tribunal may decide."[286] Efforts to establish a second international military trial were however fruitless, resulting in the establishment of various "zone trials".[287] Control Council Law No. 10, a legislative act jointly promulgated by the occupying powers,[288] was enacted in order to give effect to the IMT Charter in the zones and to "establish a uniform legal basis in Germany for the prosecution of war criminals and other similar offenders, other than those dealt with by the International Military Tribunal".[289] Art. I Control Council Law No. 10 determines that the 1945 London Agreement, to which the IMT Nuremberg Charter is annexed, is an integral part of the law. However, Art. III of Control Council Law No. 10 further stipulated that the rules and procedure of the tribunals that charge persons with offenses under Control Council Law No. 10 "shall be determined or designated by each Zone Commander for his respective Zone." Consequently Control Council Law No. 10 was complemented by laws that should govern the military courts in their respective occupation zones.[290] In addition to those "zone trials" there were

---

[286]IMT Nuremberg Charter, Art. 22; see also *Heller* (supra note 130), 17.

[287]For the reasons for this development see *Heller* (supra note 130), 17–24.

[288]On the classification of Control Council Law No. 10 as "domestic legislation" or an "international agreement" see Sect. 7.5.3.1, Statutes of the IMT, IMTFE and Control Council Law No. 10.

[289]Control Council Law No. 10, Punishment of Persons Guilty of War Crimes, Crimes Against Peace and Against Humanity, 20 December 1945, 3 Official Gazette Control Council for Germany 50–55 (1946).

[290]For the US Military Tribunals in the United States Zone see Ordinance No. 7, 18 October 1946, Art. I: "the purpose of this Ordinance is to provide for the establishment of military tribunals which shall have power to try and punish persons charged with offenses recognized as crimes in Article II of Control Council Law No. 10", printed in Trials of War Criminals Before the Nuernberg Military Tribunals Under Control Council Law No. 10 ("The Green Series"), Vol. I, October 1946 – April 1949, XXI; for the Military Government Tribunals in the French Zone of Germany see Ordinance No. 20, 25 November 1945 and Ordinance No. 36, 25 February 1946, of the French Commander-in-chief, United Nations War Crimes Commission, Law Reports of Trials of War Criminals, Vol. III (1948), 100ff; for the British law concerning the trial of war criminals by British Military Courts see Royal Warrant, 14 June 1945, Army Order 81/45 with amendments, United Nations War Crimes Commission, Law Reports of Trials of War Criminals, Vol. I (1947), 105. The Royal Warrant is applicable to all trials of war criminals under the jurisdiction of the United Kingdom; as such there is no differentiation to "zone trials" or other war crime trials, however it restricts the jurisdiction to "war crimes" and does not include crimes against humanity or the crime of aggression. Furthermore, the Allies have after some time started to transfer the competence to carry out prosecutions in their respective zones to German authorities, see the German Supreme Court for the British Occupied Zone and the German Courts in the French Occupied Zone.

also other post World War II criminal trials held by domestic courts outside the occupied zones of Germany.[291]

Consequently, in the field of post World War II jurisprudence, in addition to the international military courts sitting at Nuremberg and Tokyo, there were a multitude of different tribunals of varying relevance. It is evident that those military tribunals that followed a "general continental practice", mostly exercised jurisdiction over war crimes not by applying international law but required the violation of domestic law.[292] The British law governing the trials of war criminals by the British military courts, Army Order 81/45, also restricted the jurisdiction of the military courts to "war crimes" which it defined.[293] Strictly speaking, the law applicable in those instances is thus domestic.

The present author considers that the situation of the US military tribunals as contained in the "green series"[294] is different. Although the US have also enacted Ordinance No. 7 as domestic legislation to complement Control Council Law No. 10, the authority to try and punish persons charged with offenses depended upon recognition of the offences as crimes in Article II of Control Council law No. 10.[295] Admittedly, there has been some confusion within the jurisprudence of

---

[291]The Australian Military Court, the Canadian Military Court, the Chinese War Crimes Court, USSR Military Courts, the Netherlands Special Courts, Norwegian Courts, the Supreme National Tribunal of Poland and Danish Military Courts.

[292]For example the French Permanent Military Tribunal for the Trial of War Criminals, Ordinance of 28 August 1944, which considers that war criminals "shall be prosecuted by French military tribunals and shall be tried *in accordance with the French laws in force*" (emphasis added), see United Nations War Crimes Commission, Law Reports of Trials of War Criminals, Vol. III (1948), 93 and 95; see also the Norwegian Law on the Punishment of Foreign War Criminals, 13 December 1946 (No. 14), Art. 1: "Acts which, by reason of their character, come within the scope of Norwegian criminal legislation are *punishable according to Norwegian law*, if they were committed in Norway or were directed against Norwegian citizens or Norwegian interests", *ibid*, 81ff; see also Polish Law concerning trials of war criminals, United Nations War Crimes Commission, Law Reports of Trials of War Criminals, Vol. VII (1948), 82ff especially 88: "From the foregoing it appears that the Polish attitude towards the treatment of war criminals follows the general continental practice that before punishment is inflicted, an individual offender *must be shown to have offended against some specific provision of Polish municipal law*."

[293]Royal Warrant, 14 June 1945, Army Order 81/45 with amendments, United Nations War Crimes Commission, Law Reports of Trials of War Criminals, Vol. I (1947), 105. See, however, Judge *Hunt* in his Separate Opinion in ICTY, Appeals Chamber Decision in *Ojdanić's* Motion Challenging Jurisdiction, arguing at para 18 "that, notwithstanding the domestic origin of the laws applied in many trials of persons charged with war crimes at that time, the law which was applied must now be regarded as having been accepted as part of customary international law."

[294]Trials of War Criminals Before the Nuernberg Military Tribunals Under Control Council Law No. 10 ("The Green Series").

[295]US Military Tribunals in the United States Zone see Ordinance No. 7, 18 October 1946, Art. I: "the purpose of this Ordinance is to provide for the establishment of military tribunals which shall have power to try and punish persons charged with offenses recognized as crimes in Article II of Control Council Law No. 10", printed in Trials of War Criminals Before the Nuernberg Military Tribunals Under Control Council Law No. 10 ("The Green Series"), Vol. I, October 1946 – April 1949.

the US military tribunal as to their classification as an "international" or "national" court.[296] The "questionable international character" of the US military tribunals was one of the reasons why judges *McDonald* and *Vohrah* in the ICTY *Erdemović* case treated those cases as "ordinary" domestic judgments that would not carry more weight in relation to the determination of customary international law.[297] In contrast, Judge *Cassese* did not deny that these US military tribunals are to be considered as national courts,[298] but he attributed greater weight to those judgments in comparison to "ordinary" domestic decisions. He states: "Control Council Law No. 10 can be regarded as an international agreement among the four Occupying Powers (subsequently transformed, to a large extent, into customary law), the action of the courts established or acting under that Law acquires an international relevance that cannot be attributed to national courts pronouncing solely on the strength of national law."[299] Thus, the authority of the US Military Tribunals to adjudicate and punish stemmed directly from Control Council Law No. 10, which despite the fact of their classification as domestic courts would give the tribunals greater authoritative weight as law-determining agencies than other post World War II jurisprudence.[300] Indeed, as has aptly been demonstrated by *Heller*, most of the US military tribunals considered that they applied international law, as their authority was based on Control Council Law No. 10, which they thought enshrined pre-existing international law.[301] Interestingly, in the *Justice* Case the US Military Tribunal highlighted that Control Council Law No. 10 incorporated the provisions of the IMT Nuremberg Charter, which "must be deemed declaratory of the principles of international law in view of its recognition as such by the General Assembly

---

[296]In the *Flick Case* the US Military Tribunal stated that it "is an international tribunal established by the International Control Council, the high legislative branch of the four Allied Powers (...) [that] administers international law", while the US Military Tribunal in the *Milch* Case, Trials of War Criminals Before the Nuremberg Military Tribunals under Control Council Law No. 10, Vol. II, 353ff, stated that "[i]t must be constantly borne in mind that this is an American court of Justice, applying the ancient and fundamental concepts of Anglo-Saxon jurisprudence." *Heller* (supra note 130), 113f, considers that the US military tribunals should be regarded as "inter-allied special tribunals".

[297]ICTY, *Erdemović* Appeals Judgment, Joint Separate Opinion of Judge McDonald and Judge Vohrah, paras 52ff.

[298]See ICTY, *Kupreškić* Trial Judgment, para 541.

[299]ICTY, *Erdemović* Appeals Judgment, Separate and Dissenting Opinion of Judge Cassese, para 27.

[300]See also SCSL, *Taylor* Appeals Judgment, para 419 (footnote 1301) determining that the US military tribunals "[a]s international tribunals applying an international agreement for the prosecution of crimes against humanity and war crimes, the NMTs' jurisprudence is indicative of customary international law." See also ICTY, *Furundžija* Trial Judgment, paras 195f arguing that in contrast to the US Military Tribunals operating under the strength of Control Council Law No. 10, before British Military courts "the law applied was domestic, thus rendering the pronouncements of the British courts less helpful in establishing rule of international law on this issue."

[301]*Heller* (supra note 130), 124.

of the United Nations."[302] As held above, in so far as the provisions of Control Council Law No. 10 incorporate provisions of substantive international criminal law as already contained in the IMT Nuremberg Statute, its legal authority can be deduced from the London agreement as well as the subsequent affirmation by the General Assembly.[303] In that regard the legal authority of Control Council Law No. 10 is interrelated with the IMT Nuremberg Statute. Such a deduced, process-oriented affirmation of the underlying legal principles, however, would only work where the law of the IMT Charter and Control Council Law No. 10 overlaps. For instance the *nexus* requirement between crimes against humanity and another crime within the jurisdiction of the IMT Nuremberg was contained in the Nuremberg Charter but was absent from Control Council Law No. 10. However, since the US military tribunals have read a nexus requirement into Control Council Law No. 10[304] modern international criminal tribunals have thus overstated the legal significance of Control Council Law No. 10 for the removal of the *nexus* requirement for crimes against humanity under customary international law in that regard.[305]

Furthermore, the use of the US Military Tribunals as law-determining agencies is limited to the substantive crimes and modes of liability that are covered by Control Council Law No. 10. For example, with regard to defenses in the ICTY *Erdemović* case, judges *McDonald* and *Vohrah* were right that while the "constitution, character and competence" of the US Military Tribunals adjudicating upon the strength of Control Council Law No. 10 might rest on international law, in substance "[t]here was no statement to the effect that the tribunals applied purely international law", and that at least with regard to the question of the use of duress as a defense "they invariably drew on the jurisprudence of their own national jurisdictions."[306] It is evident that in such cases the jurisprudence of the US Military Tribunals could not be said to function as law-determining agency for the establishment of customary international law.

7.7.4 Domestic Case Law

As shown above, domestic court decisions are better viewed as a "law-creating process" than as "law-determining agencies".[307] This holds true for all domestic cases, even post World War II cases, with the exception of the US military tribunal

---

[302]US Military Tribunal, *Altstötter and Others Case*, 968. See also *Heller* (supra note 130), 123.

[303]See Sect. 7.5.3.1, Statutes of the IMT, IMTFE and Control Council Law No. 10; see also Sect. 7.6.2.2, UN General Assembly Resolutions as Law-Determining Agencies.

[304]See the references in *Heller* (supra note 213), 383.

[305]See for example ICTY, *Kupreškić* Trial Chamber Judgment, para 577.

[306]ICTY, *Erdemović* Appeals Judgment, Joint Separate Opinion of Judge McDonald and Judge Vohrah, para 54. See also *Heller* (supra note 213), 376–7.

[307]See Sect. 6.3.4.3, International Case Law as Subsidiary Means for the Determination of Customary International Law.

cases held under Control Council Law No. 10 as contained in the "green series". Even though certain cases before international criminal tribunals endorse the view that domestic decisions can be used as subsidiary means for the determination of a rule of customary law,[308] caveats on the use of domestic decisions as law-determining agencies are much more frequent.[309] The reason for such a restricted use of domestic decisions as law-determining agencies of customary international law generally lies in the fact that domestic courts base their decisions on domestic law or "interpret international rules through the prism of national legislation."[310] It is precisely the prism of national legislation that leads to the unwanted result that domestic courts apply a national interpretation of international law that would be detrimental to using that case law as a subsidiary mean for the determination of customary law.[311] Thus, considering domestic case law as material for the "law-creating process" of customary international law by international criminal tribunals is preferable. In general, domestic decisions have been treated by international criminal tribunals as an instance of State practice.[312] However, it needs to be reemphasized that domestic decisions applying international law—or what they think is international law—or a domestic transformation of international law, may provide evidence for both "law-creating process" ingredients, State practice and *opinio iuris*.[313] In certain instances the domestic courts as State organs do not only contribute to the formation of State practice through their decisions, but indicate *opinio iuris* as well when they apply law that according to the belief of the domestic court is part of or conforms to international customary law.

---

[308]See for example ICTY *Kupreškić* Trial Judgment, para 541: "In many instances no less value may be given to decisions on international crimes delivered by national courts operating pursuant to the 1948 Genocide Convention, or the 1949 Geneva Conventions or the 1977 Protocols or similar international treaties. In these instances the international framework on the basis of which the national court operates and the fact that *in essence the court applies international substantive law*, may lend great weight to rulings of such courts." (emphasis added).

[309]ICTY, *Furundžija* Trial Judgment, para 194: "one should constantly be mindful of the need for great caution in using national case law for the purpose of determining whether customary rules of international criminal law have evolved in a particular matter." ICTY, *Kupreškić* Trial Judgment, para 542, determining that tribunals "should apply a stricter level of scrutiny to national decisions than to international judgments, as the latter are at least based on the same *corpus* of law as that applied by international courts, whereas the former tend to apply national law, or primarily that law, or else interpret international rules through the prism of national legislation." See also ECCC, Case No 002 Pre-Trial Chamber Public Decision on the JCE Appeals, para 82: "These cases, in which domestic courts applied domestic law, do not amount to international case law and the Pre-Trial Chamber does not consider them as proper precedents for the purpose of determining the status of customary law in this area."

[310]ICTY, *Kupreškić* Trial Judgment, para 542.

[311]See also P. M. Moremen, National Court Decisions as State Practice: A Transnational Judicial Dialogue?, in 32 North Carolina Journal of international Law & Commercial Regulation (2006), 291.

[312]See in that regard the reference to ICTY jurisprudence in Sect. 6.3.1.1, Preliminary Remarks.

[313]A. Nollkaemper, Decisions of National Courts as Sources of International Law: An Analysis of the Practice of the ICTY, in Boas/Schabas (eds.), International Criminal law Developments in the Case Law of the ICTY (2003), 281–283.

7.8 International Law Commission

Another source that is regularly referred to by international criminal tribunals are the various drafts of and commentaries to the International Law Commission's (ILC) "Code of Crimes Against the Peace and Security of Mankind".[314] While the ILC drafts were often referred to without any further indication as to their relevance for the determination of customary international law, some chambers have given more insights: the ICTY *Delalić* Appeals Chamber determined that since the "ILC comments on the draft articles drew from existing practice, they deserve close attention".[315] However, it needs to be stressed that ILC Draft articles and commentaries thereto cannot be considered under the category of the law-creating process for the formation of customary international law. The members of the ILC are elected in their individual capacity and do not represent a State.[316] Consequently the work of the ILC itself cannot be used as evidence of the constituent elements of State practice or *opinio iuris*. International criminal tribunals have indicated that it is more appropriate to refer to the ILC drafts as subsidiary means that may constitute evidence of customary international law.[317] Despite this overwhelming support in the jurisprudence of international criminal tribunals to use the ILC drafts as "law-determining agencies, the present author considers that the ECCC Supreme Court Chamber in the *Duch* Case, with its cautious approach for the use of ILC drafts, offers a preferable solution: While it considered that ILC drafts may in certain instances be used as evidence of customary international law,[318] the task of the ILC is not merely to codify pre-existing international law but equally to promote "the progressive development of international law".[319] As the ECCC Supreme Court Chamber has rightly held, the work of the ILC may have been carried out in the "fluctuation between these two mandates" and since "the ILC did not clearly distinguish in its work when it was working under which of these mandates, the Supreme Court Chamber may not automatically conclude that the ILC draft codes

---

[314]See the references to the ILC *inter alia* in ICTY, *Tadić* Trial Judgment, para 655 determining that a State policy is not a general requirement for crimes against humanity; *Delalić* Trial Judgment, para 309 in order to strengthen the argument that war crimes can be committed in non-international armed conflicts, and para 342 when elaborating on command responsibility; *Blaškić* Trial Judgment, para 217 being "guided by the work of the ILC" to determine the elements of the crime of murder; see also SCSL, *Taylor* Appeals Judgment, para 428 viewing the 1996 Draft Code as an "authoritative international legal instrument"; see also ECCC, *Duch* Appeals Judgment, paras 114ff.

[315]ICTY, *Delalić* Appeals Judgment, para 234.

[316]See also ICTY, *Hadžihasanović* Appeals Chamber Decision, Separate and Partially Dissenting Opinion of Judge Hunt, para 26.

[317]See in that regard ICTY, *Vasiljević* Trial Judgment, para 200; *Furundžija* Trial Judgment, para 227; *Kunarac* Trial Judgment, para 537; SCSL, *Taylor* Appeals Judgment, para 428.

[318]ECCC, *Duch* Appeals Judgment, para 114.

[319]See Statute of the International Law Commission, Art. 1 as adopted by the General Assembly in Resolution 174 (II) (1947).

of international offences always capture 'extensive State practice, precedent and doctrine'."[320] It is for these reasons that the work of the ILC is problematic as subsidiary means for the determination of a rule of customary international law.

7.9   Writings of Legal Doctrine

Art. 38 (1) (d) ICJ Statute lists the "teachings of the most highly qualified publicists of the various nations" alongside judicial decisions as subsidiary means for the determination of a rule of law. While it has been argued that judicial decisions are more authoritative than legal writings,[321] it seems that at least in relation to the classics of international law legal doctrine has had a much greater influence on the creation and determination of international law.[322] As *Koskenniemi* remarked, a Grotian lawyer "would simply say that some norms exist by force of nature or social necessity."[323] However, "at the present time, the position has undergone a profound alteration compared to the era of Grotius *et al.* No contemporary scholar can create international law."[324] It is thus clear that scholarly writings might "merely" be considered as "subsidiary means". For this purpose scholars have conducted thorough studies of customary international law, "collecting instances of practice together, which states, courts and advocates may not have the ability or time to do".[325] Thus, in contrast to Grotius' times, the determination of customary law by the legal doctrine depends on the legal quality of the analysis. Ultimately the authority of scholarly research rests upon an adequate analysis of the "law creating process", the constituent elements of customary international law.[326]

---

[320]ECCC, *Duch* Appeals Judgment, paras 115 and 116.

[321]*G. G. Fitzmaurice*, Some Problems Regarding the Formal Sources of International Law, in Koskenniemi (ed.), Sources of International Law (2000), 76: a "tribunal, while it may well treat juridical opinion as something which is of interest but of no direct authority, and which the tribunal is free to disregard, will not usually feel free to ignore a relevant decisions, and will normally feel obliged to treat it as something that must be accepted, or else – for good reason – rejected, but which must in any event be taken fully into account." See also *R. Cryer*, Of Custom, Treaties, Scholars and the Gavel: The Influence of the International Criminal Tribunals on the ICRC Customary Law Study, 11 Journal of Conflict & Security Law (2006), 248.

[322]*M. Wood*, Teachings of the Most Highly Qualified Publicists, in R. Wolfrum (ed.), Max Planck Encyclopedia of Public International Law, online edition (2010), MN 8. *C. Parry*, The Sources and Evidences of International Law (1965), 103.

[323]*M. Koskenniemi*, The Pull of the Mainstream, 88 Michigan Law Review (1990), 1947.

[324]*Y. Dinstein*, The Interaction between Customary and International Law and Treaties, 322 Recueil des Cours (2006), 314. See also *T. Hoffmann*, The Gentle Civilizer of Humanitarian Law, in Stahn/van den Herik (eds.), Future Perspectives on International Criminal Justice (2010), 79–80 who, however, considers that *Cassese* is a lawyer in the tradition of Grotius and Lauterpacht.

[325]*Cryer* (supra note 321), 248 (footnote 61).

[326]*Dinstein* (supra note 324), 314–5.

The jurisprudence of international criminal tribunals clearly reveals that they drew heavily on the writings of legal doctrine, be it individual scholars,[327] a group of scholars such as the ILC,[328] or the work of the ICRC. Generally, international criminal tribunals do not indicate what role the references to the legal doctrine should play in the determination of customary international law. Since legal doctrine merely could function as a "law-determining agency", as subsidiary means for the determination of customary international law, reference to scholarly writing could only be significant if the legal doctrine conducted an analysis of the constituent elements. However, such discussion is generally missing from the jurisprudence of the international criminal tribunals.

Interestingly, with regard to the ICRC, the ICTY *Tadić* Appeals Chamber has determined that "[t]he practical results the ICRC has thus achieved in inducing compliance with international humanitarian law ought therefore to be regarded as *an element of actual international practice*; this is an element that has been conspicuously instrumental in the emergence or crystallization of customary rules."[329] From the wording it is unclear whether the Appeals Chamber treats the work of the ICRC itself as an element of "international practice", which it considers relevant for the formation of customary international law, or whether the ICRC by "inducing compliance" merely triggers subsequent State practice. However, later chambers have stated that while the commentaries of the ICRC are relevant material for the interpretation of the 1949 Geneva Conventions, "they do not constitute state practice".[330] Thus, the work of the ICRC cannot be used as relevant material with regards to the constituent elements. The ICRC Custom Study[331] also found frequent reference in the jurisprudence of international criminal tribunals. While the ICTY *Hadžihasanović* Trial Chamber considered the document to be "an authoritative source on the subject",[332] international criminal tribunals generally do not give further indication on its relevance. More often the ICRC Custom Study has

---

[327]See for example ICTY Jurisprudence in relation to the crime of genocide when elaborating on the intent to destroy, in whole or in part, *Jelisić* Trial Judgment, paras 78ff, *Krstić* Trial Judgment, paras 584ff, and *Krstić* Appeals Judgment, paras 6ff relying heavily on the scholarly writing of *S. Glaser*, Droit international pénal conventionnel (1970), *N. Robinson*, The Genocide Convention (1960), *P. Drost*, The Crime of State, Book II, Genocide (1959), and *W. Schabas*, Genocide in International Law (2000).

[328]See the references in supra note 314. Jurisprudence of the ICTY and SCSL has indicated that "at the very least" ILC drafts may be used as being indicative of the legal views of the most highly qualified publicist of the major legal systems of the world within the meaning of Art. 38 (1) (d) ICJ Statute, see ICTY, *Furundžija* Trial Judgment, para 227; SCSL, *Taylor* Appeals Judgment, para 428. *Dinstein* determines that a group of scholars may carry more authoritative weight than individual views of single scholars, *Dinstein* (supra note 324), 314–5.

[329]ICTY, *Tadić* Appeals Chamber Jurisdiction Decision, para 109 (emphasis added).

[330]See for example ICTY, *Vasiljević* Trial Judgment, para 203 (footnote 549).

[331]*J.-M. Henckaerts*, Customary International Humanitarian Law (2005) (ICRC Custom Study).

[332]ICTY, *Hadžihasanović* Trial Judgment, para 253.

been mentioned in passing, in a footnote and without further discussion.[333] The preferred approach is to use the underlying material in the ICRC Customs Study, *i.e.* the State practice and/or *opinio iuris* the ICRC relied upon, in order to determine whether on that basis a specific customary international norm could be said to exist.[334] It is thus clear that the source of the determination of customary international law is not the ICRC Custom Study itself, but it is a "documentary source"[335] of the constitutive elements to customary international law.

7.10 Concluding Remarks

It is safe to argue that the jurisprudence of international criminal tribunals lacks methodological clarity with regards to the precise legal value of the material it referred to when proving the existence of customary international criminal law. In order to subject the methodological foundations of the determination of customary international criminal law to a comprehensible examination the evidentiary instances must be clearly allocated to either the "law-creating processes"—giving evidence to the constituent elements of customary international law of State practice and *opinio iuris*—or the "law-determining agencies", *i.e.* subsidiary means for the determination of a rule of law. The earlier chapters have analyzed the most relevant material referred to by international criminal tribunals, considering the methodological value these instances may have when proving the existence of customary international criminal law.

---

[333]See for the ICTY: *Prosecutor v. Gotovina*, IT-06-90-T, Trial Chamber, Judgment, 15 April 2011, para 1779; *Đorđević* Trial Judgment, para 2066; *Boškoski* Trial Judgment, para 205; *Orić* Appeals Judgment, para 30; *Halilović* Trial Judgment, para 39; see for the SCSL, *Fofana* Appeals Judgment, para 404.

[334]See for the ICTY: *Martić* Trial Judgment, para 466 referring to military manuals as State practice contained in *J.-M. Henckaerts*, Customary International Humanitarian Law (2005) (ICRC Custom Study); *Naletilić* Appeals Judgment, Separate and Partly Dissenting Opinion of Judge Schomburg, para 15 relying on the State practice quoted in the ICRC Custom Study; see also SCSL, *Sesay* Trial Judgment, paras 213ff referring to official pronouncements of States before the UN General Assembly and Security Council as State practice contained in the ICRC Custom Study.

[335]*Pellet* describes subsidiary means as "documentary sources", see *Pellet* (supra note 24), 854, MN 305.

Chapter 8
Conclusion

The rich jurisprudence of international criminal tribunals has woken international criminal law from a long sleep. Indeed, beginning with the ICTY, the international community *via* the UN Security Council has set up an international criminal tribunal for the first time since the Nuremberg era and has stopped turning a blind eye to the enforcement of international criminal law at the international level. The ICTY paved the way for a "proliferation"[1] of various international criminal tribunals, such as the ICTR, SCSL, and ECCC, finally resulting in the creation of a permanent institution, the ICC. As held above, apart from the ICC, international criminal tribunals have generally made their convictions dependent on the existence of a crime under customary international law.[2] This study has demonstrated

---

[1]*A. Pellet*, Article 38, in Zimmerman et al (eds.), The Statute of the International Court of Justice – A Commentary (2012), 860, MN 320.

[2]See for the ICTY: *Prosecutor v. Hadžihasanović*, IT-01-47-T, Trial Chamber, Judgment, 15 March 2006, para 254: "To prove the existence of a customary rule, the two constituent elements of the custom must be established, namely, the existence of sufficiently consistent practices (material element), and the conviction of States that they are bound by this uncodified practice, as they are by a rule of positive law (mental element)"; *Hadžihasanović* Appeals Chamber Decision, para 12: "to hold that a principle was part of customary international law, it has to be satisfied that State practice recognized the principle on basis of supporting *opinio juris*"; *Furundžija* Appeals Judgment), Declaration of Judge Patrick Robinson, para 281: "in seeking to ascertain international custom [. . .] what one is looking for is a sufficiently widespread practice of states accompanied by *opinio juris*." See for the SCSL: *Norman* Appeals Chamber Decision, para 17: "The formation of custom requires both state practice and a sense of pre-existing obligation (opinio juris)." For the ECCC see Trial Chamber Decision on Armed Conflict Nexus Requirement, para 12 (footnote 40): "The content of customary international law derives from the actual practice of states and opinio juris"; see also Pre-Trial Chamber JCE Appeals Decision, para 53: "The Pre-Trial Chamber recalls that, when determining the state of customary international law in relation to the existence of a crime or a form of individual responsibility, a court shall assess existence of common, consistent and concordant state practice, or *opinio juris*, meaning that what States do and say represents the law. A wealth of state practice does not usually carry with it a presumption that *opinio juris* exists".

© Springer International Publishing AG 2017

T. Rauter, *Judicial Practice, Customary International Criminal Law and* Nullum *Crimen Sine Lege*, DOI 10.1007/978-3-319-64477-6_8

that international criminal tribunals have applied different methodological approaches when determining customary international criminal law.[3] The doctrinal foundation of certain findings of customary law by international criminal tribunals has been the point of heavy critique in the literature.[4] Whether one considers this critique as just is dependent on one's dogmatic and philosophical concept of the foundations of customary international law.[5]

The SCSL *Taylor* Appeals Chamber held that international criminal tribunals merely "act as the instruments of States"[6] and that their mandate authorized them only to "apply customary international law as it stands".[7] However this assessment hardly is consistent with reality. The judges at international criminal tribunals have been forced to adjudicate in a legal sphere in which they did not necessarily find clear legal norms.[8] As has been suggested by *Shahabuddeen* "[t]he state of international criminal law was meager at the time of the establishment of the ICTY".[9] In such a setting, resort to a judicial "activism" or "creativity"[10] with regard to the determination of customary international criminal law is quite understandable. It can even be stated that due to the meager state of international criminal law, international criminal tribunals were given no other choice in certain cases but to fill a void in international legislation, assuming in that regard the responsibility of States. The States, as the principal law-creators in the international legal sphere, neglected the task to equip them with precise international criminal norms adequate to fulfill their task to deliver justice. So the international criminal tribunals turned to the flexibility and doctrinal confusion surrounding customary international law as a source of law. Consequently, they have certainly been much more than just "the mouth that reproduces the meaning of the law" as demanded by *Montesquieu*.[11] As

---

[3]See Chap. 6, Methodological Approaches to Customary International Law by International Criminal Tribunals.

[4]W. *Schabas*, Customary Law or "Judge-Made" Law: Judicial Creativity at the UN Criminal Tribunals, in Doria (ed.), The Legal Regime of the International Criminal Court (2009), 86; *Bantekas*, Reflections on Some Sources and Methods of International Criminal and Humanitarian Law, 6 International Criminal Law Review (2006), 121ff; A. *Zahar, G. Sluiter*, International Criminal Law (2008), 105; A. *Nollkaemper*, The Legitimacy of International Law in the Case Law of the International Criminal Tribunal for the Former Yugoslavia, in Vandamme/Reestman (eds.), Ambiguity in the Rule of Law (2001), 17.

[5]An overview on the different methodological approaches to customary international law can be found in Chap. 4, The Formation of Customary International Law and Its Methodological Challenges.

[6]SCSL, *Taylor* Appeals Judgment, para 463 (emphasis added).

[7]SCSL, *Taylor* Appeals Judgment, para 464 (emphasis added).

[8]R. *Heinsch*, Die Weiterentwicklung des humanitären Völkerrechts durch die Strafgerichtshöfe für das ehemalige Jugoslawien und Ruanda (2007), 371.

[9]M. *Shahabuddeen*, Judicial Creativity and Joint Criminal Enterprise, in Darcy, Powderly (eds.), Judicial Creativity at the International Criminal Tribunals (2010), 187.

[10]See also the other contributions in Darcy, Powderly (eds.), Judicial Creativity at the International Criminal Tribunals (2010).

[11]C. *de Secondat, Baron de Montesquieu*, De l'Esprit des lois. Livre XI, Chapitre 6 (1748).

has aptly been held by *Mettraux* "[i]n the history of international criminal law, international tribunals have done more than merely give jural *imprimatur* to norms in waiting and have been much more than mere 'evidential sources' of customary law. In effect, taking advantage of the plasticity and indeterminacy of customary law, international courts and tribunals, not least the *ad hoc* Tribunals, have often acted as 'customary midwives', 'des accoucheurs de norms coutumières', so that international criminal law may owe more to judges than any other part of international law."[12] As 'customary midwives' the lines between a mere application, a development and the creation of customary international criminal law are blurred. The development of customary international criminal law through the jurisprudence of international criminal tribunals is in line with the so-called "judicilization" of international law.[13] One could even argue that contemporary judicial law-making by international tribunals is a political and legal reality in the international legal sphere.[14]

The notion of a clear dividing line between a mere application and creation of law is probably more a myth than reality. However, judicial law-making at the international level is generally concealed: As *Jennings* argued, one essential function of the judiciary is to give the impression that it is merely applying existing rules of law, even if in reality a court creates law.[15] For such concealed law-making *Shapiro* even brands judges as liars.[16] While at the international level progressive determinations of customary international law are generally unproblematic when States are in the dock, the situation could be different in international criminal proceedings. The relationship between the human rights of the accused and the progressive determination of customary international criminal law is a fraught one. However, the *nullum crimen sine iure* principle in general, and the question as to what are the concrete requirements of the *praevia* and *certa* components in relation to customary international criminal law as a legal basis in international criminal proceedings, have not gained much attention in the jurisprudence of international criminal tribunals. This study has tried to fill the *nullum crimen sine iure* principle with content, in particular with regard to customary international law as the underlying source of individual criminal responsibility. As stated above,[17] if strict requirements for *nullum crimen sine iure praevia* are applied, customary

---

[12]G. *Mettraux*, International Crimes and the *ad hoc* Tribunals (2005), 14.

[13]G. I. *Hernandez*, The Judicialization of International Law: Reflections on the Empirical Turn, 25 European Journal of International Law (2014), 919ff, discussing the following books: K. J. *Alter*, The New Terrain of International Law. Courts, Politics, Rights (2014), *Romano et al* (eds.), The Oxford Handbook of International Adjudication (2014), Y. *Shany*, Assessing the Effectiveness of International Courts (2014).

[14]See for example A. *von Bogdandy*, I. *Venzke*, Beyond Dispute: International Judicial Institutions as Lawmakers, in von Bogdandy and Venzke (eds.), International Judicial Lawmaking (2012), 3ff;

[15]As quoted by T. *Ginsburg*, Bounded Discretion in Judicial Lawmaking, 45 Virginia Journal of International Law (2004), 636.

[16]M. *Shapiro*, Judges as Liars, 17 Harvard Journal of Law & Public Policy (1994), 155ff.

[17]See Sect. 3.10.5.4, The *praevia* Requirement and Customary International Law.

international criminal law could solely be established on the basis of the traditional method for the determination of customary international law. Thus, customary international law could only be proven to exist by establishing consistent, general and enduring State practice, coupled with *opinio iuris*, that is the subjective conviction of States that their acts (*i.e.* State practice) are required by an already existing rule of international law.[18] Other methodological approaches to customary international law beyond this traditional method would necessarily violate the *nullum crimen sine iure praevia* requirement.[19] However, an analysis of the jurisprudence of international criminal tribunals reveals a hesitation on the part of the chambers to adhere to the traditional method when establishing customary international criminal law. Indeed, it can be stated that the chambers pay lip-service to the traditional two-element approach when elaborating on abstract theory,[20] but they manifestly fail to deliver concrete evidence for State practice and *opinio iuris* in practice when establishing a specific customary international criminal norm.[21] That is not to say that the chambers of international criminal tribunals were necessarily wrong in their determination of customary international law. However, since they neglect the task to establish adequate, objective evidence of concrete instances of State practice and *opinio iuris* to bolster their findings, these findings cannot be critically scrutinized in light of the traditional requirements of consistent, general and enduring State practice coupled with *opinio iuris*.[22] Furthermore, it is uncertain how by adhering to a stringent *nullum crimen sine iure praevia* requirement, they could justify the departure from the traditional requirement of 'extensive and virtually uniform' State practice when establishing customary international law as demanded by the ICJ.[23] And yet this has been done by some chambers of international criminal tribunals in relation to customary international criminal law.[24] Moreover, the application of other methodological approaches to the determination of customary international criminal law, such as the deductive approach,[25] or approaches that are primarily being based on *opinio iuris* or *opinio iuris sive necessitatis*,[26] appear questionable in light of stringent *nullum crimen sine iure praevia* requirements.

---

[18]See Sect. 4.2.1, State Practice Under a Traditional and Sect. 4.2.2, Opinio Iuris Under a Traditional.

[19]These other approaches to customary international law are discussed in Sect. 4.3, Modern Customary International Law.

[20]See references to the jurisprudence in Sect. 6.3.1.1, Preliminary Remarks.

[21]See Chap. 6, Methodological Approaches to Customary International Law by International Criminal Tribunals.

[22]This is the reason why international criminal tribunals when determining customary international criminal law should have an obligation of "methodological disclosure", see Sect. 6.1, The Disclosure of the Method.

[23]See ICJ, North Sea Continental Shelf Cases, para 74.

[24]See Sect. 6.3.1.3, High Frequency and High Consistency of State Practice.

[25]See Sect. 6.3.3, Deductive Approach.

[26]See Sect. 6.3.3.2, Value-Based Deductive Approach and Deduction from Technical Humanitarian Principles.

If one was nevertheless to accept that the international criminal tribunals adhered to *nullum crimen sine iure praevia*, it appears that the principle must be considered flexible enough to undergo a variety of different methodological approaches for the determination of customary international criminal law. Under such a more lenient definition, the central issue does not concern the *praevia* requirement. Rather it raises the problem of how to take recourse to customary international law as a legal basis for criminal convictions, with the requirements of accessibility of the international criminal norm and foreseeability of criminal punishment as demanded by *nullum crimen sine iure certa*.[27] However, it is clear that international criminal tribunals did not adhere to stringent *nullum crimen sine iure certa* requirements. Objections from the individual defendants have been rejected on the grounds of the manifest illegality/immorality of the underlying conduct, or by establishing the criminality of the underlying conduct by taking recourse to domestic criminal law.[28] Apart from the case law of the ECCC, international criminal tribunals have not tried to establish whether accessibility or foreseeability can be established on the basis of the concrete customary international criminal norm.[29] In this study different approaches as to how accessibility to the concrete customary international criminal norm and foreseeability of individual criminal responsibility can be established have been considered.[30]

In order to make the determination of customary international criminal law more comprehensible, this study has proposed an exact allocation of the evidence referred to when establishing customary international criminal norms to the constituent elements of customary international law, and to keep a precise differentiation between the "law-creating processes" and the "law-determining agencies".[31] This would not only ensure that a judgment is considered as being based on a well-founded reasoning therewith the individual can comprehend the basis of his/her conviction, but would enhance the perceived legitimacy of international criminal justice. Consequently, sound methodological approaches for the determination of customary international criminal norms are not only crucial for abstract legal theory, but enable us to determine whether the human rights of individual defendants have been infringed when international criminal tribunals have created law retroactively, or have excessively interpreted the contours of a crime or mode of liability under customary international criminal law. This is, due to the manifest immorality of the underlying conduct, hard to assert. One might even argue that too stringent *nullum crimen sine iure* requirements would have impeded the entire

---

[27]See Sect. 3.10.6.4, The *certa* Requirement and Customary International Criminal Law.

[28]See Sect. 3.10.6.3, The *certa* Requirement as a Safeguard Requirement for the Individual.

[29]See Sect. 3.10.6.4, The *certa* Requirement and Customary International Criminal Law.

[30]See Sect. 3.10.6.4, The *certa* Requirement and Customary International Criminal Law.

[31]See Chap. 7, Relevant Material for Proving the Existence of Customary International Criminal Law.

development of international criminal law. In the words of the US Military Tribunal in the Justice Case, international criminal law would have been "strangled" at birth.[32] Indeed, the case law of the ECtHR does not address the questions of accessibility and foreseeability under Art. 7 ECHR overly positivistic when international core crimes are at stake, as long as it was theoretically possible for the individual to be aware of a possible criminal prosecution.[33] In contrast, the present author considers a greater focus on the *nullum crimen sine iure certa* requirements for the customary law basis of individual criminal responsibility is necessary. This would ensure that the relativization of the accessibility/foreseeability requirements does not come at the expense of the precision of the methodological foundation when determining customary international criminal law.

It might be said that with the adoption of the Rome Statute the importance of customary international law as a legal basis for individual criminal responsibility has lost its relevance. As argued above, the Rome Statute takes an exceptional place among the statutes of international criminal tribunals: as an international convention it does not only create the jurisdictional frame for the ICC, but is in itself the source of substantial criminal norms binding on individuals of its State parties when it has jurisdiction over them. However, if the ICC were concerned with a situation involving nationals of a non-State party, in such cases it would be necessary to demonstrate that the Rome Statute reflects customary international law. In such case customary international law is the proper legal source for establishing the criminal responsibility of the national of the non-State party.[34] Furthermore, even though the State parties to the Rome Conference have agreed on a permanent international criminal court, that fact alone does not exclude the possibility that in the future international criminal *ad hoc* tribunals might be established that adjudicate upon customary international criminal law. The questions raised within this study thus have not lost their relevance, merely because the ICC has been created by its State parties.

It might even be argued that the creation of the Rome Statute, and the precise definitions within the elements of crimes, should ensure that judges at the ICC are rather applying the law as laid down in the texts, thus restricting the possibility of judicial development of law. Indeed, with these "handcuffs" on the ICC judges the State parties possibly wanted to ensure that they retain control over the development of international criminal law, a direct consequence of the progressive jurisprudence of the UN *ad hoc* tribunals, suggesting a mistrust in the judges.[35] Indeed, judicial law-making in disguise *via* customary international law by judicial

---

[32]US Military Tribunal, *Altstötter and Others Case*, 974–5.

[33]See also W. *Schabas*, The International Criminal Court. A Commentary on the Rome Statute (2010), Art. 22, 404.

[34]See Sect. 3.10.3, The *scripta* Requirement and the Sources of International Law: International Conventions as the Sole Legal Basis for Individual Criminal Responsibility?

[35]Cf. *D. Hunt*, The International Criminal Court – High Hopes, Creative Ambiguity and an Unfortunate Mistrust in International Judges, 2 Journal of International Criminal Justice (2004), 56ff.

institutions that are merely created as law-declaring institutions could only receive its legitimacy subsequently by adequate State consent.[36] One has to agree with *Arajärvi* that "the discovery of past misinterpretation of a concept – classifying a norm under customary international law when in fact it is not yet crystallized in practice and/or *opinio juris* – but which is then followed as if it were part of customary international law by states and other entities, does not denounce its normative validity."[37] Even though the underlying decision could be regarded as a misjudgment, the subsequent affirmation would render it a proper legal basis in the future. Such a possibility of judicial law-making in international criminal law had already been discussed by Judge *Pal* with regard to the IMTFE Judgment: "law can also be created illegally otherwise than by the recognized procedures—*ex injuria jus oritur*: Any law now created in this manner and applied will perhaps be the law henceforth."[38] For example, doubts on the soundness of the methodological approach of the ICTY *Tadić* Appeals Chamber in its Jurisdiction Decision,[39] determining international humanitarian law governing internal armed conflicts and the criminality thereto under customary international law, from today's standpoint have lost its relevance. As *Kress* has argued, "retrospectively, with a view to present and future customary law the significance of such criticisms is in any event rapidly decreasing."[40] The States parties to the ICC Statute affirmed the position of the *Tadić* Appeals Chamber in Rome.[41] When negotiating the war crimes provision of Art. 8 Rome Statute, which includes provisions on non-international armed conflicts, the State parties considered that the provision should be reflective of customary international law.[42] However, in addition to such active State consent, other writers argued that judicial law making in disguise *via* customary international law could also be remedied by mere *acquiescence*.[43] The late Judge *Cassese*, as presiding judge in the Appeals Chamber at the STL, advocated the same line of thinking, which amounts to a methodological *coup de main*: In relation to the

---

[36]See *G. Schwarzenberger*, The Inductive Approach to International Law (1965), 10; *Heinsch* (supra note 8), 357–358; *A. Roberts, S. Sivakumaran*, Lawmaking by Nonstate Actors: Engaging Armed Groups in the Creation of International Humanitarian Law, 37 The Yale Journal of International Law (2012), 117–118.

[37]*N. Arajärvi*, The Lines Begin to Blur? Opinio Juris and the Moralisation of Customary International Law, 12 available http://papers.ssrn.com/sol3/papers.cfm?abstract_id=1823288& rec=1&srcabs=1599679&alg=1&pos=1 (last visited 16 June 2017).

[38]Judge *R. Pal*, Dissentient Judgement (1953), 26.

[39]ICTY, *Tadić* Appeals Chamber Jurisdiction Decision.

[40]*C. Kress*, War Crimes Committed in Non-international Armed Conflict and the Emerging System of International Criminal Justice, 30 Israel Yearbook on Human Rights (2001), 107.

[41]*Kress, id*, 107; *Roberts, Sivakumaran* (supra note 36), 117. *A. M. Danner*, When Courts Make Law: How the International Criminal Tribunals Recast the Laws of War, Vanderbilt University Law School Public Law and Legal Theory, Working Paper Number 05-30 (2005), 31.

[42]*Kress, id*, 109. See also *D. Robinson, H. von Hebel*, War Crimes in Internal Conflicts: Article 8 of the ICC Statute, 2 Yearbook of International Humanitarian Law (1999), 209.

[43]*Heinsch* (supra note 8), 357–358. Generally on the issue of *acquiescence* in relation to *opinio iuris* see Sect. 4.2.2, Opinio Iuris Under a Traditional Interpretation.

customary law status of the inherent jurisdiction of international judicial bodies, he stated that "[t]he combination of a string of decisions in this field, coupled with the implicit acceptance or acquiescence of all the international subjects concerned, clearly indicates the existence of the practice and *opinio juris* necessary for holding that a customary rule of international law has evolved."[44] According to this position, due to the implicit acceptance or acquiescence and lack of protest of States, any necessary proof of State practice and *opinio juris* is renounced. Only through the judicial practice—in *Cassese's* words the "combination of a string of decisions"—could customary international law develop. Indeed, with regard to acquiescence one might fundamentally challenge whether "silence does in fact equal consent".[45] But if such an approach finds followers, States as the principal law-making entities would be required to engage with the decisions of international tribunals, to reject the findings of "rogue" international tribunals actively in order to "opt-out" of their customary law findings. Otherwise they might very well find themselves in the same position as the sorcerer's apprentice of *Goethe*: "Ah, here comes the master! I have need of Thee! From the spirits that I called Sir, deliver me!" Indeed, concerning the way customary international law is determined the question remains as to whether States as the traditional law-makers in public international law could still be considered to be the "master" of customary international law.

---

[44]STL, Decision on Appeal of Pre-Trial Judge's Order Regarding Jurisdiction and Standing, Case No. CH/AC/2010/02, 10 November 2010, para 47.

[45]*J. Kammerhofer*, Uncertainty in International Law – A Kelsenian Perspective (2011), 78.

List of References

Jurisprudence

Domestic Case Law

Austrian Supreme Court, *Austrian Treasury v. Auer*, 14 Annual Digest and Reports of Public International Law Cases (1947), Case No. 125

British Military Court, *Trial of Kapitänleutnant Eck and Others* ("Peleus Trial"), Law Reports of the Trials of War Criminals, Vol. I, 1ff

British Military Court, *Trial of Werner Rohde and Others*, Law Reports of the Trials of War Criminals, Vol. V, 54ff

British Military Court, *Trial of Otto Sandrock and Others* ("Almelo Trial"), Law Reports of the Trials of War Criminals, Vol. I, 35ff

British Military Court, *Trial of Franz Schonfeld and Others*, Law Reports of the Trials of War Criminals, Vol. XI, 64ff

British Military Court, *Trial of Max Wielen and Others* ("Stalag Luft III Case"), Law Reports of the Trials of War Criminals, Vol. XI, 33ff

Supreme Court of Canada, *R. v. Finta*, (1994) 1 S.C.R. 701

French Court of Cassation, *Soubrouillard contre Kilbourg*, Gazette du Palais (1948), Vol. II

French Court of Cassation (Criminal Chamber), Fédération Nationale des Déportés et Internés Résistants et Patriotes and Others v. Barbie, Excerpts of the judgments of 6 October 1983, 26 January 1984 and 20 December 1985, 78 International Law Reports (1988), 125ff

French Military Tribunal, in re *Roechling and others*, 15 Annual Digest and Reports of Public International Law Cases (1948)

German Supreme Court in the British Occupied Zone, K. und A., StS 18/48, Entscheidungen des Obersten Gerichtshofs für die Britische Zone. Entscheidungen in Strafsachen, Vol. I (1949)

Federal Constitutional Court of Germany, *Jorgić* Case, 2 BvR 1290/99, 12 December 2000

Italian Court of Appeals of Bologna, *Maltoni v. Companini*, 71 Foro Italiano (1948), Vol. I

Supreme Court of Israel, Attorney General of Israel v. Eichmann, Judgment, 29 May 1962, 36 International Law Reports (1968), 277ff

Netherlands Special Court of Cassation, *Trial of Hans Albin Rauter*, Law Reports of the Trials of War Criminals, Vol. XIV, 89ff

Netherlands Special Court in Amsterdam and Netherlands Special Court of Cassation, *Trial of Willy Zuehlke*, Law Reports of the Trials of War Criminals, Vol. XIV, 139ff

© Springer International Publishing AG 2017   239
T. Rauter, *Judicial Practice, Customary International Criminal Law and* Nullum Crimen Sine Lege, DOI 10.1007/978-3-319-64477-6

Norway Court of Appeal, *Johansen v. Gross*, 16 Annual Digest and Reports of Public International Law Cases (1949)

Supreme National Tribunal of Poland, *Trial of Dr. Joseph Buhler*, Law Reports of the Trials of War Criminals, Vol. XIV, 23ff

Supreme National Tribunal of Poland, *Trial of Gauleiter Greiser*, Law Reports of the Trials of War Criminals, Vol. XIII, 70f

Supreme National Tribunal of Poland, *Trial of Hauptsturmführer Amon Leopold Goeth*, Law Reports of the Trials of War Criminals, Vol. VII, 1ff

US Military Tribunal, *Altstötter and Others Case* ("The Justice Case"), Trials of War Criminals Before the Nuernberg Military Tribunal under Control Council Law No.10 ("the Green Series"), Vol. III, 1ff

US Military Tribunal, *Brandt and Others Case* ("Medical Case"), in Trials of War Criminals Before the Nuremberg Military Tribunals under Control Council Law No. 10, Vol. I, 1ff

US Military Tribunal, *Flick and Others Case*, in Trials of War Criminals Before the Nuernberg Military Tribunal under Control Council Law No.10 ("the Green Series"), Vol. VI, 1ff

US Military Tribunal, *Greifelt and Others* Case ("the RuSHA Case"), Trials of War Criminals Before the Nuremberg Military Tribunals under Control Council Law No. 10, Vol. IV, 597ff

US Military Tribunal, *Krauch and Others Case* ("The Farben Case"), in Trials of War Criminal Before the Nuernberg Military Tribunal under Control Council Law No.10 ("the Green Series"), Vol. VII and VIII

US Military Tribunal, *Krupp and Others Case*, in Trials of War Criminal Before the Nuernberg Military Tribunal under Control Council Law No.10 ("the Green Series"), Vol. IX, 1ff

US Military Tribunal, *Leeb and Others Case* ("High Command Case"), Law Reports of the Trials of War Criminals, Vol. XII, 1ff

US Military Tribunal, *List and Others Case* ("The Hostage Case"), in Trials of War Criminals Before the Nuernberg Military Tribunal under Control Council Law No.10 ("the Green Series"), Vol. XI, 757ff

US Military Tribunal, *Milch* Case, Trials of War Criminals Before the Nuremberg Military Tribunals under Control Council Law No. 10, Vol. II, 353ff

US Military Tribunal, *Ohlendorf and Others* Case ("Einsatzgruppen Case"), in Trials of War Criminals Before the Nuremberg Military Tribunals under Control Council Law No. 10, Vol. IV, 1ff

US Military Tribunal, *Pohl and Others Case*, in Trials of War Criminals Before the Nuremberg Military Tribunals under Control Council Law No. 10, Vol. V, 193ff

US Military Tribunal, *Von Weizsaecker and Others* ("Ministries Case), in Trials of War Criminals Before the Nuremberg Military Tribunals under Control Council Law No. 10, Vol. XII, 1ff

US Supreme Court, *Ex parte Quirin et al.* 317 U.S. 1 (1942)

US Supreme Court, *Ex parte Yamashita*, 327 U.S. 1 (1946)

US Supreme Court, *Fujii v. State of California*, 217 Pac. (2d) 481 (1952)

US Supreme Court, *Oyama v. State of California*, 332 US 633 (1948)

European Court of Human Rights

Association Ekin v. France, Application No. 39288/98, Judgment, 17 July 2001

Cantoni v. France, Application No. 17862/91, Judgment, 11 November 1996

C.R. v. the United Kingdom, Application No. 20190/92, Judgment, 21 October 1995

Jones and Others v. The United Kingdom, Applications Nos. 34356/06 and 40528/06, Judgment, 14 January 2014

Jorgić v. Germany, Application No. 74613/01, Judgment, 12 July 2007

Kazakov v. Russia, Application No. 1758/02, Judgment, 18 December 2008

Kokkinakis v. Greece, Application No. 14307/88, Judgment, 25 May 1993

Kolk and Kislyiy v. Estonia, Application Nos. 23052/04 and 24018/04, Decision on Admissibility, 17 January 2006

Kononov v. Latvia, Application No. 36376/04, Judgment, 17 May 2010

Naletilić v. Croatia, Application No. 51891/99, Admissibility Decision, 4 May 2000

Ould Dah v. France, Application No. 13113/03, Decision on Admissibility, 17 March 2009

SW v. the United Kingdom, Application No. 20166/92, Judgment, 22 November 1995

Tolstoy Miloslavsky v. The United Kingdom, Application No. 18139/91, Judgment, 13 July 1995

X Ltd and Y v. the United Kingdom, Application No 8710/79, Judgment, 7 May 1982

Extraordinary Chambers in the Courts of Cambodia

Case File No. 001/18-07-2007-ECCC, *Prosecutor v. Kaing Guek Eav alias Duch*

Pre-Trial Chamber, Public Decision on Appeal against Closing Order indicting Kaing, Case File No. 001/18-07-2007-ECCC/OCIJ (PTC 02), 5 December 2008

Prosecutor v. Kaing, Case File No. 001/18-07-2007/ECCC/TC, Trial Chamber, Judgment, 26 July 2010

Prosecutor v. Kaing, Case File No. 001/18-07-2007-ECCC/SC, Supreme Court Chamber, Appeals Judgment, 3 February 2012

Case File No: 002/19-09-2007-ECCC, *Prosecutor v. Nuon Chea et. al.*

Co-Investigating Judges, Order on the Application at the ECCC of the Form of Liability Known as Joint Criminal Enterprise, Case File No: 002/19-09-2007-ECCC-OCIJ, 8 December 2009

Co-investigating Judges, Closing Order, Case File No. 002/19-19-2007-ECCC-OCIJ, 15 September 2010

Pre-Trial Chamber, Public Decision on the Appeals Against the Co-Investigative Judges Order on Joint Criminal Enterprise (JCE), Case No 002/19-09-2007-ECCC/OCIJ (PTC38), 20 May 2010 (Case No. 002 Pre-Trial Chamber Public Decision on the JCE Appeals)

Nuon Chea Defence Appeal Against the Closing Order, Case No. 002/19-09-2007-ECCC/OCIJ (PTC 146), 18 October 2010

Ieng Thirith Defence Appeal from the Closing Order, Case No. 002/19-09-2007-ECCC/OCIJ (PTC 145), 18 October 2010

Ieng Sary's Appeal Against the Closing Order, Case No. 002/19-09-2007-ECCC/OCIJ (PTC 75), 25 October 2010

Pre-Trial Chamber, Public Decision on Appeals by *Nuon Chea* and *Ieng Thirith* against the Closing Order, Case No. 002/19-09-2007-ECCC/OCIJ (PTC 145 & 146), 15 February 2011

Pre-Trial Chamber, Public Decision on *Ieng Sary's* Appeal Against the Closing Order, Case No. 002/19-09-2007-ECCC/OCIJ (PTC 75), 11 April 2011 (Pre-Trial Chamber Decision on *Ieng Sary*'s Appeal Against the Closing Order)

Decision on Co-Prosecutors' Request to Exclude Armed Conflict Nexus Requirement from the Definition of Crimes Against Humanity, Trial Chamber, Case No. 002/10-09-2007/ECCC/TC, 26 October 2011 (ECCC Trial Chamber Decision Armed Conflict Nexus Requirement)

Case File No. 002/19-09-2007/ECCC/TC, Trial Chamber, Judgment, 7 August 2014

Inter-American Court of Human Rights

Re-Introduction of the Death Penalty in the Peruvian Constitution Case, 16 Human Rights Law Journal (1995), 14ff

International Arbitration

Mexico-United States General Claims Commission, International Fisheries Company (USA) v. Mexico, July 1931, 4 Reports of International Arbitral Awards, 691ff

Mexico-United States General Claims Commission, North American Dredging Company of Texas (USA) v. Mexico, March 1926, 4 Reports of International Arbitral Awards), 26ff

International Court of Justice

Ahmadou Sadio Diallo Case (Republic of Guinea v. Democratic Republic of the Congo), Judgment - Compensation owed by the Democratic Republic of the Congo to the Republic of Guinea, 19 June 2012, ICJ Reports (2012), 324ff

Application of the Convention on the Prevention and Punishment of the Crime of Genocide (Bosnia and Herzegovina v. Serbia and Montenegro), Judgment, 26 February 2007, ICJ Reports (2007), 43ff

Armed Activities on the Territory of the Congo (Democratic Republic of Congo v. Uganda), Judgment, 19 December 2005, ICJ Reports (2005), 168ff

Asylum Case (Colombia v. Peru), Judgment, 20 November 1950, ICJ Reports (1950), 266ff

Continental Shelf Case (Libya v. Malta), Judgment, 3 June 1985, ICJ Reports (1985), 13ff

Corfu Channel Case (United Kingdom v. Albania), Judgment, 9 April 1949, ICJ Reports (1949), 4ff

Fisheries Case (United Kingdom v. Norway), Judgment, 18 December 1951, ICJ Reports (1951), 116ff

Jurisdictional Immunities of the State (Germany v. Italy: Greece Intervening), Judgment, 3 February 2012, ICJ Reports (2012) (Jurisdictional Immunities Case), 99ff

Legal Consequences for States of the Continued Presence of South Africa in Namibia (South West Africa) Notwithstanding Security Council Resolution 276 (1970), Advisory Opinion, ICJ Reports (1971), 16ff

Legal Consequences of the Construction of a Wall in the Occupied Palestinian Territory, Advisory Opinion, ICJ Reports (2004), 136ff

Legality of the Threat or Use of Nuclear Weapons, Advisory Opinion, 8 July 1996, ICJ Reports (1996), 226ff

Military and Paramilitary Activities in and against Nicaragua (Nicaragua v. US), ICJ Reports (1986), Judgment, 27 June 1986, 14ff

North Sea Continental Shelf Cases (Federal Republic of Germany v. Denmark, Federal Republic of Germany v. the Netherlands), Judgment, 20 February 1969, ICJ Reports (1969), 3ff

Right of Passage over Indian Territory (Portugal v. India), Judgment, 12 April 1960, ICJ Reports (1960), 6ff

Reservations to the Convention on the Prevention and Punishment of the Crime of Genocide, Advisory Opinion, 28 May 1951, ICJ Reports (1951), 15ff

South West Africa Cases (Ethiopia and Libera v. South Africa), Judgment, 18 July 1966, ICJ Reports (1966), 6ff

International Criminal Court

ICC, Trial Chamber I, ICC-01/04-01/06, Situation in the Democratic Republic of the Congo in the Case of the *Prosecutor v. Thomas Lubanga Dyilo*, Judgment, 14 March 2012

International Criminal Tribunal for the former Yugoslavia

Prosecutor v. Aleksovski, IT-95-14/1, Trial Chamber, Judgment, 25 June 1999

Prosecutor v. Aleksovski, IT-95-14/1A, Appeals Chamber, Judgment, 24 March 2000

Prosecutor v. Blagojević & Jokić, IT-02-60-T, Trial Chamber, Judgment, 17 January 2005

Prosecutor v. Blaškić, IT-95-14-T, Trial Chamber, Judgment, 3 March 2000

Prosecutor v. Blaškić, IT-95-14-A, Appeals Chamber, Judgment, 29 July 2004

Prosecutor v. Boškoski, IT-04-82-T, Trial Chamber, Judgment, 10 July 2008

Prosecutor v. Brđanin, IT-99-36-T, Trial Chamber, Judgment, 1 September 2004

Prosecutor v. Brđanin, IT-99-36-A, Appeals Chamber, Judgment, 3 April 2007

Prosecutor v. Delalić (Čelebici), Case No. IT-96-21-T, Trial Chamber, Judgment, 16 November 1998

Prosecutor v. Delalić (Čelebici), IT-96-21-A, Appeals Chamber, Judgment, 20 February 2001

Prosecutor v. Đorđević, IT-05-87/1-T, Trial Chamber, Judgment, 23 February 2011

Prosecutor v. Đorđević, IT-05-87/1-A, Appeals Chamber, Judgment, 27 January 2014

Prosecutor v. Erdemović, IT-96-22-T, Trial Chamber, Sentencing Judgment, 29 November 1996

Prosecutor v. Erdemović, IT-96-22-A, Appeals Chamber, Judgment, 7 October 1997

Prosecutor v. Furundžija, IT-95-17/1-T, Trial Chamber, Judgment, 10 December 1998

Prosecutor v. Furundžija, IT-95-17/1, Appeals Chamber, Judgment, 21 July 2000

Prosecutor v. Galić, IT-98-29-T, Trial Chamber, Judgment, 5 December 2003

Prosecutor v. Galić, IT-98-29-A, Appeals Chamber, Judgment, 30 November 2006

Prosecutor v. Gotovina, IT-06-90-T, Trial Chamber, Judgment, 15 April 2011

Prosecutor v. Hadžihasanović, IT-01-47-PT, Trial Chamber, Decision on Joint Challenge to Jurisdiction, 12 November 2002 (*Hadžihasanović* Trial Chamber Decision)

Prosecutor v. Hadžihasanović, IT-01-47, Appeals Chamber, Interlocutory Appeal on Decision on Joint Challenge to Jurisdiction, 27 November 2002

Prosecutor v. Hadžihasanović, IT-01-47-AR 72, Appeals Chamber, Decision on Interlocutory Appeal Challenging Jurisdiction in Relation to Command Responsibility, 16 July 2003 (*Hadžihasanović* Appeals Chamber Decision)

Prosecutor v. Hadžihasanović, IT-01-47-T, Trial Chamber, Judgment, 15 March 2006

Prosecutor v. Halilović, IT-01-48-T, Trial Chamber, Judgment, 16 November 2005

Prosecutor v. Jelisić, IT-95-10-T, Trial Chamber, Judgment, 14 December 1999

Prosecutor v. Kordić, IT-95-14/2, Trial Chamber, Decision on Joint Defence Motion, 2 March 1999

Prosecutor v. Kordić, IT-95-14/2-T, Trial Chamber, Judgment, 26 February 2001

Prosecutor v. Kordić, IT-95-14/2-A, Appeals Chamber, Judgment, 17 December 2004

Prosecutor v. Krajišnik, IT-00-39-T, Trial Chamber, Judgment, 27 September 2006

Prosecutor v. Krnojelac, IT-97-25-T, Trial Chamber, Judgment, 15 March 2002

Prosecutor v. Krnojelac, IT-94-I-A, Appeals Chamber, Judgment, 17 September 2003

Prosecutor v. Krstić, IT-98-33-T, Trial Chamber, Judgment, 2 August 2001

Prosecutor v. Krstić, IT-98-33A, Appeals Chamber, Judgment, 19 April 2004

Prosecutor v. Kunarac, IT-96-23-T & IT-96-23/1-T, Trial Chamber, Judgment, 22 February 2001

Prosecutor v. Kunarac et al, IT-96-23 & IT-96-23/1, Appeals Chamber, Judgment, 12 June 2002

Prosecutor v. Kupreškić, IT-95-16-T, Trial Chamber, Judgment, 14 January 2000

Prosecutor v. Kvočka, IT-98-30/1-T, Trial Chamber, Judgment, 2 November 2001

Prosecutor v. Limaj et al, IT-03-66-T, Trial Chamber, Judgment, 30 November 2005

Prosecutor v. Limaj et al, IT-03-66-A, Appeals Chamber, Judgment, 27 September 2007

Prosecutor v. Martić, IT-95-11-R61, Trial Chamber, Decision, 8 March 1996

Prosecutor v. Martić, IT-95-11-T, Trial Chamber, Judgment, 12 June 2007

Prosecutor v. Martić, IT-95-11-A, Appeals Chamber, Judgment, 8 October 2008

Prosecutor v. Milošević, IT-98-29/1-T, Trial Chamber, Judgment, 12 December 2007

Prosecutor v. Milošević, IT-98-29/1-A, Appeals Chamber, Judgment, 12 November 2009

Prosecutor v. Milutinović et al, IT-99-37-AR72, Appeals Chamber, Decision on Dragolub Ojdanić's Motion Challenging Jurisdiction – Joint Criminal Enterprise, 21 May 2003 (*Ojdanić* Appeals Chamber Decision)

Prosecutor v. Milutinović et al, IT-05-87-PT, Trial Chamber, Decision on Ojdanić's Motion Challenging Jurisdiction: Indirect Co-perpetration, 22 March 2006

Prosecutor v. Mrkšić, IT-95-13/1-T, Trial Chamber, Judgment, 27 September 2007

Prosecutor v. Mrkšić, IT-95-13/1, Appeals Chamber, Judgment, 5 May 2009

Prosecutor v. Naletilić, IT-98-34-T, Trial Chamber, Judgment, 31 March 2003

Prosecutor v. Naletilić, IT-98-34-A, Appeals Chamber, Judgment, 3 May 2006

Prosecutor v. Orić, IT-03-68, Trial Chamber, Judgment, 30 June 2006

Prosecutor v. Perišić, Appeals Chamber, Judgment, 28 February 2013

Prosecutor v. Popović, IT-05-88-T, Trial Chamber, Judgment, 10 June 2010

Prosecutor v. Šainović, IT-05-87-A, Appeals Chamber, Judgment, 23 January 2014

Prosecutor v. Simić, IT-95-9-T, Trial Chamber, Judgment, 17 October 2003

Prosecutor v. Stakić, IT-97-24-T, Trial Chamber, Judgment, 31 July 2003

Prosecutor v. Stakić, IT-97-24-A, Appeals Chamber, Judgment, 22 March 2006

Prosecutor v. Stanišić and Župljanin, IT-08-91-T, Trial Chamber, Judgment, 27 March 2013

Prosecutor v. Strugar, IT-01-42-PT, Trial Chamber, Decision on Defence Preliminary Motion Challenging Jurisdiction, 7 June 2002

Prosecutor v. Strugar, IT-01-42-AR72, Appeals Chamber, Decision on Interlocutory Appeal, 22 November 2002

Prosecutor v. Strugar, IT-01-42-T, Trial Chamber, Judgment, 31 January 2005

Prosecutor v. Tadić, IT-94-1, Appeals Chamber, Decision on the Defence Motion for Interlocutory Appeal on Jurisdiction, 2 October 1995 (*Tadić* Appeals Chamber Jurisdiction Decision)

Prosecutor v. Tadić, IT-94-1-T, Trial Chamber, Opinion and Judgment, 7 May 1997

Prosecutor v. Tadić, IT-94-1-A, Appeals Chamber, Judgment, 15 July 1999

Prosecutor v. Vasiljević, IT-98-32-T, Judgment, Trial Chamber, 29 November 2002

International Criminal Tribunal for Rwanda

Prosecutor v. Akayesu, Case No. ICTR-96-4-T, Trial Judgment, 2 September 1998

Prosecutor v. Akayesu, Case No. ICTR-96-4-A, Appeals Chamber, Judgment, 1 June 2001

Prosecutor v. Bagilishema, ICTR-95-1A-T, Trial Chamber, Judgment, 7 June 2001

Prosecutor v. Kanyabashi, Case No. ICTR-96-15-T, Decision on Defence Motion on Jurisdiction, Trial Chamber, 18 June 1997

Prosecutor v. Karemera, Case No. ICTR-98-44-T, Trial Chamber, Decision on the Preliminary Motions By the Defence Challenging Jurisdiction in Relation to Joint Criminal Enterprise, 11 May 2004 (*Karemera* Trial Chamber Decision)

Prosecutor v. Kayishema, Case No.ICTR-95-1-T, Trial Chamber, Judgment, 21 May 1999

Prosecutor v. Musema, Case No.ICTR-96-13-T, Trial Chamber, Judgment, 27 January 2000

Prosecutor v. Nzabririnda, Case No. ICTR-2001-77-T, Trial Chamber, Sentencing Judgment, 23 February 2007

Prosecutor v. Ruggiu, Case No. ICTR-97-32-T, Trial Chamber, Judgment and Sentence, 1 June 2000

Prosecutor v. Rutaganda, Case No. ICTR-96-3-T, Trial Chamber, Judgment, 6 December 1999

Prosecutor v. Rwamakuba, ICTR-98-44-AR72.4, Appeals Chamber, Decision on Interlocutory Appeal Regarding Application of Joint Criminal Enterprise to the Crime of Genocide, 22 October 2004

Prosecutor v. Semanza, ICTR-97-20-A, Appeals Chamber, Decision, 31 May 2000

Prosecutor v. Semanza, Case No. ICTR-97-20-T, Trial Chamber, Judgment, 15 May 2003

International Military Tribunal Nuremberg

Trial of the Major War Criminals before the International Military Tribunal, Nuremberg, 14 November 1945 – 1 October 1946, "Blue Series" (1947-1948), Volumes I - XXII

International Military Tribunal for the Far East

International Military Tribunal for the Far East, Judgment of 12 November 1948, in Pritchard/ Zaide (eds.), The Tokyo War Crimes Trial, Vol. 22

Permanent Court of International Justice

Mavrommatis Palestine Concessions Case (Greece v. United Kingdom), 1924 PCIJ (ser. A) No. 2 (30 August 1924), Judgment
S.S. Lotus (France v. Turkey), 1927 PCIJ (ser. A) No. 10 (7 September 1927), Judgment

Special Court for Sierra Leone

Prosecutor v. Brima, Case No. SCSL-04-16-T, Trial Chamber, Judgment, 20 June 2007
Prosecutor v. Fofana, SCSL-2004-14-AR72(E), Appeals Chamber, Decision on Preliminary Motion on Lack of Jurisdiction Materiae: Nature of Armed Conflict, 25 May 2004
Prosecutor v. Fofana, Case No. SCSL-04-14-T, Trial Chamber, Judgment, 2 August 2007
Prosecutor v. Fofana, Case No. SCSL-04-14-A, Appeals Chamber, Judgment, 28 May 2008
Prosecutor v. Norman, Case No. SCSL-2004-14-AR72(E), Decision on Preliminary Motion Based on Lack of Jurisdiction (Child Recruitment), Appeals Chamber, 31 May 2004 (*Norman* Appeals Chamber Decision)
Prosecutor v. Sesay, Case No. SCSL-04-15-T, Trial Chamber, Judgment, 2 March 2009
Prosecutor v. Sesay, Case No. SCSL-04-15-A, Appeals Chamber, Judgment, 26 October 2009
Prosecutor v. Taylor, Case No. SCSL-03-01-A, Appeals Chamber, Judgment, 26 September 2013
Prosecutor v. Taylor, Case No. SCSL-03-01-ES, Motion for Termination of Enforcement of Sentence in the United Kingdom and for Transfer to Rwanda, 13 June 2014

Special Tribunal for Lebanon

Decision on Appeal of Pre-Trial Judge's Order Regarding Jurisdiction and Standing, Case No. CH/AC/2010/02, 10 November 2010

International Conventions

Agreement between the United Nations and the Government of Sierra Leone on the Establishment of a Special Court for Sierra Leone, 2178 UNTS 138, UN Doc. S/2002/246 (2002), Appendix II

Convention against Torture and Other Cruel, Inhuman or Degrading Treatment or Punishment, 10 December 1984, 1465 UNTS 85

Convention for the Protection of Human Rights and Fundamental Freedoms, 3 September 1952, 213 UNTS 222

Convention on the High Seas, 29 April 1958, 450 UNTS 82

Convention on the Law of the Sea, 10 December 1982, U.N. Doc. A/Conf. 62/122

Convention on the non-applicability of statutory limitations to war crimes and crimes against humanity, 26 November 1968, 754 UNTS 73

Convention on the Prevention and Punishment of the Crime of Genocide, 9 December 1948, 78 UNTS 277

Convention on the Prohibition of the Development, Production, Stockpiling and Use of Chemical Weapons and on their Destruction, 3 September 1992, 1974 UNTS 45

Convention on the Rights of the Child, 20 November 1989, 1577 UNTS 3

European Convention on Mutual Assistance in Criminal Matters, 20 April 1959, ETS 30; 41 ECA 283; 72 UNTS 185

Geneva Convention for the Amelioration of the Condition of the Wounded and Sich in Armed Forces in the Field (GC I), 12 August 1949, 75 UNTS 31

Geneva Convention for the Amelioration of the Condition of Wounded, Sick and Shipwrecked Members of Armed Forces at Sea (GC II), 12 August 1949, 75 UNTS 85

Geneva Convention Relative to the Protection of Civilian Persons in Time of War (GC IV), 12 August 1949, 75 UNTS 287

Geneva Convention Relative to the Treatment of Prisoners of War (GC III), 12 August 1949, 75 UNTS 135

Hague Convention (IV) respecting the Laws and Customs of War on Land, 18 October 1907, 36 Stat. 2277, 3 Martens Nouveau Recueil (ser. 3)

International Convention for the Suppression of Terrorist Bombing (adopted by consensus by the General Assembly Resolution 52/164 (15 December 1997))

International Convention on the Suppression and Punishment of the Crime of Apartheid, 30 November 1973, 1015 UNTS 243

International Covenant on Civil and Political Rights, 16 December 1966, 999 UNTS 171

Nuremberg Charter as annexed to the Agreement for the Prosecution and Punishment of the Major War Criminals of the European Axis (London Agreement), 8 August 1945, 39 American Journal of International Law Supplement (1945), 257ff

Nyon Arrangement, 14 September 1937, 181 LNTS, 135; Agreement Supplementary to the Nyon Agreement, 17 September 1937, 181 LNTS.

Pact of Paris, 27 August 1928, 94 LNTS. 57

Protocol Additional to the Geneva Conventions of 12 August 1949, and relating to the Protection of Victims of International Armed Conflicts (Additional Protocol I), 6 June 1977, 1125 UNTS 3

Protocol Additional to the Geneva Conventions of 12 August 1949 and Relating to the Protection of Victims of Non-International Armed Conflicts (Protocol II), 8 June 1977, 1125 UNTS 609

Protocol for the Pacific Settlement of International Disputes, 2 October 1924, 1008 League of Nations O.J. 1521 (1925) (never entered into force)

Rome Statute of the International Criminal Court, 17 July 1998, 2187 UNTS 90

Statute of the International Court of Justice, 26 June 1945, 33 UNTS 993

Treaty of Peace with Germany (Treaty of Versailles), 28 June 1919, 11 Martens Nouveau Recueil (3d)

Vienna Convention on the Law of Treaties, 23 May 1969, 1155 UNTS 331

Other International Documents

International Law Commission

Draft Code of Crimes against the Peace and Security of Mankind with commentaries, Yearbook of the International Law Commission (1996), Vol. II, Part 2 (1996 ILC Draft Code)

ILC Report on the Work of its 68th Session to the General Assembly, 2 May – 10 June and 4 July – 12 August 2016, Supplement No. 10 (A/71/10), Chapter V.

Principles of International law Recognized in the Charter of the Nürnberg Tribunal and in the Judgment of the Tribunal, Yearbook of the International Law Commission (1950), Vol. II

Report of the ILC to the General Assembly, Yearbook of the International Law Commission (1950), Volume II

Report of the Planning Group, Official Records of the General Assembly, UN Doc. A/CN.4/L.796, International Law Commission, 63rd Session, 26 April -3 June and 4 July – 12 August 2011

Report of the Study Group of the International Law Commission, Fragmentation of International Law: Difficulties Arising from the Diversification and Expansion of International Law, UN Doc. A/CN.4/L.682 (13 April 2006)

Report on the Work of its 65th Session to the General Assembly, 6 May - 7 June and 8 July – 9 August 2013, Supplement No. 10 (A/68/10)

Special Rapporteur *M. Wood*, First Report on Formation and Evidence of Customary International Law, International Law Commission, 65th Session, 6 May-7 June and 8 July-9 August 2013, Official Records of the General Assembly, UN Doc. A/CN.4/663

Special Rapporteur *M. Wood*, Second Report on Identification of Customary International Law, International Law Commission, 66th Session, 5 May-6 June and 7 July-8 August 2014, Official Records of the General Assembly, UN Doc. A/CN.4/672

Special Rapporteur *M. Wood*, Third Report on Identification of Customary International Law, International Law Commission, 67th Session, 4 May-5 June and 6 July-7 August 2015, Official Records of the General Assembly, UN Doc. A/CN.4/682

Special Rapporteur *M. Wood*, Fourth Report on Identification of Customary International Law, International Law Commission, 68th Session, 2 May-10 June and 4 July-12 August 2016, Official Records of the General Assembly, UN Doc. A/CN.4/695

Statute of the International Law Commission, adopted by the General Assembly in Resolution 174 (II), 21 November 1947, and amended by resolutions 485 (V), 12 December 1950, 984 (X), 3 December 1955, 985 (X), 3 December 1955 and 36/39, 18 November 1981

Survey of International Law in Relation to the Work of Codification of the International Law Commission, Memorandum submitted by the Secretary General, 10 February 1949, UN Doc. A/CN.4/1/Rev.1

Working Paper by Special Rapporteur *M.O. Hudson*, Yearbook of the International Law Commission (1950), Volume II, 24ff

Miscellaneous

History of the United Nations War Crimes Commission and the Development of the Laws of War (1948)

ICC, Resolution RC/Res.6, Depositary Notification C.N.651.2010 Treaties-8, ICC, Assembly of State Parties, 11 June 2010, Annex I

ICC, Report on Prosecutorial Strategy, Office of the Prosecutor of the ICC, 14. September 2006, available at: http://www.icc-cpi.int/NR/rdonlyres/D673DD8C-D427-4547-BC69-2D363E07274B/143708/ProsecutorialStrategy20060914_English.pdf (last visited: 2 December 2014)

Report of the Special Rapporteur on torture and other forms of cruel, inhuman or degrading treatment, Study on the phenomena of torture, cruel, inhuman, or degrading treatment or punishment in the world, including an assessment of conditions of detention, submitted on 5 February 2010 to the United Nations Human Rights Council, UN-Doc. A/HRC/13/39/Add.5
Special Panels in East Timor, UNTAET Regulation No. 2000/15, 6 June 2000

UN General Assembly

UN GA Res. 95, A/RES/95, Affirmation of the Principles of International Law recognized by the Charter of the Nurnberg Tribunal, 11 December 1946
UN GA Res. 177, A/RES/177, Formulation of the principles recognized in the Charter of the Nürnberg Tribunal and in the judgment of the Tribunal, 21 November 1947
UN GA Res. 217A, A/RES/3/217A, Universal Declaration of Human Rights, 10 December 1948
UN GA Res 2444, A/RES/2444, Respect for Human Rights in Armed Conflicts, 19 December 1968
UN GA Resolution 2675, A/RES/2675, Basic Principles for the Protection of Civilian Populations in Armed Conflicts, 9 December 1970
UN GA Res. 123D, A/RES/37/123D, The Situation in the Middle East, 16 December 1982

UN Secretary General

Draft International Covenant on Human Rights and Measures of Implementation, The General Adequacy of the First Eighteen Articles (Parts I and II), Memorandum by the Secretary-General, UN Doc. E/CN.4/528, 2 April 1951
Report on ICTY: Report of the Secretary-General Pursuant to Paragraph 2 of Security Council Resolution 808 (1993), 3 May 1993, UN Doc S/25704
Report on ICTR: Report of the Secretary-General Pursuant to Paragraph 5 of Security Council Resolution 955 (1994), 13 February 1995, UN Doc S/1995/134
Report on SCSL: Report of the Secretary-General on the establishment of a Special Court for Sierra Leone, 4 October 2000, UN Doc. S/2000/915

UN Security Council

Statute of the International Criminal Tribunal for the former Yugoslavia UNSC Res 827 (1993) (25 May 1993)
Statute of the International Tribunal for Rwanda UNSC Res 955 (1994) (8 November 1994)
Statute of the Special Tribunal for Lebanon, UNSC Res 1757 /(2007) (30 May 2007)

Literature

D. Akande, Sources of International Criminal Law, in Cassese (ed.), Oxford Companion to International Criminal Justice (2009), 41ff

M. Akehurst, Custom as a Source of International Law, 47 British Yearbook of International Law (1977), 1ff

J.E. Alvarez, Editorial Comment: Hegemonic International Law Revisited, 97 American Journal of International (2003), 873ff

K. J. Alter, The New Terrain of International Law. Courts, Politics, Rights (2014)

K. Ambos, General Principles of Criminal Law in the Rome Statute, 10 Criminal Law Forum (1999), 1ff

K. Ambos, Der allgemeine Teil des Völkerstrafrechts (2002)

K. Ambos, Möglichkeiten und Grenzen völkerstrafrechtlichen Rechtsgüterschutzes, in F. Neubacher and A. Klein (eds.), Vom Recht der Macht zur Macht des Rechts? (2006), 111ff

K. Ambos, Remarks on the General Part of International Criminal Law, 4 Journal of International Criminal Justice (2006), 660ff

K. Ambos, Joint Criminal Enterprise and Command Responsibility, 5 Journal of International Criminal Justice (2007), 159ff

K. Ambos, Punishment without a Sovereign? The Ius Puniendi Issue of International Criminal Law: A First Contribution towards a Consistent Theory of International Criminal Law, 33 Oxford Journal of Legal Studies (2013), 293ff

K. Ambos, Treatise on International Criminal Law, Volume 1 (2013)

D. Anzilotti, Cours de droit international (1929)

N. Arajärvi, The Lines Begin to Blur? Opinio Juris and the Moralisation of Customary International Law, available at http://papers.ssrn.com/sol3/papers.cfm?abstract_id=1823288& rec=1&srcabs=1599679&alg=1&pos=1 (last visited 16 June 2017)

G. Arangio-Ruiz, The Normative Role of the General Assembly of the United Nations and the Declaration of Principles of Friendly Relations, 3 Recueil des Courts (1972), 431ff

A. Ashworth, Principles of Criminal Law (2006)

J. Austin, The Province of Jurisprudence Determined (1832)

M. E. Badar, "Just Convict Everyone!" – Joint Perpetration: From *Tadić* to *Stakić* and Back Again, 6 International Criminal Law Review (2006), 293ff

R.B. Baker, Customary International Law in the 21st Century: Old Challenges and New Debates, 21 European Journal of international Law (2010), 173ff

I. Bantekas, Reflections on Some Sources and Methods of International Criminal and Humanitarian Law, 6 International Criminal Law Review (2006), 121ff

S. Barriga, C. Kress (eds.), The Travaux Préparatoires of the Crime of Aggression (2012)

M.C. Bassiouni, A Functional Approach to General Principles of International Law, 11 Michigan Journal of International Law (1990), 768ff

M. C. Bassiouni, "Crimes against Humanity:" The Need for a Specialized Convention, 31 Columbia Journal of Transnational Law (1994), 457ff

M. C. Bassiouni, Establishing an International Criminal Court: Historical Survey, 149 Military Law Review (1995), 49ff

M.C. Bassiouni and *P. Manikas*, The Law of the International Criminal Tribunal for the Former Yugoslavia (1996)

M C. Bassiouni, Crimes Against Humanity in International Law (1999)

M. C. Bassiouni, The Sources and Content of International Criminal Law: A Theoretical Framework, in: Bassiouni (ed.), International Criminal Law, Vol. 1 (1999), 3ff

M. C. Bassiouni, Universal Jurisdiction for International Crimes, 42 Virginia Journal of International law (2001-2002), 81ff

M. C. Bassiouni, Introduction to International Criminal Law (2003)

R. Baxter, Multilateral Treaties as Evidence of Customary International Law, 41 British Yearbook of International Law (1965-66), 275ff

R. Baxter, Treaties and Custom, 129 Recueil des Cours (1970), 25ff

J. B. Bellinger and W. J. Haynes, A US government response to the International Committee of the Red Cross study Customary International Humanitarian Law, 89 Review of the Red Cross (2007), 443ff

W. Blackstone, Commentaries on the Laws of England, Vol. 1 (1756)

L. Blutman, Conceptual Confusion and Methodological Deficiencies: Some Ways that Theories on Customary International Law Fail, 25 European Journal of International Law (2014), 529ff

G. Boas, The Difficulty with Individual Criminal Responsibility in International Criminal Law, Stahn/van den Herik (eds.), Future Perspective on International Criminal Justice (2010), 501ff

S. Bock and *L. Preis*, Strafbarkeit nach Völkergewohnheitsrecht oder Verstoß gegen das Rückwirkungsverbot? – Drittstaatenangehörige vor dem IStGH, 20 Humanitäres Völkerrecht – Informationsschriften (Journal of International Law of Peace and Armed Conflict) (2007), 148ff

M. Boot, Genocide, Crimes Against Humanity, War Crimes. Nullum Crimen Sine Lege and the Subject Matter Jurisdiction of the International Criminal Court (2002)

A. Z. Borda, The Use of Precedent as Subsidiary Means and Sources of International Criminal Law, 18 Tilburg Law Review (2013), 65ff

M. Bos, A Methodology of International Law (1984)

M.J. Bossuyt, Guide to the "Travaux Préparatoires" of the International Covenant on Civil and Political Rights (1987)

A. Boyle, C. Chinkin, The Making of International Law (2007)

B. Broomhall, Art. 22, in Triffterer (ed.), Commentary on the Rome Statute of the International Criminal Court (2008)

I. Brownlie, Principles of Public International Law (2008)

T. Buergenthal, Lawmaking by the ICJ and Other International Courts, 103 American Society of International Law Proceedings (2009), 403ff

C. Burchard, The Nuremberg Trial and its Impact on Germany, 4 Journal of International Criminal Justice (2004), 800ff

M. Byers, Custom, Power and the Power of Rules (1999)

L. Carroll, Alice's Adventures in Wonderland (1869)

A. Cassese, J.H.H. Weiler (eds.), Change and Stability in International Law-Making (1988)

A. Cassese, A Follow-Up: Forcible Humanitarian Countermeasures and Opinio Necessitatis, 10 European Journal of International Law (1999), 791ff

A. Cassese, The Martens Clause: Half a Loaf or Simply Pie in the Sky?, 11 European Journal of International Law (2000), 187ff

A. Cassese, The Influence of the European Court on Human Rights on International Criminal Tribunals – Some Methodological Remarks, in Bergsmo (ed.), Human Rights and Criminal Justice For the Downtrodden: Essays in Honour of Asbjorn Eide (2003), 19ff

A. Cassese, Black Letter Lawyering v. Constructive Interpretation, 2 Journal of International Criminal Justice (2004), 265ff

A. Cassese International Criminal Law (2008)

A. Cassese, Affirmation of the Principles of International law Recognized by the Charter of the Nürnberg Tribunal (2009), 1ff available at: http://untreaty.un.org/cod/avl/pdf/ha/ga_95-I/ga_95-I_e.pdf (last visited 16 June 2017)

A. Cassese, Editorial, Nino – In His Own Words, 22 European Journal of International Law (2011), 931ff

A. Cassese, International Criminal Law (2013)

J. Castañeda, Legal Effects of United nations Resolutions (1969)

J. I. Charney, The Persistent Objector Rule and the Development of Customary International Law, 56 British Yearbook of International Law (1985), 11ff

B. Cheng, United Nations Resolutions on Outer Space: "Instant" International Customary Law, in Cheng (ed.), International law: Teaching and Practice (1982), 237ff

V. Chetail, The Contribution of the International Court of Justice to International Humanitarian Law, 85 ICRC Review No. 850 (2003),235ff

H. G. Cohen, Finding International Law: Rethinking the Doctrine of Sources, 93 Iowa Law Review (2007), 65ff

J. Crawford, The ILC Adopts a Statute for an International Criminal Court, 89 American Journal of International Law (1995), 404ff

R. Cryer, International Criminal law vs State Sovereignty: Another Round?, 16 European Journal of International Law (2006), 979ff

R. Cryer, Of Custom, Treaties, Scholars and the Gavel: The Influence of the International Criminal Tribunals on the ICRC Customary Law Study, 11 Journal of Conflict & Security Law (2006), 239ff

R. Cryer, The Philosophy of International Criminal Law, in Orakhelashvili (ed.), Research Handbook on the Theory and History of International Law (2011), 232ff

A. D'Amato, Consent, Estoppel, and Reasonableness: Three Challenges to Universal International Law, 10 Virginia Journal of International Law (1969), 1ff

A. D'Amato, The Concept of Custom in International Law (1971)

A. D'Amato, Trashing Customary International Law, 81 American Journal of International Law (1987), 101ff

A. D'Amato, Custom and Treaty: A Response to Professor Weisburd, 21 Vanderbilt Journal of Transnational Law (1988), 459ff

J. d'Aspremont, Customary International Law as a Dance Floor, available at: http://www.ejiltalk.org/customary-international-law-as-a-dance-floor-part-i/#more-10650 (last visited 16 June 2017).

J. d'Aspremont, Formalism and the Sources of International Law (2011)

S. Dana, Beyond Retroactivity to Realizing Justice: A Theory on the Principle of Legality in International Criminal Law Sentencing, 99 The Journal of Criminal Law & Criminology (2009), 857ff

G.M. Danilenko, The Theory of International Customary Law, 31 German Yearbook of International Law (1988), 9ff

G.M. Danilenko; Law-Making in the International Community (1993)

A. M. Danner and J. S. Martinez, Guilty Associations: Joint Criminal Enterprise, Command Responsibility, and the Development of International Criminal Law, 93 California Law Review (2005), 75ff

A. M. Danner, When Courts Make Law: How the International Criminal Tribunals Recast the Laws of War, Vanderbilt University Law School Public Law and Legal Theory, Working Paper Number 05-30 (2005), 1ff

J. de Aréchaga, Custom and Treaties, in Change and Stability in International Law-Making (1988), Cassese,Weiler (eds.), 1ff

A. de Gentili, De Iure Belli (1612), Book I (Carnegie translation 1933)

I.M.L. de Souza, The Role of State Consent in the Customary Process, 44 The International and Comparative Law Quarterly (1995), 521ff

V.D. Degan, On the Sources of International Criminal Law, 4 Chinese Journal of International Law (2005), 45ff

Y. Dinstein, The ICRC Customary Humanitarian Law Study, 36 Israel Yearbook on Human Rights (2006), 6f

Y. Dinstein, The Interaction between Customary and International Law and Treaties, 322 Recueil des Cours (2006), 243ff

K. Doehring, Die Rechtsprechung als Rechtsquelle des Völkerrechts. Zur Auslegung des Art. 38 Abs. 1 Ziff. d des Statuts des Internationalen Gerichtshofs, in Reinhart (ed.), Richterliche Rechtsfortbildung – Erscheinungsformen, Auftrag und Grenzen, FS Heidelberg (1986), 541ff

O. Dörr, Article 31, in Dörr/Schmalenbach (eds.), Vienna Convention on the Law of Treaties. A Commentary (2012)

M.A. Drumbl, Atrocity, Punishment and International Law (2007)

M.A. Drumbl, A Hard Look at the Soft Theory of International Criminal Law, in: L.N. Sadat and M.P. Scharf (eds), The Theory and Practice of International Criminal Law: Essays in Honor of M. Cherif Bassiouni (2008), 1ff

P. Drost, The Crime of State, Book II, Genocide (1959)

A. Eichhofer, Die Rechtsquellen des Völkerstrafrechts, Kühner/Esser/Gerding (eds.), Völkerstrafrecht (2007), 1ff

O. Elias, The Nature of the Subjective Element in Customary International Law, 33 International and Comparative Law Quarterly (1995), 501ff

G. Endo, Nullum crimen nulla poena sine lege Principle and the ICTY and ICTR, 15 Revue Québécoise de droit international (2002), 205ff

V. Epps, The Soldier's Obligation to Die When Ordered to Shoot Civilians or Face Death Himself, 37 New England Law Review (2003), 987ff

A.L. Escorihuela, Alf Ross: Towards a Realist Critique and Reconstruction of International Law, 14 European Journal of International Law (2003), 703ff

W. N. Ferdinandusse, Direct Application of International Criminal Law in National Courts (2006)

H. Fischer, Grave Breaches of the 1949 Geneva Conventions, in McDonald, Swaak-Goldman (eds.), Substantive and Procedural Aspects of International Criminal Law (2000), Vol. I, 65ff

G.G. Fitzmaurice, Some Problems Regarding the Formal Sources of International Law, in Koskenniemi (ed.), Sources of International Law (2000), 57ff

G. Fletcher, Basic Concepts of Criminal Law (1998)

G. Fletcher, Collective Guilt and Collective Punishment, 5 Theoretical Inquiries in Law (2004), 163ff

G. Fletcher and J.D. Ohlin, Reclaiming Fundamental Principles in the Darfur Case, 3 Journal of International Criminal Justice (2005), 539ff

P. Gaeta, International Criminalization of Prohibited Conduct, in Cassese (ed), The Oxford Companion to International Criminal Justice (2009), 63ff

K. S. Gallant, The Principle of Legality in International and Comparative Criminal Law (2009)

K. S. Gallant, International Criminal Court and the Making of Public International Law: New Roles for International Organizations and Individuals, 43 John Marshall Law Review (2010), 603ff

J.C. Gardner, Judicial Precedent in the Making of International Public Law, 17 Journal of Comparative Legislation and International Law (1935), 251ff

S. Garibian, Crimes against humanity and international legality in legal theory after Nuremberg, 9 Journal of Genocide Research (2007), 93ff

C. Garraway, Military Manuals, Operational Law and the Regulatory Framework of the Armed Forces, in Hayashi (ed.), National Military Manuals on the Law of Armed Conflict (2008), 50ff

H.P. Gasser, Military Manuals, Legal Advisers and the First Additional Protocol of 1977, in Hayashi (ed.), National Military Manuals on the Law of Armed Conflict (2008), 56ff

K. Gierhake, Begründung des Völkerstrafrechts auf der Grundlage der Kantischen Rechtslehre (2005)

T. Ginsburg, Bounded Discretion in Judicial Lawmaking, 45 Virginia Journal of International Law (2004), 631ff

S. Glaser, Droit international pénal conventionnel (1970)

M. Glasius, Do International Criminal Courts Require Democratic Legitimacy, 23 European Journal of International Law (2012), 43ff

V. Gowlland-Debbas, Judicial Insights into the Fundamental Values and Interests of the International Community, in Muller et al (eds.), The International Court of Justice, Its future role after fifty years (1997), 327ff

C. Greenwood, The Development of International Humanitarian Law by the International Criminal Tribunal for the Former Yugoslavia, 2 Max Planck Yearbook of United Nations Law (1998), 97ff

E. Greppi, The Evolution of Individual Criminal Responsibility under International Law, International Review of the Red Cross, Volume 81, Issue 835 (1999), 531ff

H. Günther, Zur Entstehung von Völkergewohnheitsrecht (1970)

P. Guggenheim, Les deux éléments de la coutume en droit international, La technique et les principes du droit public: Etudes en l'honneur de Georges Scelle, Vol. 1 (1959), 275ff

A. T. Guzman, Saving Customary International Law, 27 Michigan Journal of International Law (2005), 115ff

P. Haggenmacher, La doctrine des deux éléments du droit coutumier dans la pratique de la Cour internationale, 90 Revue générale de droit international public (1986), 5ff

J. Hall, Nulla Poena Sine Lege, 47 Yale Law Journal (1937), 165ff

S. Hall, The Persistent Spectre: Natural Law, International Order and the Limits of Legal Positivism, 12 European Journal of International Law (2001), 269ff

M. Happold, International Humanitarian Law, War Criminality and Child Recruitment: The Special Court for Sierra Leone's Decision in Prosecutor v. Samuel Hinga Norman, 18 Leiden Journal of International Law (2005), 283ff

H.L.A. Hart, The Concept of Law (1961)

H.L.A. Hart, Punishment and Responsibility (1968)

P. Hauck, The Challenge of Customary International Crimes to the Principle of Nullum Crimen Sine Lege, 21 Humanitäres Völkerrecht – Informationsschriften (Journal of International Law of Peace and Armed Conflict) (2008), 58ff

N. Hayes, Creating a Definition of Rape in International Law: The Contribution of the International Criminal Tribunals, in Darcy, Powderly (eds.), Judicial Creativity at the International Criminal Tribunals (2010), 129ff

R. Heinsch, Die Weiterentwicklung des humanitären Völkerrechts durch die Strafgerichtshöfe für das ehemalige Jugoslawien und Ruanda (2007)

W. Heintschel von Heinegg, Criminal International Law and Customary International Law, in Zimmermann (ed.), International Criminal Law and the Current Development of Public International Law (2003), 27ff

K. J. Heller, The Nuremberg Military Tribunals and the Origins of International Criminal Law (2011)

J.-M. Henckaerts, Customary International Humanitarian Law (2005)

G. I. Hernandez, The Judicialization of International Law: Reflections on the Empirical Turn, 25 European Journal of International Law (2014), 919ff

J. Higashi, The Role of Resolutions of United Nations General Assembly in the Formative Process of International Customary Law, 25 Japanese Annual of International Law (1982), 11ff

R. Higgins, Rethinking the Conceptual Thinking about the Individual in International Law, in 4 British Journal of International Studies (1978), 2ff

R. Higgins, Problems & Process: International Law and How We Use It (1994)

P. Hilpold, Humanitarian Intervention: Is there a Need for a Legal Reappraisal?, 12 European Journal of International Law (2001), 437ff

T. Hoffmann, The Gentle Civilizer of Humanitarian Law, in Stahn/van den Herik (eds.), Future Perspectives on International Criminal Justice (2010), 58ff

D. Hunt, The International Criminal Court – High Hopes, Creative Ambiguity and an Unfortunate Mistrust in International Judges, 2 Journal of International Criminal Justice (2004), 56ff

K. Ipsen, Völkerrecht (2004)

R. H Jackson, Report of Robert H. Jackson United States Representative to the International Conference on Military Trials (1945)

H. Jäger, Makroverbrechen als Gegenstand des Völkerstrafrechts, Hankel/Stuby (eds.), Strafgerichte gegen Menschheitsverbrechen. Zum Völkerstrafrecht nach den Nürnberger Prozessen (1995), 325ff

H. Jäger, Hört das Kriminalitätskonzept vor der Makrokriminalität auf?, in F. Neubacher and A. Klein (eds.), Vom Recht der Macht zur Macht des Rechts? (2006), 45ff

N. Jareborg, Criminalization as Last Resort (*Ultima Ratio*), 2 Ohio State Journal of Criminal Law (2004), 521ff

R. Y. Jennings, General Course on Principles of International Law, 121 Recueil des Cours (1967), 325ff

R. Y. Jennings, The Identification of International Law, in Cheng (ed.), International law: Teaching and Practice (1982), 3ff

R. Y. Jennings, The Judiciary, National and International and the Development of International Law, 45 International Comparative Law Quarterly (1996), 1ff

B.B. Jia, The Relations between Treaties and Custom, 9 Chinese Journal of International Law (2010), 81ff

B.B. Jing, Judicial Decisions as a Source of International Law and the Defence of Duress in Murder or Other Cases Arising from Armed Conflict, in Yee and Wand (eds.), International Law in the Post-Cold War World (2001), 77ff

E. Jouannet, Universalism and Imperialism (2007)

F. Kalshoven, Reprisals and the Protection of Civilians, in Vohrah *et al* (eds.), Man's Inhumanity to Man: Essays in Honour of Antonio Cassese (2003), 481ff

J. Kammerhofer, Uncertainty in the Formal Sources of International Law: Customary International Law and Some of its Problems, 15 European Journal of International Law (2004), 523ff

J. Kammerhofer, Uncertainty in International Law – A Kelsenian Perspective (2011)

I. Kant, The Moral Law (1948) as translated by Paton

H. Kelsen, Théorie du droit international coutumier, 1 Revue internationale de la théorie du droit (1939), 253ff

H. Kelsen, Collective and Individual Responsibility in International Law with Particular Regard to the Punishment of War Criminals, 31 California Law Review (1943), 530ff

H. Kelsen, Peace through Law (1944)

H. Kelsen, The Rule Against Ex Post Facto Laws and the Prosecution of the Axis War Criminals, 2 Judge Advocate Journal (1945), 8ff

H. Kelsen, Will the Judgment in the Nuremberg Trial Constitute a Precedent in International Law?, 1 International Law Quarterly (1947), 153ff

H. Kelsen, Pure Theory of Law (1967 as translated by Knight)

H. Kelsen, Allgemeine Theorie der Normen (1979)

G. Jellinek, Allgemeine Staatslehre (1914)

L. Kirchmair, Die Theorie des Rechtserzeugerkreises - Eine rechtstheoretische Untersuchung des Verhältnisses von Völkerrecht zu Staatsrecht am Beispiel der österreichischen Rechtsordnung (2013)

F. L. Kirgis, Custom on a Sliding Scale, 81 American Journal of International Law (1987), 146ff

P. Kirsch, in Dörmann (ed.), Elements of War Crimes under the Rome Statute of the International Criminal Court: Sources and Commentary (2003), Foreword

J. Klabbers, Constitutionalism and the Making of International Law, 5 No Foundations: Journal of Extreme Legal Positivism (2008), 84ff

T. Kleinlein, Konstitutionalisierung im Völkerrecht (2012)

R. Kolb, Selected Problems in the Theory of Customary International Law, 50 Netherlands International Law Review (2003), 119ff

M. Koskenniemi, The Pull of the Mainstream, 88 Michigan Law Review (1990), 1946ff

M. Koskenniemi, From Apology to Utopia (2005)

C. Kress, War Crimes Committed in Non-international Armed Conflict and the Emerging System of International Criminal Justice, 30 Israel Yearbook on Human Rights (2001), 103ff

C. Kress, Nulla poena nullum crimen sine lege, in R. Wolfrum (ed.), Max Planck Encyclopedia of Public International Law, online edition (2010)

H. Krieger, A Conflict of Norms: The Relationship between Humanitarian Law and Human Rights Law in the ICRC Customary Law Study, 11 Journal of Conflict & Security Law (2006), 265ff

B. Krivec, Von Versailles nach Rom – Der lange Weg von Nullum crimen, nulla poena sine lege. Bedeutung und Entwicklung des strafrechtlichen Gesetzesvorbehalts im völkerrechtlichen Strafrecht (2004)

S. Lamb, Nullum Crimen, Nulla Poena Sine Lege in International Criminal Law, in Cassese (ed.), The Rome Statute of the International Criminal Court: A Commentary (2002), 733ff

H. Lauterpacht, Decisions of Municipal Courts as a Source of International Law, 10 British Yearbook of International Law (1929), 65ff

H. Lauterpacht, The Law of Nations and the Punishment of War Crimes, 21 British Yearbook of International Law (1944), 58ff

H. Lauterpacht, The Development of International Law by the International Court (1958)

H. Lauterpacht, International Law - Being the Collected Papers of Hersch Lauterpacht (ed., E. Lauterpacht), Volume 2, The Law of Peace (1975)

R. Lemkin, Axis Rule in Occupied Europe: Laws of Occupation, Analysis of Government, Proposals for Redress (1944), 79ff

B. D. Lepard, Customary International Law – A New Theory with Practical Applications (2010)

C.L. Lim, O. Elias, The Paradox of Consensualism in International Law (1998)

C.L. Lim, O. Elias, Withdrawing From Custom and the Paradox of Consensualism in International Law, 21 Duke Journal of Comparative & International law (2010), 143ff

D. Luban, Fairness to Rightness: Jurisdiction, Legality and the Legitimacy of International Criminal Law, Georgetown Law Faculty Working Papers (July 2008), 1ff

K.H. Lüders, Strafgerichtsbarkeit über Angehörige des Feindstaates, Süddeutsche Juristenzeitung, 1946, 216ff

G. Manner, The Object Theory of the Individual in International law, 46 American Journal of International Law (1952), 428ff

J.S. Martinez, Antislavery Court and the Dawn of International Human Rights Law, 117 Yale Law Journal (2008), 550ff

M. McAuliffe deGuzman, Article 21, in Triffterer (ed.), Commentary on the Rome Statute of the International Criminal Court (2008), 701ff

R. McCorquodale, An Inclusive International Legal System, 17 Leiden Journal of International Law (2004), 492ff

B. D Meltzer, A Note on Some Aspects of the Nuremberg Debate, 14 The University of Chicago Law Review (1946-1947), 455ff

M. H. Mendelson, The Subjective Element in Customary International Law, 66 British Yearbook of International Law (1995), 177ff

M. H. Mendelson, The Formation of Customary International Law, 272 Recueil des Cours (1998), 155ff

P.K. Menon, Individuals as Subjects of International Law, Revue de Droit International 1992, 295ff

T. Meron, The Geneva Conventions as Customary Law, 81 American Journal of International Law (1987), 348ff

T. Meron, Human Rights and Humanitarian Norms as Customary Law (1989)

T. Meron, International Criminalization of Internal Atrocities, 89 American Journal of International Law (1995), 554ff

T. Meron, The Continuing Role of Custom in the Formation of International Humanitarian Law, 90 American Journal of International Law (1996), 238ff

T. Meron, War Crimes Law Comes of Age (1998)

T. Meron, The Martens Clause, Principles of Humanity, and the Dictates of Public Conscience, 94 American Journal of International Law (2000), 78ff

T. Meron, International Law in the Age of Human Rights, 301 Recueil des Cours (2003), 11ff

T. Meron, Editorial Comment, Revival of Customary Humanitarian Law, 99 American Journal of International Law (2005), 817ff

T. Meron, The Humanization of International Law (2006)

G. Mettraux, International Crimes and the *ad hoc* Tribunals (2005)

M. Milanovic, Is the Rome Statute Binding on Individuals? (And Why We Should Care), 9 Journal of International Criminal Justice (2011), 25ff

A. Mokhtar, Nullum Crimen, Nulla Poena Sine Lege: Aspects and Prospects, 26 Statute Law Review (2005), 41ff

C. de Secondat, Baron de Montesquieu, De l'Esprit des lois. Livre XI, Chapitre 6 (1748)

P. M. Moremen, National Court Decisions as State Practice: A Transnational Judicial Dialogue?, in 32 North Carolina Journal of international Law & Commercial Regulation (2006), 259ff

H. Mosler, Völkerrecht als Rechtsordnung, 36 Zeitschrift für ausländische, öffentliches Recht und Völkerrecht (1976), 6ff

H. Mosler, The International Society as a Legal Community (1980)

R. *Müllerson*, The Interplay of Objective and Subjective Elements in Customary Law, in K. Wellens (ed.), International Law: Theory and Practice: Essays in Honour of Eric Suy (1998), 161ff

A. *Nollkaemper*, The Legitimacy of International Law in the Case Law of the International Criminal Tribunal for the Former Yugoslavia, in Vandamme/Reestman (eds.), Ambiguity in the Rule of Law (2001), 13ff

A. *Nollkaemper*, Decisions of National Courts as Sources of International Law: An Analysis of the Practice of the ICTY, in Boas/Schabas (eds.), International Criminal law Developments in the Case Law of the ICTY (2003), 277ff

A. *Nollkaemper*, National Courts and the International rule of Law (2011)

M. D. *Öberg*, The Legal Effects of Resolutions of the UN Security Council and General Assembly in the Jurisprudence of the ICJ, 15 European Journal of International Law (2006), 879ff

M. D. *Öberg*, The absorption of grave breaches into war crimes, International Review of the Red Cross, Volume 91, Number 873 (2009), 163ff

M. D. *Öberg*, Processing Evidence and Drafting Judgments in International Criminal Trial Chamber, 24 Criminal Law Forum (2013), 113ff

L. *Oppenheim*, 1 International Law (1995)

A. *Orakhelashvili*, Natural Law and Customary Law, 68 Zeitschrift für ausländisches, öffentliches Recht und Völkerrecht (2008), 69ff

M. *Osiel*, The Banality of Good: Aligning Incentives against Mass Atrocity, 105 Columbia Law Review (2005), 1751ff

Judge R. *Pal*, Dissentient Judgement to the IMTFE (1953)

W. H. *Parks*, The ICRC Customary Law Study: A Preliminary Assessment, 99 Proceedings of the Annual Meeting (American Society of International Law) (2005), 208ff

C. *Parry*, The Sources and Evidences of International Law (1965)

M. Payandeh, Internationales Gemeinschaftsrecht (2010)

A. *Pellet*, The Normative Dilemma: Will and Consent in International Law-Making, 12 Australian Yearbook of International Law (1991), 22ff

A. *Pellet*, Shaping the Future of International Law: The Role of the World Court in Law-Making, in Arsanjani et al. (eds.), Looking to the Future: Essays on International Law in Honor of W. M. Reisman (2011), 1065ff

A. *Pellet*, Article 38, in Zimmerman et al (eds.), The Statute of the International Court of Justice – A Commentary (2012)

N. *Petersen*, Customary Law without Custom? Rules, Principles, and the Role of State Practice in International Norm Creation, 23 American University Law Review (2008), 275ff

N. *Petersen*, The Role of Consent and Uncertainty in the Formation of Customary International Law, in Lepard (ed.), Reexamining Customary International Law (forthcoming), available at: www.coll.mpg.de/pdf_dat/2011_04online.pdf (last visited 16 June 2017)

Lord *Phillimore*, An International Court and The Resolutions of the Committee of Jurists, 3 British Yearbook of International law (1922-23), 79ff

R. *Pisillo-Mazzeschi*, Treaty and Custom: Reflections on the Codification of International Law, 23 Commonwealth Law Bulletin (1997), 549ff

F. O. *Raimondo*, General Principles of Law in the Decisions of International Criminal Tribunals (2008)

F.O. *Raimondo*, General Principles of Law, Judicial Creativity, and the Development of International Criminal Law, in Darcy, Powderly (eds.), Judicial Creativity at the International Criminal Tribunals (2010), 45ff

S. R *Ratner*, The Schizophrenias of International Criminal Law, 33 Texas International Law Journal (1998), 237ff

S. R. *Ratner, J. S. Abrams, J. L. Bischoff*, Accountability for Human Rights Atrocities in International Law: Beyond the Nuremberg Legacy (2009)

J. *Raz*, The Concept of a Legal System (1980)

T. Rensmann, die Humanisierung des Völkerrechts durch das *ius in bello* – Von der Martens'schen Klausel zu "Responsibility to Protect", 68 Zeitschrift für ausländisches öffentliches Recht und Völkerrecht (2008), 111ff

P. J. A. Ritter von Feuerbach, The Foundations of Criminal Law and the Nullum Crimen Principle, 5 Journal of International Criminal Justice (2007), 1005ff, reproducing from Lehrbuch des gemeinen in Deutschland gültigen peinlichen Rechts (1847)

A. E. Roberts, Traditional and Modern Approaches to Customary International Law: A Reconciliation, 95 American Journal of International Law (2001), 757ff

A. Roberts, S. Sivakumaran, Lawmaking by Nonstate Actors: Engaging Armed Groups in the Creation of International Humanitarian Law, 37 The Yale Journal of International Law (2012), 107ff

D. Robinson, H. von Hebel, War Crimes in Internal Conflicts: Article 8 of the ICC Statute, 2 Yearbook of International Humanitarian Law (1999), 193ff

D. Robinson, The Identity Crisis of International Criminal Law, 21 Leiden Journal of International Law (2008), 925ff

D. Robinson, The Two Liberalisms of International Criminal Law, Stahn/van den Herik (eds.), Future Perspective on International Criminal Justice (2010), 115ff

D. Robinson, A Cosmopolitan Liberal Account of International Criminal Law, 26 Leiden Journal of International Law (2013), 127ff

N. Robinson, The Universal Declaration of Human Rights (1958)

N. Robinson, The Genocide Convention (1960)

Romano et al (eds.), The Oxford Handbook of International Adjudication (2014)

E. Rosand, The Security Council as "Global Legislator": Ultra Vires or Ultra Innovative?, 28 Fordham International Law Journal (2005), 542ff

S. Rosenne, The Law and Practice of International Courts and Tribunals: Volume III, Procedure (2006)

A. Ross, A Textbook of International Law (1947)

C. Roxin, Strafrecht: Allgemeiner Teil I: Grundlagen. Der Aufbau der Verbrechenslehre (1997)

L. N. Sadat, The International Criminal Court and the Transformation of International Law: Justice for the New Millennium (2002)

L. N. Sadat (ed.), Forging a Convention for Crimes against Humanity (2013)

C. J. M. Safferling, The Justification of Punishment in International Criminal Law – Can National Theories of Justification be Applied to the International Level, 4 Austrian Review of International & European Law (2000), 126ff

C. J. M. Safferling Towards an International Criminal Procedure (2001)

C. J. M. Safferling and *S. Kirsch*, Zehn Jahre Völkerstrafgesetzbuch, 44 Juristische Arbeitsblätter (2012), 481ff

W. Schabas, Genocide in International Law (2000)

W. Schabas, An Introduction to the International Criminal Court (2004)

W. Schabas, The UN International Criminal Tribunals (2006)

W. Schabas, State Policy as an Element of International Crimes, 98 Journal of Criminal Law & Criminology (2008), 959ff

W. Schabas, Customary Law or "Judge-Made" Law: Judicial Creativity at the UN Criminal Tribunals, in Doria (ed.), The Legal Regime of the International Criminal Court (2009), 77ff

W. Schabas, The International Criminal Court. A Commentary on the Rome Statute (2010)

W. Schabas, The Contribution of the Eichmann Trial to International Law, 26 Leiden Journal of International Law (2013), 667ff

O. Schachter, International Law in Theory and Practice, 178 Recueil des Cours (1982), 9ff

O. Schachter, Entangled Treaty and Custom, Dinstein (ed.), International Law at a Time of Perplexity: Essays in Honour of Shabtai Rosenne (1988), 717ff

O. Schachter, New Custom: Power, Opinio Juris and Contrary Practice, in Theory of International Law at the Threshold of the 21st Century: Essays in Honour of Krzysztof Skubiszewski (1996), 531ff

M. P. Scharf, Seizing the "Grotian Moment": Accelerated Formation of Customary International Law in Times of Fundamental Change, 43 Cornell International Law Journal (2012), 439

M. P. Scharf, Customary International Law in Times of Fundamental Change (2013)

H. G. Schermers, The European Communities bound by Fundamental Human Rights, 27 Common Market Law Review (1990), 249ff

B. Schlütter, Developments in Customary International law (2010)

K. Schmalenbach, The Crime of Aggression Before the International Criminal Court, in: *Liber Amicorum Rüdiger* Wolfrum, Coexistence, Cooperation and Solidarity Vol. II (2012), 1259ff

M.N. Schmitt, S. Watts, State *Opinio Juris* and International Humanitarian Law Pluralism, 91 International Law Studies (2015), 171ff

A. Schüller, Das Rückwirkungsverbot im Völkerstrafrecht, in Kühner/Esser/Gerding (eds.), Völkerstrafrecht (2007), 197ff

G. Schwarzenberger, The Inductive Approach to International Law, 60 Harvard Law Review (1947), 539ff

G. Schwarzenberger, International Law as Applied by International Courts and Tribunals (1957), Vol. 1

G. Schwarzenberger, The Inductive Approach to International Law (1965)

G. Schwarzenberger, The Problem of an International Criminal Law, in: G.O.W. Mueller and E. M. Wise (eds.), International Criminal Law (1965), 3ff

G. Schwarzenberger, The Judgment of Nuremberg, Mettraux (ed.), Perspectives on the Nuremberg Trial (2008), 167ff

S. M. Schwebel, The Effect of Resolutions of the U.N. General Assembly on Customary International Law, 73 Proceedings of the Annual meeting (American Society of International Law) (1979), 301ff

M. Shahabuddeen, Precedent in the World Court (1996)

M. Shahabuddeen, Does the Principle of Legality Stand in the Way of Progressive Development of Law?, 2 Journal of International Criminal Justice (2004), 1007ff

M. Shahabuddeen, Judicial Creativity and Joint Criminal Enterprise, in Darcy, Powderly (eds.), Judicial Creativity at the International Criminal Tribunals (2010), 184ff

M. Shahabuddeen, International Criminal Justice at the Yugoslav Tribunal, A Judge's Recollection (2012)

Y. Shany, Assessing the Effectiveness of International Courts (2014)

M. Shapiro, Judges as Liars, 17 Harvard Journal of Law & Public Policy (1994), 155ff

M.N. Shaw, International Law (2008)

B. Simma and *P. Alston*, The Sources of Human Rights Law: Custom, Jus Cogens, and General Principles, 12 Australian Yearbook of International Law (1988-1989), 82ff

B. Simma, From Bilateralism to Community Interest in International Law, 250 Recueil des Cours (1994), 217ff

B. Simma, International Human Rights and General International Law, in collected Courses of the Academy of European Law, Volume IV (1995), 153ff

B. Simma and *A.L. Paulus*, The Responsibility of Individuals for Human Rights Abuses in Internal Conflicts: A Positivist View, in 93 American Journal of International Law (1999), 302

B. Simma, Universality of International Law from the Perspective of a Practitioner, 20 European Journal of International Law (2009), 265ff

K. Skubiszewski, Resolutions of the U.N. General Assembly and Evidence of Custom, International Law at the Time of its Codification – Essays in Honour of Roberto Ago (1987), 503ff

K. Skubiszewski, International Legislation, Bernhardt (ed.), Encyclopedia of Public International Law, Vol. II (1995), 1255ff

J. L. Slama, Opinio Juris in Customary International Law, 15 Oklahoma City University Law Review (1990), 603ff

R. D. Sloane, The Expressive Capacity of International Punishment: The Limits of the National law Analogy and the Potential of International Criminal Law, in 43 Stanford Journal of International law (2007), 39ff

G. Sperduti, La fonte suprema dell ordinamento internazionale (1946)

H. Spieker, Völkergewohnheitsrechtlicher Schutz der natürlichen Umwelt im internationalen bewaffneten Konflikt (1992)

M. Swart, Judicial Lawmaking in the Context of the International Criminal Tribunals for Yugoslavia and Rwanda (2006)

S. Talmon, The Security Council as World Legislature, 99 American Journal of International Law (2005), 175ff

I. Tallgreen, The Sensibility and Sense of International Criminal Law, 13 European Journal of International Law (2002), 561ff

H.W.A. Thirlway, International Customary Law and Codification (1972)

Tomka, Custom and the International Court of Justice, 12 The Law and Practice of International Courts and Tribunals (2013), 195ff

C. Tomuschat, Obligations Arising for States without or against Their Will, 241 Recueil des Cours (1993), 197ff

C. Tomuschat, International Law: Ensuring the Survival of mankind on the Eve of a New Century, 281 Recueil des Cours (1999), 9ff

C. Tomuschat, The Legacy of Nuremberg, 4 Journal of International Criminal Justice (2006), 830ff

X. Tracol, The Precedent of Appeals Chambers Decisions in the International Criminal Tribunals, 17 Leiden Journal of International Law (2004), 67ff

H. Triepel, Völkerrecht und Landesrecht (1899)

O. Triffterer, Dogmatische Untersuchungen zur Entwicklung des materiellen Völkerstrafrechts seit Nürnberg (1966)

O. Triffterer, Bestandsaufnahme zum Völkerstrafrecht, in Hankel, Stuby (eds.), Strafgerichte gegen Menschheitsverbrechen (1995), 169ff

O. Triffterer, Der ständige Internationale Strafgerichtshof – Anspruch und Wirklichkeit, in Gössel/Triffterer (eds.), Festschrift Zipf (1999), 493ff

O. Triffterer, Preliminary Remarks: The Permanent International Criminal Court – Ideal and Reality, in Triffterer (ed.), Commentary on the Rome Statute of the International Criminal Court (2008), 15ff

G.I. Tunkin, CoExistence and International Law, 95 Recueil des Cours (1958), 1ff

D. Turns, Military Manuals and the Customary Law of Armed Conflict, in Hayashi (ed.), National Military Manuals on the Law of Armed Conflict (2008), 64ff

L. van den Herik, The Contribution of the Rwanda Tribunal to the Development of International Law (2005)

G.J.H. van Hoof, Rethinking the Sources of International Law (1983)

B. Van Schaack, Crimen Sine Lege: Judicial Lawmaking at the Intersection of Law and Morals, 97 The Georgetown Law Journal (2008), 119ff

E. van Sliedregt, Individual Criminal Responsibility in International Law (2012)

S. Vattel, The Law of Nations (1916)

A. Verdross, Völkerrecht (1937)

A. Verdross, Entstehungsweisen und Geltungsgrund des universellen völkerrechtlichen Gewohnheitsrechts, 29 Zeitschrift für ausländisches öffentliches Recht und Völkerrecht (1969), 635ff

A. Verdross, Die Quellen des universellen Völkerrechts (1973)

A. Verdross, B. Simma, Universelles Völkerrecht (1984)

J. Verhoeven, Article 21 of the Rome Statute and the Ambiguities of Applicable Law, 23 Netherlands Yearbook of International Law (2002), 3ff

M. E. Villiger, Customary International Law and Treaties (1997)

A. von Bogdandy, I. Venzke, Beyond Dispute: International Judicial Institutionas as Lawmakers, in von Bogdandy and Venzke (eds.), International Judicial Lawmaking (2012), 3ff

H. von Hebel and D. Robinson, Crimes within the Jurisdiction of the Court, in Lee, The International Criminal Court: The Making of the Rome Statute: Issues, Negotiations, Results (1999), 79ff

F. von Liszt, The Rationale for the Nullum Crimen Principle, 5 Journal of International Criminal Justice (2007), 1009ff, reproducing from *F. von Liszt*, Die deterministischen Gegner der Zweckstrafe, 13 Zeitschrift für die gesamte Strafrechtswissenschaft (1983), 325ff

P. M. Wald, Tribunal Discourse and Intercourse: How the International Courts Speak to One Another, 30 Boston College International and Comparative Law Review (2007), 15ff

R. M. Walden, The Subjective Element in the Formation of Customary International Law, 12 Israel Law Review (1977), 344ff

R. M. Walden, Customary International Law: A Jurisprudential Analysis, 13 Israel Law Review (1978), 86ff

J.S. Watson, Legal Theory, Efficacy and Validity in the Development of Human Rights Norms in International Law, 3 University of Illinois Law Forum (1979), 609ff

P. Webb, International Judicial Integration and Fragmentation (2013)

P. Weil, Towards Relative Normativity in International Law, 77 American Journal of International Law (1983), 413ff

P. Weis, Nationality and Statelessness in International Law (1979)

A. M. Weisburd, Customary International Law: The Problem of Treaties, 21 Vanderbilt Journal of Transnational Law (1988), 1ff

D. Weissbrodt, The Right to a Fair Trial under the Universal Declaration of Human Rights and the International Covenant on Civil and Political Rights (2001)

G. Werle, Völkerstrafrecht (2007)

G. Werle, General Principles of International Criminal Law, in Cassese (ed.), The Oxford Companion to International Criminal Justice (2009), 54ff

G. Werle, Principles of International Criminal Law (2009)

R. K Woetzel, The Nuremberg Trials in International Law with a Postlude on the Eichmann Case (1962)

K. Wolfke, Custom in Present International Law (1964)

M. Wood, Teachings of the Most Highly Qualified Publicists, in R. Wolfrum (ed.), Max Planck Encyclopedia of Public International Law, online edition (2010)

W. T. Worster, The Inductive and Deductive Methods in Customary International Law Analysis: Traditional and Modern Approaches, Georgetown Journal of International Law (2014), 445ff

J. Wouters, C. Ryngaert, The Impact on the Process of the Formation of customary International Law, in Kamminga, Scheinin (eds.), The Impact of Human Rights Law on General International Law (2009), 111ff

J Wouters, P. De Man, International Organizations as Law-Makers, Klabbers, Wallendahl (eds.), Research Handbook on the Law of International Organizations (2011), 190ff

S. Yee, The Tu Quoque Argument as a Defence to International Crimes, Prosecution or Punishment, 3 Chinese Journal of International Law (2004), 87ff

S. Zappalà, Human Rights in International Criminal Proceedings (2007)

A. Zahar, G. Sluiter, International Criminal Law (2008)

K. Zemanek, What is State Practice and Who Makes it?, in Beyerlin et al. (eds.), Recht zwischen Umbruch und Bewahrung: Völkerrecht, Europarecht, Staatsrecht: Festschrift für Rudolf Bernhardt (1995), 289ff

G. Zyberi, The Humanitarian Face of the International Court of Justice. Its Contribution to Interpreting and Developing International Human Rights and Humanitarian Law Rules and Principles (2008)

National Legislation

Austrian Criminal Code, "Strafgesetzbuch", Federal Law Gazette No. 60/1974

British law concerning the trial of war criminals by British Military Courts, Royal Warrant, 14 June 1945, Army Order 81/45 with amendments, reprinted in United Nations War Crimes Commission, Law Reports of Trials of War Criminals, Vol. I (1947), 105ff

Cambodian Law on the Establishment of the Extraordinary Chambers with Inclusion of Amendments as promulgated on 27 October 2004 (ECCC Statute)

Control Council Law No. 10, Punishment of Persons Guilty of War Crimes, Crimes Against Peace and Against Humanity, 20 December 1945, 3 Official Gazette Control Council for Germany 50ff (1946)

French Ordinance No. 20, 25 November 1945, and Ordinance No. 36, 25 February 1946, of the French Commander-in-chief, reprinted in United Nations War Crimes Commission, Law Reports of Trials of War Criminals, Vol. III (1948), 100ff

French Penal Code, "Code pénal", official translation available at: http://www.legifrance.gouv.fr/affichCode.do?cidTexte=LEGITEXT000006070719 (last visited 16 June 2017)

German Code of Crimes against International Law, Parliamentary Documents (Bundestagsdrucksache) 14/8524 and 14/8892, Federal Gazette I (2002) 2254

German draft law for the German Code of Crimes against International Law, Bundesratsdrucksache 29/02 of 15 January 2002

Norwegian Law on the Punishment of Foreign War Criminals, 13 December 1946 (No.14), reprinted in United Nations War Crimes Commission, Law Reports of Trials of War Criminals, Vol. III (1948), 81ff

Polish Law concerning trials of war criminals, reprinted in United Nations War Crimes Commission, Law Reports of Trials of War Criminals, Vol. VII (1948), 82ff

United Kingdom Joint Service Manual of the Law of Armed Conflict (2004), JSP 383, available at https://www.gov.uk/government/publications/jsp-383-the-joint-service-manual-of-the-law-of-armed-conflict-2004-edition (last visited: 16 June 2017)

US Ordinance No. 7, 18 October 1946, reprinted in Trials of War Criminals Before the Nuernberg Military Tribunals Under Control Council Law No. 10 ("The Green Series"), Vol. I, October 1946- April 1949, XXI